AMERICAN MARKETING ASSOCIATION

DICTIONARY OF MARKETING TERMS

SECOND EDITION

Peter D. Bennett
Editor

Printed on recyclable paper

American Marketing Association
Chicago, Illinois

NTC Business Books
a division of *NTC Publishing Group* • Lincolnwood, Illinois USA

Library of Congress Cataloging-in-Publication Data

Dictionary of marketing terms / Peter D. Bennett, editor.
p. cm.
At head of title: American Marketing Association.
ISBN 0-8442-3598-9
1. Marketing—Dictionaries. I. Bennett, Peter D. II. American Marketing Association.
HF5415.D4874 1995
658.8′003—dc20 94-39784
CIP

Published in conjunction with the American Marketing Association,
250 South Wacker Drive, Chicago, Illinois, 60606.

1996 Printing

Published by NTC Business Books, a division of NTC Publishing Group
4255 West Touhy Avenue
Lincolnwood (Chicago), Illinois 60646-1975 U.S.A.

Manufactured in the United States of America.

6 7 8 9 BC 9 8 7 6 5 4 3 2

Contributors

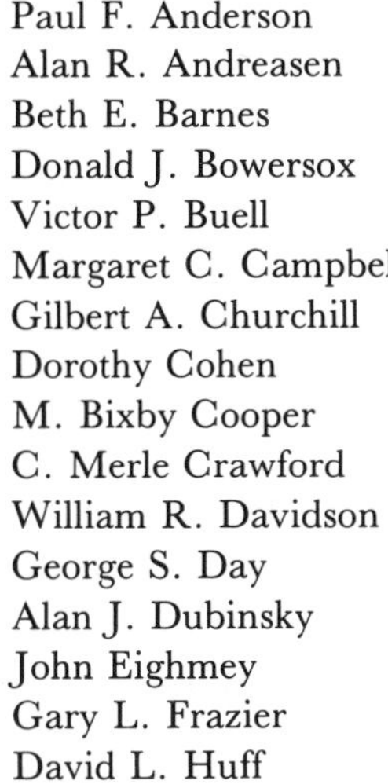

Paul F. Anderson
Alan R. Andreasen
Beth E. Barnes
Donald J. Bowersox
Victor P. Buell
Margaret C. Campbell
Gilbert A. Churchill
Dorothy Cohen
M. Bixby Cooper
C. Merle Crawford
William R. Davidson
George S. Day
Alan J. Dubinsky
John Eighmey
Gary L. Frazier
David L. Huff
Harold H. Kassarjian
Warren J. Keegan
Bernard J. LaLonde
William Lazer
Gary L. Lilien
Kent Monroe
John R. Nevin
Jerry C. Olson
J. Paul Peter
David C. Schmittlein
Don E. Schultz
Donald L. Shawver
Barton A. Weitz
David Wilemon
David T. Wilson
Yoram J. Wind

Editor

Peter D. Bennett

Preface

Human communication is never simple, and is often complicated by the fact that there is less than complete agreement on the symbols that are the building blocks of communication. The terminology of a profession, or of an academic discipline, is a major part of the shared set of symbols by which persons in the profession, or discipline, communicate with one another.

Marketing, of course, is both a profession and an academic discipline. Marketing has been blessed by a particularly close relationship between the practitioners who make up the profession and the educators who carry prime responsibility for the advancement and development of the discipline. That close relationship has been fostered and enhanced by the American Marketing Association (AMA), which was the result of a 1935 merger between the American Marketing Society (practitioners) and the National Association of Marketing Teachers (NAMT, educators). Since then, the assumption has been that one terminology has been appropriate for both the discipline and profession.

Indeed, prior to the creation of the AMA by the merger, the NAMT formed in 1931 a Committee on Definitions. The central proposition was that the more precise the language of a group, the more clear will be its collective thinking, and the more accurate will be its communication. Quoting the committee's 1961 report,

> When the members of the original committee began work in 1931, we hoped that we might achieve some degree of uniformity of usage among writers on the subject of marketing. We hoped we could avoid, in our discipline, the waste of paper and ink which plagued the field of economic theory where at least a third to a half of the verbiage of many of the textbooks were devoted to presenting and defending the author's personal definitions of the terms he used.

During the life of the committee, under both the NAMT and the AMA, it issued three published reports, in 1933, 1948, and 1961. Throughout its life, the committee was chaired by the late Dr. Ralph S. Alexander of Columbia University. The last report was titled *Marketing Definitions: A Glossary of Marketing Terms,* and was published by AMA. It was 24 pages long and included the definitions of 112 marketing terms.

It wasn't until the late 1980s that the AMA sought to bring out a replacement for that brief volume. At the request of the AMA, I undertook the task of bringing out the first edition of the *Dictionary of Marketing Terms*, which was published by the AMA in 1988. In contrast, that volume is several times the size of the 1961 *Glossary,* both in terms of pages and the number of marketing terms defined. This increase reflects the explosion of the language of a young discipline over a quarter of a century, as well as our efforts to be more inclusive, expanding on the scope of earlier publications.

That difference in the scope of the task caused a distinct difference in how the work was completed in contrast to the earlier works. For instance, the 1961 report was compiled after asking 74 AMA members to critique the 1948 report, suggesting changes and additions of new terms. The 11-person committee, after researching definitions of the added terms, was engaged in a series of meetings that totaled four or five working days to hammer out the definitions of the 112 terms. Attempting to follow such a procedure for the scope of the *Dictionary* would have been asking the marketing community to wait another quarter of a century for that work to be finished.

The first edition of the *Dictionary* actually started with the work of the 1980 AMA Ad Hoc Task Force for Marketing Definitions, chaired by Donald L. Shawver of the University of Missouri-Columbia. That group included the following individuals:

Victor P. Buell	University of Massachusetts
Edward W. Cundiff	Emory University
Thomas Greer	University of Maryland
Eugene J. Kelley	Pennsylvania State University
William Lazer	Michigan State University
Wayne Lemburg	American Marketing Association
Elmer Lotshaw	Owens-Illinois, Inc.
Vern McGinnis	Growmark, Inc.
Fred Reynolds	University of Georgia
Emily Tompkins	Journal of Marketing Research
John Wright	Georgia State University

This group provided the base on which the first edition of the *Dictionary* was built. Starting with a list of over 1,600 terms, the group worked toward a goal of reducing the list to 500 terms. Once reduced, it was the intent of the task force to prepare a glossary using methodologies much like those of the earlier works. The work of that task force was not completed. While serving as the AMA Editor of Professional Publications, the present editor became committed to a new approach that would provide the profession/discipline with a dictionary of marketing terms.

Early in the preparation of the first edition, it was decided that the committee approach would not work. Instead, this is a *compilation*, a collection of definitions of marketing terms prepared by authoritative individuals in several domains and subsets of the marketing discipline/profession. The legitimacy, and authoritative character, of this work rests squarely on the expertise of the individuals who are its collective author.

During 1993 and 1994, the second edition of the *Dictionary* was prepared. This edition is an expanded and altered work. In a few cases, the authors of the definitions have changed. At the end of each definition is a set of initials, those of the author of the definition. Two definitions included in the book, *marketing* and *marketing research*, are those adopted by the Board of Directors of the American Marketing Association. The authors and the particular marketing areas for which they prepared definitions are as follows:

Paul F. Anderson: Finance/Control

Paul F. Anderson holds a BA in economics and an MBA from Kent State University. He received his Ph.D. from Michigan State University with a major in marketing and a minor in finance and economics. He has published articles in such journals as *The Journal of Marketing, The Journal of Consumer Research, Financial Management, Engineering Economics, Accounting Historians Journal*, and *The Journal of Accounting, Auditing, and Finance*. He is a previous winner of the Alpha Kappa Psi and Harold H. Maynard awards, and is now on the faculty of The Pennsylvania State University.

Alan R. Andreasen: Social Marketing

Alan R. Andreasen is Visiting Professor at the School of Business at Georgetown University. He has written and consulted extensively on social marketing for such agencies as the National Cancer Institute, SOMARC (Social Marketing and Change), the Academy for Educational Development, United Way of America, and family planning programs in Egypt, Bangladesh, Pakistan, Jamaica, Thailand, Colombia, Mexico, and Peru. His books include *Strategic Marketing for Nonprofit Organizations* (4th ed., with Philip Kotler) and *Marketing for Social Change* (Josse Bass, 1994) and his articles include "Alternative Growth Strategies for Contraceptive Social Marketing Programs," *Journal of Health Care Marketing,* (June 1988).

Donald J. Bowersox and Bernard J. LaLonde: Physical Distribution

Dr. Donald J. Bowersox is The John H. McConnell University Professor of Business Administration at The Eli Broad Graduate School of Management, Michigan State University. He is author or co-author of twelve textbooks and over 100 articles on marketing, transportation, and logistics. He has consulted for more than 200 *Fortune 500* companies and is a frequent speaker for professional organizations. He is a recipient of the Council of Logistics Management's Distinguished Service Award.

Dr. Bernard J. LaLonde is author or co-author of a number of books and is a frequent contributor to professional journals and the trade press. He has consulted for more than 40 *Fortune 500* companies, and lectured in Canada, Europe, Japan, and Australia. Founding editor of the *Journal of Business Logistics*, he has received a number of awards for his contributions to education and research, including the Council of Logistics Management's Distinguished Service Award.

Victor P. Buell: Organization

Victor P. Buell is author of *Organizing for Marketing/Advertising Success*, three marketing management books, an award-winning *Journal of Marketing* article on product management organization, and editor of the *Handbook of Modern*

Marketing containing six chapters on organization. He conducted two in-depth marketing organization studies for member companies of the Association of National Advertisers. Professor of marketing emeritus, University of Massachusetts, he is the former corporate vice president of marketing for two major international corporations, former consultant with McKinsey & Company, and past president of the American Marketing Association.

Gilbert A. Churchill: Marketing Research
Gilbert A. Churchill, Jr., is the Arthur C. Nielsen Chair of Marketing Research at the University of Wisconsin-Madison. Professor Churchill was named Distinguished Marketing Educator by the American Marketing Association in 1986, only the second individual so honored. The award recognizes and honors a living marketing educator for distinguished service and outstanding contributions in the field of marketing education. He is a past recipient of the William O'Dell award for the outstanding *Journal of Marketing Research* article of the year, and has been a finalist for the award several other times. He is a past editor of the *Journal of Marketing Research* and is author of two leading books for marketing research: *Basic Marketing Research*, 2nd ed., 1992, and *Marketing Research: Methodological Foundations*, 5th ed., 1991, both by Dryden Press.

Dorothy Cohen: Marketing Legislation/Social Responsibility
Dorothy Cohen served as Vice President of Public Policy for the American Marketing Association. She has written a column for the Legal Developments of Marketing section of the *Journal of Marketing* for every issue since 1963, and contributed to the "Legal News" column in the *Marketing News* for many years. She is the author of numerous articles on legal issues which have influenced both policy changes at the Federal Trade Commission and programs developed by the European Economic Community to eliminate misleading advertising. She is the co-author of *Modern Marketing* and the author of *Consumer Behavior and Advertising*.

C. Merle Crawford: Product/Product Development
C. Merle Crawford is Professor of Marketing at The University of Michigan. He has also served 10 years in industry in marketing research and product management. He was the Charter President of the Product Development and Management Association, and was twice elected vice-president of the American Marketing Association. He is currently co-editor of *Journal of Product Innovation and Management*, and is the author of *New Products Management*, 2nd edition, 1987.

William R. Davidson: Marketing Institutions (Wholesale/Retail)
William R. Davidson is co-founder and Chairman Emeritus of Management Horizons, a division of Price Waterhouse. He was formerly Professor and Chairman of the Department of Marketing at The Ohio State University and has been a visiting professor at Harvard and Stanford Universities. He

is a co-author of *Marketing and Retailing Management* and is the author or co-author of more than 100 papers, monographs, or articles in professional or trade publications. He is past president of the American Marketing Association and is a member of the AMA Foundation Board of Trustees. Dr. Davidson was assisted by Professor Dale Achabal, University of Santa Clara; Professor Leonard Berry, Texas A & M University; Professor Robert Lusch, The University of Oklahoma; and Professor Barton Weitz, University of Florida.

George S. Day: Strategic Marketing

George S. Day is the Geoffrey T. Boisi Professor, Professor of Marketing and Director of the Huntsman Center for Global Competition and Innovation at The Wharton School, University of Pennsylvania. He has written extensively on strategic marketing topics and has published over 100 articles. His most recent book is *Market-Driven Strategy: Processes for Creating Value*, The Free Press, 1990.

Alan J. Dubinsky: Sales Management

Alan J. Dubinsky is Professor of Marketing at Metropolitan State University in Minneapolis. His research has appeared in *Journal of Marketing, Journal of Marketing Research, Journal of Retailing, Journal of International Business Studies, Journal of Business Research, Journal of Applied Psychology, Journal of Management*, and *Sloan Management Review*, among others. He is co-author of *Managing the Successful Sales Force*. His research interests are in the areas of personal selling and sales management.

John Eighmey: Advertising

John Eighmey is a professor of advertising in the College of Communication at the University of Alabama. His Ph.D. is in marketing from the University of Iowa. From 1984 to 1989, he was Senior Vice President and Manager of Creative Services at Young & Rubicam (Y&R) in New York, where he was responsible for the operation of the creative and production departments. From 1980 to 1984 he was Director of Account Research Services at Y&R. Professor Eighmey's advertising and marketing career began as an assistant professor of marketing at the University of Notre Dame. He later served as Deputy Assistant Director for National Advertising and program manager for advertising substantiation at the Federal Trade Commission in Washington, D.C.; as an associate professor of advertising at Northwestern University; and as a Research Director for Response Analysis Corporation in Princeton, NJ. Professor Eighmey has served as a member of the Accrediting Committee of the Accrediting Council for Education in Journalism and Mass Communication and the Publications Committee of the American Academy of Advertising. He is currently a member of the Advisory Board of the Association for Consumer Research, and a consultant to major corporations on matters relating to advertising creativity, advertising claims substantiation, advertising litigation, and public policy.

Gary L. Frazier: Channels of Distribution

Gary L. Frazier is the Richard and Jarda Hurd Professor of Distribution Management at the University of Southern California. He has been an active researcher and teacher in channels of distribution for approximately fifteen years. His research on channel structure and channel management has appeared in such journals as the *Journal of Marketing* and the *Journal of Marketing Research*. Professor Frazier is on the editorial review boards of the *Journal of Marketing, Journal of Marketing Research*, and *Journal of Retailing*. He has also served as consultant and expert witness for many organizations.

David L. Huff: Geography

David L. Huff is the Century Club Professor of Business Administration at the University of Texas at Austin. He is a specialist in the geographical dimensions of marketing. He has pioneered work on consumer spatial behavior, location decisions, and market area analysis. His publications on these subjects are quoted widely.

Harold H. Kassarjian and Margaret C. Campbell: Consumer Behavior

Harold H. Kassarjian is a professor of marketing at the Anderson Graduate School of Management at the University of California, Los Angeles. An author of numerous articles and several books, he has served as editor of the *Journal of Consumer Research,* and president of the Association for Consumer Research.

Margaret C. Campbell is an assistant professor of marketing at the Anderson Graduate School of Management at the University of California, Los Angeles. Her research includes: consumers' beliefs about marketing, intended and unintended effects of advertising techniques, and the role of perceptions of fairness and equity in marketing.

Warren J. Keegan: Global Marketing

Warren Keegan is a Fellow, Academy of International Business and Professor of International Business and Marketing and Director of the Institute for Global Business Strategy at the Lubin School of Business, Pace University, New York City and Westchester. He serves as a consultant to corporations, law firms, governments and international agencies, is a frequent speaker to business audiences and regularly appears on national and global television. He is the Prodigy on-line international business bulletin board expert on international business and author of the weekly *Global Observer* commentary for *International Business*, a core feature of the Prodigy service. Dr. Keegan's previous experience includes the positions of MIT Fellow in Africa where he served as Assistant Secretary in the Ministry of Development Planning and Secretary of the Economic Development Commission, Government of Tanzania; consultant with Boston Consulting Group; and Chairman of Douglas A. Edwards, Inc., a New York corporate real estate firm. He has an MBA and Doctorate from the Harvard Business School. Keegan's publications include *Marketing Sans Frontiers* (with Jean-Marc De Leersnyder) (Inter-

Editions, Paris, 1994); *Marketing* (second edition, Prentice-Hall, 1994); *Global Marketing Management* (fourth edition), the leading graduate-level and professional reference text on global marketing; *Advertising Worldwide; Judgements, Choices, and Decisions: Effective Management through Self-Knowledge* (John Wiley & Sons); *Global Marketing Management* (Prentice-Hall, 1995); *Principles of Global Marketing* (Prentice-Hall, 1995); and the *Dictionary of Marketing Terms.*

William Lazer and M. Bixby Cooper: Environments

Dr. William Lazer is Professor Emeritus, Marketing Systems and Future Environments, Michigan State University, and Principal, Lazer Associates International. He has been on the faculties of Michigan State University; University of Manitoba, Canada; University of Louvain, Belgium, and has lectured for scores of universities and professional associations around the world. Dr. Lazer is a past president of the American Marketing Association, served as a member of the Presidential Blue Ribbon Committee on Trade Negotiations under two U.S. Presidents, was Chairman of the Census Advisory Committee (marketing), a member of the Fulbright Advisory Committee (business) and an Advisor to the Office of the U.S. Price Commissioner, Phase II. He was the third recipient of the prestigious American Marketing Association/Irwin Award. He has published 17 books and more than 150 monographs and articles in business journals and periodicals.

Dr. M. Bixby Cooper is Associate Professor of Marketing and Logistics at Michigan State University. His research focuses on issues of customer service, distribution, and marketing management. He is co-author of *Strategic Marketing Channel Management* and his articles have appeared in numerous academic and professional journals. He is a frequent lecturer and consultant in the area of customer service and served for four years on the Executive Board of the International Customer Service Association.

Gary L. Lilien and David T. Wilson: Organizational Marketing

Gary L. Lilien is Distinguished Research Professor of Management Science in the Smeal College of Business Administration at The Pennsylvania State University and Co-founder and Research Director of Penn State's Institute for the Study of Business Markets. He is the author or co-author of six books and more than 70 articles, mainly in the area of business or organizational marketing.

David T. Wilson is the Alvin H. Clemens Professor of Entrepreneurial Studies, Professor of Marketing, and Co-founder and Managing Director of the Institute for the Study of Business Markets at The Pennsylvania State University. He has published several books and more than 50 articles on business-to-business marketing.

Kent Monroe: Pricing

Kent B. Monroe (D.B.A., Illinois) is J. M. Jones Professor of Marketing, Department of Business Administration, University of Illinois Urbana-

Champaign. He has pioneered research on the information value of price and has chapters on pricing in the text *Modern Marketing Management*, (1980); in *Marketing Handbook*, Vol. 2, *Marketing Management*, (1985); and in *Handbook of Modern Marketing*, (1986). He is the author of *Pricing: Making Profitable Decisions*, (1990). He has served as editor of the *Journal of Consumer Research* and is the editor of *Pricing Strategy & Practice: An International Journal*. He has served as a consultant and regularly conducts executive education programs on pricing.

John R. Nevin: Channels of Distribution

John R. Nevin is the Wisconsin Distinguished Professor at the University of Wisconsin-Madison. He has been an active teacher and researcher in channels of distribution for approximately fifteen years. His research on the behavioral and legal aspects of channel relations has appeared in the *Journal of Macromarketing, Journal of Marketing* and the *Journal of Marketing Research*. Professor Nevin is on the Editorial Board of the *Journal of Marketing*, and has served as consultant or expert witness for many organizations.

J. Paul Peter and Jerry C. Olson: Consumer Behavior

J. Paul Peter is the James R. McManus-Bascom Professor in Marketing at the University of Wisconsin-Madison. He has published a variety of articles on consumer behavior, marketing theory, and research methodology. One of his papers received the William O'Dell Award from the *Journal of Marketing Research* in 1986. He has co-authored several textbooks including *Consumer Behavior: Marketing Strategy Perspectives, A Preface to Marketing Management, Marketing Management: Knowledge and Skills*, and *Strategic Management: Concept and Applications*. He has served on the Editorial Review Boards of the *Journal of Marketing Research* and *Journal of Consumer Research*.

Jerry C. Olson is the Earl P. Strong Executive Education Professor and Chairman of Marketing in the Smeal College of Business Administration at Penn State University. He holds a Ph.D. in consumer psychology from Purdue University, and has published papers on consumer response to advertising, cognitive structures, and attitude theory. He is co-author with J. Paul Peter of *Consumer Behavior: Marketing Strategy Perspectives* and *Understanding Consumer Behavior* and has edited three books on consumer behavior. He has served on the editorial boards of the *Journal of Marketing*, the *Journal of Consumer Research*, the *International Journal of Research in Marketing*, and *Culture and Consumption*. He has served as president of the Association for Consumer Research.

David C. Schmittlein and Yoram J. Wind: Marketing Models

Dr. Schmittlein is a professor of marketing and Vice Dean and Director of Wharton's doctoral programs. His research concerns the development and application of models that improve marketing decisions. Since 1980 he has published more than 30 articles, primarily in journals of marketing, management, economics and statistics. He has been an area editor for *Marketing Science* and is an editorial board member for the *Journal of Marketing Research.*

Jerry Wind is The Lauder Professor and Professor of Marketing. He has served as editor-in-chief of the *Journal of Marketing*, and has served on the policy boards of *Journal of Consumer Research* and *Marketing Science*, and on the editorial boards of all major marketing journals. He is a regular contributor to the marketing literature (including 10 books and 200 papers and articles) encompassing marketing strategy, research and modeling. He has been an active consultant to many *Fortune 500* firms utilizing marketing research and modeling. Dr. Wind is also the recipient of various awards, including the prestigious Charles Coolidge Parlin Award and the 1993 American Marketing Association/Irwin Distinguished Marketing Educator Award.

Don E. Schultz and Beth E. Barnes: Sales Promotion/Public Relations

Don E. Schultz is Professor of Integrated Marketing Communications at Northwestern University's Medill School of Journalism. He is the author of several texts in the areas of advertising, sales promotion, and integrated marketing communications, including *Sales Promotion Management, Essentials of Sales Promotion, Strategic Advertising Campaigns, Essentials of Advertising Strategy* and *Integrated Marketing Communications: Putting It Together & Making It Work.* He is a frequent lecturer and consultant on advertising, sales promotion, overall promotional campaign strategy, and integrated marketing communications for companies and agencies in North America, Asia, South America, and the Pacific Rim.

Beth E. Barnes is Assistant Professor in the School of Communications at The Pennsylvania State University. She teaches courses in advertising, campaign development, and audience analysis. She writes a monthly column for *Construction Marketing Today*, "Constructive Advertising," which takes a critical look at advertisements directed at the construction industry.

Donald L. Shawver: Economic Terms

Donald L. Shawver, Professor Emeritus of Marketing at University of Missouri, Columbia, received his Ph.D. in economics from the University of Illinois in 1951. He taught marketing to students at the University of Illinois, University of Missouri, and Eastern Illinois University during six decades, from the 1940s through the 1990s. He served the American Marketing Association four years as Secretary-Treasurer, three years as Book Review Editor of the *Journal of Marketing*, and three years as Editor of Professional Publications.

Barton A. Weitz: Sales

Barton A. Weitz holds the J.C. Penney Eminent Scholar Chair at the University of Florida. He has held a variety of sales and marketing management positions for high-technology firms and has been a member of the marketing faculty at UCLA and the Wharton School. Dr. Weitz's research on personal selling and sales management has been published in leading marketing journals, and he is the former editor of the *Journal of Marketing Research*. Dr. Weitz is the co-author of one of the most widely used personal selling textbooks, *Selling: Building Relationships*. His co-author, Dr. Steve Castelberry, assisted him in developing the definitions. In addition to his academic achievements, Dr. Weitz has participated in sales management executive education programs sponsored by Northwestern University, UCLA, the Wharton School, AT&T, and General Electric.

David Wilemon: Product/Product Development

David Wilemon is Professor of Marketing and Innovation Management at Syracuse University. He also serves as Director of the Snyder Innovation Management Center. His research and professional interests are in the areas of new product development, product management, and R&D management. He has been president of the Product Development and Management Association and has served on the editorial boards of the *Journal of Marketing, Journal of Consumer Marketing, Marketing Management, Industrial Marketing Management, Journal of Product Innovation Management*, and *Transactions on Engineering Management*. The contributions of **C. Merle Crawford**, Professor of Marketing (Emeritus), The Graduate School of Business, The University of Michigan, are gratefully acknowledged.

In addition, Professor Arvind Rangaswamy of The Pennsylvania State University provided a definition for the term *data base marketing*, for which we thank him.

As editor of the volume, I am pleased to be able to publicly thank the people who contributed to this work. All members of the marketing discipline/profession owe them a debt of gratitude. My appreciation also goes to Francesca Van Gorp, AMA's Business Director of Professional Publications; Anne Knudsen, Executive Editor and Betsy Lancefield, Assistant Editor, NTC Business Books/ VGM Career Horizons, for their efforts in putting this volume together. Finally, my special thanks go to Barbara Wettlaufer, on whose shoulders fell the monumental task of making detailed examination and changes necessary to achieve uniformity among such a large number of authors.

A dictionary such as this is never complete. The language of marketing is a living thing that changes with advances in the discipline and the profession, and we hope that practitioners of both will contribute to its evolution. We welcome your comments, criticism, and suggestions. Such suggestions should be addressed to:

Peter D. Bennett, Editor
Dictionary of Marketing Terms
801 Business Administration Building
The Pennsylvania State University
University Park, PA. 16802

E-mail: pdb1@psu.edu

abandonment The discontinuance of a marketed product. It is also called product deletion or product elimination. Abandonment may occur at any time from shortly after launch (a new product failure) to many years later. The criterion for this decision is the same as for a new product: net present value of the product's estimated stream of future earnings, both direct and indirect. Simplified heuristics (e.g., number of years without a profit) may be substituted for this criterion. (See also decline stage of the **product life cycle**, **pruning decision**, and **weak product.**) [DW]

ABC See **Audit Bureau of Circulations**

ABC Analysis An approach for classifying accounts based on their attractiveness. A accounts are the most attractive while C accounts are the least attractive. (See also **account classification**.) [BAW]

ABC inventory classification A classification scheme used to implement inventory management strategies. Products are segmented into groups based upon unit sales or some other criterion. (For example, class A might be items with the highest frequency of sales, etc.) Inventory management is then guided by this segmentation. [DJB/BJL]

above-the-line cost Any cost involved in the advertising production process that is specifically listed in the budget. (See also **below-the-line cost**.) [JE]

absolute advantage When a country has the capacity to produce goods at a lower cost than another country, it is said to have an absolute production advantage. Even if a country has an absolute advantage in the production of all goods, it can still gain from specialization and trade if it has a comparative advantage in the production of any good. (See also **comparative advantage** and **competitive advantage**.) [WJK]

accelerated development The process of speeding up the new product development process. Development can be accelerated in a number of ways, such as speeding up the development process, eliminating unnecessary steps, undertaking two or more development tasks in parallel, and eliminating or minimizing decision-making delays. [DW]

accelerated development stage See **retail life cycle**

accelerated purchase A sales promotion goal achieved when consumers or channel members purchase the product before the time they would have normally bought. [DES/BEB]

acceptable price range This includes those prices that buyers are willing to pay for goods or services. (See also **price sensitivity meter** and **price thresholds**.) [KM]

acceptance operator See **linear learning model**

accessories The miscellaneous apparel-related items that are offered in department stores and apparel specialty stores including gloves, hosiery, handbags, jewelry, handkerchiefs, scarves, etc. [WRD]

accessory equipment The portable factory equipment and tools that are used in the production process and do not become part of the finished product. They are generally inexpensive, short-lived, and relatively standardized. Examples are hand tools, lift trucks, and office equipment (typewriters, desks). (See also **industrial products** and **installations**.) [GLL/DTW]

accidental sample See **convenience sample**

accommodation desk A service area in a large store for customer accommodation on such things as store information, exchanges or refunds, gift certificates, or stamping parking permits. [WRD]

account A customer, usually an institution or another organization, that purchases a company's products or services. [BAW]

account classification The categorization of a salesperson's customers into groups, based on criteria such as potential sales, for the purpose of developing a sales call plan. Comment: The classification scheme reflects the relative attractiveness of the various customers and is used to direct sales effort. (See also **ABC Analysis**.) [BAW]

account executive 1. (advertising definition) The person in an advertising agency who serves as the principal contact with a specific agency client (or more than one client) and coordinates the work of agency staff members assigned to those client(s). [JE] 2. (sales definition) A salesperson who has responsibility for the overall relationship between his or her firm and a few major accounts. Comment: An account executive coordinates financial, production, and technical capabilities of the firm to satisfy the needs of the account. [BAW]

account group The members of the various advertising agency functional departments (such as account management, creative, media planning, research, traffic, etc.) who are assigned to work on an ongoing basis on the projects related to a particular agency client. [JE]

account opener A premium or special promotion item offered to induce the opening of a new account, especially in financial institutions and stores operating on an installment-credit plan basis. [WRD]

account representative See **account executive**

account specialist See **sales organization specialized by account**

acculturation 1. (consumer behavior definition) The learning of the behaviors and mores of a culture other than the one in which the individual was raised. For example, acculturation is the process by which a recent immigrant to the U.S. learns the American way of life. [HHK/MCC] 2. (consumer behavior definition) The process by which people in one culture or subculture learn to understand and adapt to the norms, values, life styles, and behaviors of people in another culture or subculture. [JPP/JCO]

accumulation A sorting process that brings similar stocks from a number of sources together into a larger homogeneous supply. (See also **allocation, assorting, concentration, sorting,** and **sorting out**.) [GLF]

ACM See **automatic checkout machine**

acquisition 1. (product development definition) The acquiring by one firm of another firm's technology (process, facility, or material), product rights (trademarks), or entire businesses in order to increase its total sales. The acquisition may be related to the firm's current business (e.g., the acquisition of a competitor, a supplier, or a buyer) or may be unrelated (e.g., the acquisition of an entirely different business). Acquisition is a method of expanding one's product offering by means other than internal development. Any combination that forms one company from two or more previously existing companies is known as a merger. (See also **horizontal integration, merger,** and **vertical integration**.) [DW] 2. (strategic marketing definition) The acquiring by one firm of other technology (process, facility, or material), product rights (trademarks), or entire businesses in order to increase its total sales. The acquisition may be related to the firm's current business (e.g., the acquisition of a competitor, a supplier, or a buyer) or may be unrelated (e.g., the acquisition of an entirely new business). Acquisition is a method of expanding one's product offering by means other than internal development. Any combination that forms one company from two or more previously existing companies is known as a merger. (See also **diversification**.) [GSD]

acquisition value The buyers' perceptions of the relative worth of a product or service to them. It is formally defined as the subjectively weighted difference between the most a buyer would be willing to pay for the item less the actual price of the item. [KM]

action See **AIDA, attitude, behavior,** and **hierarchy of effects model**

action program See **implementation**

activation The essentially automatic process by which knowledge and meanings are retrieved from memory and made available for use by cognitive processes. (See also **spreading activation**.) [JPP/JCO]

active listening A method of listening that attempts to draw out as much information as possible by actively processing information received and stimulating the communication of additional information. [BAW]

activities, interests, and opinions (AIO) A measurable series of psychographic variables involving the interests and beliefs of consumers. [HHK/MCC]

activity based costing A cost accounting system that ties actual costs to the direct performance and value of activities. Costs are not allocated based on a formula, but are traced and charged to specific activities. [DJB/BJL]

activity goal, sales The behavioral objectives for salespeople, such as the number of calls made or number of displays set up in a day. [BAW]

activity quota A quota that focuses on the activities in which sales representatives are supposed to engage. Activity quotas focus on a salesperson's efforts rather than the sales volume outcomes of these activities. Examples of activity quotas include number of letters to potential accounts, number of product demonstrations, number of calls on new accounts, and number of submitted proposals. (See also **financial quota, sales quota,** and **sales volume quota**.) [AJD]

ad The name used to indicate an advertising message in the print media. (See also **advertisement** and **commercial**.) [JE]

ad valorem duty A duty or tax that is levied as a percentage of the value of the imported goods. It also is known as a tariff. (See also **compound duties, countervailing duties, specific duties,** and **tariff system**.) [WJK]

A. D. Little Business Profile Matrix

See **product and business portfolio models**

adaptation The process of adjusting to environmental stimuli such that the stimuli become less noticed. (See also **advertising wearout**.) [HHK/MCC]

adaptation pricing policy A pricing for the rest of the world of adapting home country prices to local competitive and market circumstances. It also is known as polycentric pricing policy. (See also **extension pricing policy** and **invention pricing policy**.) [WJK]

adapted product See **adaptive product**

adaptive control budgeting An advertising budget method whereby the advertiser uses test markets to examine the sales level and profitability of advertising spending levels that are higher and lower than the spending level currently being used by the advertiser. The advertiser may decide to adapt to either a higher or lower spending level depending on test market results. (See also **all-you-can-afford budgeting, competitive parity budgeting, objective-and-task budgeting, payout budgeting,** and **percent-of-sales budgeting**.) [JE]

adaptive experimentation An approach (and philosophy) for management decisions, calling for continuous experimentation to establish empirically the market response functions. Most common in direct marketing, it can and has been applied to advertising and other marketing mix variables. The experiment should reflect the needed variation in stimuli, cost of measuring the results, lost opportunity cost in the non-optimal cells, and management confidence in the base strategy. (See also **marketing mix models**.) [DCS/YJW]

adaptive planning An iterative process framework for organizing myriad information flows, analyses, issues, and opinions that coalesce into strategic decisions. There are four stages to this process: (1) situation assessment—the analysis of internal and environmental factors that influence business performance, combined with a comparison of past performance relative to objectives and expectations, (2) strategic thinking—identification of key issues that have a major impact on performance and the generation of creative strategic options for dealing with each issue, (3) decision making—selection of strategic thrust, choices of options, and allocation of resources in light of mutually acceptable objectives, and (4) implementation—ongoing activities that translate strategic decisions into specific programs, projects, and near-term functional action plans. The process is iterative because the implementation phase will eventually be followed by a revised situation assessment. (See also **gap analysis**.) [GSD]

adaptive product Also called adapted product, this market entry acquires its uniqueness by variation on another, more pioneering product. The degree of adaptation is more than trivial (to avoid being an emulative product or "me-too" product) but it varies greatly in significance. (See also **innovative imitation, pioneering innovativeness,** and **product adaptation**.) [DW]

adaptive selling An approach to personal selling in which selling behaviors are altered during the sales interaction or across customer interactions, based on information about the nature of the selling situation. [BAW]

ADBUDG A decision calculus model for the advertising budgeting decision. The model assumes that there is a fixed upper limit of response to saturation advertising, and it also assumes that there is a fixed lower limit to response under no advertising for an extended period. Within this range, increases in advertising spending increase response, and reductions in advertising spending lead to a decay in response over time. The model's parameters are calculated using subjective responses to a series of point-estimate questions concerning the likely impact of various advertising spending decisions (Little 1970). The effectiveness of the model's use has been discussed by Chakravarthi, Mitchell, and Staelin (1981) and Little and Lodish (1981). (See also **ADMOD, advertising models,** and **MEDIAC**.) [DCS/YJW]

ADCAD See **expert systems**

add-on In charge accounts, the purchasing of additional merchandise without paying in full for previous purchases, especially in installment-credit plan selling. [WRD]

additional markup The adding of another markup to the original markup. It is the amount of a price increase, especially in stores operating under the retail inventory method of accounting. (See also **additional markup cancellation** and **gross additional markup**.) [WRD]

additional markup cancellation A downward adjustment in price that is offset against a previously recorded additional markup. (See also **gross additional markup**.) [WRD]

additional markdown An increase of a previous markdown to further lower the selling price. [WRD]

ADI See **area of dominant influence**

adjacencies plan A store layout plan that determines which categories of merchandise will be placed adjacent to each other. [WRD]

adjustive function of attitudes See **instrumental function of attitudes**

administered vertical marketing system A form of vertical marketing system designed to control a line or classification of merchandise as opposed to an entire store's operation. Such systems involve the development of comprehensive programs for specified lines of merchandise. The vertically aligned companies, even though in a non-ownership position, may work together to reduce the total systems cost of such activities as advertising, transportation, and data processing. (See also **contractual vertical marketing system** and **corporate vertical marketing system**.) [WRD]

administration functional expense See **functional expense classification**

administrative control A term applied to studies relying on questionnaires and referring to the speed, cost, and control of the replies afforded by the mode of administration. [GAC]

administrative delays See **non tariff barriers**

ADMOD A model providing a decision support system for making advertising budget, copy, and media allocation decisions. The model assumes that an advertising campaign of given duration has as its objective specific changes in the cognitions and/or decisions in various consumer market segments. It evaluates the value of any potential media insertion schedule by aggregating over all segments (and individuals within each segment) the projected impact of the schedule for each individual (Aaker 1975). (See also **ADBUDG, advertising models, decision calculus models,** and **MEDIAC**.) [DCS/YJW]

adopter categories Persons or firms that adopt an innovation are often classified into five groups according to the sequence of their adoption of it: (1) Innovators (the first 2 to 5 percent); (2) Early adopters (the next 10 to 15 percent); (3) Early majority (the next 35 percent); (4) Late majority (the next 35 percent); (5) Laggards (the final 5 to 10 percent). The numbers are percents of the total number of actual adopters, not of the total adopter categories (the number of persons or firms in the marketplace). There is wide disagreement on the exact portion in each category. (See also **diffusion of innovation, diffusion process,** and **product adoption process**.) [DW]

adoption process This term sometimes is used to refer to a model of stages in the purchase process ranging from awareness to knowledge, evaluation, trial, and adoption. In other cases, it is used as a synonym for the diffusion process. (See also **AIDA**.) [JPP/JCO]

advance dating An arrangement by which the seller sets a specific future date when the terms of sale become applicable. For example, the order may be placed on January 5 and the goods shipped on January 10, but under the terms "2/10, net 30 as of May 1." In this case, the discount and net periods are calculated from May 1. Season dating is another name for terms of this kind. (See also **end of month dating, extra dating, future dating, memorandum purchase and dating, ordinary dating, proximo dating,** and **receipt-of-goods dating**.) [WRD]

advance order An order placed well in advance of the desired time of shipment. By placing orders in advance of the actual buying season, a buyer is enabled often to get a lower price because the buyer gives the supplier business when the latter would normally be receiving little. [WRD]

advertised brand A brand that is owned by an organization (usually a manufacturer) that uses a marketing strategy usually involving substantial advertising. An advertised brand is a consumer product, though it need not be, and is contrasted with a private brand, which is not normally advertised heavily. (See also **national brand**.) [DW]

advertisement Any announcement or persuasive message placed in the mass media in paid or donated time or space by an identified individual, company, or organization. (See also **ad** and **commercial**.) [JE]

advertiser The company, organization, or individual who pays for advertising space or time to present an announcement or persuasive message to the public. [JE]

advertising The placement of announcements and persuasive messages in time or space purchased in any of the mass media by business firms, nonprofit organizations, government agencies, and individuals who seek to inform and/or persuade members of a particular target market or audience about their products, services, organizations, or ideas. (See also **feature, promotion mix, promotional allowance,** and **promotional campaign**.) [JE]

advertising agency An organization that provides a variety of advertising-related services to clients seeking assistance in their advertising activities. A full-service advertising agency engages in the planning and administration of advertising campaigns, including setting advertising objectives, developing advertising strategies, developing and producing the advertising messages, developing and executing media plans, and coordinating related activities such as sales promotion and public relations. A limited-service advertising agency concentrates on one of the major advertising agency functions such as developing and producing advertising messages or media plans. [JE]

advertising allowance A payment made to a retail or wholesale operator by the seller of an advertised product or for use in purchasing local advertising time and space for the advertiser's product. (See also **cooperative advertising**.) [JE]

advertising appropriation See **advertising budget**

advertising budget The decision about how much money should be spent for advertising during a specific time period in order to accomplish the specific objectives of a client. This decision also involves the allocation of specific amounts of the total advertising appropriation to various media, creative approaches, times of the year, and to the production costs involved in preparing the advertising messages for placement in the various media. (See also **adaptive control budgeting, all-you-can-afford budgeting, competitive parity budgeting, objective-and-task budgeting, payout budgeting,** and **percent-of-sales budgeting**.) [JE]

advertising campaign A group of advertisements, commercials, and related promotional materials and activities that are designed to be used during the same period of time as part of a coordinated advertising plan to meet the specified advertising objectives of a client. [JE]

advertising claim A statement made in advertising about the benefits, characteristics, and/or performance of a product or service designed to persuade the customer to make a purchase. (See also **advertising message** and **puffery**.) [JE]

advertising clutter See **clutter, advertising**

advertising concept See **advertising idea** and **concept statement**

advertising contract A contractual agreement between an advertiser and the operator of any form of advertising media for the purchase of specified types of advertising time or space. [JE]

advertising copy The verbal or written component of advertising messages. [JE]

Advertising Council A nonprofit organization in the United States composed of advertisers, advertising agencies, and advertising media whose purpose is to organize and carry out public service advertising. The Council selects particular public service organizations to support, identifies volunteer advertising agencies to create advertising campaigns for each selected public service organization, and coordinates the distribution of the advertising materials to the advertising media, which donate time or space in which to disseminate each campaign to the public. (See also **public service announcement**.) [JE]

advertising/display allowance A form of trade sales promotion in which retailers are given a discount in exchange for either promoting the product in their own advertising, setting up a product display, or both. It is also known as a display allowance. [DES/BEB]

advertising effectiveness An evaluation of the extent to which a specific advertisement or advertising campaign meets the objectives specified by the client. There is a wide variety of approaches to evaluation, including inquiry tests, recall tests, and market tests. The measurement approaches include recall of ads and advertising themes, attitudes toward the advertising, persuasiveness, and impact on actual sales levels. (See also **product performance tracking** and **readership test**.) [JE]

advertising exposure See **exposure**

advertising idea The theme or concept that serves as the organizing thought for an advertisement. Ideas are used to dramatize the product-related information conveyed in advertising. [JE]

advertising manager The advertising manager participates in the development of marketing plans, acts as the principal contact with the advertising agency, provides the agency with market and product data and budget guidelines, and critiques the agency's creative and media recommendations at the time of (or prior to) their submission to marketing management. The advertising manager normally reports to the corporate or division marketing manager. Comment: Many consumer packaged goods companies with product manager setups do not have an advertising manager; rather the functions listed above are performed by product managers or brand managers for their assigned products. If, in such setups, there is an advertising manager, this executive usually is limited to providing expert counsel and services to the product managers. [VPB]

advertising media The various mass media that can be employed to carry advertising messages to potential audiences or target markets for products, services, organizations, or ideas. These media include newspapers, magazines, direct mail advertising, Yellow Pages, radio, broadcast television, cable television, outdoor advertising, transit advertising, and specialty advertising. [JE]

advertising message The visual and/or auditory information prepared by an advertiser to inform and/or persuade an audience regarding a product, organization, or idea. It is sometimes called the creative work by advertising professionals in recognition of the talent and skill required to prepare the more effective pieces of advertising. (See also **advertising claim** and **advertising copy**.) [JE]

advertising models Large numbers of models have been used to assist in making advertising decisions. Econometric and other market models, as well as decision calculus models such as ADBUDG, have been used in the determination of advertising budgets. Media selection and scheduling models have included linear and nonlinear programming-type models, such as MEDIAC, and decision calculus models. Few models, such as Aaker's ADMOD (1975), have been designed to deal simultaneously with budget, copy, and media allocation decisions. (See also **BRANDAID, diffusion model, expert systems, LITMUS, NEWPROD, NEWS,** and **Vidale-Wolfe model**.) [DCS/YJW]

advertising objective A statement prepared by the advertiser (often in association with an advertising agency) to set forth specific goals to be accomplished and the time period in which they are to be accomplished. Objectives can be stated in such terms as products to be sold, the amount of trial purchases, the amount of repeat purchases, audience members reached, the frequency with which audience members are reached, and percentages of the audience made aware of the advertising or the product. [JE]

advertising penetration The percentage of the target market that remembers a significant portion of the advertising message conveyed by an advertised campaign. [JE]

advertising, regulation of Under the

Wheeler Lea Amendment to the Federal Trade Commission Act, unfair or deceptive acts or practices (which may include advertising) are prohibited. Besides the FTC, the Alcohol Tobacco and Tax Division of the Internal Revenue Service, the FCC, the FDA, the SEC, and the U.S. Postal Service are involved in regulating advertising. [DC]

advertising specialties See **specialty advertising**

advertising strategy A statement prepared by the advertiser (often in association with an advertising agency) setting forth the (1) competitive frame, (2) target market, and (3) message argument to be used in an advertising campaign for a specific product or service. (See also **copy platform**.) [JE]

advertising substantiation The documentation by means of tests or other evidence of product performance claims made in advertising. Federal Trade Commission decisions indicate that it is a deceptive and/or unfair practice for advertisers to fail to possess reasonable documentation for product performance claims made in advertising messages before the claims are disseminated to the public. [JE]

advertising theme See **advertising idea**

advertising wearout The occurrence of consumers becoming so used to an ad that they stop paying attention to it. (See also **adaptation**.) [HHK/MCC]

Advisor A descriptive model explaining the level of marketing communication expenditures for industrial products. Two of the more important explanatory variables are the size of the product market (i.e., dollar sales in the previous year) and the number of potential customers that the marketing effort is to reach (Lilien 1979). (See also **marketing mix models**.) [DCS/YJW]

advisory authority See **staff authority**

advocacy advertising A type of advertising placed by businesses and other organizations that is intended to communicate a viewpoint about a controversial topic relating to the social, political, or economic environment. (See also **institutional advertising**.) [JE]

affect 1. (consumer behavior definition) The feelings a person has toward an attitude object such as a brand, advertisement, salesperson, etc. Affect is growing in importance in attempts to understand and predict consumer behavior. [HHK/MCC] (2). (consumer behavior definition) The affective responses include states such as emotions, specific feelings, and moods that vary in level of intensity and arousal. (See also **Wheel of Consumer Analysis**.) [JPP/JCO]

affective conflict A state of conflict that exists when a channel member feels stress, frustration, tension, or hostility toward another channel member. (See also **latent conflict, manifest conflict,** and **perceived conflict**.) [GLF]

affiliated buying See **cooperative buying**

affiliated store A store operated as a unit of a voluntary group or franchise group. Also, it may be a store controlled by another store but operated under a separate name. [WRD]

affinities A tendency for similar or complementary retail stores to be located in close proximity to one another. For example, furniture stores in a city may be located in close proximity to one another in order to facilitate consumer comparison shopping. (See also **location affinities**.) [WRD]

after sales support The services offered by the selling firm after the sale has been made to promote goodwill, ensure customer satisfaction, and develop customer loyalty. Comment: This requires a salesperson to monitor order processing; to ensure proper installation and initial use of products; and to provide maintenance, repair services, and information on the care and use of products. [BAW]

after-market The potential future sales generated by owners of equipment for repair and replacement parts. [DLS]

agency cost The dollar reduction in welfare experienced by the principal due to the inherent nature of the agency relationship with management. [PFA]

agency of record (AOR) An advertising agency assigned specific media buying responsibilities by a client. [JE]

agency theory A theory of the firm that seeks to explain corporate activities as arising out of the natural conflicts between the principals (stockholders) and agents (managers) of a firm. [PFA]

agent 1. (sales definition) A person acts as a representative of a firm or individual. [BAW] 2. (retailing definition) A business unit that negotiates purchases, sales, or both but does not take title to the goods in which it deals. 3. (retailing definition) A person agent; one who represents the principal (who, in the case of retailing, is the store or merchant) and who acts under authority, whether in buying or in bringing the principal into business relations with third parties. (See also **agency theory** and **manufacturer's agent**.) [WRD] 4. (global marketing definition) A company or individual that represents a company in a particular market. Normally an agent does not take title to goods. [WJK]

agents and brokers Independent middlemen (intermediaries) who do not take title to the goods they handle, but do actively negotiate the purchase or sale of goods for their clients. [GLF]

aggregation A concept of market segmentation that assumes that most consumers are alike. Retailers adhering to the concept focus on common dimensions of the market rather than uniqueness, and the strategy is to focus on the broadest possible number of buyers by an appeal to universal product themes. Reliance is on mass distribution, mass advertising, and a universal theme of low price. [WRD]

aging 1. In retailing, aging is the length of time merchandise has been in stock. 2. The aging of certain products is part of the curing—e.g., tobacco, liquor, cheese. 3. The classification of accounts receivable according to the number of days outstanding. [WRD]

agreement See **negotiation**

agricultural advertising See **business-to-business advertising**

AGVS See **automated guided vehicle system**

AHP See **analytic hierarchy process**

AI See **artificial intelligence**

AIDA An approach to understanding how advertising and selling supposedly work. The assumption is that the consumer passes through several steps in the influence process. First, Attention must be developed, to be followed by Interest, Desire, and finally Action as called for in the message. Another, but similar, scheme was developed by Lavidge and Steiner in 1961, later to be dubbed the AIDA: Hierarchy of Effects Model by Palda in 1966. This approach involves the hierarchy of effects: awareness, knowledge, liking, preference, conviction, and finally purchase in that order. Note the similarity to the adoption process. (See also **formula selling**

and **hierarchy of effects model.**) [HHK/MCC]

aided recall See **recall test**

AIO See **activities, interests, and opinions**

Airline Deregulation Act (1978) This act ended classical economic regulation of the airline industry by gradually phasing out price and entry controls and eventually abolishing the Civil Aeronautics Board [DC]

aisle table A table in a major store aisle, between departments, used to feature special promotional values. [WRD]

all-purpose revolving account A regular 30-day charge account. If paid in full within 30 days from date of statement, the account has no service charge, but when installment payments are made, a service charge is made on the balance at the time of the next billing. [WRD]

all-you-can-afford budgeting An approach to the advertising budget that establishes the amount to be spent on advertising as the funds remaining after all other necessary expenditures and investments have been covered in the comprehensive budget for the business or organization. (See also **adaptive control budgeting, competitive parity budgeting, objective-and-task budgeting, payout budgeting,** and **percent-of-sales budgeting.**) [JE]

alliance A long-term relationship maintained by a commitment among two or more firms to voluntarily give up some of their operational autonomy in an effort to jointly pursue specific goals. The alliance goal is to cooperatively build upon the combined resources of participating firms to improve the performance quality and competitiveness of the channel. [DJB/BJL]

alliances The pooling of complementary resources by two firms in an arrangement that falls short of a full merger or acquisition. Alliances typically involve coordinated activity from very early in the process of new technology development. (See also **diversification.**) [GSD]

allocation A sorting process that consists of breaking a homogeneous supply down into smaller and smaller lots. (See also **accumulation, assorting, dispersion,** and **sorting out.**) [GLF]

alpha error See **Type I error**

alpha factor See **exponential smoothing**

alteration cost The net cost of altering goods for customers for repair of items in stock. The cost includes labor, supplies, and all expenses, including costs for this service when purchased outside the store. [WRD]

alteration department See **alteration room**

alteration room A section, run in conjunction with one or more selling departments, that alters merchandise to customers' wishes, especially for men's and women's apparel. [WRD]

ambiance An overall feeling or mood projected by a store through its aesthetic appeal to human senses. [WRD]

American National Standards Institute See **ANSI.X12**

analog approach A method of trade area analysis that is also known as the similar store or mapping approach. The analysis is divided into four steps: 1) describing the current trade areas by using a technique known as customer spotting; 2) plotting the customer on a map; 3) defining the primary trade zone, secondary trade zone, and tertiary trade zone; and 4) matching the characteristics of stores in the trade areas with a potential new store to estimate its sales potential. [WRD]

American Technology Preeminance Act (1992) This act requires that, as of 1994, packaging labels in consumer commodities must be expressed in both inch or pound symbols and the metric system. [DC]

analysis of selected cases An intensive study of selected examples of the phenomenon of interest. [GAC]

analysis of variance (ANOVA) A statistical test employed with interval data to determine if k ($k > 2$) samples came from populations with equal means. [GAC]

analytic hierarchy process (AHP) A three-step process for making resource allocation decisions. First, the organization's objectives, sub-objectives and strategies are organized hierarchically. Next, the decision maker evaluates, in a pairwise fashion, each of the elements in a particular stratum of the hierarchy with respect to its importance in accomplishing each of the elements of the next-higher stratum. Finally, a model is applied to these pairwise judgments that produces a set of importance (or priority) weights for each element of each stratum in the hierarchy (Wind and Saaty 1980). Areas of application in marketing include the product portfolio decision, selection of new products to develop, and generation and evaluation of various marketing mix strategies. (See also **marketing mix models, probit model, product and business portfolio models, resource allocation models,** and **sales force models.**) [DCS/YJW]

ANC Andean Common Market

anchor The reference price or reference product in consumers' comparisons. (See also **anchoring effect.**) [KM]

anchor store A large and well-known retail operation located in a shopping center and serving as an attracting force to draw consumers to the center. [WRD]

anchoring effect The result when buyers make comparisons of prices or products against a reference price or reference product. The result of this comparison is usually weighted toward the anchor, creating an anchor bias, the anchoring effect. [KM]

ancillary service 1. (physical distribution definition) A service offering provided by modal operators in addition to basic transportation services. The provision of such services typically includes sorting, storing product prior to delivery, marking or tagging the product, and collecting rate shipment. [DJB/BJL] 2. (retailing definition) The service such as layaway, gift wrap, credit, and others not directly related to the actual sale of a specific product within the store. Some of these services are charged for and some are not. [WRD]

ANOVA See **analysis of variance**

ANSI.X12 (American National Standards Institute) The basic electronic data interchange format utilized in North America for communication transmissions. [DJB/BJL]

Anti-Merger Act (1950) Commonly called the Celler-Kefauver Act, this act amends the Clayton Act to prohibit mergers and acquisitions in restraint of competition by the purchase of assets or of stocks. [DC]

anticipation A discount in addition to the cash discount if a bill is paid prior to the expiration of the cash discount period, usually at the rate of 6 percent per annum—e.g., at this rate, for 60 days prepayment, which is 1/6 of an interest year, the anticipation ratio would be 1 percent of the face amount. [WRD]

anticompetitive leasing arrangement A lease that limits the type and amount of competition a particular retailer faces within a trading area or shopping center. [WRD]

antidumping duties The penalty duties on goods that have been declared in violation of antidumping laws. The duties that take the form of special additional import charges equal to the dumping margin. (See also **dumping**). [WJK]

antidumping laws The laws passed by a host government to protect local industries from dumping. (See also **dumping**.) [WJK]

antitrust laws Federal antitrust policy is set forth in four laws: the Sherman Antitrust Act, the Clayton Act, the Federal Trade Commission Act, and the Robinson-Patman Act. These laws are negative in character and outlaw restraints of trade, monopolizing, attempting to monopolize, unfair methods of competition, and, where they may substantially lessen competition or tend to create a monopoly, price discrimination, exclusive dealing, and mergers. [DC]

AOG See **arrival of goods**

AOR See **agency of record**

apothecary In America, until recent times, a compounder of drugs. The predecessor of **pharmacy** or **pharmacist**. [WRD]

applied research and development See **research and development**

approach, sales The initial stage in a sales interaction. Comment: The objectives of the approach are securing approval for the sales call, getting the prospect's attention and interest, and building rapport with the prospect. (See also **balance sheet method, benefit approach, compliment approach, consultative selling, customer orientation, formula selling, high-pressure selling, multilevel selling, problem solution approach,** and **systems selling**.) [BAW]

approval sale A sale subject to later approval or selection, the customer having unlimited return privileges. [WRD]

approved vendor list A list of suppliers with whom purchasing agents are allowed to close contracts. [GLL/DTW]

apron A form attached to an invoice or copy of purchase order in retail stores, containing details to check before payment. It is sometimes called a rider. [WRD]

APT See **arbitrage pricing theory**

AR See **average revenue**

arbitrage pricing theory (APT) A theory stating that the expected return on any asset or security is given by the following formula:

$$E_a = E_0 + (E_{p1} - E_0)\beta_{a1} + (E_{p2} - E_0)\beta_{a2} + \ldots + (E_{pk} - E_0)\beta_{ak}$$

where

E_a = the expected return on an asset a,

E_0 = the expected return on a riskiest asset,

$\beta_{a1} \ldots \beta_{ak}$ = the beta coefficients for each of the k factors, and

$E_{p1} \ldots E_{pk}$ = the expected returns on portfolios of securities which have a beta coefficient of 1 when regressed on the kth factor and a beta of zero on all others.

The APT is designed as a replacement for the untestable capital asset pricing model. In essence, the APT says that asset returns are a linear function of various macroeconomic factors (e.g., industrial production, the spread between long- and short-term interest rates, expected and unexpected inflation, the spread between high- and low-grade bonds). At the present time the model's empirical validity, testability, and the number and identity of its return generating factors are controversial issues in financial economics. [PFA]

arbitrage The simultaneous purchase and sale of the same commodity or security in two different markets in an attempt to profit from price differences in the two markets. [DLS]

arcade shopping center An enclosed shopping area with a number of stores in lanes under archways and with one roof overhead. (See also **community shopping center, factory outlet center, mall-type shopping center, neighborhood shopping center, off-price shopping center, regional shopping center, strip-type shopping center,** and **super regional shopping center**.) [WRD]

area of dominant influence (ADI) The geographic area surrounding a city in which the broadcasting stations based in that city account for a greater share of the listening or viewing households than do broadcasting stations based in other nearby cities. (See also **designated market area**.) [JE]

area sampling A form of a cluster sample in which areas (for example, census tracts, blocks) serve as the primary sampling units. The population is divided into mutually exclusive and exhaustive areas using maps, and a random sample of areas is selected. If all the households in the selected areas are used in the study, it is one-stage area sampling, while if the areas themselves are subsampled with respect to households, the procedure is two-stage area sampling. [GAC]

arrival of goods (AOG) This is applicable to the cash discount period, indicating that the discount will be granted if payment is made within the number of days specified, calculated from the time the goods arrive at the destination. It is used for the purpose of accommodating distantly located customers. The net payment period, however, is computed from the time of shipment. [WRD]

art See **artwork**

art director A person possessing good taste who is skilled in the visualization of advertising ideas. [JE]

articulated railcar An extended rail chassis that can haul up to ten containers on a single flexible unit. This reduces the weight and the time required to interchange railcars. [DJB/BJL]

artificial intelligence (AI) An area of computer science concerned with designing smart computer systems. AI systems exhibit the characteristics generally associated with intelligence in human learning, reasoning, and solving problems. (See also **expert system**.) [DJB/BJL]

artwork Any illustration (including design elements, drawing, painting, photography) used in the production of print advertising. The term is often used in the short form *art*. [JE]

as is The merchandise that is offered for sale without recourse to an adjustment or a refund. The goods may be irregular, shopworn, or damaged, but that is understood. [WRD]

ASAR See **automated storage and retrieval equipment**

A.S.E.A.N. See **Association of South East Asian Nations**

aspirational group A reference group that an individual consumer wants to join or be similar to. (See also **dissociative group**.) [JPP/JCO]

assembler An establishment engaged primarily in purchasing farm products or seafood in growers' markets or producing regions. The assembler usually purchases in relatively small quantities, concentrates large supplies, and thus assembles economical shipments for movement into a major wholesale market center. (See also **commission buyer of farm products**.) [WRD]

assertiveness See **social styles matrix**

ASSESSOR A model for predicting the market share of a new frequently purchased product using pretest market information. Perceptions and preferences of potential customers are measured via interview and a simulated shopping experience conducted at a central location. The prediction is based on the sample participants' reaction to advertising (exposure to advertisements for several brands), estimated level of product trial (based on the simulated shopping experience), estimated repeat purchase level (via follow-up interview), and brand preference judgments (Silk and Urban 1978). Evidence on the model's predictive validity has been reported by Urban and Katz (1983). (See also **LITMUS, new product forecasting models, Newprod, NEWS, SPRINTER Mod III, STEAM,** and **Tracker**.) [DCS/YJW]

assignment The formal transfer of property, as for benefit of creditors, especially accounts receivable as collateral for a loan. [WRD]

associated buying office A type of resident buying office that is cooperatively maintained in a central market by a group of noncompeting independent stores. It is controlled and financed by the stores, each store paying a prorated share of the office expenses. [WRD]

Association of South East Asian Nations (A.S.E.A.N.) An association of countries established in 1967 at Bangkok, Thailand, to accelerate economic progress and to increase the stability in the South East Asian region. [WJK]

assorting A sorting process that consists of building an assortment of products for use in association with each other. (See also **accumulation, allocation, concentration,** and **sorting out**.) [GLF]

assortment 1. (retailing definition) The range of choice offered to the consumer within a particular classification of merchandise. In terms of men's shirts, for example, it is the range of prices, styles, colors, patterns, and materials that is available for customer selection. 2. (retailing definition) The range of choice among substitute characteristics of a given type of article. (See also **variety**.) [WRD] 3. (channels of distribution definition) A combination of similar and/or complementary products that, taken together, have some definite purpose for providing benefits to specific markets. (See also **sorting**.) [GLF]

ATM See **automated teller machine**

atmosphere The physical characteristics of the store such as architecture, layout, signs and displays, color, lighting, temperature, noise, and smells creating an image in the customer's mind. [WRD]

atmospherics The store architecture, layout, lighting, color scheme, temperature, access, noise, assortment, prices, special events, etc., that serve as stimuli and attention attractors of consumers to a retail store. [WRD]

A-T-R See **awareness-trial-repeat**

attention The process by which a consumer selects information in the environment to interpret. Also, it is the point at which a consumer becomes aware or conscious of particular stimuli in the environment. (See also **AIDA**.) [JPP/JCO]

attitude 1. (consumer behavior definition) A person's overall evaluation of a concept; an affective response involving general feelings of liking or favorability. [JPP/JCO] 2. (consumer behavior definition) A cognitive process involving positive or negative valences, feelings, or emotions. An attitude toward an object always involves a stirred-up state—a positive or negative feeling or motivational component. It is an interrelated system of cognition, feelings, and action tendencies. (See also **belief, category-based processing, consistency theory, ego-defensive function of attitudes, functional theory of attitudes, instrumental function of attitudes, knowledge function of attitudes,** and **value-expressive function of attitudes**.) [HHK/MCC]

attitude models See **multiattribute attitude models**

attitude toward objects (A_o) Consumer's overall evaluations of an object such as a product or store. [JPP/JCO]

attitude toward the ad (A_{ad}) Consumers' overall evaluations of an advertisement, not the brand being promoted. [JPP/JCO]

attracting nonusers of the product category See **market penetration strategy**

attracting users of competitive brands See **market penetration strategy**

attraction model A market share model that predicts a particular brand's market share as the quotient of that brand's "attraction" divided by the sum of the "attraction" level for all brands in the market. The attraction level for a brand is often in turn expressed as a function of customer characteristics, the marketing mix, and the competitive environment. Conditions under which an attraction model can be expected to hold have been described by Bell, Keeney, and Little (1975). (See also **Multiplicative Competitive Interaction model**.) [DCS/YJW]

attributable costs See **direct costs**

attribute See **product attributes**

attribution theory A theory, or group of several theories, stemming from Heider's (1958) belief in the importance of understanding individuals' "naive theories" of causality. Attribution theory assumes that individuals attempt to understand their environments in an analytical fashion, arriving at explanations of causality through a fairly logical process. Kelly (1967, 1972) provided an influential elaboration of the process by which individuals infer causality. Based on this, attribution theory suggests that individuals make inferences of causality based on the extent to which events co-vary across individuals, situations, and over time. [HHK/MCC]

auction A market in which goods are sold to the highest bidder. The auction usually is well publicized in advance or held at specific times well known in the trade. Exchange is effected in accordance with definite rules, with sales made to the highest bidder. (See also **commercial auction** and **forced sale**.) [WRD]

auction company A business establishment engaged in selling merchandise on an agency basis by the auction method. (See also **commercial auction**.) [WRD]

audience The number and/or characteristics of the persons or households who are exposed to a particular type of advertising media or media vehicle. [JE]

audience accumulation The total number of different persons or households exposed to a media vehicle or to a particular advertising campaign during a specified period of time. [JE]

audience duplication The total number of persons or households exposed more than once to the same media vehicle or to a particular advertising campaign during a specified period of time. [JE]

audimeter An electronic monitoring device used to measure the time periods during which a television set is being used and the specific channel to which it is tuned at each moment. [JE]

Audit Bureau of Circulations (ABC) An organization sponsored by advertisers, advertising agencies, and print media publishers that verifies the audience circulation figures claimed by newspapers and magazines. [JE]

audited sales The reconciliation of daily cash and charge sales against the recorded total on the sales registers. This reconciliation is accomplished in a back office procedure at the end of the day. [WRD]

auditing (post and pre) Transportation freight bills are checked to assure billing accuracy. **Preauditing** determines the proper rate and charges prior to payment of a freight bill. **Postauditing** makes the same determination after payment. [DJB/BJL]

augmented product This is the view of a product that includes not only its core benefit and its physical being, but adds other sources of benefits such as service, warranty, and image. The augmented aspects are added to the physical product by action of the seller, e.g., with company reputation or with service. (See also **core product**.) [DW]

authorization A process by which credit sales are approved either through a telephone system from the selling floor to the credit office or by an automated system tied into a point-of-sale system. [WRD]

authorized dealer A dealer who has a franchise to sell a manufacturer's product. The authorized dealer is usually the only dealer or one of a few selected dealers in a trading area. [WRD]

automated guided vehicle system (AGVS) A materials handling system that does not require a driver. The AGVS is automatically routed and positioned at destination by an optical or magnetic guidance system. [DJB/BJL]

automated storage and retrieval equipment (ASAR) An automated unit-load handling system using high-rise, structured steel vertical racks that improves materials-handling productivity, provides maximum storage density per square foot of floor space, and minimizes the direct labor required for handling. [DJB/BJL]

automated teller machine (ATM) A machine that allows use of special cards by consumers to make deposits, withdraw cash, or transfer funds among accounts via electronic funds transfer. [WL/MBC]

automatic checkout machine (ACM) A system whereby customers have the opportunity to check themselves out of a store by scanning their purchases with the point-of-sale system, entering their customer identification card, and receiving clearance to exit the store. [WRD]

automatic merchandising machine operator An establishment primarily engaged in the retail sales of products by means of automatic merchandising units, also referred to as vending machines. (See also **automatic selling**.) [WRD]

automatic reorder The reorder of staple merchandise on the basis of predetermined minimum stock and specified reorder quantities without the intervention of the buyer except for periodic revision of items to be carried and the minimum and reorder quantities. This can be handled manually by reorder clerks or automatically by computer methods. [WRD]

automatic reordering system A system for ordering staple merchandise when a predetermined minimum quantity of goods in stock is reached. An automatic reorder can be generated by a computer on the basis of a perpetual inventory system and reorder point calculations. [WRD]

automatic selling The retail sale of goods or services through coin- or currency-operated machines activated by the ultimate consumer-buyer. (See also **automatic merchandising machine operator** and **vending machine**.) [WRD]

Automobile Information Disclosures Act (1958) This act mandates the display of various kinds of information on every new automobile including the suggested price of the car and of all optional equipment, and transportation costs. [DC]

autonomic decision making A pattern of decision making within a family in which an equal number of decisions are made individually by each spouse. (See also **syncratic decision making**.) [JPP/JCO]

average cost per unit Total cost, i.e., the sum of fixed costs and variable costs at a given level of output, divided by the number of units. [DLS]

average fixed cost The total fixed cost divided by the number of units produced and sold. (See also **average total cost; average variable cost; buyers' costs; common costs; cost; direct costs; direct fixed costs; direct variable costs; fixed cost; total;** and **indirect traceable costs**.) [KM]

average frequency See **frequency**

average revenue (AR) 1. (economic definition) The total revenue divided by the number of units marketed. [DLS] 2. pricing definition) The total revenue divided by the number of units sold. (See also **marginal revenue**.) [KM]

average total cost The total cost divided by the number of units produced and sold. (See also **average fixed cost, average variable cost, buyers' costs, common costs, cost, direct costs, direct fixed costs, direct variable costs,** and **indirect traceable costs**.) [KM]

average variable cost The total variable cost divided by the number of units produced and sold. (See also **average fixed cost; average total cost; buyers' costs; common costs; cost; direct costs; direct fixed costs; direct variable costs; indirect traceable costs;** and **variable cost, total**.) [KM]

average-cost pricing A practice of adding a "fair" or "reasonable" markup to the average cost of a product. [DLS]

award See **contest**

aware stage See **buyer readiness stage**

awareness See **adoption process, AIDA, awareness-trial-repeat,** and **hierarchy of effects model**

awareness-trial-repeat (A-T-R) A paradigm consisting of three key steps by the intended user. The steps take the person or firm from a state of ignorance about a new product to the point of product adoption. Awareness (cognition) may be of the product generally, its brand, and one or more of its attributes. Trial means some form of test purchase or use, following upon favorable affect stemming from knowledge regarding the attributes. Repeat means the trial was sufficiently successful to warrant one or more repeat purchases. There are other, similar, paradigms (for example attention, interest, desire, action) but these are not new product specific and do not cover the entire product adoption process. (See also **AIDA**.) [DW]

B-roll Videotaped footage that is not included in the final edited version of a company's video news release (VNR). B-roll is given to television stations along with the VNR to give the stations the option of putting together their own version of the story, giving more time to aspects the station feels will be of particular interest to their viewers. [DES/BEB]

baby boom The period from the end of World War II until the early 1960s when the number of births increased significantly, resulting in a population surge characterized as "the baby boom generation." [WL/MBC]

back order 1. (retailing definition) A part of an order that the vendor has not filled on time and that the vendor intends to ship as soon as the goods in question are received, manufactured, or procured. [WRD] 2. (physical distribution definition) An order not filled or shipped at time originally requested and "kept on the books" to be shipped later. [DJB/BJL]

back haul 1. The rerouting of a freight shipment back over a route that it has completed. 2. The use of a firm's empty delivery equipment to haul back purchases of merchandise from suppliers who are located near customer destinations. [WRD]

back-haul provision Current transportation regulation authorizes a freight allowance for customer pick up of specific commodities rather than delivered pricing. This provision often increases utilization of transportation capacity. [DJB/BJL]

backdoor selling 1. Sales to ultimate consumers by wholesalers who hold themselves out to be sellers only to retailers. 2. A salesperson's practice of avoiding a purchasing agent by visiting departments in plants to obtain orders without authorization from the purchasing agent. [WRD]

backgrounder sheet A brief review of an organization's history, mission, financial support, or other information provided to the media with other publicity materials in order to supply basic information that may be used in a news story. It is also known as a fact sheet. [DES/BEB]

backward integration See **integration**

backward vertical integration See **vertical integration**

bait advertising An alluring but insincere offer to sell whereby the advertiser does not intend to sell the advertised product at the advertised price; the purpose is to increase customer traffic. It also is called bait and switch advertising. [WRD]

bait and switch A deceptive sales practice whereby a low-priced product is advertised to lure customers to a store, where they are then induced to buy higher priced models by disparaging the less-expensive product. [DC]

bait and switch advertising The advertising of a product or service at an unusually low price with an intention to switch the customer to a higher priced item when the customer comes to the store to buy the advertised item. This practice is illegal if customers find it difficult or impossible to buy the advertised item. (See also **bait advertising**.) [JE]

balance of payments 1. (economic definition) The difference between monetary transactions of one country with the rest of the world in a given time period. [DLS] 2. (global marketing definition) A record of all the economic transactions between a country and the rest of the world. For the world as a whole, theoretically, imports must equal exports. The balance of payments can be divided into the so-called current account and capital account. The **current account** is for goods and services, the **capital account** is for money and investments. (See also **balance of trade** and **foreign direct investment**.) [WJK]

balance of trade The balance of merchandise imports and exports. (See also **balance of payments**.) [WJK]

balance sheet method An approach used by salespeople to gain commitment from a buyer by asking the buyer to think of the pros and cons of various alternatives. It is often referred to as the Ben Franklin method. (See also **approach, sales; benefit approach; compliment approach; consultative selling; customer orientation; formula selling; high-pressure selling; multilevel selling; problem solution approach;** and **systems selling**.) [BAW]

Balance Theory See **cognitive dissonance** and **consistency theory**

balanced stock The composition of merchandise inventory in the colors, sizes, styles, and other assortment characteristics that will satisfy customer wants. [WRD]

banner A series of cross tabulations between a criterion or dependent variable, and several, sometimes many, explanatory variables in a single table. [GAC]

bar code An information technology application that uniquely identifies various aspects of product characteristics as well as additional information regarding delivery and handling instructions. The information is read by scanning devices and greatly increases the speed, accuracy, and productivity of the distribution process. (See also **universal product code**.) [DJB/BJL]

barriers to competition The economic, legal, technical, psychological, or other factors that reduce competitive rivalry below the level that would otherwise occur naturally. Barriers include branding, advertising, patents, entry restrictions, tariffs, and quotas. Product differentiation is a barrier to competition. (See also **barriers to entry** and **product differentiation**.) [WL/MBC]

barriers to entry The economic, legal, psychological, technical, and other forces that limit access to markets, and hence reduce the threat of new competition. (See also **barriers to competition**.) [WL/MBC]

barter 1. (advertising definition) The practice of trading time or space in advertising media for merchandise or other nonmonetary forms of compensation. Syndicated television or radio programs are often carried by television and radio stations on a barter basis with the local stations receiving the syndicated program including some commercials in return for being able to sell the remaining commercial positions to other advertisers. [JE] 2. (global marketing definition) A type of trade transaction in which there is a direct exchange of goods or services between two parties. Although no money is involved, both partners construct an approximate shadow price for products flowing in each direction, without the use of money; e.g., A West German company sells a $60 million steel making complex to Indonesia and is paid in 3,000,000 barrels of Indonesia oil. (The shadow price of the oil would thus be $20 per barrel.) (See also **countertrade** and **switch trading**.) [WJK]

basement store A formerly typical department store division (not necessarily located in a basement) that is organized separately from the main store departments. It handles merchandise in lower price lines, features frequent bargain sales, purchases and offers considerable distress or job lot merchandise, and usually offers a much more limited range of services and breadth of assortment than main store departments. [WRD]

basic low stock The lowest level of inventory judged permissible for an item. It indicates a conception of the smallest number of units that could be on hand without losing sales at the lowest sales period of the year or season. [WRD]

basic stock list An assortment plan for staple merchandise that is continuously maintained in stock, usually for a period of a year or more. [WRD]

basing-point pricing A variation of delivered pricing. The delivered price is the product's list price plus transportation from a basing point to the buyer. The basing point is a city where the product is produced. But, in basing-point pricing, the product may be shipped from a city other than the basing point. (See also **multiple basing-point pricing system**.) [KM]

basis of segmentation See **market segmentation**

batting average See **hit rate**

Bayesian probability A probability based on a person's subjective or personal judgments and experience. [GAC]

BCG See **growth-share matrix**

BDI See **brand development index**

behavior The overt acts or actions of consumers that can be directly observed. (See also **consistency theory** and **Wheel of Consumer Analysis**.) [JPP/JCO]

behavior modeling See **sales training**

behavior monitoring See **behavioral self-management**

behavioral analysis A sales management evaluation and control method for monitoring sales force performance. A behavioral analysis involves evaluating the actual behavior of salespeople as well as their ultimate performance in terms of sales volume. Examples of behavioral analysis techniques include self-rating scales, supervisor ratings, and field observations. [AJD]

behavioral intention A cognitive plan to perform a behavior or action ("I intend to go shopping later"), created through a choice/decision process that focuses on beliefs about the consequences of the action. (See also **purchase intention** and **Theory of Reasoned Action**.) [JPP/JCO]

behavioral self-management A process by which a salesperson adopts certain procedures to control his or her behavior in order to achieve favorable results (such as improved performance). Examples of behavioral self-management techniques include salespeople's monitoring their own behavior (e.g., recording the amount of time spent calling on customers), setting personal goals (e.g., determining the number of new accounts to open), and rehearsing the desired behavior (e.g., practicing a sales presentation). Use of behavioral self-management affords sales managers additional time to engage in particularly important managerial activities and provides sales personnel opportunity to practice successful time management. [AJD]

belief 1. (consumer behavior definition) A cognition or cognitive organization about some aspect of the individual's world. Unlike an attitude, a belief is always emotionally or motivationally neutral. Krench and Crutchfield define belief as a generic term that encompasses knowledge, opinion, and faith—an enduring organization of perceptions and cognition about some aspect of the individual's world. It is the pattern of the meanings of a thing, the cognition about that thing. [HHK/MCC] 2. (consumer behavior definition) The perceived association between two concepts. A belief is synonymous with knowledge or meaning in that all refer to consumers' interpretations of important concepts. [JPP/JCO]

belongingness See **hierarchy of needs, Maslow's need hierarchy,** and **psychological drives**

below-the-line cost Any cost in the advertising production process that is not specifically itemized in the production budget. (See also **above-the-line cost.**) [JE]

Ben Franklin method See **balance sheet method**

benefit approach A sales approach in which the salesperson states a benefit of the product or service that will satisfy a prospect's need. (See also **approach, sales; balance sheet method; compliment approach; consultative selling; customer orientation; formula selling; high-pressure selling; multilevel selling; problem solution approach;** and **systems selling.**) [BAW]

benefit, product The value provided to a customer by a product feature. [BAW]

benefit segmentation The process of grouping consumers into market segments on the basis of the desirable consequences sought from the product. For example, the toothpaste market may include one segment seeking cosmetic benefits such as white teeth and another seeking health benefits such as decay prevention. [JPP/JCO]

benefit summary method A method used by salespeople to secure a prospect's commitment by reviewing the agreed-upon benefits of the salesperson's proposal. (See also **direct request method.**) [BAW]

Bernoulli process A probabilistic model in which the probability *p* that an event of interest occurs remains the same over repeated observations. That is, *p* stays the same over time, and does not depend on the outcome of past observations. This stationary, zero order model has been used to represent brand choice behavior or media viewing behavior by individuals (Greene 1982; Lilien and Kotler 1983). (See also **Beta binominal model.**) [DCS/YJW]

best seller list See **never-out list**

best sellers See **key items** and **never-out list**

Beta binomial model A probability mixture model commonly used to represent patterns of brand choice behavior or media exposure patterns. The model assumes that each individual's behavior follows a Bernoulli process. That is, an individual performs some behavior of interest (e.g., buying a brand of interest) with probability *p* on each possible opportunity (e.g., occasion on which a purchase is made from the product category of interest). The number of times that the behavior of interest is exhibited, out of a given number of opportunities, has the binomial distribution for any individual. The model further assumes that the probability values *p* vary across individuals according to a beta distribution (Greene 1982; Massy, Montgomery, and Morrison 1970). A generalization of this model to represent choice among more than two items is termed the Dirichlet multinomial model. These models are used to predict future brand choice or media exposure patterns based on individuals' past behavior. (See also **Bernoulli process** and **probability mixture model**.) [DCS/YJW]

beta coefficient A measure of the systematic risk (the risk that cannot be diversified away by holding a diversified portfolio) of an asset or security—where the variance of the return distribution is used as the risk surrogate. Beta is generally estimated as the slope coefficient of a linear regression of the asset or security's return on the market's return for some "representative" number of periods:

$$R_{ij} = \alpha_j + \beta_j R_{im}$$

where:

R_{ij} = the return on security j during period i,

α_j = the intercept coefficient for security j,

β_j = the beta coefficient for security j, and

R_{im} = the return on all market securities during period i.

beta distribution See **Beta binomial model**

beta error See **Type II error**

better business bureaus These are nonprofit organizations sponsored by local businesses. They currently number 150 and offer a variety of consumer education programs and materials, handle consumer inquiries, mediate and arbitrate complaints, and maintain records of consumer satisfaction and dissatisfaction with individual companies. [DC]

bid A legal document in which a seller agrees to provide products and/or services to a potential buyer at a specific price under specified conditions. [BAW]

bidding An invitation to potential suppliers to submit their offers and a price for a particular opportunity. A closed bid is formal, written, and sealed, and usually all closed bids are opened and reviewed at the same time, with the contract being awarded to the lowest bidder who meets the specifications. An open bid is usually more informal and is used when specific requirements are hard to rigidly define or when products vary substantially. (See also **sealed-bid pricing**.) [GLL/DTW]

bill of exchange An unconditional order in writing addressed by one person (the drawer) to another (the drawee), signed by the person giving it, requiring the person to whom it is addressed to pay on demand, or at a fixed or determinable future time, a sum certain in money to, or to the order of, a specified person or to bearer. (See also **documentary collections**.) [WJK]

bill of lading 1. (global marketing definition) A vital document in international trade that is required to establish legal ownership and facilitate financial transactions. The bill of lading serves the following purposes: (1) as a contract for shipment between the carrier and the shipper; (2) as a receipt from the carrier for shipment; and (3) as a certificate of ownership or title to the goods. [WJK] 2. (physical distribution definition) The basic document in the purchase of transportation services. It describes commodities and quantities shipped as well as the terms and conditions of carrier liability. Current law allows the bill of lading to be electronically generated and transmitted. [DJB/BJL]

bill of materials (BOM) An assessment of the combination of assemblies, subassemblies, parts, and materials needed to support planned production as detailed in the materials requirement plan. [DJB/BJL]

billed cost The price appearing on a vendor's bill before deducting cash discounts, but after deducting any trade discounts and quantity discounts from the list price. [WRD]

billed cost of inventory See **cost inventory**

binomial distribution See **Beta binomial model**

biological drives See **physiological motives**

bird dog An individual who, for a fee, provides sales leads to a salesperson. The individual also is called a spotter. [BAW]

black market The availability of merchandise at higher than ordinary prices when difficult or impossible to purchase it under normal market circumstances. This commonly involves illegal transactions. [WRD]

blanket order A general order placed with a manufacturer without specifying detailed instructions, such as sizes, styles, and shipping dates, all of which are to be furnished later, often in several orders for specific shipments. [WRD]

bleed advertisement The print ads or brochures for which the color, graphics, and/or artwork extends to the edge of the page. Such pages have no unprinted margins or borders and are usually sold at a premium price. [JE]

block plan A store layout plan that delineates the actual sizes, shapes, and locations of all store components. (See also **boutique store layout, bubble plan, free-flow pattern, free-form, gridiron pattern,** and **loop layout**.) [WRD]

blocked currency A currency regulated by its government in a manner that precludes it being taken out of the country or converted to other currencies. [DLS]

blueline A print of an ad, brochure, or other advertising materials produced on photosensitive paper (hence the blue color). It is used to confirm the location of all artwork, headlines, graphics, and text components before printing. (See also **galley proof**.) [JE]

blunder An error that arises when editing, coding, key punching, or tabulating the data. [GAC]

body copy The text of a piece of print advertising that provides more detailed information than provided by headlines and subheads. [JE]

body language The nonverbal signals communicated in sales interactions through facial expressions, arms, legs, and hands. (See also **nonverbal communications**.) [BAW]

BOM See **bill of materials**

bonus 1. (sales definition) A special compensation option that is a payment made at the discretion of management for achieving or surpassing some set level of performance. Whereas commissions are typically paid for each sale that is made, a bonus is generally not paid until the salesperson surpasses some level of total sales or other aspect of performance. The size of the bonus, however, might be determined by the extent to which the salesperson exceeds the minimum level of performance required to earn the bonus. Thus, bonuses are usually additional incentives to motivate salespeople to reach high levels of performance rather than a part of the basic compensation plan. [AJD] 2. (sales definition) An element in a salesperson's compensation that is paid infrequently in a lump sum, often based on subjective judgments of performance. (See also **combination compensation plan, commission, incentive compensation, incentive plan,** and **salary**.) [BAW]

bonus pack A special container, package, carton, or other holder in which the consumer is given more of the product for the same or perhaps even lower price per ounce or unit than in the regular container. (See also **flagging**.) [DES/BEB]

book See **portfolio**

book inventory An inventory that is compiled by adding units and/or the cost or retail value of incoming goods to previous inventory figures and deducing them from the units and/or cost or retail value of outgoing goods. Or, the units and/or cost or retail value of goods on hand at any time per the perpetual inventory system records. [WRD]

booking The act of order-taking, especially for delivery at a later date. Frequently the amount of production is based on the booking of advance orders. [WRD]

boomerang method A method used by salespeople to respond to customer objections by turning the objection into a reason for acting immediately. (See also **direct denial, feel-felt-found method, indirect denial, pass up method,** and **postpone method**.) [BAW]

Boston Consulting Group See **growth-share matrix**

bounce back coupon See **bounce back offer**

bounce back offer A coupon or other selling device included in a customer ordered product, premium, refund, or other package that attempts to sell more of the same or another product to the recipient. (See also **fulfillment**.) [DES/BEB]

boundary spanning A concept describing job tasks or responsibilities beyond the traditional managerial area. Boundary spanning can be internal to the firm (extending beyond traditional organizational departments) or external to the firm (crossing between channel members). [DJB/BJL]

boutique Actually, in French the word means "little shop," but in American retailing, the term has come to mean a carefully selected group of merchandise with unusual displays and fixtures, informal and attractive decor, and an atmosphere of individualized attention in the personalized manner of the image created in the operation. (See also **boutique store layout**.) [WRD]

boutique store layout A form of retail store layout pattern that brings together complete offerings from one vendor or for one use in one section as opposed to having the items in separate departments. For example, a tennis boutique in a department store will feature rackets, balls, shoes, and tennis outfits. (See also **block plan, bubble plan, free-flow pattern, free-form, gridiron pattern,** and **loop layout**.) [WRD]

Box-Jenkins method A method for forecasting sales that relies on procedures for identifying models that best fit a set of time series data and statistical tests to examine the adequacy of the fitted models, where the models consist of a combination of autoregressive and moving average terms. (See also **sales forecast**.) [GAC]

boycott A refusal to deal with, or cooperate with, a firm or nation to signal extreme disapproval of its policies and actions. Boycotts induce change, as, for example, when consumers boycott a retail chain to gain redress for perceived inequities. [WL/MBC]

BPI See **buying power index**

bracket creep The movement of consumers to higher and higher income tax brackets during periods of inflation regardless of the lack of any real increase in income. This phenomenon is less serious since the 1986 tax reform, which greatly reduced the number of tax brackets. [WL/MBC]

brainstorming A group method of problem solving, used in product concept generation. It is sometimes thought to be an open, free-wheeling idea session, but more correctly is a specific procedure developed by Alex Osborn, with precise rules of session conduct. Now it has many modifications in format of use, each variation with its own name. [DW]

branch house An establishment maintained by a manufacturer, separate from the headquarters establishment and used primarily for the purpose of stocking, selling, delivering, and servicing the manufacturer's product. [WRD]

branch house wholesaler A national, regional, or sectional wholesaler who operates a number of variously located establishments to provide better customer service in all parts of the territory covered. It differs from a chain wholesaler in that each branch is closely supervised as an extension of the main wholesale house. [WRD]

branch sales manager See **field sales manager**

branching question A technique used to direct respondents to different places in a questionnaire based on their response to the question at hand. [GAC]

brand A name, term, design, symbol, or any other feature that identifies one seller's good or service as distinct from those of other sellers. The legal term for brand is trademark. A brand may identify one item, a family of items, or all items of that seller. If used for the firm as a whole, the preferred term is trade name. (See also **advertised brand; brand extension; brand generic; brand image; brand name; brand personality; branded merchandise; branding, individual; branding, line family; competitive brands; distributor's brand; family brand; fighting brand; flanker brand; generic brand; house brand; individual brand; local brand; manufacturer's brand; national brand; product hierarchy;** and **unadvertised brand**.) [DW]

brand choice The selection of one brand from a set of alternative brands. [JPP/JCO]

brand choice models These stochastic models of individual brand choice focus on the brand that will be purchased on a particular purchase occasion, given that a purchase event will occur. This type of model includes Bernoulli processes and Markov models. Models in this category vary in their treatment of population heterogeneity, purchase event feedback, and exogenous market factors (Lilien and Kotler 1983). (See also **Bernoulli process, Beta binomial model, Defender, Dirichlet multinomial model, elasticon, Elimination-By-Aspects model, Hendry model, linear learning model, logit model, Luce's Choice Axiom, Mar-**

kov model, Negative Binomial Distribution model, nested logit model, probability mixture model, and zero order model.) [DCS/YJW]

brand contacts Any information-bearing experience that a customer or prospect has with the brand, the product category, or the sponsoring organization that relates to the marketer's product or service. (See also **database**.) [DES/BEB]

brand decision See **buying decisions**

brand decision model See **decision calculus models**

brand development index (BDI) A measure of the extent to which the sales of products in a market category have captured the total potential in a geographical area, based on the population of that area and the average consumption per user nationally. The brand development index is usually calculated for separate metropolitan areas, and is used to determine high-potential (underdeveloped) areas for new product entries or for primary demand promotions. [DW]

brand equity The value of a brand. From a consumer perspective, brand equity is based on consumer attitudes about positive brand attributes and favorable consequences of brand use. [JPP/JCO]

brand extension A product line extension marketed under the same general brand as a previous item or items. To distinguish the brand extension from the other item(s) under the primary brand, one can either add a secondary brand identification or add a generic. Thus an Epson FX-85 printer is an extension of Epson that used the secondary brand of FX-85, while Jello Instant Pudding is an extension of the Jello brand that uses a generic term. A brand extension is usually aimed at another segment of the general market for the overall brand. (See also **family brand** and **individual brand**.) [DW]

brand generic This is the second half of a product's identifying title. Brand is the first half, and identifies one seller's version, while the generic is the second half and identifies the general class of item. [Example: Jello (brand) gelatin dessert (generic)]. This is not to be confused with generic brand (such as on some low-price items in supermarkets), for which there is no individual brand. [DW]

brand image The perception of a brand in the minds of persons. The brand image is a mirror reflection (though perhaps inaccurate) of the brand personality or product being. It is what people believe about a brand—their thoughts, feelings, expectations. [DW]

brand indifference A purchasing pattern characterized by a low degree of brand loyalty. (See also **brand switching**.) [JPP/JCO]

brand label See **label**

brand loyalty 1. (sales promotion definition) The situation in which a consumer generally buys the same manufacturer-originated product or service repeatedly over time rather than buying from multiple suppliers within the category. [DES/BEB] 2. (consumer behavior definition) The degree to which a consumer consistently purchases the same brand within a product class. (See also **brand indifference** and **brand switching**.) [JPP/JCO]

brand management organization See **product management organization**

brand manager See **product manager**

brand mark The brand mark is that part of a brand name that cannot be spoken. It most commonly is a symbol, picture, design, distinctive lettering, color, or a combination of these. [DW]

brand name The brand name is that part of a brand that can be spoken. It includes letters, numbers, or words. The term trademark covers all forms of brand (brand name, brand mark, etc.), but brand name is the form most often meant when trademark is used. [DW]

brand personality This is the psychological nature of a particular brand as intended by its sellers, though persons in the marketplace may see the brand otherwise (called brand image). These two perspectives compare to the personalities of individual humans: what we intend or desire, and what others see or believe. [DW]

brand positioning See **product positioning**

brand switching A purchasing pattern characterized by a change from one brand to another. (See also **brand indifference** and **brand loyalty**.) [JPP/JCO]

brand-switching matrix A two-way table that indicates which brands a sample of people purchased in one period and which brands they purchased in a subsequent period, thus highlighting the switches occurring among and between brands as well as the number of persons who purchased the same brand in both periods. [GAC]

BRANDAID A decision support system for determining the marketing mix for a particular brand. The model has submodels dealing with advertising spending level, price, and salesperson effort (i.e., dollars per customer per year). Its parameters can be calibrated by combining historical data (e.g., on sales, market share, advertising spending, etc.) with structured subjective judgments (Little 1975). (See also **advertising models, decision calculus models, marketing mix models, promotion models,** and **sales force models**.) [DCS/YJW]

branded merchandise Goods that are identified by brands. This contrasts with generic brands, which are identified only by commodity type. [DW]

branding, family See **family brand**

branding, generic See **generic brand**

branding, individual Using separate brands for each product, without a family brand to tie them to other brands of that firm. Individual brands are used when the products are different physically, are of different quality levels, are targeted for different users or uses, or vary in some other way that might cause confusion or loss of sales if brought together under a family brand umbrella. [DW]

branding, line family Using a family brand to cover only some of a firm's products. It contrasts with those cases where the term *family brand* is used only to designate the firm's entire product line. (See also **brand**.) [DW]

break-bulk The process of dividing larger quantities into smaller quantities in the transportation-warehousing system as goods get closer to the final market. [DJB/BJL]

break-even analysis A method of examining the relationships between fixed costs, variable costs, volume, and price. The objective of the analysis is to determine the break-even point at alternative prices and a given cost structure. [KM]

break-even point The sales volume at which total revenues are equal to total costs. [KM]

breaking bulk See **allocation**

breaking sizes Running out of stock on particular sizes. [WRD]

Bretton Woods Agreement An agreed statement of aims for postwar monetary policy which resulted from an international monetary and financial conference held at Bretton Woods, New Hampshire, in July 1944. Its aims were: (1) to make all currencies freely convertible and thereby encourage multilateral trade; (2) to keep exchange rates stable; (3) to provide some means of assisting a country with temporary difficulties with its balance of payments; and (4) to encourage economic growth and development. (See also **International Bank for Reconstruction and Development**.) [WJK]

bribe A payment made to buyers to influence their purchase decisions. [BAW]

broad class See **product class**

broadcast quality The media industries' standard for material that can be aired. Technical format and content are both aspects of broadcast quality. For example, 3/4-inch tape is broadcast quality, VHS tape is not. Publicity submissions that are not broadcast quality generally will not be used. [DES/BEB]

broadcast television A method of distributing television signals by means of stations that broadcast signals over channels assigned to specific geographic areas. (See also **cable television**.) [JE]

brochure See **house publication**

broken case lot selling Breaking of cases to sell smaller quantities, done by many wholesalers to accommodate retailers who cannot afford to buy in full shipping case lots. [WRD]

broken lot An amount less than some understood standard unit of sale. [WRD]

broker A middleman who serves as a go-between for the buyer or seller. The broker assumes no title risks, does not usually have physical custody of products, and is not looked upon as a permanent representative of either the buyer or seller. (See also **agents and brokers**.) [WRD]

brown goods Merchandise in the consumer electronic audiovisual field, such as televisions, radios, stereo sets, etc. The name came from the brown (furniture color) cases in which such merchandise is frequently manufactured. At one time the term also included all furniture. [DW]

Brussels Nomenclature A tariff classification system developed by an international committee of experts under the sponsorship of the Customs Cooperation Council. The rules were used by most GATT members up until January 1989, when the Harmonized Tariff System went into effect. (See also **General Agreement on Tariffs and Trade**.) [WJK]

BTN See **Brussels Nomenclature**

bubble plan A store layout plan that shows the rough placement and adjacency of key elements of a proposed store. (See also **block plan, boutique store layout, free-flow pattern, free-form, gridiron pattern,** and **loop layout**.) [WRD]

budget The detailed financial component of the strategic plan that guides the allocation of resources and provides a mechanism for identifying deviations of actual from desired performance so corrective action can be taken. A budget assigns a dollar figure to each revenue and expense related activity. A budget is usually prepared for a period of one year by each component of an organization. Like the action program, a budget provides both a guide for action and a means of assessing performance. [GSD]

build market position See **investment strategy**

build strategy See **portfolio analysis**

bulk marking The practice of placing the price only on the original shipping containers or at least bulk packages; individual units are not marked until the merchandise is transferred from reserve to forward stock. It is also referred to as deferred marking. [WRD]

bundle See **mixed bundling**

bundling Offering several complementary products together or offering additional services in a single "package deal." The price of the bundle is typically lower than the sum of the prices of the individual products or services included in it. Groups of services or products may be bundled in different combinations appealing differently to different segments in order to price discriminate among these segments and to avoid cherry picking. (See also **mixed bundling, multiple-unit pricing** and **price bundling**.) [GLL/DTW]

bureaucratic organization This term is associated with government, where official decision making is circumscribed by laws, rules, and regulations which often result in inflexibility, "red tape", and slowness to act. The term is sometimes applied to the hierarchical business structure, which is thought to lead to slow decision making and slow response to change. It should be noted, however, that business—unlike government—operates in a competitive environment that does not reward slow decision making if it results in poor sales or customer service. Comment: To combat any tendency towards bureaucracy, particularly in large corporations, companies have speeded up decision making by measures such as decentralized and flatter organization structures along with computerized information and communication systems that alert management quickly to problems requiring resolution. (See also **centralized management; decentralized management; decentralized sales organization; divisional organization; flat organization; functional organization; geographical organization; hierarchical organization; market management organization; marketing organization, forms of; matrix organization; nonbusiness marketing organization;** and **product management organization**.) [VPB]

bushelman A formerly common term referring to a repairer of garments, especially in the alteration room for men's clothing. [WRD]

business analysis This is a term of many meanings, and in marketing it is usually associated in some way with the evaluation of new product proposals. In format, it may consist of a five-year, discounted cash flow, net present value-type of financial analysis, or it may be a more comprehensive analysis of the entire situation surrounding the proposed product. Chronologically, it may come early in the development process (when it is used to decide whether expensive research and development should be undertaken), and/or late in the product development cycle when the commercialization decision is being made. [DW]

Business Conditions Digest The U.S. Department of Commerce's monthly publication of economic time series covering such data as business and consumer expectations, cyclical indicators, national income, foreign trade, and price movements. [WL/MBC]

business cycle A rhythmic wave-like pattern of changes in business conditions over a period of time. (See also **depression, prosperity, recession,** and **recovery**.) [DLS]

business defamation Statements made that are unfair or untrue about a competitor, its products, or its salespeople. [BAW]

business definition Specifies the present and/or prospective scope of a strategic business unit's activities in terms of the boundaries of the arena in which the business elects to compete. The definition also serves to direct attention to the true function of the business—that is, the way that the business meets the needs of its target customers. A complete definition requires choices about the business position a long four dimensions: (1) customer functions—addressing the benefits being provided; (2) customer segments—specifying the customer groups seeking similar benefits and sharing characteristics that are strategically relevant; (3) technology—specifying the alternative ways in which a particular function can be performed; and (4) vertical business system—specifying where the business chooses to participate in the sequence of stages in the vertical business system (or value-added system). (See also **adaptive planning** and **strategy**.) [GSD]

business goals See **goal** and **growth objectives**

business manager See **matrix organization**

business market See **industrial market**

business market segmentation See **industrial market segmentation**

business marketing See **industrial marketing**

business planning process See **strategic planning**

business portfolio matrices See **portfolio analysis**

business portfolio models See **product and business portfolio models**

business reply card See **preprint advertising**

business reply envelope See **preprint advertising**

business service The intangible product (service), such as banking and maintenance, that is purchased by organizations that produce other products. It is a type of industrial product. [DW]

business start-up See **venture**

business strengths See **distinctive competences**

business system See **value chain analysis**

business-to-business advertising An area of advertising for products, services, resources, materials, and supplies purchased and used by businesses. This area includes: (1) industrial advertising, which involves goods, services, resources, and supplies used in the production of other goods and services; (2) trade advertising, which is directed to wholesalers and retailers who buy the advertised product for resale to consumers; (3) professional advertising, which is directed to members of various professions who might use or recommend the advertised product; and, (4) agricultural advertising, which is directed to farmers as business customers of various products and services. [JE]

buy See **media buy**

buy one-get one free A sales promotion offer made to either the retailer or the consumer in which purchase of one unit of the product is encouraged or rewarded by providing a second unit of the same product free of charge. [DES/BEB]

buy-back allowance A form of trade sales promotion in which channel members are offered an incentive to restock their store or warehouse with the product to the level in place prior to a count and recount promotion offer. [DES/BEB]

buyclasses Buying situations that are distinguished on four characteristics: newness to decision makers, number of alternatives to be considered, uncertainty inherent in the buying situation, and the amount of information needed for making a buying decision. There are three buyclasses: new task purchase, modified rebuy, and straight rebuy. A **new task purchase** is a problem or requirement that has not arisen before such that the buying center does not have any relevant experience with the product or service. A **modified rebuy** is a situation such that the buying center has some relevant experience to draw upon. The alternatives considered, however, are different, or changed from the ones considered the last time a similar problem arose. A **straight rebuy** is the purchase of standard parts; maintenance, repair, and operating items and supplies; or any recurring need that is handled on a routine basis. (See also **buygrid framework** and **information search**.) [GLL/DTW]

buyer The organizational member that carries out the purchase procedures of a product. A buyer may or may not make the buying decision. The buyer will manage the buying process, e.g., place the order and process the paperwork. (See also **buying center, buying roles, consumer,** and **procurement**.) [GLL/DTW]

buyer behavior This term is often used as an alternative to consumer behavior, but also is used when the purchaser is not the ultimate consumer but rather an industrial buyer, a buying center, or other middleman between the seller and the ultimate user. It is defined by some as the more general term, with consumer behavior and organizational buyer behavior as subsets. [HHK/MCC]

buyer intention A measure of a buyer's intention to buy a product or service. It can be measured as the subjective probability that a buyer's beliefs and attitudes will be acted upon in a purchasing framework. (See also **buyers intention survey** and **intention**.) [GLL/DTW]

buyer readiness stage The buyer's stage regarding readiness to buy a certain product or service. At any time, people are in different stages: unaware, aware, informed, interested, predisposed to buying, and intending to buy. [GLL/DTW]

buyer's remorse The insecurity that a buyer feels about the appropriateness of the purchase decision after the decision has been made. It also is called post purchase dissonance. (See also **cognitive dissonance**.) [BAW]

buyer's utility See **product line optimization**

buyer's welfare models See **product line optimization**

buyers intention survey A survey of buyers to measure their purchase intentions. The best results are obtained if the buyers have clearly formulated intentions. (See also **buyer intention**.) [GLL/DTW]

buyers market Economic conditions that favor the position of the retail buyer (or merchandiser) rather than the vendor. In other words, economic conditions are such that the retailer can demand and usually get concessions from suppliers in terms of price, delivery, and other market advantages. It is the opposite of a sellers market. [WRD]

buyers' costs The costs that buyers incur when acquiring and using products and services. Such costs include the price of the item being acquired, cost of information search, shipping costs, transportation costs, installation costs, and postpurchase costs that may affect buyers' perceptions of value of the item being acquired. (See also **acquisition value, average fixed cost, average total cost, average variable cost, common costs, cost, direct costs, direct fixed costs, direct variable costs,** and **indirect traceable costs**.) [KM]

buyers' intentions method See **users' expectations method**

buyflow The communication network between all individuals involved in a buying decision and the actions that take place during the course of making the purchase decision. (See also **buying center**.) [GLL/DTW]

buygrid framework A conceptual model that describes the organizational buying process. It consists of two dimensions: buyclasses and buyphases. The **buyclasses** are new task purchase, modified rebuy, and straight rebuy. The **buyphases** are need recognition, need definition, need description, seller identification, proposal solicitation, proposal evaluation and selection, ordering procedures, and performance review. (See also **buying center** and **problem recognition, in organizational buying**.) [GLL/DTW]

buying allowance A form of trade sales promotion in which the retailer is offered a discount on the purchase of the product at a particular point in time. The discount is often tied to the purchase of a particular number of units. [DES/BEB]

buying calendar A plan of a store buyer's market activities, generally covering a six-month merchandising season based on a selling calendar that indicates planned promotional events. [WRD]

buying center The group of individuals that consists of all organizational members who are involved in any way, to any extent, in any phase of a specific buying decision. (See also **buyer, buyflow, buygrid framework, buying committee, buying roles,** and **information search**.) [GLL/DTW]

buying committee 1. (industrial definition) An officially appointed group that is responsible for purchasing goods and services. [GLL/DTW] 2. (retailing definition) A committee that has the authority for final judgment and decision on such matters as adding or eliminating new products. It is especially common in supermarket companies and department store resident buying offices. [WRD] (See also **buying center** and **committee buying**.)

buying criteria The factors considered by buyers in their evaluation of alternative suppliers, such as dependability, product quality, cost, vendor production capacity, after-sale service, vendor reliability and integrity, reciprocity, and emotional factors. They can be categorized as product-related, e.g., technical specifications; company-related, e.g., reputation, and salesperson-related, e.g., expertise and trustworthiness. [GLL/DTW]

buying decisions The different buying situations a buyer would face in the course of purchasing a product or service to satisfy a need. Three buying decisions can be distinguished: (1) **product decision**, deciding on which product(s) will be purchased with available resources; (2) **brand decision**, deciding on which brand(s) will be purchased among competing brands of the same product; and (3) **supplier decision**, deciding on which supplier(s) will be patronized among competing suppliers. [GLL/DTW]

buying functional expense See **functional expense classification**

buying habits See **routinized response behavior**

buying influence The buying center members or their sources of information who have influence upon the other buying center members such that these other individuals can change in their behavior and/or attitudes in the process of making a specific buying decision. (See also **influence, interpersonal, in the buying center**.) [GLL/DTW]

buying motives The forces that have been activated into a state of tension causing the buyer to seek satisfaction of a specific need. Organizational buyers are influenced by both rational appeals (e.g., economic factors such as cost, quality, and service) and emotional appeals (e.g., status, security, and fear). (See also **motivation**.) [GLL/DTW]

buying plan A breakdown of the dollar open-to-buy figure of a department or merchandise classification to indicate the number or value of units to purchase in different classifications and subclassifications. [WRD]

buying policy index A leading indicator of business activity, published monthly by National Bureau of Economic Research, based on the proportion of purchasing agents reporting their buying commitments for the months ahead. [WL/MBC]

buying power 1. (consumer behavior definition) A term found in economic psychology implying the income available for discretionary spending among segments in the population. It is a measure of the ability and willingness to buy goods or services. [HHK/MCC] 2. (industrial definition) Refers to the relative influence an individual or a job function (engineering, purchasing, production) has in a purchase decision. Power may be based on reward abilities (granting monetary or perceptual benefits), coercion (imposing punishment), legitimacy (formal authority), personality (based on individual characteristics or status), or expertise (special knowledge or expertise). (See also **purchasing power**.) [GLL/DTW]

buying power index (BPI) 1. (retailing definition) An index indicating the percentage of total U.S. retail sales occurring in a specific geographic area. It is used to forecast demand for new stores and to evaluate the performance of existing stores. [WRD] 2. (industrial definition) A weighted index that converts three basic elements—population, effective buying income, and retail sales—into a measurement of a market's ability to buy. The index is expressed as a percentage of total U.S. potential and is published annually by *Sales and Marketing Management* magazine. [GLL/DTW]

buying period The sum of the reorder period and the delivery period, under periodic stock counting methods of unit control. [WRD]

buying roles The activities that one or more person(s) might perform in a buying decision. Six buying roles can be distinguished: (1) **initiator**, the person who first suggests or thinks of the idea of buying the particular product or service; (2) **influencer**, a person whose views influence other members of the buying center in making the final decision; (3) **decider**, the person who ultimately determines any part of or the entire buying decision—whether to buy, what to buy, how to buy, or where to buy; (4) **buyer**, the person who handles the paper work of the actual purchase; (5) **user**, the person(s) who consumes or uses the product or service; and (6) **gatekeeper**, the person(s) who controls information or access, or both, to decision makers and influencers. (See also **buying center**.) [GLL/DTW]

buying signal A verbal or visual cue that indicates a potential customer is interested in purchasing a product or service. Comment: A buying signal indicates that a salesperson should begin to close the sale. [BAW]

buying style The way a customer buys a given product or service. Buying styles range from deliberate buying to impulsive buying. [GLL/DTW]

buyphases See **buygrid framework**

cable television A method of distributing television signals by means of coaxial or fiber-optic cables. Cable subscribers can receive a wide variety of cable television channels, and some cable systems enable subscribers to both receive and send information by means of the cable connection between the cable system office and individual households. Some cable television services are even including telephone connection capabilities as an option available to subscribers. (See also **broadcast television**.) [JE]

Cable Television Consumer Protection and Competition Act (1992) An act containing complex, interrelated provisions that revise rules concerning cable television, broadcast television, and new television technologies. The Federal Communications Commission is required to prescribe regulations and resolve disputes. (See also **consumer protection legislation**.) [DC]

CACM Central American Common Market

cadre A salesperson who receives a relatively large amount of latitude, support, and attention from his or her sales manager. Cadres receive special treatment from their managers because they are perceived to be particularly competent, motivated, and trustworthy. In return for the special treatment, cadres are expected to perform assignments that are outside the formal job description. Cadres are the opposite of hired hand salespeople. [AJD]

CAI See **computer assisted interviewing**

call frequency The number of sales calls per time period made on a particular customer. Comment: The call frequencies assigned to customers are used by salespeople to plan their own route and sales call schedules. (See also **circular routing, leapfrog routing, routine call pattern, routing,** and **zoning**.) [BAW]

call option In foreign currency market, a call option gives the buyer of the call the right, but not the obligation, to buy the foreign currency up to the call's expiration date. (See also **foreign exchange market**.) [WJK]

call report A salesperson's report of a sales call made on a customer. [BAW]

call system A system of equalizing sales opportunities among salespeople—e.g., some stores rotate salespeople, giving each an equal opportunity to meet arriving customers. [WRD]

CALLPLAN A decision calculus model providing a decision support system for determining the amount of time that a salesperson should spend with current customers and sales prospects. The model's parameters are calculated using subjective responses to a series of point estimate questions concerning the likely impact of various numbers of customer visits on sales from each customer (Lodish 1971). Evidence regarding the model's effectiveness has been reported by Fudge and Lodish (1977). (See also **decision calculus models, decision support system, DETAILER, GEOLINE,** and **sales force models**.) [DCS/YJW]

cancellation A notification to a vendor that a buyer does not wish to accept ordered merchandise. Also, it is merchandise declared surplus by retailers, often sold in broken lots to discount houses or liquidators. (Out-of-style or slightly damaged shoes are frequently sold as "cancellation shoes".) [WRD]

canned sales presentation A standardized sales presentation that includes all the key selling points arranged in the order designed to elicit the best response from the customer. (See also **customized sales presentation; need satisfaction selling; outlined presentation; presentation, sales;** and **stimulus response sales approach**.) [BAW]

canned sales talk A prepared sales talk repeated from memory. [WRD]

cannibalization The loss of sales in established products experienced by a firm resulting from its own introduction of new products that are partial or complete substitutes. That is, the new product "steals" some of the sales of the established product. [GSD]

canvasser See **house-to-house salesperson**

capabilities See **competitive position**

capacity requirements planning (CRP) The evaluation of planned production to determine if it can be accomplished within the capacity limitations of manufacturing facilities. A capacity load projection is completed for each item in the master production schedule. The calculated load requirement is compared to available capacity, thus determining underutilization or overutilization of facilities. [DJB/BJL]

capital 1. The produced wealth that assists directly in further production and that furnishes satisfaction or gratification to the user only indirectly or incidentally, if at all. 2. The owner's investment in a business. 3. All economic goods in existence at a given period of time used by society for production. [DLS]

capital account See **balance of payments**

capital asset pricing model (CAPM) A theory that states that the expected return on any asset or security is given by the following formula:

$$E\,(R_j = R_f + [E(R_m) - R_f]\,B_j$$

where:

$E\,(R_j)$ = the expected return on any security j,

R_f = the risk-free rate of interest (often estimated by the return on U.S. Treasury bills),

$E\,(R_m)$ = the expected return on all securities in the market (often estimated by the return on the Standard & Poor's 500-stock index), and

B_j = the beta coefficient for security j.

It is generally conceded in finance that the CAPM is effectively untestable. [PFA]

capital consumption allowance The sum of depreciation on major capital goods plus capital goods destroyed or damaged plus depreciation on minor capital goods. (See also **net national product**.) [DLS]

capital goods The instruments of production that make up an organization's plant and operating capacity. (See also **capital consumption allowance** and **installations.) [DLS]**

capital intensive A product or an industry in which plant and equipment requirements are large relative to labor. [DLS]

capital turnover The number of times

total capital investment is divisible into sales; the greater this figure, the smaller the net profit on sales required to meet a given return on investment. [WRD]

capitalism See **economic organization**

CAPM See **capital asset pricing model**

CAPM approach to investment analysis A technique that employs the CAPM equation to calculate the risk-adjusted, after-tax required rate of return in the net present value equation. This approach replaces the use of the traditional weighted average cost of capital. Beta is usually estimated as the average of the betas for firms already operating (exclusively) in the market in which the investment will be made. [PFA]

captive market The potential clientele of retail or service businesses located in hotels, airports, railroad stations, etc., where consumers do not have reasonable alternative sources of supply. [WRD]

career plateau A situation in which the likelihood of a salesperson's receiving increased responsibility (e.g., a promotion, a bigger territory) is low. Career plateauing can lead to substantial opportunity costs for sales personnel on the company. Factors contributing to a career plateau include both personal (e.g., low motivation, feelings of job burnout) and organizational (e.g., inadequate sales training, little company growth) characteristics. [AJD]

CARICOM Caribbean Economic Community

carload The shipment by rail of a full load. This usually qualifies for lower freight rate than smaller shipments. [DJB/BJL]

carousel The materials handling equipment that delivers the desired item to the order picker. Typically a carousel consists of a series of bins mounted on an oval track. The entire carousel rotates, bringing the bin to the operator. [DJB/BJL]

carriage trade An old expression that refers to a wealthy class of patrons accorded special services. [WRD]

carrier In transportation, a car, truck, vessel, plane, helicopter, or train. [WRD]

carry over models Models in which the effect of a marketing mix variable is assumed to last beyond a single time period. A transformation often applied in modeling the effect of lagged marketing expenditures (e.g., advertising expenditures in previous periods) on the current period's sales is the Koyck transformation. When it is assumed that the effect of the marketing expenditure decays geometrically over time (i.e., loses a constant proportion of its remaining impact in each subsequent period), then the Koyck transformation allows the analyst to estimate all of those lagged marketing expenditure effects using a single one-period-lagged-sales term to predict current sales. The transformation thus greatly simplifies the task of estimating lagged effects in sales response models. The validity of the assumptions required for the transformation to be appropriate has, however, been challenged. For reviews see Parsons and Schultz (1976, Chapter 8) or Lilien and Kotler (1983, Chapter 4). [DCS/YJW]

carrying charge The sum paid for credit service on certain charge accounts. It is an interest usually charged on the unpaid balance. [WRD]

cartel A combination of separate firms who collusively set prices and control output with the intent of maximizing mutual profits. [DLS]

cash before delivery (C.B.D.) See **cash in advance, cash with order,** and **collect on delivery**

cash cow See **growth-share matrix**

cash discount A premium for advance payment at a rate that is usually higher than the prevailing rate of interest. It also is a reduction in price allowed the buyer for prompt payment. [WRD]

cash excess See **overage**

cash flow The cash generated by after-tax earnings plus depreciation minus cash used within the business. Or more simply, the movement of cash into and out of the business. Where the "in-flows" (receipts) have exceeded the "out-flows" (disbursements) in a specified period of time, the cash flow is said to be positive and provides additional net cash. When the disbursements exceed the receipts in a specified period of time, the cash flow is said to be negative and reduces net cash. [GSD]

cash in advance (C.I.A.) Payment before receipt or delivery of goods or services. Used interchangeably with cash before delivery, and applies in the same instance as the latter. (See also **cash with order** and **collect on delivery**.) [WRD]

cash on delivery The practice of collecting for the price of the merchandise plus the relevant transportation charges. It is commonly referred to as C.O.D. (See also **collect on delivery**.) [KM]

cash register bank An assortment of change for the use of the salesperson or transaction station operator. It is prepared at the end of the day by the person operating a cash register or prepared by a cashier for the cash register operator. [WRD]

cash terms The payment of cash for the purchase of goods, usually within a certain time period—e.g., 10 to 14 days. [WRD]

cash with order (CWO) The seller demands that cash covering the cost of merchandise and delivery accompany the customer's order; cash before delivery and cash in advance apply similarly. [WRD]

cashless economy See **electronic funds transfer**

catalog A publication containing the descriptions or details of a number or range of products used to increase mail order sales, phone sales, and/or in-store traffic of the sender. [DES/BEB]

catalog showroom A retail outlet that consumers visit to make actual purchases of articles described in catalogs mailed to their homes or available for reference in the store. [WRD]

categorization A cognitive process by which objects, events, and persons are grouped together and responded to in terms of their class membership rather than their uniqueness. [JPP/JCO]

category killer A type of destination store that is usually large and that concentrates on one category, thus making it possible to carry both a broad assortment and deep selection of merchandise, coupled with low price and moderate service. (See also **mail-order house**.) [WRD]

category manager This manager reports to the marketing manager and is responsible for the marketing of the several brands falling under a generic product category such as coffee, dessert, and oral hygiene. This manager (companies sometimes use other titles, for example, unit business manager) is responsible for maximizing the total profit from the mix of brands in the category. This may be done by allocating funds and marketing effort according to the profit potential of each brand in the mix; also deleting weak brands and adding new brands with higher profit potential. The category manager is chosen for business as well as marketing skills and works closely (sometimes as a member of a team) with other functional managers such as production, finance, and research and development to achieve maximum profitability for the product category. (See also **divisional organization; group product manager; marketing organization, forms of; matrix organization; new product manager; product management organization;** and **product manager**.) [VPB]

category signage A signage system that is used to call out and locate specific merchandise categories in a store. [WRD]

category-based processing A cognitive process in which an individual attempts to categorize new stimuli. If a stimulus can be considered as an example of an existing category, it is evaluated by the affect associated with the category, rather than by careful consideration of its attributes (as in piecemeal processing). The category schema is the basis for evaluation. (See also **attitude**.) [HHK/MCC]

causal research A research design in which the major emphasis is on determining a cause-and-effect relationship. (See also **descriptive research** and **exploratory research**.) [GAC]

C.B.D. See **cash before delivery** or **central business district**

cease and desist order An order from an administrative agency or court prohibiting the continuation of a particular course of conduct. [DC]

Celler-Kefauver Act (1950) See **Anti-Merger Act (1950)**

census A complete canvass of a population. [GAC]

census block Usually a well-defined rectangular area bounded by streets or roads. However, it may be irregular in shape and may be bounded by physical features such as railroads or streams. Census blocks do not cross boundaries of countries, tracts, or block numbering areas. [DLH]

census metropolitan area (CMA) The main labor market area of an urbanized core having at least 100,000 population. Each constituent municipality has at least 40 percent of its labor force working in the urbanized core. [DLH]

census tract A small, relatively permanent area into which metropolitan statistical areas (MSAs) and certain other areas are divided for the purpose of providing statistics for small areas. When census tracts are established, they are designed to be homogeneous with respect to population characteristics, economic status, and living conditions. Census tracts generally have between 2,500 and 8,000 residents. [DLH]

center of influence method A prospecting method used by salespeople in which the salesperson cultivates well-known, influential people who are willing to provide sales leads. (See also **cold-canvassing, curiosity approach, endless chain method, introduction approach, product approach,** and **referral approach**.) [BAW]

centers of commerce See **central place theory**

central business district (CBD) For statistical purposes, this area is specifically defined for individual cities. Because there are not generally accepted rules for determining what a CBD area should include or exclude, the U.S. Bureau of the Census did not provide rigid specifications for defining the CBD but provided a general characterization of the CBD, describing it as an area of very high land valuation; an area characterized by a high concentration of retail businesses, offices, theaters, hotels, service businesses; and an area of high traffic flow; and required that the CBD ordinarily should be defined to follow existing census tract lines; i.e., to consist of one or more whole census tracts. (See also **concentric zone theory**.) [WRD]

central buying A type of central market representation in which the authority and responsibility for merchandise selection and purchase are vested in a central market office, rather than in the individual store units represented by the central office. It is also referred to as consolidated buying. [WRD]

central market A place where a large number of suppliers are concentrated. The location may be a simple area, such as a merchandise mart, or it may be located in the same general section of a city. For example, New York is still the primary central market for many types of merchandise, especially women's wear. [WRD]

central office edit The thorough and exacting scrutiny and correction of completed data collection forms, including a decision about what to do with the data. [GAC]

central place theory 1. (retailing definition) A model that ranks communities according to the assortment of goods available in each. At the bottom of the hierarchy are communities that represent the smallest central places (centers of commerce). They provide the basic necessities of life. Further up the hierarchy are the larger central places, which carry all goods and services found in lower-order central places plus more specialized ones that are not necessary. (See also **concentric zone theory, dialectic process, gravity model, natural selection theory, retail accordion theory, retail life cycle,** and **wheel of retailing theory**.) [WRD] 2. (geography definition) A normative theory that explains the size, number, and spacing of distribution centers to serve a dispersed population. (See also **multiple purpose trip**.) [DLH]

central route to persuasion One of two types of cognitive processes by which persuasion occurs. In the central route, consumers focus on the product messages in the ad, interpret them, form beliefs about product attributes and consequences, and integrate these meanings to form brand attitudes and intentions. (See also **peripheral route to persuasion**.) [JPP/JCO]

centralized adjustment system A centralized office that handles complaints, whether placed by telephone, mail, or a personal visit to the store. It would not apply to routine matters, such as the return of merchandise in good condition and within the limits of the store's policy governing approval sales, exchanges, and so on. [WRD]

centralized management The practice of referring matters for decision to higher levels of management, particularly to corporate management. (See also **bureaucratic organization; decentralized management; divisional organization; flat organization; functional organization; geographic organization; hierarchical organization; market management organization; marketing organization, forms of; matrix organization; multibusiness organization; nonbusiness marketing organization;** and **product management organization**.) [VPB]

centralized sales organization A sales force, reporting to corporate or group management, that sells the products of two or more divisions. This may be appropriate when the products of the divisions are distributed through the same channels. (See also **decentralized sales organization; full-line sales organization; partially integrated division; sales organization, forms of; sales organization specialized by account; sales organization specialized by market;** and **sales organization specialized by product**.) [VPB]

cents-off offer A consumer sales promotion technique offering a certificate good for a discount off the posted purchase price of a particular product. (See also **coupon**.) [DES/BEB]

CERCLA See **Comprehensive Environmental Response, Compensation and Liability Act (1980)**

certificate of origin A document that specifies the origin of a product. [WJK]

C.F.R. See **cost and freight**

chain discount A series of trade discount percentages or their total—e.g., if a list (catalog) price denotes $100 and is subject to a 40-15-15 discount to dealers, the total or chain discount is $56.65—i.e., $100 - 40% = $60, $60 - 15% = $51, $51 - 15% = $43.35. (See also **on-percentage**.) [WRD]

chain of command See **hierarchical organization**

chain store A store that is a single store unit of a chain store system. (See also **multiunit establishment**.) [WRD]

chain store system A group of retail stores of essentially the same type, centrally owned and with some degree of centralized control of operation. The term chain store may also refer to a single store as a unit of such a group. (See also **multiunit establishment**.) [WRD]

chain wholesaler See **branch house wholesaler**

chance constrained programming See **mathematical programming**

channel control The actual impact that a channel member achieves on an associated channel member's beliefs, attitudes, and behavior. (See also **channel power**.) [GLF]

channel cooperation The willingness of channel members to work together to ensure important channel functions are performed. [GLF]

channel effectiveness A channel performance dimension based on how well the channel satisfies customer needs and wants, such as for lot size, delivery time, location convenience, and assortment breadth. (See also **channel efficiency, channel productivity,** and **channel profitability**.) [GLF]

channel efficiency A channel performance dimension focusing on how well the firm minimizes costs associated with performing necessary channel functions. (See also **channel effectiveness, channel productivity,** and **channel profitability**.) [GLF]

channel equity See **channel performance**

channel flows The marketing functions performed by manufacturers, wholesalers, retailers, and other channel members within the channel. Eight universal channel flows that have been identified include physical possession, ownership, promotion, negotiation, financing, risking, ordering, and payment. (See also **channel functions** and **channel specialization**.) [GLF]

channel functions The job tasks or activities that need to be performed in the channel. (See also **channel flows**.) [GLF]

channel member commitment The degree to which a channel relationship is stable, loyalty has been built, and each channel member is willing to make sacrifices to maintain the exchange. [GLF]

channel member dependence A channel member's need to maintain a particular channel relationship in order to achieve desired goals. [GLF]

channel member satisfaction A channel member's affective state reflecting its overall approval or disapproval of a channel relationship with another firm. [GLF]

channel of distribution An organized network (system) of agencies and institutions which, in combination, perform all the functions required to link producers with end customers to accomplish the marketing task. (See also **channel performance**.) [GLF]

channel of distribution model See **distribution models**

channel performance An outcome measure of the channel of distribution. The performance of a distribution channel can be assessed by considering a number of performance dimensions, including channel effectiveness, channel efficiency, channel productivity, and channel profitability. [GLF]

channel power The ability of a particular channel member to control or influence the decision making and behavior of another channel member, or one channel member's potential for influence with another channel member. (See also **channel control**.) [GLF]

channel productivity A channel performance dimension based on the degree to which the channels' total investment in the various inputs necessary to achieve a given distribution objective can be optimized in terms of outputs. (See also **channel effectiveness, channel efficiency**, and **channel profitability**.) [GLF]

channel profitability A channel performance dimension based on the financial performance of channel members in terms of ROI, liquidity, leverage, growth in sales and profits, etc. (See also **channel effectiveness, channel efficiency**, and **channel productivity**.) [GLF]

channel specialization The channel members' choice of unique positions in the channel based on their capacities, interests, goals, expectations, values, and frames of references. Hence, each performs those tasks (participates in those channel flows) which it can perform at a comparative advantage. [GLF]

checking-list item See **never-out list**

checklist A memory-jogger list of items, used to remind an analyst to think of all relevant aspects. It finds frequent use as a tool of creativity in concept generation and as a factor-consideration list in concept screening. (See also **screening of ideas**.) [DW]

cherry picking A buyer selection of only a few items from one vendor's line and others from another line, failing to purchase a complete line or classification of merchandise from one resource. It also sometimes describes a customer's tendency to buy only items on sale. [WRD]

child protection A term covering the totality of measures necessary for a child's physical, moral, and mental well-being. [DC]

Child Protection Act (1966) This act amended the Federal Hazardous Substances Act by stating toys and other children's articles that contained hazardous substances were banned. [DC]

choice Choice involves evaluating alternative actions or behaviors and forming a behavioral intention or plan to engage in the selected behavior. Choice is the outcome of purchase decision making. [JPP/JCO]

choice alternatives The different behaviors considered by consumers in decision making; they are usually the products or brands considered for purchase. [JPP/JCO]

choice criteria The specific attributes or consequences used by consumers to evaluate and choose from a set of alternatives. [JPP/JCO]

choice heuristic See **heuristic**

choice rule A method by which an individual is hypothesized to make choices or decisions. A choice rule specifies the manner in which the individual evaluates each alternative under consideration. (See also **conjunctive rule, disjunctive rule, lexicographic rule, noncompensatory rules,** and **piecemeal processing**.) [HHK/MCC]

C.I.A. See **cash in advance**

C.I.F. See **cost insurance freight**

CIM See **computer integrated manufacturing**

CIP See **consumer information processing**

circular routing A method for scheduling sales calls that involves circular patterns. (See also **call frequency, leapfrog routing, routine call pattern, routing,** and **zoning**.) [BAW]

circulation The number of copies of a print advertising medium that are distributed. Paid circulation refers to the number of copies that are purchased by readers. (See also **controlled circulation**.) [JE]

claim See **advertising claim**

class membership See **categorization**

class rate All the products transported by common carriers that are classified for purposes of transportation pricing. The charge in dollars and cents per hundredweight to move a specific product classification between two locations is the class rate. (See also **commodity rate, exception rate,** and **line-haul rate**.) [DJB/BJL]

classic merchandise The merchandise that is not influenced by style changes, for which a demand virtually always exists. [WRD]

classical conditioning 1. (consumer behavior definition) A process through which a previously neutral stimulus, by being paired with an unconditioned stimulus, comes to elicit a response very similar to the response originally elicited by the unconditioned stimulus. [JPP/JCO] 2. (consumer behavior definition) A traditional learning approach often credited to the work of Ivan Pavlov. It is the belief that when a stimulus that elicits a response is paired with another stimulus, the second stimulus will elicit behavior similar to the original response. [HHK/MCC]

classical probability A probability determined by the relative frequency with which an event occurs when an experiment is repeated under controlled conditions. [GAC]

classification A grouping of merchandise into a homogeneous category usually smaller than a department. It is particularly useful for control purposes. (See also **classification control, dissection control,** and **merchandise classification**.) [WRD]

classification control A form of dollar inventory control in which the dollar value of each classification of goods is smaller than the total stock of the department—e.g., the sporting goods department may be divided into several classifications or dissections, such as golf, fishing, active sport, etc. (See also **dissection control** and **merchandise classification.**) [WRD]

Clayton Act (1914) This act specifically outlaws discrimination in prices, exclusive and tying contracts, intercorporate stockholdings, and interlocking directorates "where the effect . . . may be to substantially lessen competition or tend to create a monopoly." (See also **antitrust laws, contract, tying,** and **Robinson-Patman Act**.) [DC]

Clean Air Act (1970) This act requires the Environmental Protection Agency to establish air-quality standards based on considerations of public health. [DC]

clearance sale An end-of-season sale to make room for new goods. It is also pushing the sale of slow-moving, shopworn, and demonstration model goods. [WRD]

clearing arrangement See **switch trading**

clearinghouse The central processing location where coupons or other sales promotion offers are collected, analyzed, and sorted for payment or fulfillment. [DES/BEB]

client The term used to indicate an advertiser who is being served by an advertising agency. [JE]

close The culmination of a sales presentation in which a salesperson attempts to get a customer to commit to buying a product or service. [BAW]

close-out An offer at a reduced price to clear slow-moving or incomplete stock. It is also an incomplete assortment, the remainder of a line of merchandise that is to be discontinued, offered at a low price to ensure immediate sale. [WRD]

closed bid See **bidding**

closed stock Items sold only in sets, with no assurance to the customer that the same pattern and quality can be bought at any later time. Thus there is no provision for replacing broken pieces. (See also **open stock**.) [WRD]

closed-door discount house A type of discount store that sells only to consumers who purchase a membership card. (See also **wholesale club**.) [WRD]

"closed-loop" MRP See **manufacturing resource planning**

closing See **close**

club plan selling An arrangement in which a consumer is awarded prizes or granted discount buying privileges by getting new customers to join the club. The club is the group of customers served by the selling organization, and one joins by making purchases. [WRD]

cluster analysis A body of statistical techniques concerned with developing natural groupings of objects based on the relationships of the *p* variables describing the objects. (See also **conjoint analysis, correlation analysis, discriminant analysis, factor analysis,** and **regression analysis**.) [GAC]

cluster sample A probability sample distinguished by a two-step procedure in which (1) the parent population is divided into mutually exclusive and exhaustive subsets, and (2) a random sample of subsets is selected. If the investigator then uses all of the population elements in the selected subsets for the sample, the procedure is one-stage cluster sampling; if a sample of elements is selected probabilistically from the subsets, the procedure is two-stage cluster sampling. (See also **area sampling, simple random sample, stratified sample,** and **systematic sample**.) [GAC]

clutter The condition that exists when many ads or commercials are placed too closely together in space or time. [JE]

clutter, advertising The extent to which multiple messages compete for the consumers' (limited) attention. It often is used to indicate multiple competing messages in one medium (such as television) or place. [HHK/MCC]

CMA See **census metropolitan area**

CMSA See **consolidated metropolitan statistical area**

C.O.D. See **collect on delivery**

co-op See **cooperative advertising**

co-op coupons Offers from a group of noncompetitive or mutually enhancing group of sellers who have either joined or been gathered together to offer a greater value than any could alone. (See also **coupon**.) [DES/BEB]

co-op mailing The distribution of coupons or other sales promotion offers for a variety of products through a single mailing piece. [DES/BEB]

coalitions See **alliances**

code 128 The standard bar code carton symbology utilized in warehousing, shipping, and receiving. [DJB/BJL]

coding A technical procedure by which data are categorized; it involves specifying the alternative categories or classes into which the responses are to be placed and assigning code numbers to the classes. [GAC]

coefficient of income sensitivity The average percentage that sales of a product vary over a period of time relative to a one percent change in personal disposable income. [DLS]

coercive influence strategy A means of communication that puts direct pressure on the target to perform a specific behavior or set of behaviors with adverse consequences of noncompliance stressed or implied and mediated by the source. (See also **influence strategy** and **noncoercive influence strategy**.) [GLF]

COFC See **container-on-flatcar**

cognition 1. (consumer behavior definition) The sum total of an individual's beliefs, attitudes, perceptions, needs, goals, and learned reactions about some aspect of the individual's world. A cognition is the pattern of meaning of a thing. [HHK/MCC] 2. (consumer behavior definition) The mental processes of interpretation and decision making, including the beliefs and meanings they create. (See also **awareness-trial-repeat** and **Wheel of Consumer Analysis**.) [JPP/JCO]

cognitive dissonance 1. (consumer behavior definition) A psychologically uncomfortable state produced by an inconsistency between beliefs and behaviors, producing a motivation to reduce the dissonance. [JPP/JCO] 2. (consumer behavior definition) A term coined by Leon Festinger to describe the feeling of discomfort or imbalance that is presumed to be evident when various cognitions about a thing are not in agreement with each other. For example, knowledge that smoking leads to serious physical ailments is dissonant with the belief that smoking is pleasurable and the psychophysiological need to smoke. Cognitive dissonance is similar to Heider's work on Balance Theory and Osgood and Tannenbaum's Congruity Theory. Dissonance is presumed to be an uncomfortable state that the individual strives to reduce. (See also **buyer's remorse, consistency theory,** and **post-purchase evaluation**.) [HHK/MCC]

cognitive processes The mental activities by which external information in the environment is transformed into meanings or patterns of thought and combined to form judgments about behavior. (See also **central route to persuasion, comprehension,** and **peripheral route to persuasion**.) [JPP/JCO]

cognitive response The thoughts a consumer has to a persuasive message such as support arguments or counterarguments. [JPP/JCO]

cohort 1. (consumer behavior definition) A fellow consumer or group of consumers grouped along some variable. For example, age cohort would be a group of consumers of approximately the same age. [HHK/MCC] 2. (marketing research definition) An aggregate of individuals who experience the same event within the same time interval. [GAC]

COLA See **cost-of-living allowance**

cold-canvassing A method of prospecting under which a salesperson calls on totally unfamiliar organizations and prospects. (See also **center of influence method, curiosity approach, endless chain method, introduction approach, product approach,** and **referral approach**.) [BAW]

collaborative agreements A cooperation strategy between companies to jointly pursue a common goal. It is also referred to as strategic alliances or global strategic partnerships. [WJK]

collect on delivery (C.O.D.) The buyer must make payment for the purchase at time of delivery of goods. It is considered a poor substitute for cash before delivery or cash in advance because if the purchaser refuses, the seller incurs return freight charges and any deterioration of the product in the process. (See also **cash on delivery** and **sight draft-bill of lading**.) [WRD]

collect rate shipment A freight bill is a carrier's method of charging for transportation services. If it is collect, the buyer is responsible and must pay transport costs upon arrival of the shipment. [DJB/BJL]

collusion An agreement between competitors, made after contacting customers, concerning their relationships with the customers. (See also **conspiracy**.) [BAW]

color sep See **color separation**

color separation A negative of one of the four colors (black, blue, red, and yellow) used in the four-color printing process to reproduce color photographs and other color elements. [JE]

column inch A unit of print advertising space that is one column wide and one inch in height. [JE]

combination compensation plan 1. (sales definition) A compensation plan for salespeople that combines a base salary with commissions and/or a bonus. (See also **incentive compensation.**) [BAW] 2. (sales definition) A sales force compensation plan that offers a base salary plus some proportion of incentive pay consisting of commissions, bonuses, or both. When salary plus commission is used, the commissions are typically tied to sales volume or profitability, just as with a straight commission plan. The only difference is that the commissions are smaller in a combination plan than when the salesperson is compensated solely by commission. (See also **straight salary plan**.) [AJD]

combination export management firm See **manufacturer's export representative**

commercial The name used to indicate an advertising message in the radio, broadcast television, and cable television media. (See also **ad** and **advertisement**.) [JE]

commercial auction An agent business unit that effects the sale of goods through an auctioneer, who, under specified rules, solicits bids or offers from buyers and has the power to accept the highest bids of responsible bidders and, thereby, consummates the sale. (See also **auction** and **auction company**.) [WRD]

commercial pool See **pool**

commercialization A stage (usually the last) in the development cycle for a new product. Commonly, it is thought to begin when the product is introduced into the marketplace, but actually starts when a management commits to marketing the item. Subsequent activity during commercialization includes manufacturing and distribution, as well as promotion. It may precede the product announcement date by months. (See also **new product development**.) [DW]

commercialized product concept statement See **concept statement commercialized**

commissary store A retail outlet owned and operated by one of the armed forces to sell food and related products to military personnel at special prices. (See also **post exchange**.) [WRD]

commission The compensation paid to salespeople based on a fixed formula related to the salesperson's activity or performance. Comment: The basis for calculating a commission is frequently a fixed percentage of sales or gross margin generated. Salespeople may have to achieve a prespecified level of performance before they are eligible to receive a commission. (See also **bonus, combination compensation plan, incentive compensation,** and **salary**.) [BAW]

commission buyer of farm products A wholesale establishment primarily engaged in buying farm products on a commission basis from farmers for others. (See also **assembler**.) [WRD]

commission buying office An office that receives its remuneration in the form of commissions on orders placed from manufacturers rather than from retailers. [WRD]

commission house An agent who usually exercises physical control over and negotiates the sale of the goods the agent handles. The agent generally enjoys broader powers as to prices, methods, and terms of the sale than does the broker, although the agent must obey instructions issued by the principal. The agent often arranges delivery, extends necessary credit, collects, deducts fees, and remits the balance to the principal. (See also **factor**.) [WRD]

commission merchant See **commission house**

commission method of compensation The traditional compensation method whereby advertising agencies have been paid on the basis of a percentage of the cost of media time and/or space they purchased for a client. The usual commission has been 15 percent of the total cost of the media space and time purchased. Recently, clients have been moving toward the negotiation of specific fees for the services rendered by advertising agencies. (See also **fee method of compensation**.) [JE]

commissioner A specialized type of buying agency that brings the buyer in contact with proper vendors in foreign markets and acts as an interpreter. Also, the commissioner facilitates the procedures of foreign exchange and shipping. [WRD]

committee buying The situation whenever the buying decision is made by a group of people rather than by a single buyer. A multiunit operation is usually the type of firm that uses this procedure. (See also **buying committee**.) [WRD]

commodity exchange An organization usually owned by the member-traders that provides facilities for bringing together buyers and sellers, or their agents, of specified standard commodities for promoting trades in accordance with prescribed rules—either spot or future, or both—in these commodities. (See also **organized market**.) [WRD]

commodity product See **staple good**

commodity rate A transportation rate published for specific commodities without regard to classification. Carriers commonly publish commodity rates when a large quantity of product moves between the two locations on a regular basis. When a commodity rate exists, it supersedes the corresponding class rate or exception rate. (See also **line-haul rate**.) [DJB/BJL]

common area (of shopping center) The area within a shopping center that is not for rental by tenants but is available for common use by all tenants, their customers, and invitees. [WRD]

common carrier A company that offers to transport property for revenue at any time and any place within its operating authority without discrimination. A common carrier is authorized to conduct for-hire transportation after receiving certification as fit, willing, and able. (See also **independent carrier**.) [DJB/BJL]

common costs The common or general costs that support a number of activities or profit segments. These costs cannot be traced to a product or segment. (See also **average fixed cost, average total cost, average variable cost, buyers' costs, cost, direct costs, direct fixed costs, direct variable costs,** and **indirect traceable costs**.) [KM]

common law This term refers to that part of the law that grew up without benefit of legislation and resulted from court decisions; these rulings then became the precedent for subsequent litigation. According to legal theory, the colonists brought the common law of England with them to America. [DC]

common market A group of countries that have harmonized tariff policies among members, established common tariffs for nonmembers and permit the free flow of factors of production among members. (See also **custom union**.) [WJK]

communication A method of data collection involving questioning of respondents to secure the desired information using a data collection instrument called a questionnaire. [GAC]

community market See **public market**

community relations A firm's interactions with the locality in which it operates, with emphasis on disseminating company information to foster trust in the company's activities. [DES/BEB]

community service activities See **public service announcement**

community shopping center One of the several standard classes of shopping centers recognized by The Urban Land Institute. The community shopping center usually has a junior department store or a discount store as the major tenant. The community shopping center is typically about 150,000 square feet of store area but ranges from 100,000 square feet to 450,000 square feet. (See also **arcade shopping center, factory outlet center, mall-type shopping center, neighborhood shopping center, off-price shopping center, regional shopping center, strip-type shopping center,** and **super regional shopping center**.) [WRD]

commuters' zone See **concentric zone theory**

comp See **comprehensive layout**

company image See **consumer relations**

company potential See **sales potential**

company-related buying criteria See **buying criteria**

comparative advantage 1. (global marketing definition) A theory that holds that a country can gain from trade even if it has an absolute disadvantage in the production of all goods, or, that it can gain from trade even if it has an absolute advantage in the production of all goods. (See also **absolute advantage** and **competitive advantage**.) [WJK] 2. (economic definition) A term that relates to both the greater absolute advantages or the smaller absolute disadvantages that a country has in economic activities as compared with other countries. (See also **law of comparative advantage**.) [DLS]

comparative advertising 1. (consumer behavior definition) An advertisement in which there is specific mention or presentation of competing brand(s) and a comparison is made or implied. [HHK/MCC] 2. (advertising definition) An approach to the advertising message that persuades the audience by comparing the performance of two or more brands of a product or service. The reference brand may be the previous formula used by the advertiser, an unnamed competitor of the advertiser, or a specific and named competitor of the advertiser. [JE]

comparative prices Statements in advertisements or signs comparing specific prices with previous prices, other prices, or prices goods are estimated to be worth. [WRD]

comparative rating scale A scale requiring subjects to make their ratings as a series of relative judgments or comparisons rather than as independent assessments. (See also **constant sum method, graphic-rating scale, Guttman scale, interval scale, itemized rating scale, nominal scale, ordinal scale, ratio scale, Stapel scale,** and **summated rating**.) [GAC]

comparison shopping Includes two major types of activity, merchandise shopping and service shopping: 1. **Merchandise shopping** activities rendered by an organized shopping bureau includes checks of new items being offered by competing stores; reports on advertised promotions of competitors; comparison price shopping, etc. 2. **Service shopping** is normally performed by shoppers who pose as customers and report the quality of selling service on standard forms. [WRD]

compensation/incentive models See **sales force models**

compensatory import charges Taxes that correspond to various internal taxes, such as value-added taxes and sales taxes. [WJK]

compensatory integration procedure See **compensatory rule**

compensatory model See **compensatory rule**

compensatory process See **compensatory rule**

compensatory rule In evaluating alternatives, the compensatory rule suggests that a consumer will select the alternative with the highest overall evaluation on a set of choice criteria. Criteria evaluations are done separately and combined arithmetically such that positive evaluations can offset or balance (compensate for) negative evaluations. This term is also called compensatory integration procedure, compensatory model, and compensatory process. (See also **noncompensatory rules**.) [JPP/JCO]

competences of firm See **distinctive competences**

competition The rivalry among sellers trying to achieve such goals as increasing profits, market share, and sales volume by varying the elements of the marketing mix: price, product, distribution, and promotion. It is the product of vying for customers by the pursuit of differential advantage, i.e., changing to better meet consumer wants and needs. In economic theory, various competitive states such as monopolistic competition, oligopoly, perfect competition, and monopoly are delineated based on the degree of control that sellers have over price. (See also **imperfect competition**.) [WL/MBC]

competitive advantage 1. (strategic marketing definition) A competitive advantage exists when there is a match between the distinctive competences of a firm and the factors critical for success within the industry that permits the firm to outperform its competitors. Advantages can be gained by having the lowest delivered costs and/or differentiation in terms of providing superior or unique performance on attributes that are important to customers. (See also **competitive strategy, differential advantage, first-mover advantage, follower advantage,** and **invisible assets**.) [GSD] 2. (global marketing definition) A total offer, vis-a-vis relevant competition, that is more attractive to customers. It exists when the competencies of a firm permit the firm to outperform its competitors. (See also **absolute advantage** and **comparative advantage**.) [WJK]

competitive advertising See **consumer sales promotion**

competitive analysis The analysis of factors designed to answer the question, "how well is a firm doing compared to its competitors?" The analysis goes well beyond sales and profit figures in assessing the firm's ratings on such factors as price, product, technical capabilities, quality, customer service, delivery, and other important factors compared to each of the major competitors. [WL/MBC]

competitive bidding The practice of competition in which firms submit offers or bids that detail the services and product specifications to be offered at a stated price. [KM]

competitive brands The brands that are considered as alternatives by buyers in a particular market segment; sometimes called the evoked set. Occasionally, it is used to mean a (smaller) set of products which a particular seller wishes to be competing with; more rarely, it means the full set of competitors in fact competing in a given market. [DW]

competitive duplication See **sustainable competitive advantage**

competitive environment The number and strength of rival firms competing in the market for a product. (See also **duopoly, imperfect competition, monopolistic competition, monopoly, monopsony, oligopolistic competition, oligopolistic environment, oligopoly, oligopsony, perfect competition, pure competition,** and **workable competition**.) [DLS]

competitive forces See **market attractiveness**

competitive frame The list of specific brands with which a given brand competes most directly for customers. (See also **advertising strategy**.) [JE]

competitive intelligence The systematic gathering of data and information about all aspects of competitors' marketing and business activities for the purposes of formulating plans and strategies and making decisions. [WL/MBC]

competitive parity budgeting An advertising budget method whereby an advertiser chooses to use a level of spending on advertising that is similar to the advertising spending level being used by major competitors. (See also **adaptive control budgeting, all-you-can-afford budgeting, objective-and-task budgeting, payout budgeting,** and **percent-of-sales budgeting**.) [JE]

competitive position The position of one business relative to others in the same industry. There are a multitude of factors contributing to (and which can be used to measure) competition. The major categories are (1) **market position**—relative share of market, rate of change of share, variability of share across segments, perceived differentiation of quality/service/price, breadth of product, and company images; (2) **economic and technological position**—relative cost position, capacity utilization, technological position, and patented technology, product, or process; and (3) **capabilities**—management strength and depth, marketing strength, distribution system, labor relations, relationships with regulators. (See also **PIMS Program**.) [GSD]

competitive sales promotion See **consumer sales promotion**

competitive strategy A plan that attempts to define a position for the business that utilizes the competitive advantages that the business has over its competitors. [GSD]

complement of markup percentage One hundred percent less markup percentage on retail. (See also **cost multiplier**.) [WRD]

complementary products 1. (product development definition) The products that are manufactured together, sold together, bought together, or used together. One aids or enhances the other. (See also **assortment** and **substitute products**.) [DW] 2. (economic definition) Those products whose demands are positively related, i.e., an increase in quantity demanded by the market of product A results in an increase in the quantity demanded for product B. [DLS] 3. (environments definition) A product that is used or sold jointly with other products, such as razors and blades, or toothbrushes and toothpaste. [WL/MBC]

complete protection See **warranty**

completed fertility The average number of births for all women in a society. (See also **crude birth rate, fertility rate, replacement level fertility,** and **total fertility rate**.) [WL/MBC]

completely randomized design An experimental design in which the experimental treatments are assigned to the test units completely at random. (See also **experiment**.) [GAC]

compliance See **foot-in-the-door technique**

compliment approach A sales approach in which the salesperson begins the sales call by complimenting the prospect. (See also **approach, sales; balance sheet method; benefit approach; consultative selling; customer orien-**

tation; formula selling; high-pressure selling; multilevel selling; problem solution approach; and **systems selling.**) [BAW]

component parts The industrial products (or subassemblies) that either are ready for direct assembly into the finished product or require only a minor amount of further processing. Examples are switches, transistors, motors, gears, nuts, bolts, and screws. (See also **fabricating materials, parts,** and **processed materials.**) [GLL/DTW]

component prototype See **prototype**

compound duties The duties that provide for specific, plus ad valorem duties to be levied on the same articles. (See also **countervailing duties, specific duties,** and **tariff system.**) [WJK]

comprehension The cognitive processes involved in interpreting, understanding, and making sense of concepts, events, objects, and persons in the environment. (See also **elaboration** and **hierarchy of effects model.**) [JPP/JCO]

Comprehensive Crime Control Act (1984) An act establishing the United States Sentencing Commission, a permanent independent federal agency whose central purpose is to establish sentencing policies and practices "by promulgating detailed guidelines prescribing appropriate sentences for offenders convicted of federal crimes." Federal Sentencing Guidelines for application to organizations convicted of violating federal criminal law went into effect in 1991. [DC]

Comprehensive Environmental Response, Compensation & Liability Act (CERCLA) (1980) At act designed to curtail offenses to the environment. Under CERCLA, any person who is responsible for a release or threat of release of a hazardous substance and fails, without sufficient cause, to properly provide removal or remedial action may be liable for punitive damages. [DC]

comprehensive layout A detailed mock-up of a print ad presented to clients in order to gain their approval for the advertising approach before significant production costs are incurred for obtaining artwork and typesetting. (See also **dummy, layout, mechanical, rough, storyboard,** and **thumbnail.**) [JE]

computer assisted interviewing (CAI) The conduct of surveys using computers to manage the sequence of questions and in which the answers are recorded electronically through the use of the keyboard. [GAC]

computer integrated manufacturing (CIM) An approach to managerial control that focuses on the automated flow of information among participants in the stages of manufacturing. [DJB/BJL]

computerized buying The use of computers in managing the purchasing process. Such tasks as calculating current inventory figures, computing economic order quantities, preparing purchase orders, developing requests for vendor quotations, expediting orders, and generating printouts of dollars spent on vendors and products can be part of the system. Some systems may have decision support models to assist in analysis of purchase alternatives. [GLL/DTW]

concentrated marketing See **marketing segmentation strategies**

concentration The process of bringing goods from various places together in one place. It includes the sorting processes of accumulation and assorting. [GLF]

concentration, economic A measure of the dominance of a market exercised by the top few firms in an industry. [DLS]

concentration ratio 1. (environments definition) A statistical measure, such as the percentage of a total industry's sales accounted for by the largest three firms in the industry, representing the degree of concentration of a market. (See also **market concentration**.) [WL/MBC] 2. (strategic marketing definition) The proportion of industry shipments accounted for by the four largest firms in that industry, expressed as a percentage. This measure describes the structure of competition and yields insights into the intensity of rivalry in an industry. [GSD]

concentration strategy In this strategy, a company chooses to pursue a large share of one or more submarkets rather than chasing a small share of a large market. The strategy can be somewhat risky if the demand in the submarket falls away or if one or more competitors enter the submarket. [GSD]

concentric diversification See **diversification**

concentric zone theory A theory of urban land-use patterns, developed by William Burgess, that states that a city will assume the form of five concentric urban zones: the central business district, the zone in transition, the zone of working persons' homes, the zone of better residences, and the commuters' zone. Growth is accomplished by the expansion of each zone into the next zone. (See also **central place theory, dialectic process, gravity model, natural selection theory, retail accordion theory, retail life cycle,** and **wheel of retailing theory**.) [WRD]

concept A briefly stated idea or theme for possible use as the organizing idea for an advertisement or advertising campaign. (See also **advertising idea** and **attitude, belief,** and **product concept**.) [JE]

concept evaluation stage A stage of the new product development cycle in which ideas for new products are evaluated. Initially, the product idea may be evaluated on the basis of words, pictures, or models. The purpose of the concept evaluation stage is to determine whether an idea is worth further investment. The concept evaluation stage follows the idea generation stage. [DW]

concept generation See **idea generation**

concept statement A verbal and/or pictorial statement of a concept (for a product or for advertising) that is prepared for presentation to potential buyers or users to get their reaction prior to its being implemented. Product concepts are followed by prototypes; advertising concepts by one of several forms of semi-finished production. [DW]

concept statement, commercialized A term used in distinguishing two types of product concept statements. A commercialized product concept statement is prepared in an advertising format, as a persuasive statement. A noncommercialized product concept statement is prepared in neutral, nonpersuasive format. [DW]

concept test A qualitative or quantitative examination of consumer reactions to a proposed advertising idea. [JE]

concept test-based forecasting models See **new product forecasting models**

concept testing and development The process in which a concept statement is presented to potential buyers or users, for their reactions. These reactions permit the developer to estimate the sales value of the concept (whether product or advertising) and to make changes in it so as to enhance its sales value. (See also **screening of ideas**.) [DW]

conceptual definition See **constitutive definition**

conditional sale contract An agreement under which the title does not pass to the buyer until the buyer has fulfilled his/her contract obligations. The buyer assumes complete responsibility upon delivery, must maintain the article purchased, and must make regular payments. If the buyer defaults, the seller may repossess, use the proceeds of a sale of the item to satisfy the remaining obligation, and refund the excess, if any, above the cost of repossession and sale, to the buyer. If the proceeds of a sale are insufficient, the buyer is still technically liable to the seller for the remainder. [WRD]

confirmation In consumer satisfaction theory, confirmation refers to a situation in which a product performs exactly as it was expected to, i.e., prepurchase expectations are confirmed. (See also **disconfirmation**.) [JPP/JCO]

confirmation (of order) From a retailer's standpoint, the official order of a store for goods made out on the retailer's order form and countersigned by the buyer and merchandise manager. It is distinguished from the memoranda that buyers often make out on vendors' order blanks that are not official orders and are not binding on the store. From the vendor's standpoint, it is the acknowledgment of a buyer's order by the vendor. It is the buyer's legal acceptance of the offer made by the buyer generally in writing. [WRD]

conflicting incoming stimuli See **selective perception**

conglomerate A firm with large diversified holdings acquired through acquisitions and mergers. It is also known as a multimarket firm. [WL/MBC]

conglomerate diversification See **diversification**

conglomerate merger The merger of companies in unrelated businesses, such as the merger of automobile manufacturers with electronics products manufacturers, or of airlines with hotels and car rental companies. [WL/MBC]

Congruity Theory See **cognitive dissonance**

conjoint analysis A statistical technique in which respondents' utilities or valuations of attributes are inferred from the preferences they express for various combinations of these attributes. (See also **cluster analysis, correlation analysis, discriminant analysis, elasticon, factor analysis, POSSE, product design modes, product line optimization,** and **regression analysis**.) [GAC]

conjoint analysis-based simulation models See **product and business portfolio models**

conjunctive rule A decision-making rule of thumb or heuristic in which the consumer is assumed to set up minimum cutoffs for each of several attributes or dimensions of a product or thing. If the brand or item does not meet all of the minimum criteria, it is rejected. The evaluation rule leads to an acceptable or nonacceptable decision. For example, a conjunctive rule may be that a slice of bread must have at least 3 grams of protein, minimum percentages of specific vitamins, less than 100 mg sodium, and less than 75 calories per slice to be acceptable. A brand must meet all of these minimum attributes or it is unacceptable. A shortfall in one attribute is not offset by excessive endowment in another attribute. (See also

choice rule, disjunctive rule, expectancy-value model, lexicographic rule, noncompensatory rules, and **piecemeal processing**.) [HHK/MCC]

conscience See **ego**

conscious parallelism 1. (legislation definition) Evidence of concert of action implied from business behavior, such as setting parallel prices, without proof of an express agreement. [DC] 2. (strategic marketing definition) The pattern within an industry in which firms prefer to "follow" other firms (typically the market leader) rather than pursue a different course. The reason for behaving in this manner is that there is little opportunity and/or little gain to be made by adopting a different strategy from the others in the industry. It is most often observed as similarity in pricing actions. [GSD]

consent order An order issued after a defendant agrees to discontinue a complained-of practice without admitting any violation of the law. [DC]

consideration 1. (sales definition) A sales manager leadership style wherein sales managers are supportive, friendly, and considerate of their sales personnel; they consult with them and represent their interests; and they recognize their contributions. In essence, a sales manager using this kind of leadership style exhibits relationship-oriented behavior. (See also **contingent reward leadership, initiating structure, laissez faire leadership, management-by-exception leadership,** and **transformational leadership**.) [AJD] 2. (retailing definition) Something of value received or given at the request of the promiser in reliance on and in return for the promiser's promise. It may be a payment of money, or merely an exchange of promises, as when a buyer orders goods and the vendor confirms the order. The buyer promises to buy and take the goods, and the vendor promises to sell and ship them. [WRD]

consideration set The group of alternatives that a consumer evaluates in making a decision. [JPP/JCO]

consignee A person or firm to whom shipments are made. [DJB/BJL]

consignment 1. (channels of distribution definition) A method of selling whereby a manufacturer provides an intermediary with the merchandise while retaining title to the goods. The intermediary is free to sell the product and to pay only for goods actually sold. [GLF] 2. (retailing definition) The products shipped for future sale or other purpose, title remaining with the shipper (consignor), for which the receiver (consignee), upon acceptance, is accountable. The consignee may be the eventual purchaser, may act as the agent through whom the sale is effected, or may otherwise dispose of the products in accordance with an agreement with the consignor. [WRD]

consignment sale In this sale, title remains with the vendor until the goods are resold by the retailer; however, any unsold portion of the goods may be returned to the vendor without payment. [WRD]

consistency theory A theory that purports that attitudes, values, and behavior tend to be consistent in the cognitive structures of the individual. (See also **cognitive dissonance**.) [HHK/MCC]

consistent stimuli See **selective perception**

consolidated buying See **central buying**

consolidated delivery service A private business organized to deliver products for retailers. A fee is charged for every package delivered. [WRD]

consolidated metropolitan statistical area (CMSA) An area that contains two or more overlapping and/or interlocking primary metropolitan statistical areas. (See also **metropolitan statistical area** and **standard metropolitan statistical area**.) [DLS]

consolidation 1. (physical distribution definition) The small shipments combined or consolidated into larger shipments to reduce transportation expenditures. Larger volume shipments typically qualify for quantity discounts. Generally the larger the shipment the lower the freight rate per hundredweight. [DJB/BJL] 2. (environments definition) The joining of two or more independent business firms into a new firm. Unlike a merger, the acquired company does not maintain its identity. [WL/MBC]

consolidator A person or firm providing the service of combining small shipments into larger shipments to reduce transportation expenditures. [DJB/BJL]

conspicuous consumption A term believed to have been coined by Veblen implying consumption for the sake of displaying to others wealth, power, or prestige. Usually it is applied to expensive or luxury goods rather than everyday items. (See also **hedonistic consumption**.) [HHK/MCC]

conspiracy An agreement between competitors, made prior to contacting customers, concerning their relationships with the customers. (See also **collusion**.) [BAW]

constant dollar value The adjustment of dollar values by purchasing power to eliminate or allow for the effects of price changes on data in dollars reported over time. This is sometimes referred to as real dollars. [WL/MBC]

constant dollars Dollars that have been adjusted statistically to a base period in an attempt to remove the effects of inflation and deflation. [DLS]

constant sum method A type of comparative rating scale in which an individual is instructed to divide some given sum among two or more attributes on the basis of some criterion (e.g., their importance to him or her). (See also **graphic-rating scale, Guttman scale, interval scale, itemized rating scale, nominal scale, ordinal scale, ratio scale, Stapel scale,** and **summated rating**.) [GAC]

constitutive definition A definition in which a given construct is defined in terms of other constructs in the set, sometimes in the form of an equation that expresses the relationship among them. (See also **operational definition**.) [GAC]

construct validation An approach to validating a measure by determining what construct, concept, or trait the instrument is in fact measuring. (See also **content validity, convergent validity, discriminant validity, external validity, internal validity, pragmatic validity,** and **validity**.) [GAC]

consultative selling A customized sales presentation approach in which the salesperson is viewed as an expert and serves as a consultant to the customer. The salesperson identifies the prospects's needs and recommends the best solution even if the best solution does not require the salesperson's products or services. (See also **approach, sales; balance sheet method; benefit approach; compliment approach; customer orientation; formula selling; high-pressure selling; multilevel sell-**

ing; problem solution approach, and **systems selling**.) [BAW]

consumable supplies The products that are used up or consumed in the operation of a business. Examples are cleaning compounds, business forms, soaps, and small tools. [GLL/DTW]

consumer Traditionally, the ultimate user or consumer of goods, ideas, and services. However, the term also is used to imply the buyer or decision maker as well as the ultimate consumer. A mother buying cereal for consumption by a small child is often called the consumer although she may not be the ultimate user. (See also **consumer behavior**.) [HHK/MCC]

consumer awareness See **product performance tracking**

consumer behavior 1. (consumer behavior definition) The dynamic interaction of affect and cognition, behavior, and the environment by which human beings conduct the exchange aspects of their lives. 2. The overt actions of consumers. [JPP/JCO] 3. (consumer behavior definition) The behavior of the consumer or decision maker in the market place of products and services. It often is used to describe the interdisciplinary field of scientific study that attempts to understand and describe such behavior. (See also **buyer behavior**.) [HHK/MCC]

Consumer Behavior Odyssey A team of researchers that traveled across the country in the summer of 1986 interviewing, filming, and recording the behavior of consumers engaging in various consumption activities. [HHK/MCC]

consumer "bill of rights" President John F. Kennedy's directive to the Consumer Advisory Council in 1962 setting forth the federal government's role in consumerism in aiding consumers to exercise their rights to safety, to be informed, to choose, and to be heard. [DC]

consumer buying behavior See **consumer behavior**

consumer choice model A model attempting to represent how consumers use and combine information about alternatives in order to make a choice among them. [HHK/MCC]

consumer cooperative A marketing organization owned and operated for the mutual benefit of consumer-owners who have voluntarily associated themselves for the purpose. [WRD]

consumer credit Credit used by individuals or families for the satisfaction of their own wants. Also, it is the granting of credit by retailers, banks, and finance companies for this purpose. [WRD]

Consumer Credit Protection Act (1968) This act, also known as the Truth-in-Lending Act, requires full disclosure of terms and conditions of finance charges, and restricts the garnishment of wages. (See also **consumer protection legislation**.) [DC]

consumer decision making See **decision making, consumer**

consumer decision making unit The decision maker in the family, organization, or group. The decision making unit need not necessarily be a single individual, but may be a committee or informal set of individuals that makes the final choices. Often the decision reflects not only the attributes of the products being considered, but also the influence patterns found in formal groups and informal groups. (see also **decision making, consumer**.) [HHK/MCC]

consumer demand See **sales promotion**

consumer education The formalized teaching efforts to provide consumers with skills and knowledge to allocate their resources wisely in the marketplace. [DC]

consumer expenditure survey A survey of a representative sample of the U.S. population conducted by the U.S. Bureau of the Census for the Bureau of Labor Statistics to provide a continuous flow of data on the buying habits of American consumers. The survey consists of two components: an interview panel survey of five interviews every three months, and a diary or record keeping survey of households for two consecutive one-week periods. [WL/MBC]

consumer finance company A lending agency licensed under state laws to engage in the business of lending money to consumers. It is also referred to as a personal finance company. [WRD]

Consumer Goods Pricing Act (1975) This act repealed the Miller-Tydings Resale Price Maintenance Act and the McGuire-Keogh Fair Trade Enabling Act, thereby removing federal antitrust exemption for resale price maintenance agreements. (See also **fair trade laws**.) [DC]

consumer group interaction See **consumer relations**

consumer information The policies aimed at providing consumers with marketplace information and fostering effective utilization leading to improved consumer choice. [DC]

consumer information processing (CIP) The mental processes by which consumers interpret information from the environment to make it meaningful and integrate that information to make decisions. [JPP/JCO]

consumer motivation The needs, wants, drives, and desires of an individual that lead him or her toward the purchase of products or ideas. The motivations may be physiologically, psychologically, or environmentally driven. [HHK/MCC]

consumer movement A mix of people, ideas, and organizations representing previously unrepresented groups or concerns and having change or reform as common ends. [DC]

consumer price index (CPI) A statistical measure maintained by the U.S. government that shows the trend of prices of goods and services (a *market basket*) purchased by consumers. [GLS]

consumer/product relationship The relationship between consumers and a product or brand. It is how consumers perceive the product as relating to their goals and values. The consumer/product relationship is important to consider in developing marketing strategies. [JPP/JCO]

consumer product A product produced for, and purchased by, households for their use. (See also **convenience product, emergency product, impulse product, shopping product, specialty product**, and **staple good**.) [DW]

Consumer Product Safety Act (1972) This act established the Consumer Product Safety Commission and transferred a number of product safety functions previously assigned to other agencies to this commission. (See also **consumer protection legislation**.) [DC]

Consumer Product Safety Commission (CPSC) A federal regulatory agency that conducts investigations on consumer product safety, tests consumer products, provides training in product safety, promulgates product safety standards, and collects data relating to causes and prevention of injury associated with consumer products. (See also **Consumer Product Safety Act**.) [DC]

consumer protection The body of federal, state, and local government legislation designed to assure safety, purity, quality, and efficacy of many products and services and the reliability of statements in advertising about them. [DC]

consumer protection legislation The basic consumer protection legislation enacted by the federal government is the Federal Trade Commission Act, which prohibits unfair or deceptive acts or practices. Others include the Consumer Credit Protection Act, the Consumer Product Safety Act, environmental protection acts, the Federal Food, Drug and Cosmetics Act, the Magnuson-Moss Warranty Federal Trade Commission Improvement Act, the National Traffic and Motor Vehicle Safety Act, the Pure Food and Drug Act, the Cable Television Consumer Protection and Competition Act, the Telephone Disclosure and Dispute Resolution Act, and the Nutrition Labeling and Education Act. [DC]

consumer relations The communications efforts used to support the sale of a product or service. This generally includes product publicity, company image advertising, interaction with consumer groups, and customer inquiry response systems. [DES/BEB]

consumer sales promotion Externally directed incentives offered to the ultimate consumer. These usually consist of offers such as coupons, premiums, rebates, etc., designed to gain one or more of the following: product trial; repeat usage of product; more frequent or multiple product purchases; introduce a new/improved product; introduce new packaging or different size packages; neutralize competitive advertising or sales promotions; capitalize on seasonal, geographic, or special events; encourage consumers to trade up to a larger size, more profitable line, or another product in the line. (See also **accelerated purchase, buy one-get one free, cents-off offer, contest, continuity plan, cross-selling deal, cross ruff, free sample, game, refund, sales promotion,** and **sample**.) [DES/BEB]

consumer satisfaction 1. (consumer behavior definition) The degree to which a consumer's expectations are fulfilled or surpassed by a product. (See also **confirmation** and **disconfirmation**.) [JPP/JCO] 2. (consumer behavior definition) The post-purchase evaluation of a consumer action by the ultimate consumer or the decision maker. The beliefs, attitudes, and future purchase patterns; word-of-mouth communication; and legal and informal complaints have been related to the post-purchase satisfaction/dissatisfaction process. [HHK/MCC]

Consumer Sentiment Index The Index of Consumer Sentiment (ICS) was developed at the University of Michigan Survey Research Center to measure the confidence or optimism (pessimism) of consumers in their future well-being and coming economic conditions. The index measures short- and long-term expectations of business conditions and the individual's perceived economic well-being. Evidence indicates that the ICS is a leading indicator of economic activity as consumer confidence seems to precede major spending decisions. [HHK/MCC]

consumer sovereignty The dominant role of the consumer in dictating the type and quality of goods and services produced in an economic system. [DC]

consumer's surplus The gap between total utility a given consumer gets and total market value. Consumer's surplus is created by the fact that the last consumer buys at a price where the amount of utility of the good and market price are equal; consumers who would have paid more for earlier units have to pay only the market price and receive a surplus. [DLS]

consumerism The widening range of activities of government, business, and independent organizations that are designed to protect individuals from practices that infringe upon their rights as consumers. Or, the organized efforts of consumers seeking redress, restitution, and remedy for dissatisfaction they have accumulated in the acquisition of their standard of living. [DC]

consumers' goods Goods that directly satisfy human wants in consumption and that assist in further production only indirectly or incidentally, if at all. [DLS]

consumers' surplus The difference between the maximum price that consumers are willing to pay and the lower amount they actually pay. (See also **value-in-use**.) [KM]

consumption The direct and final use of goods or services in satisfying the wants of free human beings. [DLS]

consumption function A schedule of the amounts of their disposable income that individuals tend to devote to consumption at various levels of income. (See also **propensity to consume**.) [DLS]

continuous demand The demand for products that have a long, relatively stable history of sales. [DLS]

container-on-flatcar (COFC) A shipment of goods in a container on a rail flatcar. Shipments moving as COFC receive special rates. (See also **double stack, intermodal transportation, piggyback,** and **trailer-on-flatcar**.) [DJB/BJL]

containerization The physical grouping of master cartons into one unit load for materials handling or transport. The basic objective is to increase materials handling efficiency. [DJB/BJL]

containerizing The practice in transportation of consolidating a number of packages into one container that is sealed at the point of origin and remains sealed until it reaches the point of destination. [WRD]

content analysis The analysis of articles and news stories in various media used as a method of identifying positive and negative mentions about an organization, product, service, or issue. It is a method used to measure impact of publicity and other promotional and public relations efforts. [DES/BEB]

content validity An approach to validating a measure by determining the adequacy with which the domain of the characteristic is captured by the measure; it is sometimes called face validity. (See also **construct validation, convergent validity, discriminant validity, external validity, internal validity, pragmatic validity,** and **validity**.) [GAC]

contest A consumer sales promotion technique requiring the participant to use specific skills or ability to solve or complete a specified problem to qualify for a prize or award. (See also **dealer tie-in, game,** and **sweepstakes**.) [DES/BEB]

contest, sales See **sales contest**

contingency contract An agreement to deliver goods or services at a price to be determined either by the actual costs incurred while performing the service or producing the product or by the measured value realized after the service has been performed or the product has been used. [KM]

contingency planning Development of plans to provide an alternative to the main plan in the event of threats or opportunities that were thought to have a low probability of occurring at the time of the preparation of the main plan. The contingency plan deals not with unforeseen events, but with events that were foreseen but considered unlikely to occur. [GSD]

contingency pricing The setting of a price based either on actual costs incurred after the service has been performed or the product produced or on the measured value the buyer realizes because of the service or product. [KM]

contingent reward leadership A leadership style wherein sales managers maintain close supervision with their salespeople. In essence, using this leadership style entails identifying and clarifying job tasks for the salespeople, defining the objectives, recommending how to execute job assignments, and indicating how successful performance will lead to attainment of desired job rewards. (See also **consideration, initiating structure, laissez faire leadership, management-by-exception leadership,** and **transformational leadership**.) [AJD]

continuity 1. (advertising definition) A script for a television commercial. 2. The timing pattern used in a media plan to schedule the exposure of the advertising messages during the time period covered by the media plan. (See also **continuous media pattern, flighting,** and **pulsing**.) [JE] 3. (channels of distribution definition) The degree to which a channel relationship is expected to last into the future. [GLF]

continuity plan Any type of consumer sales promotion technique that encourages customers to purchase products on a continuing basis or over time. The plan often is based on some sort of saving or accumulation scheme such as trading stamps, points, coupons, or the like. (See also **frequent shopper program**.) [DES/BEB]

continuous innovation See **innovation**

continuous media pattern A timing pattern used in a media plan whereby the advertising messages are scheduled continuously throughout the time period covered by the media plan. (See also **continuity, flighting,** and **pulsing**.) [JE]

continuous replenishment (CR) A finished product inventory management system where high volume items are shipped in addition to requested replenishment products in anticipation of actual demand. High volume items are utilized to provide the benefits of full truckload deliveries. [DJB/BJL]

contraceptive social marketing (CSM) The application of commercial marketing technology to the promotion of contraceptive products (condoms, birth control pills, etc.) as part of public or private nonprofit family planning programs. [ARA]

contract The agreement between two or more persons that creates an obligation to do or not to do a particular thing. Its essentials are competent parties, subject matter, legal consideration, mutuality of agreement, and mutuality of obligation. [DC]

contract carrier 1. (physical distribution definition) A contract carrier performs transportation services on a selected basis after receiving authorization in the form of a permit. The contract refers to the agreement between the shipper and a contract carrier. (See also **independent carrier**.) [DJB/BJL] 2. (retailing definition) A transportation company that provides shipping service to one or various shippers on a contract basis. It does not maintain regularly scheduled service and its rates are more easily adapted to specific situations than are those of the common carrier. [WRD]

contract department A unit in a department store set up to sell in quantity to institutions such supplies as food, bedding, floor coverings; a department that arranges for the sale of goods in quantity to large buyers at special prices. [WRD]

contract manufacturing A joint venture method by which work is contracted to a qualified manufacturer to produce the product(s) that the firm wishes to market. Contract manufacturing offers a chance to enter a market faster with less risk, but has the drawback of less control over the manufacturing process. [GLL/DTW]

contract, tying This exists when a person agrees to sell one product, the "tying product," only on the condition that the vendee also purchase another product, the "tied product." It is also called a tie-in arrangement and is generally illegal under the Sherman Antitrust Act or Clayton Act. [DC]

contractual vertical marketing system 1. (retailing definition) A form of vertical marketing system in which independent firms at different levels in the channel operate contractually to obtain the economies and market impacts that could not be obtained by unilateral action. Under this system, the identity of the individual firm and its autonomy of operation remain intact. (See also **administered vertical marketing system, corporate vertical marketing system,** and **franchise**.) [WRD] 2. (channels of distribution definition) A marketing channel that achieves vertical coordination between independent firms at different channel levels through the use of contractual agreements. The three principal types of contractual systems are **franchise system, retailer sponsored cooperative,** and **wholesaler sponsored cooperative**. (See also **vertical marketing system** and **voluntary group**.) [GLF]

contribution The amount of revenue left over from the sale of a product after the direct costs and indirect costs related to the product have been subtracted out. [KM]

contribution pricing A method of determining the price of a product or service that uses the direct costs or indirect traceable costs related to the production and sale of the product or services as the relevant costs. [KM]

control See **goal** and **objective**

control group A group of subjects in an experiment who are not exposed to any of the experimental treatments or alternatives whose effects are to be measured; the control group is used to assess what part of the total observed effect was due to things other than the experimental variable(s). (See also **experimental group**.) [GAC]

controllable cost The cost that varies in volume, efficiency, choice of alternatives, and management determination. It is also any cost an organizational unit has authority to incur and/or ability to change. [WRD]

controlled circulation The distribution of a newspaper or magazine, usually free, to selected individuals who are members of an audience of special interest to advertisers. (See also **circulation**.) [JE]

controlled test market A market in which an entire marketing test program is conducted by an outside service. (See also **simulated test marketing** and **standard test market**.) [GAC]

convenience product A consumer good and/or service (such as soap, candy bar, and shoe shine) that is bought frequently, often on impulse, with little time and effort spent on the buying process. A convenience product usually is low-priced and is widely available. (See also **consumer product, emergency product, impulse product, shopping product, specialty product,** and **staple good**.) [DW]

convenience sample A nonprobability sample that is sometimes called an accidental sample because those included in the sample enter by accident in that they just happen to be where the study is being conducted when it is being conducted. (See also **judgment sample, quota sample, sequential sample,** and **snowball sample**.) [GAC]

convenience store A retail institution whose primary advantage to consumers is locational convenience. It is usually a high-margin, high inventory turnover retail institution. [WRD]

convergent validity The confirmation of the existence of a construct determined by the correlations exhibited by independent measures of the construct. (See also **construct validation, content validity, discriminant validity, external validity, internal validity, pragmatic validity,** and **validity**.) [GAC]

conversion of non-users See **market development**

conversion rate See **hit rate**

converter In the textile and paper trades, a wholesaling firm engaged in manufacturing activities to a significant degree. Also, a firm or merchant who purchases grey cotton cloth (woven but not finished) and has it bleached, dyed, printed, or mercerized before sale. [WRD]

conveyor A materials handling device widely used in shipping and receiving operations. Conveyors are classified as power or gravity, with roller or belt movement. [DJB/BJL]

conviction See **AIDA** and **hierarchy of effects model**

cooperative An establishment owned by an association of customers of the establishment whether or not they are incorporated. In general, the distinguishing features of a cooperative are patronage dividends based on the volume of expenditures by the members and a limitation of one vote per member regardless of the amount of stock owned. [WRD]

cooperative advertising An approach to paying for local advertising or retail advertising whereby the advertising space or time is placed by a local retail store but is partly or fully paid for by a national manufacturer whose product is featured in the advertising. (See also **advertising allowance** and **dealer tie-in**.) [JE]

cooperative buying Any and all consolidations of orders by a number of stores or store buyers in separate stores. It is also called affiliated buying. [WRD]

cooperative chain A group of retailers who on their own initiative have banded together for the purpose of buying, merchandising, or promoting. It is also called a cooperative group. [WRD]

cooperative exporting The cooperation of domestic firms for the purpose of international exports. Firms that compete domestically may collaborate internationally. [WJK]

cooperative game theory See **game theoretic models**

cooperative group A contractual marketing system in which retailers combine to form a wholesale warehouse operation. Its services to retailer members are primarily large-scale buying and warehousing operations. (See also **cooperative chain**.) [GLF]

cooperative marketing The process by which independent producers, wholesalers, retailers, consumers, or combinations of them act collectively in buying or selling or both. [WRD]

cooperative wholesaler A wholesale business owned by retail merchants. Typically, the wholesale establishment buys in its own name. Examples exist in the food, drug, and hardware lines. [WRD]

copy platform A statement prepared by the advertiser (often in association with an advertising agency) setting forth the advertising strategy, a summary of the rationale for the strategy, and related background information. (See also **advertising strategy**.) [JE]

copy research The testing of audience reactions to advertising messages while the advertising is being developed (called pre-testing) or after the advertising has been produced in final form (called post-testing). [JE]

copy testing See **copy research**

copyfitting The process of calculating how much space a given amount of text will require on a printed page and rewriting the copy, if necessary, to fit into the available space. [JE]

copyright 1. (legislation definition) A copyright offers the owner of original work that can be printed, recorded, or "fixed" in any manner the sole right to reproduce and distribute the work, to display or perform it, and to authorize others to do so, during the author's lifetime and for fifty years thereafter. [DC] 2. (product development definition) An exclusive right to the production or sale of literary, musical, or other artistic work, or to the use of a print or label. Occasionally, it is applied to a brand, but brands are usually protected by registration in the Patent and Copyright Office as a trademark. [DW]

Copyright Amendments Act of 1992 This act allows for automatic renewal of copyright works eligible for renewal between years 1995 and 2005. Any copyright secured between January 1, 1963 and December 31, 1977 has been extended automatically for 47 years. [DC]

copywriter A person with good verbal abilities who is talented in creating advertising ideas and skilled at writing advertising copy. [JE]

core benefit See **core product**

core product The central benefit or purpose for which a consumer buys a product. The core product varies from purchaser to purchaser. The core product or core benefit may come either from the physical good or service performance, or from the augmented dimensions of the product. (See also **augmented product**.) [DW]

corporate advertising See **institutional advertising**

corporate buy agreement A contractual buy-sell agreement in which the volume needs of multiple sites are aggregated. Usually, the buyer negotiates a favorable price and commits to a minimum annual purchase volume. [GLL/DTW]

corporate culture The patterns and norms that govern the behavior of a corporation and its employees; particularly, the shared values, beliefs, and customs. [WL/MBC]

corporate marketing system A marketing channel that achieves vertical coordination through the joint ownership and operation of two or more channel members on different levels of distribution. [GLF]

corporate mission See **corporate purpose**

corporate purpose The *raison d'etre* of a firm that describes the scope of the firm and its dominant emphasis and values. The purpose (or mission) of an organization is a function of five elements: (1) the history of the organization; (2) the current preferences of the management and/or owners; (3) environmental considerations; (4) the resources of the organization; and (5) the distinctive competences of the organization. (See also **corporate strategy**.) [GSD]

corporate relations The use of communication and public relations techniques to build favorable attitudes toward a particular company with competitors, consumers, the financial community, stockholders, and other publics. [DES/BEB]

corporate strategy The overall plan that integrates the strategies of all the businesses within the corporation. It usually describes the overall mission, the financial and human resource strategies and policies that affect all businesses within the corporation, the organization structure, the management of the interdependencies among businesses, and major initiatives to change the scope of the firm such as acquisitions and divestments. (See also **corporate purpose**.) [GSD]

corporate vertical marketing system A form of vertical marketing system in which all or most of the functions from production to distribution are at least partially owned and controlled by a single enterprise. Corporate systems typically operate manufacturing plants, warehouse facilities, and retail outlets. (See also **administered vertical marketing system, contractual vertical marketing system,** and **vertical marketing system**.) [WRD]

corrective advertising An advertising message placed by an advertiser in order to correct a deceptive or unfair advertising message previously disseminated by the advertiser. This type of advertising is used when the Federal Trade Commission finds that certain advertising messages used by an advertiser require correction. [JE]

corrective steps See **warranty**

correlation analysis A statistical technique used to measure the closeness of the linear relationship between two or more intervally scaled variables. (See also **cluster analysis, conjoint analysis, discriminant analysis, factor analysis, regression analysis,** and **spurious correlation**.) [GAC]

cost The money expended to produce and market a product or service. (See also **average fixed cost, average total cost, average variable cost, buyers' costs, common costs, direct costs, direct fixed costs, direct variable costs,** and **indirect traceable costs**.) [KM]

cost analysis A sales management evaluation and control method for monitoring sales force performance. A cost analysis involves monitoring the costs of various selling functions across individual salespeople, districts, products, and customer types. When put together with the data from a sales analysis, this procedure allows a firm to judge the profitability of various products, customer types, and territories. (See also **sales force evaluation**.) [AJD]

cost and freight (C.F.R.) The terminology is the same as cost insurance freight except the seller is not responsible for risk or loss at any point outside the factory. (See also **delivery duty paid**.) [WJK]

cost center A division, department, or subdivision thereof; a group of machines, people, or both; a single machine, operator, or any other unit of activity into which a business is divided for cost assignment and allocation. [WRD]

cost code The item cost information indicated on price tickets in code. A common method of coding is the use of letters from an easily remembered word or expression with nonrepeating letters corresponding to numerals. The following is illustrative:

y o u n g b l a d e
1 2 3 4 5 6 7 8 9 0 [WRD]

cost complement See **cost multiplier**

cost department A manufacturing or processing department within a retail store that is operated on the cost method of accounting. Also, one of the independent departments selling merchandise or service (principally service) but carrying no inventories at retail value—e.g., restaurant, barber shop, fur storage, and beauty parlor. [WRD]

cost insurance freight (C.I.F.) Under this contract the risk of loss or damage to goods is transferred to the buyer once the goods have passed the ship's rail. But the seller has to pay the expense of transportation for the goods up to the port of destination, including the expense of insurance. (See also **cost and freight** and **delivery duty paid**.) [WJK]

cost inventory The actual cost or market value, whichever is lower, of the inventory on hand at any time. The term seldom refers to the original price paid for the merchandise, but rather the present depreciated worth. If the original price is to be designated, the term generally used is billed cost of inventory. [WRD]

cost method of inventory Determination of the cost of inventory on hand by marking the actual cost on each price ticket in code and computing inventory value using these unit cost prices. [WRD]

cost multiplier The complement of the markup percent. This figure indicates the average relationship of cost to retail value of goods handled in the accounting period. It is also referred to as the cost complement or cost percent. (See also **complement of markup percentage**.) [WRD]

cost of industrial sales call The cost includes the salaries, commissions, bonuses, travel expenses, and entertainment expenses that a company encounters each time a salesperson makes a face-to-face presentation to one or more persons. [GLL/DTW]

cost of information search See **buyers' costs**

cost of living The money required to maintain a particular standard of living expressed in terms of the purchase of specified goods and services. [WL/MBC]

cost oriented strategy An approach to improving performance by reducing the costs per unit. The cost advantage can be used to improve profit margins or increase market share by cutting prices. (See also **experience curve analysis**). [GSD]

cost percent See **cost multiplier**

cost-of-living allowance (COLA) An adjustment to wages and earnings, particularly during periods of rapid increases in prices, to keep them in line with the cost of living. [WL/MBC]

cost-per-rating point (CPR or **CPRP)** A method of comparing the cost effectiveness of two or more alternative media vehicles in radio or television. CPRP is computed by dividing the cost of the time unit or commercial by the rating of the media vehicle during that time period. [JE]

cost-per-thousand (CPM) A simple and widely used method of comparing the cost effectiveness of two or more alternative media vehicles. It is the cost of using the media vehicle to reach 1,000 people or households. The CPM of any vehicle is computed by dividing the cost of placing a specific ad or commercial in the media vehicle by the vehicle's audience size and multiplying the result by 1,000. [JE]

cost-plus A method of determining the selling price of goods or services whereby cost is increased by an agreed-upon increment. [WRD]

cost-plus pricing A method of determining the price of a product or service that uses direct costs, indirect costs, and fixed costs whether related to the production and sale of the product or service or not. These costs are converted to per unit costs for the product and then a predetermined percentage of these costs is added to provide a profit margin. The resulting price is cost per unit plus the percentage markup. [KM]

count and recount promotion A trade sales promotion technique in which inventory is counted at the beginning of the promotion and recounted at the end of the promotion period. Discounts are then allowed based on the total quantity of product moved during the promotion period. (See also **buy-back allowance**.) [DES/BEB]

counter purchase A form of countertrade in which the selling firm agrees to purchase, at a later time, goods from the buyer equal to the amount of the original sale. [KM]

counterargument See **cognitive response**

counterpurchase A transaction in which each delivery is paid for in cash. In most counterpurchase transactions, two separate contracts are signed, one in which the supplier sells products for a cash settlement (the original sales contract), the other in which the supplier agrees to purchase and market unrelated products from the buyer (a separate, parallel contract). This is also termed parallel barter or parallel trading. [WJK]

countertrade This is a broad term incorporating a real distinction from barter, because money or credit is involved in the transaction. Countertrade broadly defines an arrangement in which firms both sell to and buy from their overseas customers. It is a sale of goods and services tied to an offsetting transaction, spelled out in a countertrade agreement. For example, a company sells jet engines to a foreign country and agrees as a condition of the sale to purchase goods or services of a designated value or quantity as a full or partial offset. (See also **switch trading**.) [WJK]

countervailing duties The duties levied to offset subsidies granted in the exporting country. (See also **ad valorem duty, compound duties, specific duties,** and **tariff system**.) [WJK]

countervailing power 1. (economic definition) The power exercised by large organizations with diverse and conflicting interests in the marketplace. [DLS] 2. (environments definition) The ability of individuals, companies, or groups to offset the power of large enterprises or large purchasers. [WL/MBC]

country of origin effect The effect that the country of origin of the product has on the buyer's quality perceptions of the product. [WJK]

coupon A printed certificate entitling the bearer to a stated price reduction or special value on a specific product, generally for a specified period of time. The value of the coupon is set and redeemed by the seller. (See also **bounce back offer, cents-off offer, co-op coupons, co-op mailing, consumer sales promotion, continuity plan, cross ruff, face value, free standing insert, in-store coupon, pass-along deal, solo coupon, specialty distributed coupon, take one pad,** and **trade coupon**.) [DES/BEB]

coupon fraud A planned misredemption of coupon offers designed to illegally obtain the value of a coupon without adhering to the published rules for redemption. [DES/BEB]

coupon payment See **clearinghouse**

coupon redemption The use of a seller's value certificate at the time of purchase to obtain either a lower price or greater value than normal. Also, this term is used to describe the act of accepting a seller's certificate by a retailer or other intermediary. (See also **misredemption, redemption rate,** and **retailer's handling charge**.) [DES/BEB]

crisis management An attempt by an organization to reduce, minimize, or control the impact of a calamitous event through various communication techniques. [DES/BEB]

courtesy days The days on which stores extend to credit customers the privilege of making purchases at sale prices in advance of public advertising of the sale. [WRD]

coverage The degree to which a particular advertising medium delivers an audience within a particular geographic area or within a specific target market. [JE]

CPI See **consumer price index**

CPM See **cost-per-thousand**

CPR See **cost-per-rating point**

CPRP See **cost-per-rating point**

CPS See **current population survey**

CPSC See **Consumer Product Safety Commission**

CR See **continuous replenishment**

creative boutique A limited-service advertising agency that focuses its work on the development of highly effective (creative) advertising messages for its clients. [JE]

credit A method of purchasing wherein the product or service is acquired for the promise of paying money for the acquisition at a later time. [KM]

credit bureau An organization that collects, maintains, and provides credit information to members or subscribers; sometimes cooperatively owned by users of the service. It maintains an up-to-date file containing a so-called master card (of credit information) for each consumer who has asked for credit from local merchants who use the service of the bureau. [WRD]

credit limit The maximum quantity of credit that may be allowed to be outstanding on an individual customer account. [WRD]

credit union A cooperative savings and loan organization formed for the purpose of encouraging thrift among members and making loans to them at relatively low rates of interest. [WRD]

criterion related validity See **pragmatic validity**

critical success factors See **key success factors**

cross impact analysis A forecasting technique often used in futures research that logically studies the effects of the interaction of specified events with each other. The wide variety of impacts that can occur are analyzed and assessed to determine the overall effect. It has been used to assess market and product opportunities. (See also **futurology**.) [WL/MBC]

cross ruff A consumer sales promotion technique in which a noncompetitive product is used as the vehicle to distribute a coupon, sample, or other sales promotion offer for another product. (See also **free sample**.) [DES/BEB]

cross selling 1. (retailing definition) The process of selling between and among departments to facilitate larger transactions and to make it more convenient for the customer to do related item shopping. (See also **inter-selling**.) [WRD] 2. (sales promotion definition) A consumer sales promotion technique in which the manufacturer attempts to sell the consumer products related to a product the consumer already uses or which the marketer has available. (See also **consumer sales promotion**.) [DES/BEB]

cross tabulation A count of the number of cases that fall into each of several categories when the categories are based on two or more variables considered simultaneously. (See also **banner**.) [GAC]

cross-elasticity of demand A measure of the extent to which a change in the price of one product affects the sale of another—e.g., a small percentage change in the price of Product A may result in a large change in the sales of Product B. [DLS]

cross-functional integration See **integrated development**

cross-price elasticity See **elasticon**

cross-sectional study An investigation involving a sample of elements selected from the population of interest that are measured at a single point in time. (See also **longitudinal study** and **sample survey**.) [GAC]

CRP See **capacity requirements planning**

crude birth rate The number of live births per year per thousand population. (See also **completed fertility, fertility rate, replacement level fertility,** and **total fertility rate**.) [WL/MBC]

CSM See **contraceptive social marketing**

cue A technical term from psychological learning theory for the stimulus that impels some sort of action. An advertisement may be the cue leading to desire for or purchase of a product. [HHK/MCC]

cultural ecology The study of the process by which a society adapts to its environment by social transformations and evolutionary changes. [WL/MBC]

cultural environment The aggregate of patterns and norms that regulate a society's behavior including the values, beliefs, and customs that are shared and transmitted by the society. (See also **demographic environment, economic environment, natural environment,** and **political environment**.) [WL/MBC]

cultural lag The differences in the rates of change in various parts of the same culture, such as the relatively slow rate of acceptance of products or ideas by some market segments compared to others. It is also used to indicate the failure of a society to keep up with technological and environmental changes in its economic, social, legal, and political policies. [WL/MBC]

culture 1. (consumer behavior definition) The set of learned values, norms, and behaviors that are shared by a society and are designed to increase the probability of the society's survival. (See also **acculturation, rituals, socialization,** and **subculture**.) [JPP/JCO] 2. (consumer behavior definition) The institutionalized ways or modes of appropriate behavior. It is the modal or distinctive patterns of behavior of a people including implicit cultural beliefs, norms, values, and premises that govern conduct. It includes the shared superstitions, myths, folkways, mores, and behavior patterns that are rewarded or punished. [HHK/MCC]

cumulative audience See **reach**

cumulative markon The total of markon on the beginning inventory in any accounting period plus the aggregate purchase markon during the period, including additional markups, before any markdowns. It is the difference between the total cost and the total original retail value of all goods handled to date, commonly expressed as a percentage of cumulative original retail. [WRD]

cumulative markup The average percentage markup for the period. It is the total retail price minus cost divided by retail price. [WRD]

cumulative quantity discount A reduction in the price to be paid for purchases that exceed a given level of volume over a specified period of time. This form of discount is also referred to as a deferred discount or a patronage discount. (See also **quantity discount**.) [KM]

cumulative reach See **reach**

curiosity approach A method for approaching a prospect in which the salesperson arouses the prospect's interest by making a statement that piques the prospect's curiosity. (See also **center of influence method, cold-canvassing, endless chain method, introduction approach, product approach,** and **referral approach**.) [BAW]

currency devaluation A reduction in the value of one currency vis-a-vis other currencies. Devaluation takes place when currency values adjust in foreign exchange markets in response to supply and demand pressure, or in the case of regulated currency rates, when the government decides to change the rate. (See also **currency revaluation**.) [WJK]

currency revaluation An increase in the value of one currency vis-a-vis other currencies. Revaluation takes place when currency values adjust in the foreign exchange markets in response to supply and demand pressures. (See also **currency devaluation**.) [WJK]

current account See **balance of payments**

Current Population Reports See **current population survey**

current population survey (CPS) A monthly nationwide survey of a scientifically selected sample of about 71,000 housing units in 729 areas, covering about 1,200 counties and cities in every state and the District of Columbia. The U.S. Bureau of the Census issues a series of publications on the results under the title *Current Population Reports*. [WL/MBC]

custom union A market that is created when countries agree to eliminate trade and tariff barriers among the participating countries and impose uniform tariffs on nonmember countries. The custom union is an important element in a broader framework of economic integration. (See also **common market**.) [WJK]

customary pricing The practice of establishing a price for a product or service and not changing it over a relatively long time. Prices are changed by varying the quantity or quality of the product rather than the monetary value. [KM]

customer The actual or prospective purchaser of products or services. [BAW]

customer functions See **business definition** and **product-market definition**

customer inquiry response systems See **consumer relations**

customer loyalty See **after sales support**

customer orientation A sales approach in which the customer's needs and interest are paramount. (See also **approach, sales; balance sheet method; benefit approach; compliment approach; consultative selling; formula selling; high-pressure selling; multilevel selling; problem solution approach;** and **systems selling**.) [BAW]

customer satisfaction The degree to which there is match between the customer's expectations of the product and the actual performance of the product. Expectations are formed based on information consumers receive from salespersons, friends, family, opinion leaders, etc., as well as past experience with the product. This is an important measure of the ability of a firm to successfully meet the needs of its customer. (See also **after sales support** and **product performance tracking**.) [GSD]

customer segments See **business definition** and **product-market definition**

customer service 1. (physical distribution definition) A customer-oriented corporate philosophy that integrates and manages all of the elements of the customer interface within a predetermined cost-service mix. [DBL/BJL] 2. (product development definition) The identifiable, but essentially intangible, activities that are offered by a seller in conjunction with a product, such as delivery and repair. These activities may be priced separately, but usually are not, and are provided only with a product that is being sold. These activities are not to be confused with intangible products (services), the types of products for which the activity is the primary purpose of a sale. The sale of service products may be accompanied by the provision of customer services, an example being the courteous treatment a bank client receives when entering the lobby for the purchase of any of several service products such as check cashing or a loan. (See also **marketing services**.) [DW] 3. (retailing definition) The set of retail activities that increase the value customers receive when they shop and purchase merchandise. [WRD]

customer spotting See **analog approach**

customer switching costs The costs that tend to tie buyers to one supplier. These costs tend to be high when the product is durable or specialized, when the customer has invested a lot of time and energy in learning how to use the product, or when the customer has made special-purpose investments that are useless elsewhere. [GSD]

customer traffic See **traffic (customer)**

customer-driven innovation See **demand-pulled innovation**

customization Tailoring the product to the special and unique needs of the customer. Each buyer is potentially a unique segment. [GLL/DTW]

customized portfolio models See **product and business portfolio models**

customized sales presentation A sales presentation developed from a detailed analysis or survey of the specific prospect's needs. (See also **canned sales presentation; need satisfaction selling; outlined presentation; presentation, sales;** and **stimulus response sales approach**.) [BAW]

Customs Cooperation Council See **Brussels Nomenclature**

cutthroat competition The temporary reduction of prices, often to unreasonable levels, such as below costs, for the purpose of eliminating competitors so as to be able to control a product's or service's price. [WL/MBC]

CWO See **cash with order**

cycles, business See **business cycle**

cycles, economic See **business cycle**

cyclical business A business in which sales and profits are determined largely by the fluctuations of business conditions or the business cycle. [WL/MBC]

damaged goods See **as is**

damaged merchandise See **distressed merchandise**

DAR See **day-after-recall**

data system The part of a decision support system that includes the processes used to capture and the methods used to store data coming from a number of external and internal sources. [GAC]

database A compendium of information on current and prospective customers that generally includes demographic and psychographic data as well as purchase history and a record of brand contacts. (See also **LEXIS** and **NEXIS**.) [DES/BEB]

database marketing An approach by which computer database technologies are harnessed to design, create, and manage customer data lists containing information about each customer's characteristics and history of interactions with the company. The lists are used as needed for locating, selecting, targeting, servicing, and establishing relationships with customers in order to enhance the long-term value of these customers to the company. The techniques used for managing lists include: 1. database manipulation methods such as select and join, 2. statistical methods for predicting each customer's likelihood of future purchases of specific items based on his/her history of past purchases, and 3. measures for computing the life-time value of a customer on an ongoing basis. [AR]

dating 1. (sales promotion definition) A type of trade sales promotion in which the retailer is allowed to buy a certain amount of product from the manufacturer and then pay for that product over a prolonged period of time. [DES/BEB] 2. (retailing definition) The dates in which discounts can be taken or the full invoice amount is due. (See also **advance dating, end of month dating, extra dating, future dating, memorandum purchase and dating, ordinary dating, proximo dating, receipt-of-goods dating,** and **season dating**.) [WRD]

day-after-recall (DAR) A method of testing the performance of an ad or a commercial whereby members of the audience are surveyed one day after their exposure to an ad or commercial in an advertising vehicle to discover how many of the audience members remember encountering that specific ad or commercial in the advertising vehicle. [JE]

deal An inducement such as a price reduction, free goods offer, or other special offering made by a seller to a channel member or the ultimate consumer, generally for a limited period of time. (See also **consumer sales promotion, deal prone, diversion, forward buying, incremental sales,** and **trade sales promotion**.) [DES/BEB]

deal merchandise A product that a seller may offer at a reduced price or that may have been specially bundled, processed, or manufactured for a limited period of time. (See also **trade sales promotion**.) [DES/BEB]

deal prone A description of the behavior of that group of consumers who make product purchase decisions on the basis of whether or not a particular product is being sold under some sort of deal condition. [DES/BEB]

deal proneness A consumer's general inclination to use promotional deals such as buying on sale or using coupons. [JPP/JCO]

dealer loader A premium or other reward that is used to encourage a retailer to develop a special display or product offering. Commonly, the item is a reusable product that forms the basis for the display. When the event is over, the retailer is allowed to keep the premium. (See also **trade sales promotion**.) [DES/BEB]

dealer tie-in The local support by a retailer for an advertiser's promotional program through use of in-store display materials, cooperative advertising, local contests, identification in media advertisements, and so on. (See also **trade sales promotion**.) [DES/BEB]

decay of a learned response See **learning decay**

decay of advertising effects See **learning decay**

deceitful diversion of patronage A practice in which a retailer publishes or verbalizes falsehoods about a competitor in an attempt to divert patrons from that competitor. [WRD]

decennial census The complete count of the population every ten years by the U.S. Bureau of the Census, as is provided by the U.S. Constitution. This enumeration and compilation of information about the characteristics of the U.S. population is a rich source of information for marketing. [WL/MBC]

decentralized adjustment system A system in which customers take their complaints directly to the selling department involved. Salespeople may make most of the adjustments, although the final approval of the department head or selling supervisor is often a requirement. [WRD]

decentralized management The practice of delegating decision-making authority to lower levels of management and, in some cases, to nonmanagers authorized to make decisions, such as salespeople. Comment: It is particularly important in marketing that decisions are made by managers or others close to the company's markets. (See also **bureaucratic organization; centralized management; divisional organization; flat organization; functional organization; geographic organization; hierarchical organization; market management organization; marketing organization, forms of; matrix organization; multibusiness organization; nonbusiness marketing organization;** and **product management organization**.) [VPB]

decentralized sales organization In this organization, each division has its own sales force. This is appropriate when company divisions sell different products to different markets through different channels, and when the divisions are large enough to afford their own sales forces. (See also **centralized sales organization; full-line sales organization; partially integrated division; sales organization, forms of; sales organization specialized by account; sales organization specialized by market;** and **sales organization specialized by product**.) [VPB]

deception An unethical sales practice involving withholding information or telling "white lies." [BAW]

deceptive advertising The advertising

intended to mislead consumers by falsely making claims, by failure to make full disclosure, or by both. [DLS]

deceptive pricing Savings claims, price comparisons, "special" sales, "two-for-one" sales, "factory" prices, or "wholesale" prices are unlawful if false or deceptive. When these terms are used, the terms and conditions of the sale must be made clear at the outset. False preticketing—the practice of marking merchandise with a price higher than that for which it is intended—is unlawful. [DC]

decider See **buying roles**

decision calculus models The quantitative models of a process that are calibrated by examining subjective judgments about outcomes of the process (e.g., market share or sales of a firm) under a variety of hypothetical scenarios (e.g., advertising spending level, promotion expenditures). Once the model linking process outcomes to marketing decision variables has been calibrated, it is possible to derive an optimal marketing recommendation (Little 1970; Chakravarthi, Mitchell, and Staelin 1981; Little and Lodish 1981). Examples for advertising decisions include ADBUDG, ADMOD, and MEDIAC. Examples for overall brand/product decisions are BRANDAID and STRATPORT. Examples for salesforce decisions include CALLPLAN and DETAILER. (See also **advertising models, decision support system, marketing mix models,** and **resource allocation models**.) [DCS/YJW]

decision maker See **consumer, consumer behavior,** and **consumer decision making unit**

decision making See **adaptive planning**

decision making, consumer 1. (consumer behavior definition) The process of selecting from several choices, products, brands, or ideas. The decision process may involve complex cognitive or mental activity, a simple learned response, or an uninvolved and uninformed choice that may even appear to be stochastic or probabilistic, i.e., occurring by chance. (See also **gatekeeper** and **low involvement consumer behavior**.) [HHK/MCC] 2. (consumer behavior definition) The process by which consumers collect information about choice alternatives and evaluate those alternatives in order to make choices among them. [JPP/JCO]

decision support system (DSS) 1. (marketing research definition) A coordinated collection of data, system tools, and techniques with supporting software and hardware by which an organization gathers and interprets relevant information from business and the environment and turns it into a basis for making management decisions. (See also **data system, dialog system,** and **model system**.) [GAC] 2. (models definition) A system, usually based on a model and computer software package, that describes the implications of specific marketing decisions and/or recommends specific marketing actions, using a set of input information. This information may either reside permanently in the DSS or be input for the particular scenario of interest (or both). The information can consist of primary information (e.g., sales and cost information from company records, or subjective judgments by managers about the likely impact of increased advertising spending) and/or secondary information (e.g., sales of competitors' products from a syndicated database constructed via store audits). An important aspect of many decision support systems is the facilitation of "what if" analyses; i.e., the sensitivity of optimal marketing strategy to the assumptions in the input information. (See also **ADMOD, BRANDAID, CALLPLAN, decision calculus models, DETAILER, GEOLINE, marketing mix models, MEDIAC, POSSE,** and **STRATPORT**.) [DCS/YJW]

decision variables, marketing These correspond to the major marketing functions that influence revenue and profit. They are summarized in the well-known four P's: product, price, promotion, and place (distribution). Other marketing decision variables may include service policies, credit, and so forth. [GSD]

decision-making unit See **buying center**

decline stage The fourth stage of a product life cycle. Sales of the product fall off from their levels during the maturity (third) stage. This may lead to abandonment or efforts at rejuvenation of the product. (See also **retail life cycle** and **weak product**.) [DW]

decompositional model See **forecasting models**

defend market position See **investment strategy**

Defender A model representing customers' brand choice decisions as a function of brand attributes. Key features include the incorporation of heterogeneous customer preferences and the representation of attribute levels in a "per dollar" multiattribute space. Based on the model, several qualitative, normative implications hold regarding the optimal competitive response by "defending" brands against a new market entrant (Hauser and Gaskin 1984; Hauser and Shugan 1983). (See also **brand choice models**.) [DCS/YJW]

deferred billing A billing method that enables customers to buy merchandise and not pay for it for several months, with no interest charge. [WRD]

deferred dating See **extra dating**

deferred discount See **cumulative quantity discount**

deferred marking See **bulk marking**

deflation An economic condition characterized by a continuous downward movement of the general price level. (See also **inflation**.) [DLS]

delivered price A quoted or invoice price that includes delivery costs to the F.O.B. point, the latter being a freight terminal, warehouse, or another location commonly accepted in the particular trade or specifically agreed upon between buyer and seller. [WRD]

delivered pricing A form of geographical pricing in which the price quoted by the manufacturer includes both the list price and the transportation costs. In such cases, the prices are quoted as F.O.B. destination, meaning the manufacturer bears the responsibility of selecting and paying for the method of transporting the product. (See also **basing-point pricing, F.O.B. origin pricing,** and **F.O.B. with freight allowed**.) [KM]

delivery duty paid Under this contract the seller undertakes to deliver the goods to the buyer at the place he or she names in the country of import with all costs, including duties, paid. The seller is responsible under this contract for getting the import license if one is required. (See also **cost and freight** and **cost insurance freight**.) [WJK]

delivery period The normal time between the placing of an order and the receipt of stock. [WRD]

delivery reliability The degree to

which a seller delivers a product according to the schedule promised at the time of sale. [DW]

Delphi technique 1. (environments definition) A frequently used method in futures research to obtain the consensus opinion of a group of experts about likely future developments. A series of questionnaires is used with controlled feedback given to participants between rounds of questions. (See also **forecasting models** and **futurology**.) [WL/MBC] 2. (marketing research definition) A method of forecasting that relies on repeated measurement and controlled feedback among those participating along the following lines: (1) each individual prepares a forecast; (2) the forecasts are collected, and an anonymous summary is prepared by the person supervising the process; (3) the summary is distributed to each person who prepared a forecast; and (4) those participating in the process are asked to study the summary and submit a revised forecast. The process is repeated until the forecasts converge. [GAC]

demand 1. (economic definition) A schedule of the amounts that buyers would be willing to purchase at a corresponding schedule of prices, in a given market at a given time. 2. (business executive definition) The number of units of a product sold in a market over a period of time. (See also **effective demand, elasticity coefficient, law of demand, primary demand,** and **selective demand**.) [DLS]

demand analysis A study of the reasons underlying the demand for a product with the intent of forecasting and anticipating sales. [DLS]

demand creation The use of price reductions and/or other incentives, such as premiums, rebates, etc., to create or increase immediate sales response for the product or service among consumers or resellers. (See also **sales promotion**.) [DES/BEB]

demand curve A graph of the quantity of a product taken by buyers in the market at various prices, given that all other factors are held constant. (See also **supply curve**.) [DLS]

demand density A measure of the extent to which potential demand for the retailer's goods and services is concentrated in certain census tracts, ZIP codes, or other geographic parts of the community. [WRD]

demand/destination areas The departments in stores in which demand for their products or services are created before customers get to their destination. [WRD]

demand factors The elements that determine the consumers' willingness and ability to pay for products. [DLS]

demand, industrial The demand includes the goods and services that are required by all individuals and organizations that are engaged in the production of other goods and services. [GLL/DTW]

demand-backward pricing The act of setting a price by starting with the estimated price consumers will pay and working backwards with retail and wholesale margins. [DLS]

demand-oriented pricing A method of pricing in which the seller attempts to set price at the level that the intended buyers are willing to pay. It is also called value-in-use pricing or value-oriented pricing. (See also **perceived-value pricing**.) [KM]

demand-pulled innovation Innovation that is caused or at least stimulated by the needs, wants, or desires of customers. This contrasts with supply-pushed innovation. Other terms for these two ideas are market- or customer-driven innovation and technology-driven innovation. [DW]

demarketing 1. (economic definition) A term used to describe a marketing strategy when the objective is to decrease the consumption of a product. [DLS] 2. (social marketing definition) The process of reducing the demand for products or services believed to be harmful to society. [ARA]

demographic edition See **regional edition**

demographic environment The human population characteristics that surround a firm or nation and that greatly affect markets. The demographic environment includes such factors as age distributions, births, deaths, immigration, marital status, sex, education, religious affiliations, and geographic disperson—characteristics that are often used for segmentation purposes. (See also **cultural environment, economic environment, natural environment,** and **political environment**.) [WL/MBC]

demographics The study of total size, sex, territorial distribution, age, composition, and other characteristics of human populations; the analysis of changes in the make-up of a population. (See also **database**.) [WL/MBC]

demography 1. (economic definition) The study of people in the aggregate, including population size, age, sex, income, occupation, and family life-cycle. [DLS] 2. (consumer behavior definition) The study of population characteristics such as age distribution, income, death rate, etc. [HHK/MCC]

demonstration model goods See **clearance sale**

demonstration, sales See **sales demonstration**

demonstrations, as retailer sales promotion An exhibition of a product in use or in its ultimate form as an inducement to prospective purchasers. Examples are preparation and dispensing of food products in supermarkets, sampling of beverages in liquor stores, or demonstration of cooking equipment in department stores—all intended to call additional attention to the product or service. [DES/BEB]

demurrage A carrier charge incurred when freight cars are retained beyond the specified time allowed for loading or unloading. Railroads charge demurrage for delays in excess of 48 hours in returning a car to service. [DJB/BJL]

department store A retail establishment that carries several lines of merchandise, such as women's ready-to-wear and accessories, mens' and boys' clothing, piece goods, small wares, and home furnishings, all of which are organized into separate departments for the purpose of promotion, service, accounting, and control. For Census purposes, it is an establishment normally employing 25 or more people and engaged in selling some items in each of the following lines of merchandise: furniture, home furnishings, appliances, radio and TV sets, a general line of apparel for the family, household linens, and dry goods. An establishment with total sales of less than $10,000,000 in which sales of any one of these groupings is greater than 80 percent of total sales is not classified as a department store. [WRD]

department store ownership group An aggregation of centrally owned stores in which each store continues to be merchandised and operated primarily as an individual concern with central guidance rather than central management or direction. [WRD]

departmentalized specialty store A term used to designate a concern organized in the same way as a department store but handling a narrower range of merchandise. [WRD]

departmentalizing The process of classifying merchandise into somewhat homogeneous groups known as departments. [WRD]

depression A phase of the business cycle characterized by a rapid decline in gross national product and employment. (See also **prosperity, recession,** and **recovery**.) [DLS]

depth interview An unstructured personal interview in which the interviewer attempts to get subjects to talk freely and to express their true feelings. [GAC]

derived demand The demand for one product that is derived from the purchase of another. The demand for industrial products is created by the purchase of consumer products that use or incorporate industrial products in them or in their manufacture. [DW]

descriptive billing A type of charge statement prepared for the customer in which a printout of the period's (usually a month) purchases appear on one statement with a description of the item purchased, the date, and the price but the original sales check is not included in the statement; only the description is. [WRD]

descriptive labeling The use of descriptive information (e.g., size, ingredients, or use) on labels. This contrasts with grade labeling, in which code letters or numbers are used to describe the relative quality of goods. [DW]

descriptive model See **Advisor**

descriptive research A research design in which the major emphasis is on determining the frequency with which something occurs or the extent to which two variables covary. (See also **causal research** and **exploratory research**.) [GAC]

designated market area (DMA) The geographic area surrounding a city in which the broadcasting stations based in that city account for a greater share of the listening or viewing households than do broadcasting stations based in other nearby cities. It also is the specific geographic area to which a county in the United States is exclusively assigned on the basis of the television viewing habits of the people residing in the county. (see also **area of dominant influence**.) [JE]

desire See **AIDA** and **hierarchy of effects model**

destination merchandise A type of merchandise that motivates or triggers a trip to a specific store. [WRD]

destination store A store to which a consumer generally makes a special trip with the intent of shopping. [WRD]

detail salesperson The missionary salesperson employed by a pharmaceutical company to call on physicians and attempt to get them to prescribe their firm's products. [BAW]

DETAILER A decision calculus model providing a decision support system for allocating a salesforce's selling effort across the items in a firm's product line. The model's parameters are calibrated using subjective responses to a series of questions concerning projected sales under various levels of detailing effort and over various time periods (Montgomery, Silk, and Zaragoza 1971). (See also **CALLPLAN, decision calculus models, decision support system, GEOLINE,** and **sales force models**.) [DCS/YJW]

detailing The personal sampling and other promotional work among doctors, dentists, and other professional persons done for pharmaceutical concerns, in order to secure goodwill and possible distribution or prescription of the product. [WRD]

detention A carrier charge incurred when trailers of motor carriers are retained beyond the specified loading or unloading time. The permitted time is specified in the tariff and normally is limited to a few hours. [DJB/BJL]

deterrence strategy See **market defense**

developing country A country with semideveloped markets whose 1987 GNP per capita ranged from $1,001 to $2,500. The characteristics of this category of country are: (1) more than 33 percent of the population is engaged in agriculture and less than 30 percent of the population is urban; (2) at least 50 percent of the population is literate; and (3) there are often highly developed industrial sectors and consumer markets are also of significant size on a per capita basis. (See also **industrialized country, postindustrialized country, preindustrialized country,** and **underdeveloped country**.) [WJK]

development function See **prototype**

development time The time it takes to develop a new product, usually expressed in months. Development time is a function of several factors, such as product complexity, newness, clarity of customer requirements, effectiveness of new product development process, prototyping quality, highly effective development leadership, priority, and prior experience. [DW]

developmental research and development phase See **research and development**

DEX/UCS The standard for electronic exchange that utilizes a uniform communications system to allow suppliers who ship direct store delivery to communicate invoice data to retailers at their receiving facilities. [DJB/BJL]

dialectic process An evolutionary theory based on the premise that retail institutions evolve. The theory suggests that new retail formats emerge by adopting characteristics from other forms of retailers in much the same way that a child is the product of the pooled genes of two very different parents. (See also **central place theory, concentric zone theory, gravity model, natural selection theory, retail accordian theory, retail life cycle,** and **wheel of retailing theory**.) [WRD]

dialog system The part of a decision support system that permits users to explore the databases by employing the system models to produce reports that satisfy their particular information needs. It is also called a language system. [GAC]

dichotomous question A fixed-alternative question in which respondents are asked to indicate which of two alternative responses most closely corresponds to their position on a subject. (See also **multichotomous question**.) [GAC]

differential advantage 1. (product development definition) A property of any product that is able to claim a uniqueness over other products in its category. To be a differential advantage, the uniqueness must be communicable to customers and have value for them. The differential advantage of a firm is often called its distinctive competences. [DW] 2. (economic definition) An advantage unique to an organization; an advantage extremely difficult to match by a competitor. [DLS] (See also **competitive advantage, distinc-**

tiveness, and **product differentiation**.)

differentiated advantage See **competitive advantage**

differentiated marketing See **market segmentation strategies**

differentiated oligopoly An oligopoly that produces and markets products that consumers consider close, but less than perfect, substitutes—e.g., automobiles. (See also **undifferentiated oligopoly**.) [DLS]

diffusion model A model representing the contagion or spread of something through a population. Diffusion models in marketing often are applied to the adoption of a new product, or the exposure of potential customers to some information about a product (e.g., an advertising message). Numerous specific mathematical formulations have been applied to diffusion processes, and these are reviewed by Lilien and Kotler (1983 Chapter 19) and Mahajan and Wind (1986). The most widely cited of these models was introduced to marketing by Bass (1969). It incorporates explicitly an innovation effect and an imitation effect. When both effects are present, the time path of adoption follows an S-shaped curve. (See also **advertising models** and **new product forecasting models**.) [DCS/YJW]

diffusion of innovation The process by which the use of an innovation is spread within a market group, over time and over various categories of adopters. (See also **adopter categories**.) [DW]

diffusion process The process by which new ideas and products become accepted by a society. (See also **adopter categories** and **adoption process**.) [JPP/JCO]

diminishing marginal utility A situation in which the marginal utility, i.e., the extra utility added by consumption of a last unit, tends to decrease. (See also **law of diminishing marginal utility**.) [DLS]

diminishing return A situation in which after a point the extra output resulting from an increase in some input(s) relative to other fixed inputs tends to become less and less. (See also **law of diminishing return, point of diminishing return,** and **point of negative return**.) [DLS]

diminishing utility A situation in which consumption of successive new units of a good causes total utility to grow at an increasingly slower rate, i.e., psychological factors cause a consumer to have a lesser appreciation to the later units. (See also **law of diminishing marginal utility** and **marginal utility**.) [DLS]

direct advertising A mass or quantity promotion, not in an advertising medium, but issued from the advertiser by mail or personal distribution to individual customers or prospects. Also, it is the advertising literature appearing in folders, leaflets, throw-aways, letters, and delivered to prospective customers by mail, salespeople, dealers, or tucked into mailboxes. [WRD]

direct channel A channel whereby goods and services are sold directly from producer to final user without involvement of other independent middlemen. (See also **indirect channel**.) [GLF]

direct cost method of inventory A system under which the cost value of each item sold is recorded along with the selling price so an accurate costing of sales may be obtained. [WRD]

direct costs Costs incurred by and solely for a particular product, department, program, sales territory, or customer account. These may be fixed costs or variable costs. They also are called traceable costs or attributable costs. (See also **average fixed cost, average total cost, average variable cost, buyers' costs, common costs, contribution, contribution pricing, cost, direct fixed costs, direct variable costs,** and **indirect traceable costs**.) [KM]

direct denial A method for answering prospect objects by making strong statements indicating that the prospect has made an error. (See also **boomerang method, feel-felt-found method, indirect denial, pass up method,** and **postpone method**.) [BAW]

direct exporting The type of exporting in which firms enter foreign markets directly and do their own export marketing. The firm itself undertakes the complete export marketing task, which is extensive. Direct exporting includes choosing appropriate foreign markets, selecting agents or distributors to represent the firm in those markets, motivating and controlling those distributors choosing the product line for the target markets, setting prices and determining promotional strategies for those markets, handling international shipping and finance, and preparing export documentation. (See also **indirect exporting**.) [WJK]

direct fixed costs Costs that are incurred by and solely for a particular product or segment but which do not vary with an activity level. (See also **average fixed cost, average total cost, average variable cost, buyers' costs, common costs, cost, direct costs, direct variable costs,** and **indirect traceable costs**.) [KM]

direct mail advertising The use of the mail delivered by the U.S. Postal Service or other delivery services as an advertising media vehicle. [JE]

direct marketing 1. (retailing definition) A form of nonstore retailing in which customers are exposed to merchandise through an impersonal medium and then purchase the merchandise by telephone or mail. [WRD] 2. (channels of distribution definition) The total of activities by which the seller, in effecting the exchange of goods and services with the buyer, directs efforts to a target audience using one or more media (direct selling, direct mail, telemarketing, direct-action advertising, catalog selling, cable selling, etc.) for the purpose of soliciting a response by phone, mail, or personal visit from a prospect or customer. [GLF]

direct product profitability (DPP) 1. (physical distribution definition) The managerial accounting practice of allocating costs to specific products. It is a method of evaluating distribution alternatives such as direct store delivery. It is also used to allocate shelf space in retail stores based on profitability. [DJB/BJL] 2. (retailing definition) The profit on sale of a product after deducting the cost of the goods and only the expenses directly related to that particular product or product line. [WRD]

direct request method A method for obtaining commitment from a customer by simply asking for the purchase order. (See also **benefit summary method**.) [BAW]

direct response advertising An approach to the advertising message that includes a method of response such as an address or telephone number whereby members of the audience can respond directly to the advertiser in order to purchase a product or service offered in the advertising message. Direct response advertising can be conveyed to members of a target market by a wide variety of advertising media, including television, radio, magazines, mail delivery, etc. (See also **general advertising, infomercial,** and **offer**.) [JE]

direct sales force A sales force consisting of salespeople employed by the company for whom they sell products or services. [BAW]

direct selling 1. (sales definition) A marketing approach that involves direct sales of goods and services to consumers through personal explanation and demonstrations, frequently in their home or place of work. [BAW] 2. (retailing definition) The process whereby the firm responsible for production sells to the user, ultimate consumer, or retailer without intervening middlemen. (See also **nonstore retailing**.) [WRD]

direct selling establishment An establishment primarily engaged in the retail sale of merchandise by telephone or house-to-house canvass or in the workplace. (See also **nonstore retailing**.) [WRD]

direct selling organization A nonstore retailing establishment that solicits orders and distributes its products direct to consumers. [WRD]

direct store delivery (DSD) 1. (physical distribution definition) A system whereby goods are delivered to the buyer's store instead of going through a warehouse or distribution center. This can result in less handling and faster deliveries, but does not necessarily result in lower costs. [DJB/BJL] 2. (retailing definition) Delivery by a vendor directly to a retail store of a customer, as opposed to delivery to a distribution center operated by the customer. [WRD]

direct variable costs Costs that vary directly with an activity level. (See also **average fixed cost, average total cost, average variable cost, buyers' costs, common costs, cost, direct costs, direct fixed costs,** and **indirect traceable costs**.) [KM]

directional and departmental signage A signage system that helps guide the shopper through the shopping trip and locate specific departments of interest. [WRD]

Dirichlet multinomial model A probability mixture model commonly used to represent patterns of brand choice behavior. Over repeated occasions on which purchases are made from the product category, the set of brands chosen are assumed to follow the multinomial distribution for any given individual. The model also assumes that individuals differ from each other in their set of brand choice probabilities. These probabilities are taken to have a Dirichlet distribution across individuals. The Dirichlet is a parsimonious distribution for the set of brand choice probabilities: for n brands there are n Dirichlet distribution parameters; $n - 1$ of which indicate the average share of choices for each brand, and the nth indicating the amount of heterogeneity in preference across individuals. The model thus can be used to predict brand choice patterns exhibited over time by a set of individuals (Jeuland, Bass, and Wright 1980; Goodhardt, Ehrenberg, and Chatfield 1984). (See also **Beta binomial model** and **brand choice models**.) [DCS/YJW]

disagreement See **negotiation**

disbursement See **cash flow**

disclaimer statement See **strict liability**

disconfirmation In consumer satisfaction theory, disconfirmation refers to a situation in which a product performs differently than expected prior to purchase. Positive disconfirmation occurs when the product performs better than expected; negative disconfirmation occurs when the product performs worse than expected. (See also **confirmation** and **dissatisfaction**.) [JPP/JCO]

discontinuous See **product innovation**

discontinuous innovation See **innovation**

discount A reduction in price. (See also **face value** and **price structure**.) [KM]

discount house A retailing business unit, featuring consumer durable items, competing on a basis of price appeal and operating on a relatively low markup and with a minimum of customer service. [WRD]

discount store Generally, a large retail store open to the public that incorporates aspects of supermarket merchandising strategy to a high degree, attempts to price merchandise at a relatively low markup, carries stock, and renders only limited types of consumer services, usually on the basis of a specific extra charge. It can be distinguished from regular retailers only by its consistent emphasis upon discount prices and its self-designation as a discount store. Much of the distinctive character has disappeared with the development of other forms of mass market retailing. [WRD]

discrete choice behavior model See **nested logit model**

discrete-lot-sizing An inventory management technique to help determine order quantities. The procurement objective is to obtain a quantity of components that equals the net requirement needed at a specific time. Purchase quantities will vary from order to order because of fluctuations in component requirements. [DJB/BJL]

discretionary buying power The money in the hands of consumers after the payment of taxes and the purchase of necessities; popularly called hot money or loose money. (See also **disposable personal income, money income, national income, personal disposable income, personal income,** and **real income**.) [DLS]

discretionary income See **discretionary buying power**

discretionary spending See **buying power**

discriminant analysis A statistical technique employed to model the relationship between a dichotomous or multichotomous criterion variable and a set of p continuous predictor variables. (See also **cluster analysis, conjoint analysis, correlation analysis, factor analysis, logit model,** and **regression analysis**.) [GAC]

discriminant consequences The consequences that differ across a set of alternatives that may be used as choice criteria. [JPP/JCO]

discriminant validity A criterion imposed on a measure of a construct requiring that it not correlate too highly with measures from which it is supposed to differ. (See also **construct validation, content validity, convergent validity, external validity, internal validity, pragmatic validity,** and **validity**.) [GAC]

discriminative stimulus A stimulus that by its mere presence or absence changes the probability of a behavior. For example, a 50 percent off sign in a store window could be a discriminitive stimulus. [JPP/JCO]

diseconomies of scale The losses that stem from producing a larger amount rather than a small amount, i.e., higher per unit costs for a product are incurred as the scale of operations is increased. (See also **economies of scale**.) [DLS]

disengagement stage See **salesperson career cycle**

disjunctive rule As compared with the conjunctive rule or lexicographic rule, the disjunctive heuristic (or rule of thumb) assumes that the consumer develops acceptable standards for each dimension (which may be higher than the minimum cutoff levels for the conjunctive heuristic). According to Bettman, if a product, brand, or alternative passes that standard for any attribute, it is accepted. The evaluation process yields groups of acceptable and unacceptable alternatives and hence the evaluation is derived rather than direct. (See also **choice rule, expectancy-value model, noncompensatory rules,** and **piecemeal processing**.) [HHK/MCC]

dispersion The process of breaking down a supply of goods into smaller lots. It includes the sorting processes of allocation and sorting out. [GLF]

display A special exhibit of a product at the point of sale, generally over and above standard shelf stocking. (See also **dealer loader, dealer tie-in, end-aisle display, event creation, feature,** and **trade sales promotion**.) [DES/BEB]

display allowance See **advertising/display allowance**

display stock The stock placed on various display fixtures that customers can directly examine. [WRD]

display type The type on a printed page, brochure, poster, or other advertising material that is larger than the type used for the body copy. [JE]

disposable income See **disposable personal income**

disposable personal income (DPI) 1. Personal income less federal, state, and local taxes. 2. A consumer's total money income less taxes paid to all government agencies; popularly shortened to *disposable income*. (See also **discretionary buying power, national income, personal disposable income,** and **real income**.) [DLS]

disproportionate stratified sampling A stratified sample in which the individual strata or subsets are sampled in relation to both their size and their variability; strata exhibiting more variability are sampled more than proportionately to their relative size, while those that are very homogeneous are sampled less than proportionately. [GAC]

dissatisfaction This occurs when prepurchase expectations are negatively disconfirmed (the product performs worse than expected). (See also **confirmation, consumer satisfaction, disconfirmation, expectation-disconfirmation model,** and **post-purchase evaluation**.) [JPP/JCO]

dissection control The subdividing of existing departments into relatively narrow groupings, then the establishing of dollar stock control records for each grouping. (see also **classification, classification control,** and **merchandise classification**.) [WRD]

dissociative group A reference group that an individual does not want to join or be similar to. (See also **aspirational group**.) [JPP/JCO]

dissonance reduction See **cognitive dissonance**

distant line extension See **line extension**

distinctive competences The strengths of the firm. That is, the particular characteristics of the firm that make it uniquely adapted to carry out its task(s) and to fulfill its purpose(s) in the industry within which it participates. The converse to the firm's distinctive advantages are its weaknesses, which inhibit and limit the ability of the firm to fulfill its purpose. (See also **differential advantage**.) [GSD]

distinctiveness A uniqueness that one product or one firm has over others. The distinctiveness may exist in any attribute, and may only be perceived, not real. (See also **differential advantage**.) [DW]

distinctiveness phase of the fashion cycle See **fashion cycle**

distress merchandise The goods that are (or soon will be) past the point where they can be sold at anything close to normal prices. This includes perishable, unfashionable, damaged, and unseasonal merchandise that still may have some market value. [DW]

distribution 1. (economic definition) A study of how factors of production are priced in the market place, i.e., the determination of rents, wages, interest, and profits. 2. (marketing definition) The marketing and carrying of products to consumers. 3. (business definition) The extent of market coverage. [DLS]

distribution center A facility for the receipt, storage, and redistribution of goods to company stores or to customers. It may be operated by retailers, manufacturers, or distribution specialists. (See also **central place theory**.) [WRD]

distribution channel See **channel of distribution**

distribution manager See **physical distribution manager**

distribution models In modeling the key decisions of which channel of distribution to choose, management can use any of the general models for option generation and evaluation. Specialized models have been developed, however, for specific distribution decisions such as site selection and logistics. Most of the gravitational site selection models follow Huff (1964), who developed a model in which the attraction of a site is proportional to the size of the retail center and inversely proportional to the customers' distance from the site. This model has been extended to incorporate not only size of retail site, but also image. These models are extensions of the Multiplicative Competitive Interaction model. Logistics-related optimization models have also been developed for warehouse locations and inventory management. Most of the models are based on mathematical programming or simulations. (See also **Multiplicative Competitive Interaction model, NEWPROD,** and **NEWS**.) [DCS/YJW]

distribution of income The apportionment of money and real income of an economy among individuals. [DLS]

distribution requirements planning (DRP) A planning technique that seeks to time-phase movement of products from manufacturing through the distribution channel. The objective is to forward allocate as little inventory as practical while satisfying customer service goals. [DJB/BJL]

distributive education A formerly common federally assisted program of education for workers in the distributive trades occupations at the high school and adult training level augmented by state and local support. Class work in school facilities is combined with concurrent work experience. [WRD]

distributive trades The establishments that are engaged principally in marketing (wholesale trade, retail trade, and service industries). [WRD]

distributor A wholesale middleman, especially in lines where selection or exclusive distribution is common at the wholesale level and the manufacturer expects strong promotional support. It is often a synonym for wholesaler. (See also **supply house** and **wholesale merchant**.) [WRD]

distributor's brand A brand that is owned and controlled by a reseller (distributor) such as a retailer or a wholesaler, as opposed to a brand owned by the manufacturer. The term applies only to the brand itself, not to the product or to its content. It is often called a private brand or private label, and (with exceptions such as Sears' brands) is usually not advertised heavily. [DW]

distributorship A type of franchise system wherein franchisees maintain warehouse stock to supply other franchisees. The distributor takes title to the goods and provides services to other customers. [WRD]

district sales manager See **field sales manager**

diversification A means whereby a business builds its total sales by identifying opportunities to build or acquire businesses that are not directly related to the company's current businesses. The major classes of diversification are concentric, horizontal and conglomerate. **Concentric diversification** results in new product lines or services that have technological and/or marketing synergies with existing product lines, even though the products may appeal to a new customer group. **Horizontal diversification** occurs when the company acquires or develops new products that could appeal to its current customer groups even though those new products may be technologically unrelated to the existing product lines. **Conglomerate diversification** occurs when there is neither technological nor marketing synergy and requires reaching new customer groups. (See also **acquisition, alliances, integration, merger,** and **product/market matrix**.) [GSD]

diversion 1. (physical distribution definition) The changing of the destination of a shipment while it is enroute and prior to arrival at the originally planned destination. [DJB/BJL] 2. (sales promotion definition) The situation in which agents or retailers in one part of the country buy a product under deal conditions and then resell the product to channel members in another part of the country where the manufacturer is not offering the deal. [DES/BEB]

diversion-in-transit A change of direction from the original destination while freight is in transit. [WRD]

diverters 1. An unauthorized, but legal, member of a marketing channel. 2. Firms that buy unwanted merchandise from retailers and manufacturers and resell the merchandise to other retailers. [WRD]

divest strategy The sale or liquidation of businesses or product lines in order to limit losses or in order to avoid predicted losses and/or because the resources freed up can be better used in other businesses. (See also **harvesting strategy, investment strategy,** and **portfolio analysis**.) [GSD]

division See **divisional organization**

division manager See **divisional organization**

divisional organization A form of organization that breaks the company into two or more business units (commonly called divisions). A division is a profit center and the division manager is responsible for attaining profit goals. A division may be responsible for a share of the company's existing product lines or for a separate business. The division manager reports to a top corporate executive. A division may be organized functionally or (as it expands) with the assistance of product managers, market managers, or category managers. (See also **bureaucratic organization; centralized management; decentralized management; flat organization; functional organization; geographic organization; hierarchical organization; market management organization; marketing organization, forms of; matrix organization; multibusiness organization; nonbusiness marketing organization;** and **product management organization**.) [VPB]

DMA See **designated market area**

DMU See **decision-making unit**

documentary collections (drafts) This is a method of payment using a bill of exchange. A bill of exchange is a negotiable instrument that is easily transferable from one party to another. [WJK]

dog See **growth-share matrix**

dollar control The control of sales, stocks, markdowns, and markups in terms of dollars rather than in terms of pieces or items. (See also **merchandise control**.) [WRD]

domesticated markets The markets that once were competitive that have been restructured as a result of voluntary, long-term binding agreements. A significant proportion of all transactions in these markets are planned and administered on the basis of negotiated rules of exchange. The benefits are reduced uncertainty, reduced transactions costs, and access to economies of scale. [GSD]

domestics A subdivision of the piece goods classification of department store merchandise, including muslins, sheets, pillowcases, tubing, cotton, outing flannel, etc. [WRD]

donor market A target audience asked to give money, goods, body organs, or blood to an organization or individual without expecting a tangible benefit in return. Comment: Donor marketing can be carried out by for-profit organizations. For-profit organizations can also be the recipients of the donations (although this is rare). [ARA]

door-to-door selling See **direct selling**

double exponential distribution See **logit model**

double stack A system for stacking two containers vertically on a single railcar. This system doubles the carrying capacity of each railcar and significantly reduces product damage. (See also **container-on-flatcar**.) [DJB/BJL]

double-barreled question A question that calls for two responses and thereby creates confusion for the respondent. [GAC]

downsizing An act of eliminating levels, units, groups, or individuals in an organization. [DLS]

downturn See **recession**

DPI See **disposable personal income**

DPP See **direct product profitability**

draw The money paid to salespeople against future commissions, usually in a period when commissions are low, in order to ensure that they may take home a specified minimum level of pay each month. [BAW]

drive See **motivation**

drop shipment 1. (physical distribution definition) Limited-function wholesalers known as drop shippers seldom take physical possession of the goods. They often specialize in heavy or bulky commodities that require the economies of volume shipment. The drop shipper buys the carload, but does not take physical possession. The order, or drop shipment, is shipped direct from the supplier to the customer. [DJB/BJL] 2. (retailing definition) A special type of wholesaler who deals in large lots shipped direct from the factory to the customer of the drop shipper, takes title to the goods, assumes responsibility for the shipment after it leaves the factory, extends credit, collects the account, and incurs all the sales costs necessary to secure orders. [WRD]

DRP See **distribution requirements planning**

DSD See **direct store delivery**

DSS See **decision support system**

dual career path, sales The provision of a choice made available to junior salespeople in an organization to receive more pay and recognition through promotions to managerial positions or through promotions within the sales rank with compensation being similar at similar levels along each path. [BAW]

dual distribution 1. (channels of distribution definition) This describes a wide variety of marketing arrangements by which a manufacturer or a wholesaler reaches its final markets by employing two or more different types of channels for the same basic product. [GLF] 2. (retailing definition) Under this type of distribution program, manufacturers sell directly to contractors and other large accounts at prices equal to or less than those available to retailers in the same market who are reselling the manufacturers' products. [WRD]

dual sourcing See **sourcing**

dummy A preliminary layout for an ad, brochure, poster, or other printed advertising material showing the position and size of the headlines, subheads, body copy, and artwork. (See also **comprehensive layout, mechanical, rough storyboard,** and **thumbnail.**) [JE]

dumping 1. (economic definition) The practice of selling a product at a lower price overseas than at home. [DLS] 2. (global marketing definition) The practice of selling merchandise in foreign markets at lower prices than those charged in the domestic markets. (See also **antidumping duties** and **antidumping laws.**) [WJK]

duopoly A market situation in which there are only two marketers of an economic good, while demand conditions remain competitive. (See also **imperfect competition, monopolistic competition, monopoly, monopsony, oligopolistic competition, oligopolistic environment, oligopoly, oligopsony, perfect competition, pure competition,** and **workable competition.**) [DLS]

duplication See **audience duplication**

durable good A consumer good that is used over an extended rather than a brief period of time. It is usually, but not necessarily, of more substantial manufacture. Examples are automobiles and furniture. (See also **hard goods** and **nondurable good.**) [DW]

dwell time The amount of time customers spend waiting in line. [WRD]

dwelling unit A single home, apartment, townhouse, or other unit in which a single person, family, or cohesive set of unrelated individuals reside. Typically, many goods are purchased in common. [HHK/MCC]

dyadic relationship A relationship between two interacting and mutually influencing organizational entities. Most buyer-seller relationships in organizational markets are dyadic, while in the consumer marketplace individual buyers rarely have the power to influence sellers. [GLL/DTW]

dynamic programming See **mathematical programming** and **product line optimization**

early adopters The second identifiable subgroup within a population that begins use of an innovation. They follow innovators and precede the early majority. Their role is to be opinion leaders and have influence over the early majority. (See also **adopter categories, adoption process,** and **product adoption process**.) [DW]

early majority The third identifiable subgroup within a population that adopts an innovation. They are preceded by early adopters and innovators. The early majority like to await the outcome of product trial by the two earlier groups, yet are not as slow to adopt as the next two groups, late majority and laggards. (See also **adopter categories, adoption process,** and **product adoption process**.) [DW]

early markdown A markdown taken early in the season or while the demand for the merchandise is still relatively active. [WRD]

early sales-based forecasting models See **new product forecasting models**

earned income The income resulting from work or services performed as contrasted with income from such sources as investments or rent. [WL/MBC]

EBA model See **Elimination-By-Aspects model**

ecology The study of the relations among living species and their physical and biotic environments, particularly adaptations to environments through the mechanisms of various systems. Consideration is given to environmental impact on development, behavior, and spatiotemporal and demographic relations. [WL/MBC]

econometric market models See **advertising models, forecasting models, marketing mix models,** and **Vidale-Wolfe model**

economic and technological factors See **market attractiveness**

economic and technological position See **competitive position**

economic concentration See **concentration, economic**

economic concept of rent A term reflecting the maximum amount that can be spent by a retail store for yearly rent expenses. It is calculated by subtracting from planned sales all projected nonrent costs including a projected or planned profit figure. [WRD]

economic determinism A philosophy, perspective, or belief that economic forces ultimately are determinants of social and political change. [WL/MBC]

economic environment The economic environment encompasses such factors as productivity, income, wealth, inflation, balance of payments, pricing, poverty, interest rates, credit, transportation, and employment; it is the totality of the economic surroundings that affect a company's markets and its opportunities. (See also **cultural environment, demographic environment, natural environment,** and **political environment**.) [WL/MBC]

economic goods The goods that are so scarce relative to human wants that human effort is required to obtain them. [DLS]

economic indicator The data collected over time that reflect economic activity and general business conditions. [DLS]

economic infrastructure The internal facilities of a country available for conducting business activities, especially the communication, transportation, distribution, and financial systems. [DLS]

economic integration See **custom union** and **political union**

economic man A model of human behavior assumed by economists in analyzing market behavior. The economic person is a rational person who attempts to maximize the utility received from his/her monetary outflows and sacrifices. (See also **social man.**) [DLS]

economic order quantity The order quantity that minimizes the total costs of processing orders and holding inventory. [WRD]

economic organization The way in which the means of production and distribution of goods are organized, such as capitalism or socialism. [WL/MBC]

economic shoppers The shoppers who try to maximize the ratio of total utility and dollars of expenditure. [DLS]

economic stage of the fashion cycle See **fashion cycle**

economic status See **census tract**

economic union See **political union**

economic well-being See **Consumer Sentiment Index**

economic-lot-sizing An inventory management technique used to determine order quantity or order period which minimizes the total cost of inventory maintenance and ordering. This requires continuous demand. [DJB/BJL]

economics 1. The science that deals with human wants and satisfaction. 2. The science that deals with a person's efforts to satisfy his/her wants through the use of the scarce resources of nature. [DLS]

economies of scale 1. (economic definition) The savings derived from producing a large number of units—e.g., in a situation in which all inputs are doubled, output may be more than doubled. (See also **diseconomies of scale** and **experience curve effect.**) [DLS] 2. (global marketing definition) The decline in per unit product costs as the absolute volume of production per period increases. [WJK]

economy pack A merchandising phrase pointing out savings by including several products as one item in one wrapping. [WRD]

ecosystem The complex of interactions of all the organisms with their environments and with each other. Technically, it is a subunit of the biosphere or a unit of a landscape. The interactions of members of a distribution channel, or the interaction of a company and its products with consumer environments are examples of marketing applications. [WL/MBC]

ECOWAS Economic Community of West African States

ECU See **European Currency Unit**

EDI See **electronic data interchange**

Edifact See **Electronic Data Interchange for Administration, Commerce and Transport**

editing The inspection and correction, if necessary, of each questionnaire or observation form. [GAC]

EDLP See **every day low price**

EEC European Economic Community

effective demand People with money and the inclination to buy. (See also **demand**.) [DLS]

effective frequency An advertiser's determination of the optimum number of exposure opportunities required to effectively convey the advertising message to the desired audience or target market. (See also **frequency**.) [JE]

efficient market hypothesis In its so-called "semi-strong" form, this hypothesis states that in setting security prices at any time, the market correctly uses all publicly available information about the underlying corporations whose stocks are traded in the market. In the absence of inside information, this implies that investors cannot consistently achieve performance in excess of the market "average" for any given level of risk. The "semi-strong" hypothesis enjoys wide acceptance in financial economics. [PFA]

EFTA See **European Free Trade Association**

ego According to Freudian Theory, the ego is one prong of the three parts of the personality. The ego is the executive, or the planner, compromising between the demands for immediate gratification of the id and the pristine rigidity of the superego (conscience or moral self). (See also **ego defenses**.) [HHK/MCC]

ego defenses The tools the ego has available to defend the individual from psychological stresses such as the forces of the id (libido) and the superego. Ego defenses are psychological constructs such as identification, rationalization, reaction formation, repression, sublimation, etc. (See also **ego-defensive function of attitudes** and **projection**.) [HHK/MCC]

ego defensive drives See **ego defenses**

ego-defensive function of attitudes The protection of the individual self provided by attitudes. The ego-defensive function protects the individual from threats by concealing the "true" self and any socially undesirable feelings and wants. It is one of the functions of attitudes proposed by the functional theory of attitudes. (See also **ego defenses, instrumental function of attitudes, knowledge function of attitudes,** and **value-expressive function of attitudes**.) [HHK/MCC]

eighty-twenty principle The situation in which a disproportionately small number (e.g., 20 percent) of salespeople, territories, products, or customers generate a disproportionately large amount (e.g., 80 percent) of a firm's sales or profits. This phenomenon can be identified and addressed by conducting a sales analysis and cost analysis. [AJD]

elaboration The degree of elaboration determines the number of meanings or beliefs formed during comprehension. [JPP/JCO]

Elaboration Likelihood Model (ELM) A model of attitude formation and change that proposes that the process by which attitudes change depends upon the message recipient's level of motivation. According to Petty and Cacioppo, the authors of the ELM, when motivation is high, the message recipient will pay attention and respond to the quality of message arguments. When motivation is low, the message recipient will be more responsive to peripheral elements of the message (e.g., music, spokesperson attractiveness, etc.). [HHK/MCC]

elastic demand 1. A situation in which a cut in price increases the quantity taken in the market enough that total revenue is increased. 2. A situation in which a given change in the price of an economic good is associated with a more than proportionate change in the quantity that buyers would purchase. 3. A situation in which the percentage of quantity taken "stretches" more than the percentage drop in price. (See also **elastic supply, elasticity coefficient,** and **inelastic demand**.) [DLS]

elastic supply 1. A situation in which a percentage increase in price attracts a greater percentage of products offered to the market. 2. A situation in which the percentage of goods offered "stretches" more than the percentage increase in price. (See also **elastic demand** and **inelastic supply**.) [DLS]

elasticity The degree that an economic variable changes in response to a change in another economic variable. [KM]

elasticity coefficient 1. A measure of the responsiveness of the quantity of a product taken in the market to price changes. 2. (technical definition) E is the limit as the change in price tends to zero of a ratio composed of two ratios: the change in quantity/quantity, divided by change in price/price. E is always negative: if the absolute value of E is greater than one, demand is said to be elastic; if exactly equal to one, unitary price elasticity prevails; if less than one, demand is said to be inelastic. (See also **elastic demand** and **inelastic demand**.) [DLS]

elasticity of demand See **price elasticity of demand**

elasticity of expectation A measure of the changes in prices of goods and changes in the quantity taken by the market stemming from expectations by consumers. [DLS]

elasticon A conjoint analysis-based model for estimating self- and cross-price elasticity. Subjects are asked to indicate their likelihood of buying each brand (when each brand is priced at some experimental level). A first order Markov model represents the price-induced brand switching. The price-demand model is fitted by generalized least-squares to the share of choices (Mahajan, Green, and Goldberg 1982). (See also **brand choice models**.) [DCS/YJW]

electronic data interchange (EDI) 1. (physical distribution definition) The intercompany, application-to-application exchange of business transactions in a standard data format. [DJB/BJL] 2. (retailing definition) The interfirm computer-to-computer transfer of information, as between or among retailers, wholesalers, and manufacturers. [WRD]

Electronic Data Interchange for Administration, Commerce and Transport (Edifact) The basic electronic data interchange format utilized globally or internationally for communication transmissions. [DJB/BJL]

electronic funds transfer The use of electronic means, such as computers, telephones, magnetic tape and so on, rather than checks, to transfer funds, or to authorize or complete a transaction. This development has given rise to the concept of the cashless economy. (See also **automated teller machine** and **point of sale transfer**.) [WL/MBC]

Elimination-By-Aspects (EBA) model A brand choice model that represents the ultimate selection decision as a series of eliminations. Each alternative available for choice is viewed as having some set of aspects (e.g., product features). At each stage of the choice process an aspect is selected (with probability proportional to that aspect's importance for this consumer), and all alternatives still being considered that do not possess the selected aspect are eliminated. The process continues until only one alternative remains, and that remaining item is assumed to be the one chosen by the consumer (Tversky 1972). Although more difficult to calibrate and apply than Luce's Choice Axiom model for choices, it does avoid the independence from irrelevant alternatives property of the latter model, which is often seen as an appealing feature of the EBA model. It has led to the development of other hierarchical/sequential choice models, including the Hierarchical Elimination Model (Tversky and Sattath 1979) and Generalized Elimination Model (Hauser 1986). (See also **logit model**.) [DCS/YJW]

ELM See **elaboration likelihood model**

embargo The prohibition of shipment of goods or services to designated countries. [WJK]

embryonic market life cycle stage See **market evolution**

EMC See **export management company**

emergency product A good (such as a portable generator) or a service (such as ambulance delivery) in which an essentially nondeliberative purchase decision is based on critical and timely need. (See also **consumer product, convenience product, impulse product, shopping product, specialty product,** and **staple good**.) [DW]

emotion See **attitude**

emotional appeals See **buying motives**

emotionally neutral See **belief**

employee discount A certain discount from retail price offered by most general merchandise retailers to employees. It is a kind of retail reduction from the point of view of accounting. Usually stores grant a larger percentage on personal wearing apparel than on gifts purchased by the employee. [WRD]

empty nest stage See **family life cycle**

emulation stage of the fashion cycle See **fashion cycle**

emulative product A new product that imitates another product already on the market. It is somewhat different from previous products (not a pure "me-too" product), but the difference is not substantial or significant. (See also **adaptive product, innovative imitation,** and **pioneering innovativeness**.) [DW]

end of month dating (EOM) The cash discount and the net credit periods begin on the first day of the following month rather than on the invoice date. EOM terms are frequently stated in this manner: "2/10, net 20, EOM." Suppose an order is filled and shipped on June 16 under these terms. In such a case, the cash discount may be taken any time through July 10 and the net amount is due on July 30. (See also **advance dating, dating, extra dating, future dating, memorandum purchase and dating, ordinary dating, proximo dating, receipt-of-goods dating,** and **season dating**.) [WRD]

end sizes Those sizes that are usually large, small, or extraordinary in some respect. (See also **fringe sizes** and **out sizes**.) [WRD]

end user A person or organization that consumes a good or service that may consist of the input of numerous firms. For example, an insurance company may be the end user for a keyboard for a personal computer, originally produced for and sold to the personal computer manufacturer. [GLL/DTW]

end-aisle display An exhibit of a product set up at the end of the aisle in a retail store to call attention to a special offering or price. (See also **display** and **trade sales promotion**.) [DES/BEB]

endless chain method A method of prospecting in which a salesperson asks customers to suggest other customers who might be interested in the salesperson's offerings. (See also **center of influence method, cold-canvassing, curiosity approach, introduction approach, product approach,** and **referral approach**.) [BAW]

enduring involvement The general, personal relevance of a product or activity. (See also **situational involvement**.) [JPP/JCO]

Engel's Law The observation that the proportion of income spent on food declines as income rises with given tastes or preferences. This law or tendency was formulated by Ernst Engel (1821-1896) in a paper published by him in 1857. [WJK]

entering new segments See **market development**

enterprise group See **keiretsu**

environment The complex set of physical and social stimuli in the external world of consumers. (See also **Wheel of Consumer Analysis**.) [JPP/JCO]

environmental analysis The gathering and analyzing of data about a company's or nation's external environment to identify trends and their impact upon an organization or country. Included among the environmental forces considered are the political, cultural, social, demographic, economic, legal, international, and ecological factors. [WL/MBC]

environmental factors See **market attractiveness**

environmental impact analysis The assessment of the impact of a strategy or decision on the environment, especially the ecological consequences of the strategy or decision. [WL/MBC]

Environmental Protection Agency (EPA) A federal agency formed in1970 that regulates the amount of pollutants manufacturers can emit. (See also **consumer protection legislation** and **Federal Environmental Pesticide Control Act**.) [DC]

environmental monitoring The activities aimed at keeping track of changes in external factors that are likely to affect the markets and demand for a firm's products and services. Among the external factors usually considered are the economic, social, demographic, political, legal, cultural, and technological forces. [WL/MBC]

environmental motives See **consumer motivation**

environmental scanning See **environmental monitoring**

environmental stimulus See **external stimulus**

environmentalism 1. (legislation definition) This refers to public concern over protecting, enhancing, and improving the environment, which includes conserving natural resources, eliminating pollution and hazardous substances, historic preservation, and preventing the extinction of plant and animal species. [DC] 2. (environments definition) That part of consumerism that concentrates on ecology issues such as air, water, and noise pollution and the depletion of natural resources. Marketing decisions and action, such as new product offerings, can impact directly on physical environments. [WL/MBC]

EOM dating See **end of month dating**

EPA See **Environmental Protection Agency**

episodic knowledge The mental representations of the specific events in a person's life. (See also **semantic knowledge**.) [JPP/JCO]

Equal Credit Opportunity Act (1974) This act prohibits discrimination by a creditor against any applicant for credit on the basis of sex or marital status. [DC]

equal time Section 315 of the Federal Communication Commission Act provides that if a broadcaster permits a legally qualified candidate for any public office to use a broadcasting station, he shall afford equal opportunity to use the broadcasting station to all other candidates for that office. (See also **fairness doctrine** and **Federal Communications Commission**.) [DC]

equalized workload method A method of determining sales force size that is based on the premise that all sales personnel should have an equal amount of work. The method requires that management estimate the work required to serve the entire market. The total work calculation is typically treated as a function of the number of accounts, the frequency with which each account should be called on, and the length of time that should be spent on each call. This estimate is then divided by the amount of work an individual salesperson should be able to handle to determine the total number of salespeople required. (See also **incremental productivity method**.) [AJD]

equilibrium point A situation in which the quantity and price offered by sellers equals the quantity and price taken by buyers. [DLS]

equilibrium price A price that equates supply and demand, i.e., the price at which the market clears. [DLS]

equipment The durable goods used to support manufacturing, logistics, administrative, and other business processes. The definition includes fixed equipment such as generators and drill presses, light factory equipment such as hand tools and lift trucks, and office equipment such as typewriters and desks. (See also **light equipment**.) [GLL/DTW]

equivalence A measure of reliability that is applied to both single instruments and measurement situations. When applied to instruments, the equivalence measure of reliability is the internal consistency or internal homogeneity of the set of items forming the scale; when applied to measurement situations, the equivalence measure of reliability focuses on whether different observers or different instruments used to measure the same individuals or objects at the same point in time yield consistent results. (See also **instrument variation** and **method variance**.) [GAC]

erratic demand A pattern of demand for a product that is varied and unpredictable—e.g., the demand for large automobiles. [DLS]

establishment stage See **salesperson career cycle**

esteem needs See **hierarchy of needs** and **Maslow's need hierarchy**

ethics This relates to moral action, conduct, motive, and character. It also means professionally right or befitting, conforming to professional standards of conduct (*Kraushnaar* v. *La Vin* 181 Misc. 508,42, N.Y. S.2d, 857,859) [DC]

ethnocentric orientation A home country orientation or an unconscious bias or belief that the home country approach to business is superior. (See also **geocentric orientation, polycentric orientation,** and **regiocentrism orientation.**) [WJK]

ethnocentric pricing policy See **extension pricing policy**

ethnography A detailed, descriptive study of a group and its behavior, characteristics, culture, etc. [HHK/MCC]

eurocurrency A national currency deposited outside the country of denomination: for example, U.S. dollars deposited in a foreign bank. (See also **eurodollars.**) [WJK]

eurodollars U.S. dollar deposits held in banks outside the United States. (See also **eurocurrency.**) [WJK]

European Community An association of European countries, viz. Germany, France, Italy, Belgium, Luxembourg, the Netherlands, the United Kingdom, Ireland, and Denmark, with uniform trade rules built upon the elimination of internal tariff barriers and the establishment of common external barriers. Its goal is to integrate and harmonize the economic, social, and political life of members. On the economic front, the goal is the elimination of all barriers and restrictions on the movement of goods and services. (See also **European Currency Unit.**) [WJK]

European Currency Unit (ECU) A weighted average currency unit created by weighting the current exchange rate of the twelve European Community member country currencies based on country GNP and trade. The ECU is a unit of value that fluctuates less than individual European Community currencies because it is a weighted average. (See also **European Community.**) [WJK]

European Free Trade Association (EFTA) An association established by the Stockholm Convention of 1959, with member countries being Austria, Finland (associate member), Iceland, Norway, Portugal, Sweden, and Switzerland. EFTA's objective is to bring about free trade in industrial goods and an expansion of trade in agricultural goods. [WJK]

European Union See **European Community**

evaluation See **adoption process, goal,** and **objective**

evaluation and control of sales force performance See **sales management**

evaluation of alternative suppliers, in organizational buying Formal supplier evaluation is the rating of alternative suppliers on preset criteria in order to evaluate their technical, financial, and managerial abilities. It is a way to substitute facts for feelings in selecting suppliers. [GLL/DTW]

evaluation rule See **conjunctive rule, disjunctive rule, lexicographic rule,** and **noncompensatory rules**

even price See **odd-even pricing**

event creation The use of communication techniques such as news releases, press conferences, etc., to call attention to activities to promote a company, product, or service. Also, it is the development of a special activity, showing, display, or exhibit designed to demonstrate products or to connect the product to favorable products or activities. (See also **press party.**) [DES/BEB]

evergreen See **feature story**

every day low price (EDLP) 1. (retailing definition) A policy or strategy of retail pricing whereby presumably low prices are set initially on items and maintained, as opposed to the occasional offering of items at special or reduced sales prices. [WRD] 2. (sales promotion definition) A pricing approach in which the product is offered to retailers and consumers at a consistently low cost rather than reducing price periodically through sales promotion activities. [DES/BEB]

evoked set 1. (consumer behavior definition) The set of alternatives that are activated directly from memory. [JPP/JCO] 2. (consumer behavior definition) The set of possible products or brands that the consumer may be considering in the decision process. It is the set of choices that has been evoked and is salient as compared with the larger number of available possible choices. For example, from the many brands of breakfast cereals on supermarket shelves, it is the half a dozen brands (or so) that the buyer may remember and be considering for purchase. (See also **competitive brands**.) [HHK/MCC]

ex-parte A regulatory practice of pretesting proposed regulatory rules in an effort to get reactions and comments from shippers, carriers, and other interested parties. [DJB/BJL]

exception rate A transportation charge based on a class rate but reduced due to special circumstances, usually local or regional competitive conditions. (See also **commodity rate** and **line-haul rate**.) [DJB/BJL]

exchange All activities associated with receiving something from someone by giving something voluntarily in return. [DLS]

exchange control The control of movement of funds and of purchases of currency by a government. Exchange control may be utilized in support of any of the following objectives: (1) to keep exchange rates stable, (2) to keep the currency undervalued to stimulate exports, or (3) to keep the currency overvalued to handicap exports and encourage imports. [WJK]

exclusion orders See **non tariff barriers**

exclusionary distribution See **non tariff barriers**

exclusive dealing A restriction that is imposed by a supplier on a customer forbidding the customer from purchasing some type of product from any other supplier. This restriction is subject to an examination of whether it substantially lessens competition or restrains trade. Exclusive dealing should not be confused with exclusive distributorships, a term applied to arrangements in which a supplier promises not to appoint more than one dealer in each territory. [DC]

exclusive distribution 1. (channels of distribution definition) A form of market coverage in which a product is distributed through one particular wholesaler or retailer in a given market area. (See also **intensive distribution** and **selective distribution**.) [GLF] 2. (retailing definition) The practice whereby the vendor agrees to sell the goods or services within a certain territory only through a single retailer or a limited number of retailers. It may also apply to wholesalers. [WRD]

exempt carrier A transportation provider not subject to direct regulation regarding operating rights or pricing policies. It must, however, comply with licensing and safety laws. If engaged in interstate movement, the carrier must publish its rates. (See also **independent carrier**.) [DJB/BJL]

exhibit The gathering and displaying of products, people, or information at a central location for viewing by a diverse audience. (See also **end-aisle display** and **event creation**.) [DES/BEB]

Eximbank See **Export Import Bank**

expandibility of demand The degree to which the demand schedule can be shifted through the use of marketing mix variables such as advertising and personal selling. [DLS]

expectancy A salesperson's estimate of the likelihood that if he or she increases his or her effort on some job activity, a higher level of performance will occur. In essence, expectancy is the linkage between effort and salesperson performance. For example, a salesperson might estimate that there is a 50 percent probability (expectancy) that if he or she spends 10 percent more time calling on new accounts, his or her sales volume will rise by 15 percent. Expectancies can influence a salesperson's level of motivation. (See also **instrumentality, salesperson motivation,** and **valence**.) [AJD]

expectancy-value model This is one of the major schools of motivation emerging from the work of Kurt Lewin. According to Wilkie, the major proposition is that the strength of the tendency to act in a certain way depends on the strength of the expectancy that the act will be followed by a given consequence (or goal) and the value of that goal to the individual. It assumes that the consumer behaves purposively and evaluates, say, the purchase of a particular brand in terms of how desirable the consequences of the purchase of that brand are for him or her. (See also **conjunctive rule, disjunctive rule, lexicographic rule,** and **noncompensatory rules**.) [HHK/MCC]

expectation-disconfirmation model A model that proposes that satisfaction depends upon the consistency between expectations and performance. Dissatisfaction is proposed to result when product performance is below expectations, whereas satisfaction arises when performance equals or exceeds expected performance. (See also **satisfaction/dissatisfaction**.) [HHK/MCC]

expediter An expediter is one who works to speed up a shipment for delivery. [DJB/BJL]

expense account An account maintained by salespeople that includes travel, entertainment, and other expenses which they incur for business purposes and for which they are reimbursed by their employers. [BAW]

expense center A collection of controllable costs that are related to one particular area of work or kind of store service. [WRD]

expense center accounting The grouping of expenses by their necessity in performing a particular kind of store service. For example, some expense centers are management, property and equipment, accounts payable, etc. Natural expenses are typically included as a part of the concept (e.g., payroll). [WRD]

experience curve analysis The application of the experience curve effect, to understand (1) how the components of the total cost of a company's product are affected by cumulative experience, (2) the relationship of industry experience and average industry prices and costs, and (3) how competitive cost comparisons relate to current costs of direct competitors to their cumulative experience. (See also **cost oriented strategy** and **experience curve effect**.) [GSD]

experience curve effect A systematic decline in the cost per unit that is achieved as the cumulative volume (and therefore experience) increases. There are three sources of the experience curve effect: (1) *learning*—the increasing efficiency of labor that arises chiefly from practice; (2) *technological improvements*—including process innovations, resource mix changes, and product standardization; and (3) *economies of scale*—the increased efficiency due to size. (See also **experience curve analysis**.) [GSD]

experience-curve pricing 1. (pricing definition) A method of pricing in which the seller sets the price sufficiently low to encourage a large sales volume in anticipation that the large sales volume would lead to a reduction in average unit costs. Generally this method of pricing is used over time by periodically reducing the price to induce additional sales volumes that lead to lower per unit costs. [KM] 2. (economic definition) A price-setting method using a markup on the average total cost as forecast by cost trends over time as sales volume accumulates. [DLS]

experience survey A series of interviews with people knowledgeable about the general subject being investigated. [GAC]

experiment A scientific investigation in which an investigator manipulates and controls one or more independent variables and observes the dependent variable for variation concomitant to the manipulation of the independent variable(s). (See also **instrument variables, manipulation check,** and **method variance**.) [GAC]

experimental demand curve A price-volume relationship estimated by simulating actual market conditions in an experiment or other form of pricing research. [KM]

experimental design A research investigation in which the investigator has direct control over at least one independent variable and manipulates at least one independent variable. (See also **completely randomized design** and **factoral design**.) [GAC]

experimental group A group of subjects in an experiment who are exposed to an experimental treatment or alternative whose effect is to be measured and compared. (See also **control group**.) [GAC]

experimental mortality An experimental condition in which test units are lost during the course of an experiment. [GAC]

expert systems 1. (models definition) Interactive computer systems that, by applying a variety of knowledge elements (e.g., facts, rules, models) within a specified domain, can solve a problem with an expertise comparable to that of an acknowledged human expert. As part of the developments in artificial intelligence, expert systems have been developed in various fields (medicine, defense, manufacturing, etc.) In recent years, a number of marketing expert systems have been developed, including ADCAD (an expert system for the design of advertising appeals and executions) (Burke, Rangaswamy, Wind, and Eliashberg 1990). [DCS/YJW] 2. (marketing research definition) A computer-based artificial intelligence system that attempts to model how experts in the area process information to solve the problem at hand. [GAC]

explicit costs The costs that are generally of a contractual or definite nature, including expenses for such items as wages, telephone bills, light bills, and supplies. They are explicitly carried on the accounting records as costs and are charged against the operation of the business because they are obvious and definite in amount. [WRD]

exploration stage See **salesperson career cycle**

exploratory research A research design in which the major emphasis is on gaining ideas and insights; it is particularly helpful in breaking broad, vague problem statements into smaller, more precise subproblem statements. (See also **causal research** and **descriptive research**.) [GAC]

exponential smoothing A forecasting technique to estimate future sales using a weighted average of previous demand and forecast accuracy. The new forecast is based on the old forecast incremented by some fraction of the differential between the old forecast and sales realized. The factor used to calculate the new forecast is called an alpha factor. (See also **forecasting models**.) [DJB/BJL]

export agent A manufacturers' agent who specializes in marketing goods abroad. (See also **import agent, import broker,** and **import commission house**.) [DLS]

export commission representative See **manufacturer's export representative**

export distributor See **manufacturer's export representative**

Export Import Bank (Eximbank) The primary U.S. government agency in the business of providing funds for international trade and investment. It also plays a key role in the U.S. export credit insurance program and is the primary administrator for the foreign currencies abroad that are generated by the U.S. surplus farm commodities. [WJK]

export management company (EMC) A firm that manages exports for other firms. It produces no product of its own but serves as an international marketing intermediary. It acts as the export department of the client firm and may even use its letterhead. [WJK]

export marketing The integrated marketing of goods and services that are produced in a foreign country. Each element of the marketing mix (product, price, promotion, and channels of distribution) is potentially variable. (See also **export selling**.) [WJK]

export selling Selling to a foreign country with the focus on the product and the emphasis on selling. The key elements of marketing mix (product, price, promotion, and channels of distribution) are all the same as in the home market. Only the place or distribution is adjusted in export selling. (See also **export marketing**.) [WJK]

export trading company A firm that buys another firm's merchandise and assumes all responsibility for the marketing and distribution of the product abroad. [WJK]

exposure Any opportunity for a reader, viewer, or listener to see and/or hear an advertising message in a particular media vehicle. [JE]

exposure distribution See **frequency**

expressed guarantee See **expressed warranty** and **guarantee**

expressed warranty 1. (retailing definition) A guarantee supplied by either the retailer or the manufacturer that details the terms of the warranty in simple and easily understood language so customers know what is and what is not covered by the warranty. [WRD] 2. (product development definition) The spoken or written promises made by the seller of a product about what will be done if the product proves to be defective in manufacture or performance. This contrasts with promises that are only implied by common knowledge of the product or by customary practices in a trade. Expressed warranties are usually restricted to stated periods of time. (See also **implied warranty** and **warranty**.) [DW]

expropriation Government acquisition of private property without payment of prompt and full compensation to owners. [WJK]

extension pricing policy A pricing policy that requires that the price of an item be the same around the world and that the customer absorb freight and import duties. This is also known as ethnocentric pricing policy. (See also **adaptation pricing policy** and **invention pricing policy**.) [WJK]

extensive problem solving 1. (consumer behavior definition) A choice involving substantial cognitive and behavioral effort. (See also **limited problem solving** and **routinized choice behavior**.) [JPP/JCO] 2. (consumer behavior definition) In the choice process, this includes those decisions that consume considerable cognitive activity and thought, as compared to routinized response behavior and habitual decision making. [HHK/MCC]

external action program See **public affairs**

external data Data that originate outside the organization for which the research is being done. (See also **internal data**.) [GAC]

external factors See **situation analysis**

external stimulus A cue or stimulus or prod to action that is external to the individual such as a bright light or an advertisement. An internal stimulus would be one from within the individual such as hunger pangs, the feeling of fear, or glee. [HHK/MCC]

external threats See **risk analysis**

external validity One criterion by which an experiment is evaluated; the criterion refers to the extent, to what populations and settings, to which the observed experimental effect can be generalized. (See also **construct validation, content validity, convergent validity, discriminant validity, internal validity, pragmatic validity,** and **validity**.) [GAC]

externality See **social impact of marketing**

extinction The process by which a learned response or learned behavior pattern is extinguished or unlearned (or forgotten). Extinction is the psychological term for unlearning. It is the process of forgetting and although there is some controversy over whether or not forgetting naturally occurs over time, it is accepted that extinction can be induced. [HHK/MCC]

extra dating A form of deferred dating. The purchaser is allowed a specified number of days before the ordinary dating begins. To illustrate, in the sale of blankets the terms "2/10—60 days extra" may be offered by the vendor. This means that the buyer has 60 days plus 10 days, or 70 days, from the invoice date in which to pay the bill with the discount deducted. (See also **advance dating, dating, end of month dating, future dating, memorandum purchase and dating, proximo dating, receipt-of-goods dating,** and **season dating**.) [WRD]

extrinsic reward A reward that is external to the individual such as money, food, or a pat on the head. An intrinsic reward is one that is internal within the person such as feeling good for a job well done. [HHK/MCC]

fabricating materials Processed materials required for producing goods and services that are not considered component parts. Examples are steel plates, chemicals, glass, coke, sheet metal, plastics, and leather. (See also **industrial products.**) [GLL/DTW]

face validity See **content validity**

face value The printed financial value of a coupon (actual savings). The face value can be either a specific monetary amount, a percentage discount, or combination offer with another product. [DES/BEB]

facilitating agent A business firm that assists in the performance of distribution tasks other than buying, selling, and transferring title (e.g., bank, transportation company, warehouse). [GLF]

fact sheet See **backgrounder sheet**

factor 1. A specialized financial institution engaged in factoring accounts receivable and lending on the security of inventory. 2. A type of commission house that often advances funds to the consignor, identified chiefly with the raw cotton and naval stores trades. [WRD]

factor analysis A body of statistical techniques concerned with the study of interrelationships among a set of variables, none of which is given the special status of a criterion variable. (See also **cluster analysis, conjoint analysis, correlation analysis, discriminant analysis,** and **regression analysis.**) [GAC]

factoral design An experimental design that is used when the effects of two or more variables are being simultaneously studied; each level of each factor is used with each level of each other factor. [GAC]

factoring A specialized financial function whereby manufacturers, wholesalers, or retailers sell accounts receivable to financial institutions, including factors, banks, and sales finance companies, often on a nonrecourse basis. [WRD]

factors of production The productive resources of an economy, usually classified as land, labor, and capital. Management is frequently included as a fourth factor of production. [DLS]

factory outlet center A shopping center that specializes in manufacturers' outlets that dispose of excess merchandise or that may serve as an alternate channel of distribution. (See also **arcade shopping center, community shopping center, mall-type shopping center, neighborhood shopping center, off-price shopping center, outlet store, regional shopping center, strip-type shopping center,** and **super regional shopping center.**) [WRD]

factory pack The multiple packaging of one product, or of one product and another product of the same firm, or one product and a sample or premium. The packaging is done at the factory and arrives in the trade channel already in the promotional form. [DW]

fad A product (e.g., unique doll and

video arcade) whose popularity is intense but temporary. A fad comes in fast, receives much attention and publicity, and goes out fast. The time period is highly variable, and a fad can repeat at intervals of several years as the hula hoop does. (See also **fashion cycle.**) [DW]

Fair Credit Reporting Act (1970) This act is designed to ensure accuracy of credit reports and to allow consumers the right to learn the nature of the information and challenge and correct erroneous information. [DC]

Fair Debt Collection Practices Act (1978) An act that specifies that a third party debt collector (i.e., one who collects debts owed to another), cannot communicate with the consumer in connection with the debt at any unusual time or place, and may not harass or abuse any person in connection with the collection of the debt. [DC]

Fair Packaging and Labeling Act (1966) This act requires that labels on consumer commodities identify the type of product being sold, the name and address of the supplier, and where applicable, the quality and contents of each serving. The act also authorizes the FTC and FDA to issue regulations concerning specific products covering items such as ingredient statements, package size standards, "slack-fill" packaging, and sales price representations. [DC]

fair trade laws Federal and state statutes permitting suppliers of branded goods to impose resale price maintenance contracts fixing minimum retail prices. The Consumer Goods Pricing Act of 1975 outlawed such practices. (See also **resale price maintenance laws.**) [DC]

fairness doctrine This doctrine requires broadcasters to afford reasonable opportunity for the discussion of conflicting views on issues of public importance. In 1987, the Federal Communications Commission abandoned its fairness doctrine: however, there have been efforts by legislators to place the doctrine into law. (See also **equal time.**) [DC]

faith See **belief**

FAK See **freight-all-kinds rate**

family A group of at least two people in a household based on marriage, cohabitation, blood relationships, or adoption. [JPP/JCO]

family brand A brand that is used on two or more individual products. The product group may or may not be all of that firm's product line. The individual members of the family also carry individual brands to differentiate them from other family members. In rare cases there are family brands that have as members other family brands, each of which has individual brands. Automobiles fit the latter situation, as with Oldsmobile (family) Cutlass (family) Ciera (individual). (See also **brand; brand extension; branding, individual; branding, line family;** and **multibrand strategy.**) [DW]

family decision making The processes, interactions, and roles of family members involved in making decisions as a group. [JPP/JCO]

family life cycle 1. (consumer behavior definition) A sociological concept that describes changes in families across time. Emphasis is placed on the effects of marriage, divorce, births, and deaths on families and the changes in income and consumption through various family stages. [JPP/JCO] 2. (consumer behavior definition) Families account for a very large percentage of all consumer expenditures. Much of this spending is systematic and stems from natural needs that change as a family unit goes through its natural stages of life. These range from the young single and the newly married stages to the full nest as the children are born and grow, to the empty nest and the final solitary survivor stage. Each transition prompts changes in values and behavior. [HHK/MCC]

family packaging The use of one design or other key packaging element to integrate the packaging of two or more individual items. The packages clearly belong to one set, but there are usually some individualizations, especially in brand name. [DW]

family roles See **roles**

F.A.S. See **free alongside ship**

fashion An accepted and popular style. [WRD]

fashion coordination The function of analyzing fashion trends in order to ensure that the merchandise offered for sale in various related apparel departments is of comparable style, quality, and appeal. [WRD]

fashion cycle The process by which a particular design, activity, color, etc., comes into some popularity and then phases out. This cycle of adoption and rejection is quite similar to the product life cycle, but the fashion cycle uses different terms to describe its phases: (1) **distinctiveness phase,** in which the style is eagerly sought; (2) **emulation stage,** in which its popularity grows; and (3) **economic stage,** in which it becomes available at lower prices to the mass market. (See also **fad.**) [DW]

fashion product A subcategory of a shopping product. This subcategory contains items that are wanted by consumers for their fashion aspects. [DW]

fast food outlet A food retailing institution featuring a very limited menu, preprepared or quickly prepared food, and take-out operations. [WRD]

FCB grid See **Foote, Cone & Belding grid**

FCC See **Federal Communications Commission**

FCPA See **Foreign Corrupt Practices Act**

FDA See **Food and Drug Administration**

fear appeals Communications material that attempts to persuade or manipulate by using frightening message content (e.g., not using Brand X deodorant will lead to a miserable social life). The relationship between fear and persuasibility seems to be curvilinear such that moderate levels of fear appear to be more effective than the use of either mild fear or strong fear. The difficulty is in the definitions and measurement of what are mild, moderate, and extreme fear appeals. [HHK/MCC]

feature The use of advertising, displays, or other activity, generally by a retailer, to call special attention to a product, generally for a limited period of time. [DES/BEB]

feature, product A fact or technical specification about a product. [BAW]

feature story A type of publicity material that can be used by the media at their convenience because it is not time-related. A feature is often human interest-related and contains more background information than typically found in a news release. It is also known as an evergreen because of its relatively long life span. [DES/BEB]

Federal Cigarette and Labeling and Advertising Act (1967) This act required a warning statement on cigarette packages and prohibited the advertising of cigarettes and little cigars on electronic media under the jurisdiction of the Federal Communications Commission. In 1986, these restrictions were extended to smokeless tobacco. [DC]

Federal Communications Commission (FCC) A federal regulatory agency responsible for supervising radio and television broadcasting. (See also **equal time, fairness doctrine,** and **Federal Cigarette and Labeling and Advertising Act.**) [DC]

Federal Energy Regulatory Commission (1971) This commission replaced the Federal Power Commission established in 1920 and is responsible for issuing licenses for the development of water and electrical power and prohibiting operators from restricting output or restraining trade in electrical energy. [DC]

Federal Environmental Pesticide Control Act (1976) This act requires registration of a pesticide before it can be distributed, sold, or offered for sale or shipped or received in any state. Responsibility for pesticide control is placed with the Environmental Protection Agency. [DC]

Federal Food, Drug and Cosmetics Act (1938) This act brought therapeutic devices and cosmetics within the regulatory authority of the FDA and strengthened the FDA's enforcement powers. (See also **consumer protection legislation.**) [DC]

Federal Hazardous Substance Act (1960) This act requires cautionary labeling of household chemical products. (See also **Child Protection Act.**) [DC]

Federal Maritime Commission This commission regulates foreign and offshore domestic trade. It authorizes the setting of international sea freight rates and regulates against imposition of illegal rebates and discrimination by carriers. (See also **Shipping Act.**) [DC]

Federal Power Commission See **Federal Energy Regulatory Commission**

federal regulatory agencies Administrative agencies that create and enforce the bulk of the laws that make up the legal environment of business. More than one hundred federal agencies exercise some degree of control over private economic activities. [DC]

Federal Trade Commission (FTC) The FTC is responsible for enforcing the Federal Trade Commission Act, which prohibits "unfair methods of competition" and "unfair or deceptive acts or practices." (See also **Fair Packaging and Labeling Act, Fur Products Labeling Act, Magnuson-Moss Warranty-Federal Trade Commission Improvement Act, substantiation, trade regulation rule,** and **Wool Products Labeling Act.**) [DC]

Federal Trade Commission Act (1914) This act placed a blanket prohibition against "unfair methods of competition" and created the FTC to enforce it. (See also **antitrust laws, consumer protection legislation, Flammable Fabrics Act, Miller-Tydings Resale Price Maintenance Act,** and **Wheeler Lea Act.**) [DC]

fee method of compensation The compensation method whereby advertising agencies are paid by their clients on the basis of negotiated fees for the specific services rendered. (See also **commission method of compensation.**) [JE]

feel-felt-found method A method used by salespeople to helpfully respond to prospect objections by showing how other prospects held similar views before buying the product or service. (See also **boomerang method, direct de-**

nial, indirect denial, pass up method, and **postpone method.**) [BAW]

feeling See **attitude**

fertility rate The ratio of the births during a year to the total number of women ages 15 to 49. (See also **completed fertility, crude birth rate, replacement level fertility,** and **total fertility rate.**) [WL/MBC]

field edit A preliminary edit, typically conducted by a field supervisor, that is designed to detect the most glaring omissions and inaccuracies in a completed data collection instrument. [GAC]

field experiment A research study in a realistic situation in which one or more independent variables are manipulated by the experimenter under as carefully controlled conditions as the situation will permit. [GAC]

field observations See **behavioral analysis**

field sales manager A title assigned to sales managers at regional, district, branch, or unit levels in companies with large sales forces. While the lowest level of field sales management provides direct supervision of salespeople, each level has a role in the overall field sales management job of recruiting; selecting; training; compensating; motivating; assigning of territories, quotas, and expense budgets; and the measurement and control of salespeople. In companies using specialized sales forces there may be field sales management titles assigned by product lines, markets, or accounts. (See also **general sales manager.**) [VPB]

field salesperson A salesperson who is responsible for contacting and selling goods and services to customers in their place of business or residence. (See also **inside salesperson.**) [BAW]

field warehousing 1. (economic definition) A financing device whereby a field warehouse receipt is pledged as security for a loan. [DLS] 2. (retailing definition) An arrangement by which the owner of goods leases a portion of the storage facility to a licensed warehouser who places a representative in charge, posts signs stating that a designated portion of the warehouse is in the charge of the outside organization, and adds to or takes from stock as directed by the financial institution that has the stock as collateral. [WRD]

FIFO See **first in, first out**

fighting brand A line extension of a main brand that is marketed by one producer to compete directly with the lower-priced products of other producers in a given market. The fighting brand usually has a separate brand identity and a low price. Its quality is usually lower than that of the main brand; it may only be temporarily on the market; and its purpose is to hold customers without having to lower the price of the main brand. [DW]

fill rate An inventory's availability goal used when setting customer service objectives, e.g., 99 percent product fill rate or filling 99 out of 100 customer orders. [DJB/BJL]

filler sheet A collection of brief (less than 100 words), newsworthy items related to the product or service being promoted. The media use filler sheet material when there are empty spaces in print layouts or broadcast time. [DES/BEB]

final purchase See **AIDA** and **hierarchy of effects model**

financial analyst A person who investigates, evaluates, and advises clients on the value and risk of investment offerings. [DES/BEB]

financial leases See **leasing**

financial quota A quota that focuses on financial criteria such as gross margin or contribution to overhead. Financial quotas are used to make salespeople conscious of the cost and profit implications of what they sell. Financial quotas are often stated in terms of direct selling expenses, gross margin, or net profit. They are most applicable when the firm's market penetration approaches saturation levels. In such instances, increasing sales or market share is difficult, so an emphasis on selling efficiency and cost control becomes a logical mechanism for increasing profits. (See also **activity quota, sales quota,** and **sales volume quota.**) [AJD]

financing See **channel flows** and **channel functions**

finished prototype See **prototype**

first in, first out (FIFO) A method for valuing inventory that assumes that the oldest merchandise is sold before the more recently purchased merchandise. [WRD]

first-mover advantage The ability of pioneering firms to gain long-term competitive advantages due to early entry. Mechanisms that lead to first-mover advantage include preemption of competition, development of a leadership reputation, increased brand loyalty due to customer switching costs, proprietary experience curve effects, and a sustainable lead in technology due to patents and trade secrets. (See also **follower advantage** and **invisible assets.**) [GSD]

Fishbein's learning theory of attitudes See **instrumental function of attitudes** and **multiattribute models of attitudes**

fit, willing and able Under current motor carrier regulations, applicants to the Interstate Commerce Commission seeking new or expanded rights must prove they are fit, willing, and able to perform the proposed service. They are no longer required to prove the service is necessary and in the public interest. [DJB/BJL]

fixed capital Durable capital that may be used repeatedly over a considerable period of time. [DLS]

fixed cost, average The total fixed cost divided by the number of units produced and marketed. (See also **fixed cost, total.**) [DLS]

fixed cost contribution per unit The selling price per unit less the variable cost per unit. [DLS]

fixed cost, total The sum of costs incurred by a firm that tend to remain at the same level (fixed) no matter how many units of a product are produced and marketed. (See also **fixed cost, average** and **total cost.**) [DLS]

fixed equipment See **equipment**

fixed exchange rate An exchange rate that is fixed by government policy and that is not free to fluctuate in response to market forces. (See also **floating exchange rate.**) [WJK]

fixed stock A definite amount of a good already produced, on hand, and ready for sale. It cannot be increased in the short run and can be decreased only by sale. [DLS]

fixed-alternative question A question in which the responses are limited to stated alternatives. (See also **dichotomous question, multichotomous question,** and **open-ended question.**) [GAC]

flagging The use of special graphic techniques on the product package or store shelf to call attention to a particular offer such as a reduced price, bonus pack, etc. [DES/BEB]

flagship store In a local department store organization, the main or downtown store, especially when it is large or dominant in relation to other company stores. [WRD]

Flammable Fabrics Act (1953) This act made illegal the production or distribution of any article of apparel which is "so highly flammable as to be dangerous when worn," under the Federal Trade Commission Act. [DC]

flanker brand A line extension. Sometimes the term is meant to cover only those line extensions that are not premium-priced or low-priced. (See also **brand.**) [DW]

flanking An indirect strategy aimed at capturing market segments whose needs are not being served by competitors. Flanking can be executed by targeting either a geographical segment or a consumer segment (group) that is not being well served by competitors, when the competitor is unwilling or unable to retaliate. [GSD]

flash report As soon as the day's sales figures have been read on whatever kind of register is in use, a tentative, unaudited report is released to give management the day's results for comparison with budget or perhaps last year's sales figure. [WRD]

flat organization This term (and the term **horizontal organization**) refers to an organization with few or no intervening levels of management between the top executive and the workers. It presents a stark contrast to the classic hierarchical organization and bureaucratic organization with their layers of managers each of whom supervises a lower layer, leading finally to the supervision of workers. The underlying concept of the flat organization is that trained workers with assigned goals, and with the authority to achieve the goals in their own way, will—working individually or in groups—be more productive than workers who are closely supervised by managers. Comment: A truly flat organization would be feasible only for a small business or service organization or institution in which all employees report directly to the boss. For a large organization wishing to delegate more authority down the line, a more descriptive term would be "flatter" organization. Layers of management are reduced to the minimum and workers are given more authority and responsibility to achieve their assigned goals. It should be noted, however, that in the case of a business (particularly where stock is issued to the public) the hierarchy cannot be dispensed with entirely. The corporation is charged with many fiduciary and legal requirements. Consequently, top management must provide policies, direction, and controls to ensure that managers and workers at all levels understand and comply with these requirements. (See also **bureaucratic organization; centralized management; decentralized management; divisional organization; functional organization; geographic organization; hierarchical organization; market management organization; marketing organization, forms of; matrix organization; multibusiness organization; nonbusiness marketing organization** and **product management organization.**) [VPB]

flat rate A price charged for advertising space or time that does not include discounts based on the quantity of space or time purchased by the advertiser. (See also **open rate.**) [JE]

flexible pricing A practice of selling at different prices to different customers. This practice could be suspect under the Robinson-Patman Act. [DLS]

flight See **flighting**

flighting An advertising continuity or timing pattern in which advertising messages are scheduled to run during intervals of time that are separated by periods in which no advertising messages appear for the advertised item. Any period of time during which the messages are appearing is called a flight, and a period of message inactivity is usually called a hiatus. (See also **continuity, continuous media pattern,** and **pulsing.**) [JE]

floating exchange rate An exchange rate that is determined by private supply and demand and that is free to respond to market forces. (See also **fixed exchange rate** and **foreign exchange risk.**) [WJK]

floor audit The use of floor sales registers for all transactions, both cash and credit, so as to obtain from the register readings the total sales for each salesperson, department, and type of sale. [WRD]

F.O.B. See **free-on-board**

F.O.B. destination A shipping term that indicates the seller pays the freight to the destination. Title does not pass until the merchandise reaches its destination; thus, the seller assumes all risks, loss, or damage while goods are in transit, except for the liability of the carrier. [WRD]

F.O.B. origin pricing A form of geographical pricing in which the seller quotes prices from the point of shipment. Free-on-board (F.O.B.) means it is the buyer's responsibility to select the mode of transporting the goods, choose the specific carrier, handle all claims, and pay all shipping charges. (See also **delivered pricing.**) [KM]

F.O.B. with freight allowed A form of delivered pricing in which the buyer arranges and pays for the transportation, but deducts these transportation costs from the invoice total and remits the net amount. [KM]

focus group 1. (consumer behavior definition) A method of gathering qualitative data on the preferences and beliefs of consumers through group interaction and discussion usually focused on a specific topic or product. Also, it is a group of respondents brought together for this purpose. [HHK/MCC] 2. (marketing research definition) A personal interview conducted among a small number of individuals simultaneously; the interview relies more on group discussion than on a series of directed questions to generate data. It is also called group indepth interview. [GAC]

focus strategies See **niche strategies**

folkways See **mores**

follower advantage The ability of nonpioneering market entrants to gain long-term competitive advantages due to late entry. Mechanisms that lead to follower advantage include resolution of demand and market uncertainty, shifts in technology or customer needs, the ability to free-ride on first-mover investments in buyer education and infrastructure development, and learning from the pioneer's product, positioning, or marketing mistakes. (See also **first-mover advantage.**) [GSD]

font See **type face**

Food and Drug Administration (FDA) This administration, created by the Pure Food and Drug Act of 1906, has the power to set standards for foods and food additives, to establish tolerances for deleterious substances and pesticides in foods, and to prohibit the sale of adulterated and misbranded foods, drugs, cosmetics, and devices. All new drugs must be submitted to the FDA for approval, and applications must be supported by extensive laboratory testing indicating efficacy and safety. (See also **Fair Packaging and Labeling Act.**) [DC]

food court In a shopping center, a concentration of restaurants and food service facilities in a particular area apart from stores, usually with a shared eating area. [WRD]

foot-in-the-door technique A technique in which compliance is gained for a relatively large request by first gaining compliance to a relatively minor request; the compliance with the minor request positively affects later compliance with the larger request. For example, getting someone to make a small donation to a charity can be used to increase the probability that he/she will donate more later. The first, small request is the foot in the door. [HHK/MCC]

Foote, Cone & Belding (FCB) grid A two-dimensional grid developed by the Foote, Cone, & Belding advertising agency for analyzing consumers and products. The grid divides products on the basis of whether they are higher or lower in involvement and on the basis of whether they are "think" products or "feel" products. [JPP/JCO]

forced sale A sale of products at less than market price due to the urgent need for a merchant to liquidate merchandise assets, generally to meet the demand of creditors. It is also the sale of goods or property under order from the court: an ordered public auction sale. [WRD]

forecasting See **Delphi technique**

forecasting models In forecasting sales, share, or other marketing objectives, a variety of models have been used, including time series models (e.g., moving averages, exponential smoothing, decompositional), econometric models (e.g., regression, input-output), and judgmental models (e.g., Delphi technique). Most common of the econometric models are those including marketing mix variables of the firm and its competitors, thus offering diagnostic insights. A brief review of the various forecasting models is offered in Lilien and Kotler (1983, Chapter 10). (See also **simulated test market.**) [DCS/YJW]

foreclosing avenues for attack See **market defense**

Foreign Corrupt Practices Act (FCPA) (1977) 1. (legislation definition) This act made it illegal for members of any United States business firm to pay money or give gifts, or promise to do so, to any foreign official, foreign political party, or candidates for foreign political office in order to obtain or retain business. [DC] 2. (global marketing definition) The U.S. law that makes it a crime for U.S. corporations to bribe an official of a foreign government or political party to obtain or retain business in a foreign country. [WJK]

foreign direct investment Investing in a country with control or influence over the direction of the investment. For balance of payments purposes, any holding of more than 20 percent of the shares of a company is considered direct as opposed to portfolio investment. (See also **balance of payments.**) [WJK]

foreign exchange Any currency that is purchased or sold in the foreign exchange market. [WJK]

foreign exchange market The buyers and sellers of currencies that are traded for both spot and future delivery on a continuous basis. (See also **call option** and **foreign exchange.**) [WJK]

foreign exchange risk The economic risks arising from fluctuating exchange rates. (See also **floating exchange rate.**) [WJK]

foreign marketing The phenomenon of marketing in an environment different from that of the home or base environment. [WJK]

foreign trade zones (FTZs) An area where goods can be made, stored, assembled, refined, or repackaged and then exported without incurring customs duties or taxes. Maquiladoras in Mexico are an example. [WJK]

forgetting See **extinction** and **learning decay**

fork-lift truck A materials handling device to move unit loads. It is capable of moving loads both horizontally and vertically. The most common power sources are propane gas and electricity. [DJB/BJL]

formative research The market research, usually on target customers, carried out before a marketing program is begun in order to help formulate effective strategy and tactics. [ARA]

formula selling A selling approach in which the sales presentation is designed to move the customer through the stages in the decision-making process such as get the customer's attention, develop interest, build desire, and secure action (AIDA). (See also **approach, sales; balance sheet method; benefit approach; compliment approach; consultative selling; customer orientation; hierarchy of effects model; high-pressure selling; multilevel selling; problem solution approach;** and **systems selling.**) [BAW]

forward buying 1. (industrial definition) The practice of buying materials in a quantity exceeding current requirements in order to receive volume discounts or to ensure availability. [GLL/DTW] 2. (sales promotion definition) A situation in which retailers buy more of a product on deal than they intend to sell during the deal period. These additional products are warehoused or stored and sold later at full price or margin. [DES/BEB]

forward integration See **integration**

forward order See **forward buying**

forward stock 1. (physical distribution definition) Inventory placed in the channel of distribution in advance of customer commitment. [DJB/BJL] 2. (retailing definition) Merchandise carried on the selling floor, rather than in a reserve stockroom. [WRD]

forward vertical integration See **vertical integration**

franchise The privilege, often exclusive, granted to a distributor or dealer by a franchisor to sell the franchisor's products within a specified territory. A franchise is an example of a contractual vertical marketing system. (See also **affiliated store, authorized dealer,** and **distributorship.**) [WRD]

franchise system See **contractual vertical marketing system**

franchisee See **franchising**

franchising A contractual system of distributing goods and services whereby one party (the franchisor) grants to another party (the franchisee) the right to distribute or sell certain goods or services; the franchisee agrees to operate the business according to a marketing plan substantially prescribed by the franchisor; and the franchisee operates the business substantially under a trademark or trade name owned by the franchisor. [GLF]

franchisor See **franchising**

free alongside ship (F.A.S.) Under this contract the seller must place goods alongside, or available to, the vessel or other mode of transportation and pay all charges up to that point. The seller's legal responsibility ends once he or she has obtained a clean wharfage receipt. [WJK]

free goods An additional amount of product offered as a reward to the consumer or reseller for purchasing a certain product or volume of product. (See also **deal** and **sales promotion.**) [DES/BEB]

free merchandise A trade sales promotion technique in which an additional amount of the product is offered without additional cost as an incentive to purchase a minimum quantity. The incentive is typically offered for a limited period of time. [DES/BEB]

free sample A consumer sales promotion technique in which a regular or specially sized quantity of the product is given away without cost to prospective purchasers. (See also **consumer sales promotion, cross ruff,** and **sample.**) [DES/BEB]

free standing insert (fsi) 1. (sales promotion definition) A preprinted advertising page(s), commonly offering coupons or other promotional activities, that is inserted into a separate publication, such as a newspaper. [DES/BEB] 2. (advertising definition) Preprint advertising of one or more pages that is loosely inserted between the pages of a newspaper or magazine. [JE]

free trade area The area of jurisdiction encompassing a group of countries that have agreed to abolish all internal barriers to trade between the member countries. [WJK]

free-flow pattern A store layout arrangement consisting of a series of circular, octagonal, oval, or U-shaped fixture patterns, resulting in curving aisles characterized by a deliberate absence of uniformity. (See also **block plan, boutique store layout, bubble plan, free-form, gridiron pattern,** and **loop layout.**) [WRD]

free-form A store design used primarily in specialty stores or within the boutiques of larger stores that arranges fixtures and aisles in an asymmetrical pattern. (See also **block plan, boutique store layout, bubble plan, free-flow pattern, gridiron pattern, loop layout,** and **store layout.**) [WRD]

free-on-board (F.O.B.) This implies loading on a transportation vehicle at some designated point. After the letters f.o.b., there is generally a designation of a place where title and control pass to the buyer. For example, **f.o.b. plant** means that the control and title to the goods pass to the buyer at the seller's plant origin. [DJB/BJL]

freight absorption pricing A policy of pricing in which the seller picks up the tab for transportation. This is usually done in order to meet the delivered price of a local competitor. [DLS]

freight bill The document used by carriers to charge for transportation services provided. [DJB/BJL]

freight classification All products transported by common carriers are grouped together into common freight classifications based upon the characteristic of the product that influences cost of handling and transport. [DJB/BJL]

freight forwarder 1. (physical distribution definition) The freight forwarder combines small shipments from different shippers into larger shipments for scale economies in the purchase of intercity transportation. The freight forwarder functions as a wholesaler of transportation services. [DJB/BJL] 2. (global marketing definition) Specialists in traffic operations, customs clearances and shipping, and tariffs and schedules. They assist exporters in determining and paying freight, fees, and insurance charges. They usually handle freight from port of export to overseas port of import. In the U.S. they are licensed by the Federal Maritime Commission. [WJK]

freight-all-kinds rate (FAK) A mixture of different products are delivered in a combination to a single or limited number of destinations. Rather than determine the classification and rate for each product, an average rate is applied for the total shipment. This simplifies paperwork associated with the bill of lading and freight bills. [DJB/BJL]

frequency The number of times a person, household, or member of a target market is exposed to a media vehicle or an advertiser's media schedule within a given period of time. This number is usually expressed as an average frequency (the average number of exposures during the time period) or as a frequency distribution (the number of people exposed once, twice, three times, etc.). (See also **effective frequency**.) [JE]

frequency distribution See **frequency**

frequent shopper program A continuity incentive program offered by a retailer to reward customers and encourage repeat business. The reward is usually based on either purchase volume or number of store visits. (See also **continuity plan**.) [DES/BEB]

Freudian theory See **psychoanalytic theory**

fringe sizes The sizes that are either very large or very small, if offered at all, are offered in very limited depth because of the thin market demand for them. Some stores specialize in fringe sizes or out sizes—e.g., tall women's shops; petite size shops. (See also **end sizes**.) [WRD]

fringe stocks Those categories of merchandise from which a small percentage of sales come. [WRD]

fringe trade area See **tertiary trade zone**

fsi See **free standing insert**

FTC See **Federal Trade Commission**

FTZs See **foreign trade zones**

fulfillment The gathering of orders or offers from a sales promotion event and the process of completing the event by distributing items integral to the event such as premiums, rebates, bounce back offer, or ordered merchandise. (See also **clearinghouse** and **refund**.) [DES/BEB]

full coverage See **market coverage strategies** and **product-market grid**

full nest stage See **family life cycle**

full promise See **warranty**

full-cost pricing An approach whereby prices are determined after all functional costs have been allocated. [DLS]

full-line forcing A form of tying arrangement in which a supplier forces a dealer to carry the full line of products. This has not been treated as *per se* unlawful by the courts; the restriction may be upheld as reasonable when the supplier can demonstrate a legitimate business need for the dealers to carry the full line. [DC]

full-line pricing In this situation, all items in a given line are priced relative to each other, or are discounted as a total package. Changes on any one item take into consideration the prices of the other items in the line, and the seller's intention is to enhance sale of the total line. (See also **product-line pricing**. [KM]

full-line sales organization In this organization, each company or division salesperson sells all products to all accounts in a geographic territory. This is an appropriate strategy when the product line is not large, is nontechnical, and is sold through one channel of distribution. It is a lower cost strategy than specializing by product, market, or type of account. (See also **centralized sales organization; decentralized sales organization; partially integrated division; sales organization, forms of; sales organization specialized by account, sales organization specialized by market;** and **sales organization specialized by product.**) [VPB]

full-line wholesaler See **general-line wholesaler**

full-service (of retailing) The offering of an adequate number of salespeople and sales supporting services to give customers the full range of expected services. It is usually compared to limited services, which implies some expected services are not offered—e.g., credit. [WRD]

full-service advertising agency See **advertising agency**

functional authority See **line authority** and **staff authority**

functional discount The discount given to middlemen or others who act in the capacity of performing distributive services that would otherwise have to be performed by the manufacturer itself. The discount sometimes prevails regardless of the quantities involved. (See also **trade discount**.) [WRD]

functional expense classification A type of expense classification system that identifies the purpose of an expenditure. The major functions promoted by the National Retail Merchants Association are (1) administration, (2) occupancy, (3) publicity, (4) buying, and (5) selling. [WRD]

functional middleman A middleman who ordinarily assists directly in effecting a change in ownership but does not take title to the goods in which the middleman deals. The middleman specializes in the performance of a single marketing function or a limited number of such functions, one of which is usually related to the transfer of title. [WRD]

functional organization In a functionally organized company, the managers of each major function (such as marketing, production, research and development, and finance) report to the chief executive, who provides overall direction and coordination. Similarly, in a functionally organized marketing department, the managers of the major marketing functions (such as sales, advertising, marketing research, and product planning) report to the marketing manager. Comment: The advantage of this form is that it provides specialization by function, while coordination of functions is provided by the chief executive. The same can be said for the functional marketing department in which direction and coordination of marketing functions is provided by the marketing manager. (See also **bureaucratic organization; centralized management; decentralized management; divisional organization; flat organization; geographic organization; hierarchical organization; market management organization; marketing organization, forms of; matrix organization; multibusiness organization; nonbusiness marketing organization;** and **product management organization**.) [VPB]

functional perceived risk See **perceived risk**

functional product grouping The categorizing and displaying of merchandise by common end users. [WRD]

functional strategies See **strategy**

functional theory of attitudes A theory of attitudes based on the idea that attitudes develop to satisfy certain functions, e.g., needs or goals, for the individual. According to this theory, attitudes reflect the underlying motives of the individual, thus, the theory is sometimes referred to as a motivational approach to attitudes. (See also **ego-defensive function of attitudes, instrumental function of attitudes, knowledge function of attitudes,** and **value-expressive function of attitudes**.) [HHK/MCC]

fundraising The techniques used to solicit contributions or other support for an organization from outside interests. [DES/BEB]

funnel approach An approach to question sequencing that gets its name from its shape, starting with broad questions and progressively narrowing down the scope. [GAC]

Fur Products Labeling Act (1951) This act gave the Federal Trade Commission jurisdiction to promulgate rules designed to disclose in labels what kind of fur is actually in a fur product. [DC]

future dating A dating method that allows the buyer additional time to take advantage of the cash discount or to pay the net amount of the invoice. (See also **advance dating, dating, end of month dating, extra dating, memorandum purchase and dating, ordinary dating, proximo dating, receipt-of-goods dating,** and **season dating.**) [WRD]

future transaction A commitment to take or deliver a currency at a specified future date. [WJK]

futures research See **futurology**

futurism A philosophy or perspective that focuses on the importance of serious thinking about and planning for the future. [WL/MBC]

futurology The prediction of future developments by an intensive study of past and present trends, using a variety of techniques, from imagination to the Delphi technique to computer simulations. Perspectives of the future are useful in contingency planning and have been used for strategic long range planning. It is used interchangeably with **futures research.** (See also **cross impact analysis.**) [WL/MBC]

galley proof A copy of the individual pages of an ad, brochure, poster, or other printed material used for final proofreading of the text before final negatives are made for the printing process. (See also **blueline**.) [JE]

game A consumer sales promotion technique that involves collection, matching, or use of skill to complete a project or activity with the goal of a prize or reward for the player. (See also **contest** and **swecpstakes**.) [DES/BEB]

game theoretic models Models that use game theory to predict the actions of either cooperative or competitive individuals (or firms). In cooperative game theory, the agreements that emerge from colluding individuals are examined. Noncooperative game theory is concerned with the actions of rational, intelligent individuals competing independently. A key element of this theory is the Nast equilibrium, i.e., a set of strategies, one for each individual, such that no individual would then unilaterally like to change the strategy. Typically, the individuals are assumed to adopt strategies in accordance with this equilibrium (assuming that such an equilibrium exists). For an overview of game theory in marketing, see Moorthy (1985). [DCS/YJW]

gama distribution See **Negative Binomial Distribution model**

gap analysis The difference in performance between the "momentum" strategy, which requires no shift in resource priorities or direction, and a strategy based on preliminary objectives identified in the adaptive planning process. This gap can be narrowed by either altering objectives in light of what can be achieved or by adopting a strategy with different objectives. (See also **growth objectives**.) [GSD]

garbology The study of consumer behavior and preferences for foods and products by examining disposed goods and other items found in the trash and garbage. [HHK/MCC]

garment district The leading apparel and textile center in the country located in New York City along or near Seventh Avenue in the 34th Street vicinity. [WRD]

gatekeeper Usually, the individual who controls the flow of information from the mass media to the group or individual. It also is used to indicate the individual who controls decision making by controlling the purchase process. In a traditional family, the mother often functions as the gatekeeper between the child and his/her exposure to the mass media and the purchase of toys or products. In an organization, the purchasing agent is often the gatekeeper between the end user and the vendor of products or services. (See also **buying roles**.) [HHK/MCC]

GATT See **General Agreement on Tariffs and Trade**

GDP See **gross domestic product**

general advertising Advertising messages that do not contain direct response offers. (See also **direct response advertising**.) [JE]

General Agreement on Tariffs and Trade (GATT) An institutional framework that provides a set of rules and principles committed to the liberalization of trade between countries. (See also **Brussels Nomenclature** and **Uruguay Round**.) [WJK]

general costs See **common costs**

General Electric's strategic business planning grid See **market attractiveness-competitive position matrix**

general merchandise store An establishment primarily selling household linens and dry goods, and either apparel and accessories or furniture and home furnishings. Establishments that meet the criteria for department stores, except as to employment, are included in this classification. Included for Census purposes are establishments whose sales of apparel or of furniture and home furnishings exceed half of their total sales, if sales of the smaller of the two lines in combination with dry goods and household linens accounts for 20 percent of total sales. [WRD]

general merchandise wholesaler A wholesaler that carries a variety of goods in several distinct and unrelated merchandise lines. [WRD]

general sales manager This manager has overall responsibility for corporate, group, or division sales. Sales management at this level is concerned with developing sales policies, strategies, and plans that support the overall marketing plan. In a small company the general sales manager may supervise all salespeople directly. As the number of salespeople increases, however, supervision of salespeople must be delegated to field sales managers. In a functionally organized company, the general sales manager reports to the marketing manager or the chief executive. In a divisionalized corporation, the general sales manager reports to the division marketing manager or to the division manager. In a divisionalized company with a centralized sales organization, the general sales manager reports to the chief executive or to a group executive. (See also **divisional organization, field sales manager, functional organization,** and **sales manager.**) [VPB]

general store An establishment primarily selling a general line of merchandise, the most important being food. The more important subsidiary lines are notions, apparel, farm supplies, and gasoline. Sales of food account for at least one-third and not more than two-thirds of total sales. This establishment is usually located in rural communities. [WRD]

general trading companies See **sogo-sosha**

general-line wholesaler A wholesaler who carries a complete stock of one type of merchandise, corresponding roughly to a substantial majority of the total merchandise requirements of customers in a major line of trade or industry classification. [WRD]

general-specific-general theory See **retail accordion theory**

Generalized Elimination Model See **Elimination-By-Aspects Model**

generalized extreme value distribution See **nested logit model**

generalized least-squares See **elasticon**

generic advertising An approach to preparing advertising messages that concentrates on the customer benefits that apply to all brands in a product category, as opposed to benefits that are unique to specific brands. (See also **primary advertising**.) [JE]

generic brand A product that is named only by its generic class (e.g., drip-grind coffee, barber shop). Other products have both an individual brand and a generic classification (Maxwell House drip-grind coffee, Maurice's barber shop). Generic brand products are often thought to be unbranded, but their producer or reseller name is usually associated with the product, too. This approach is usually associated with food and other packaged goods, but many other consumer and industrial products and services are marked as generics. (See also **brand, brand generic,** and **branded merchandise**.) [DW]

generic strategies Generalized plans that work across a range of industries and markets. They provide management with a set of strategic options, one (or a combination) of which can be chosen for application in a specific situation. Generic strategies do not provide specifics and the detail needed to be developed for any specific situation. [GSD]

generic terms, as brand names See **brand generic**

geocentric orientation A management orientation based upon the assumption that there are similarities and differences in the world that can be understood and recognized in an integrated world strategy. The geocentric orientation or world orientation is a synthesis of the ethnocentric orientation (home country) and polycentric orientation (host country). (See also **regiocentrism orientation**.) [WJK]

geodemography An availability of demographic consumer behavior and life style data by arbitrary geographic boundaries that are typically quite small. [GAC]

geographic edition See **regional edition**

geographic organization A company organized into geographical units that report to a central corporate headquarters. Normally each unit produces the same or similar products as the others, and the unit manager controls both the manufacturing and sales operations. Marketing functions other than sales are usually centralized at the corporate level. Comment: Reasons for geographic organization include high shipping costs or the need for quick delivery for reasons of freshness (e.g., baked goods), both of which require that plants be located near customers. (See also **bureaucratic organization; centralized management; decentralized management; divisional organization; flat organization; functional organization; hierarchical organization; market management organization; marketing organization, forms of; matrix organization; multibusiness organization; nonbusiness marketing organization;** and **product management organization**.) [VPB]

geographical organization See **horizontal structure of the sales organization**

geographical pricing See **delivered pricing** and **F.O.B. origin pricing**

GEOLINE A model providing a decision support system for creating service and sales territory boundaries. The approach aggregates small standard geographic units (SGUs) into sales territories while maximizing the compactness of the territories (i.e., the ease of covering the territory from the standpoint of travel), subject to the constraint that each created territory have the same overall sales activity level (or some other single criterion). (Hess and Samuels 1971). (See also **CALLPLAN, DETAILER** and **sales force models**.) [DCS/YJW]

georeference classification For analysis purposes, the data covering such things as sales, customers, product, and demographics are often classified on a geographical basis. Distribution of such data by individual markets provides the geographical structure of demand that must be serviced. The most useful geographical classification structures for logistical modeling are customer point locations, county, standard metropolitan statistical area, economic trading area, ZIP code, and grid structure. [DJB/BJL]

gift An item of value that is offered by the seller as an inducement to influence the consideration or purchase of a product or service. (See also **in-pack premium, near-pack premium, on-pack premium, pass-along deal, premium** and **self-liquidator**.) [DES/BEB]

GLA See **gross leasable area**

global account See **national account**

global advertising The use of advertising appeals, messages, art, copy, photographs, stories, and video and film segments on a global scale. (See also **international advertising**.) [WJK]

global brand A brand that is marketed according to the same strategic principles in every part of the world. (See also **local brand**.) [WJK]

global corporation A stage of development of a company doing business outside the home country. (See also **international corporation, multinational corporation,** and **transnational corporation**.) [WJK]

global direct marketing Direct marketing across national borders. [WJK]

global marketing 1. (global marketing definition) A marketing strategy that consciously addresses global customers, markets, and competition in formulating a business strategy. [WJK] 2. (consumer behavior definition) An approach to international strategy that argues for marketing a product in essentially the same way everywhere in the world. [JPP/JCO]

global marketing information systems A system designed to acquire, store, catalog, analyze, and make available to decision makers information from global sources within and external to the firm for use as the basis for planning and decision making. [WJK]

global product portfolio See **portfolio management**

global retailing Any retailing activity that spans national boundaries. (See also **international retailing**.) [WJK]

global strategic partnerships A linkage between two companies to jointly pursue a common goal on a global scale. They also are called strategic alliances and collaborative agreements. [WJK]

global strategy A strategy that seeks competitive advantage with strategic moves that are highly interdependent across countries. These moves include most or all of the following: a standardized core product that exploits or creates homogenous tastes or performance requirements, significant participation in all major country markets to build volume, a concentration of value-creating activities such as R&D and manufacturing in a few countries, and a coherent competitive strategy that pits the worldwide capabilities of the business against the competition. (See also **multidomestic strategy**.) [GSD]

GMROI See **gross margin return on inventory investment**

GNP See **gross national product**

goal A concrete, short-term point of measurement that the business unit intends to meet in pursuit of its objectives.

An overall objective converts into specific short-run goals. (See also **cognition**.) [GSD]

gondola A gondola is an island type of self service counter with tiers of shelves back-to-back. [WRD]

good guy-bad guy routine A negotiation strategy in which one member of a sales team makes an attractive offer to the prospect (a good guy) and another member discusses the difficulty in making such an attractive offer (a bad guy). The objective of the strategy is to get the prospect to accept the good guy's proposal. (See also **low-balling** and **win-win negotiation**.) [BAW]

good(s) A product that has tangible form, in contrast to services that are intangible. (See also **product hierarchy**.) [DW]

goodwill See **after sales support**

government information on industrial markets The set of data about industrial markets that the government collects and distributes. It tends to be organized around the Standard Industrial Classification (SIC) system. [GLL/DTW]

government market This market includes purchases by the governmental units—federal, state, and local—that procure or rent goods and services in carrying out the main functions of the government. The federal government accounts for almost 40 percent of the total spent by all levels of government, making it the nation's largest customer. Federal, state, and local government agencies buy a wide range of products and services. They buy bombers, sculpture, chalkboards, furniture, toiletries, clothing, fire engines, vehicles, and fuel. (See also **organizational market**.) [GLL/DTW]

government program See **public service announcement**

grade class See **grade labeling**

grade labeling A system of identification that describes products by their quality, using agreed-on numbers or letters. The grade classes (standards) and the requirements for each are usually assigned by a government or trade group, and the actual scoring is sometimes done by inspectors. Grade labeling leads to product standardization and ease of comparison by the buyer, often the purpose of the labeling. (See also **descriptive labeling** and **grading**.) [DW]

grading The classifying of a product by examining its quality. It is often done with a program of grade labeling, though individual firms can grade their own products by a private system if they wish, e.g., Good, Better, Best. [DW]

graphic-rating scale A scale in which individuals indicate their ratings of an attribute by placing a check at the appropriate point on a line that runs from one extreme of the attribute to the other. (See also **comparative rating scale, constant sum method, Guttman scale, interval scale, itemized rating scale, nominal scale, ordinal scale, ratio scale, Stapel scale,** and **summated rating**.) [GAC]

gravitational site selection model See **distribution models**

gravity model A theory about the structure of market areas. The model states that the volume of purchases by consumers and the frequency of trips to the outlets are a function of the size of the store and the distance between the store and the origin of the shopping trip. (See also **central place theory, concentric zone theory, dialectic process, natural selection theory, retail accordion theory, retail life cycle,** and **wheel of retailing theory**.) [WRD]

gray market good Merchandise that possesses a valid U.S. registered trademark and is made by a foreign manufacturer, but is imported into the United States without permission of the U.S. trademark owner. [WRD]

green marketing 1. (retailing definition) The marketing of products that are presumed to be environmentally safe. [WRD] 2. (social marketing definition) The development and marketing of products designed to minimize negative effects on the physical environment or to improve its quality. [ARA] 3. (environments definition) The efforts by organizations to produce, promote, package, and reclaim products in a manner that is sensitive or responsive to ecological concerns. [WL/MBC]

Green River ordinance A municipal ordinance regulating or forbidding house-to-house selling, canvassing, or soliciting of business. It was first enacted in Green River, Wyoming. [WRD]

greeter A person who greets customers when entering the store and provides information and/or assistance. [WRD]

gridiron pattern A store layout of fixtures and aisles in a repetitive or rectilinear pattern, best illustrated by a variety store or the grocery department in a typical supermarket. Secondary aisles run at right angles to aisles, and each aisle is usually of the same width for its length. (See also **block plan, boutique store layout, bubble plan, free-flow pattern, free-form,** and **loop layout**.) [WRD]

gross additional markup The original amount of additional markup taken before subtraction of any additional markup cancellations to determine net additional markup. (See also **retail inventory method of accounting**.) [WRD]

gross cost of merchandise handled The cost value of the opening inventory plus purchases and additions at billed cost. (See also **gross cost of merchandise sold** and **retail inventory method of accounting.**) [WRD]

gross cost of merchandise sold The gross cost of merchandise handled less the closing inventory at cost. The gross cost of merchandise sold is subtracted from net sales to calculate maintained markup. Maintained markup is then adjusted by cash discounts and workroom costs to determine gross margin of profit. (See also **retail inventory method of accounting.**) [WRD]

gross domestic product (GDP) 1. An estimate of the total national output of goods and services produced in a single country in a given time period and valued at market price. 2. GDP equals gross national product less net property income from abroad. [DLS]

gross investment The total market value of all capital goods included in the gross national product in a given period. (See also **net investment.**) [DLS]

gross leasable area (GLA) The area of a shopping plaza that is assigned to stores, excluding exits, corridors, and open space. [DLH]

gross margin of profit The difference between net sales and total cost of goods sold. (See also **gross cost of merchandise sold.**) [WRD]

gross margin return on inventory investment (GMROI) For each dollar invested in merchandise inventory, the equivalent dollars generated in gross margin. It is usually stated as the gross margin as a percentage of the average inventory investment at cost. [WRD]

gross markdown The original amount

of markdown taken before subtraction of any markdown cancellations to determine net markdown. [WRD]

gross national product (GNP) 1. The money value of a nation's entire output of final commodities and services in a given period. 2. Personal consumption expenditures plus gross private domestic investment plus net exports of goods plus government purchases of goods and services. The U.S. Department of Commerce has published continuously the national income statistical series since 1947. In former years gross national product was emphasized by politicians, the press, etc.; in more recent years gross domestic product has been emphasized. (See also **net national product.**) [DLS]

gross profit 1. Net sales minus cost of goods sold. 2. The difference between purchase price of an item and the sale price. [DLS]

gross rating point (GRP) A measure of the total amount of the advertising exposures produced by a specific media vehicle or a media schedule during a specific period of time. It is expressed in terms of the rating of a specific media vehicle (if only one is being used) or the sum of all the ratings of the vehicles included in a media schedule. It includes any audience duplication and is equal to the reach of a media schedule multiplied by the average frequency of the schedule. [JE]

group, as in organization See **team, as in organization**

group brand manager See **group product manager**

group buying The consolidating of buying requirements of several to many individual stores. [WRD]

group indepth interview See **focus group interview**

group membership See **stereotype**

group product manager This manager reports to the marketing manager and supervises several product managers and/or brand managers in companies, or divisions of companies in which there are more product managers and/or brand managers than the marketing manager can supervise directly. (See also **category manager.**) [VPB]

growth market life cycle stage See **market evolution**

growth objectives The needed and desired performance results to be reached by means outside the present products and markets. Objectives are identified by a direct translation of business goals from the growth strategy. The growth objectives guide decision making so a firm can reduce the gap between the forecasts of profit contribution of present products and markets from the overall objectives. (See also **gap analysis.**) [GSD]

growth stage See **product life cycle**

growth stage of product life cycle The second stage of the product life cycle, during which sales are increasing at an increasing rate, profits are increasing, and competitors enter the market. Product differentiation takes place, and price competition begins. Industry profits usually taper off as the product category enters the third (mature) stage, during which sales increases come only at a declining rate and eventually cease. [DW]

growth strategy Market share expansion is the prime objective under this strategy, even at the expense of short-term earnings. The firm may seek to expand market share through a number of alternative routes. First, the firm may seek new users who may previously have been loyal to other brands, or tended to switch, or were not users of the category at all. The second way in which the firm can expand its market share is to expand usage by current users: for instance, by identifying and promoting new uses. (See also **growth objectives** and **market penetration**.) [GSD]

growth-share matrix Each business or product in this portfolio matrix is classified jointly by the rate of present or forecast market growth and a measure of market share dominance. The Boston Consulting Group (BCG), which developed this model, chose market growth as an indicator of the need for cash while relative market share is an indicator of profitability and cash generating ability. Businesses are classified into one of four quadrants, and labeled according to their cash flow characteristics.

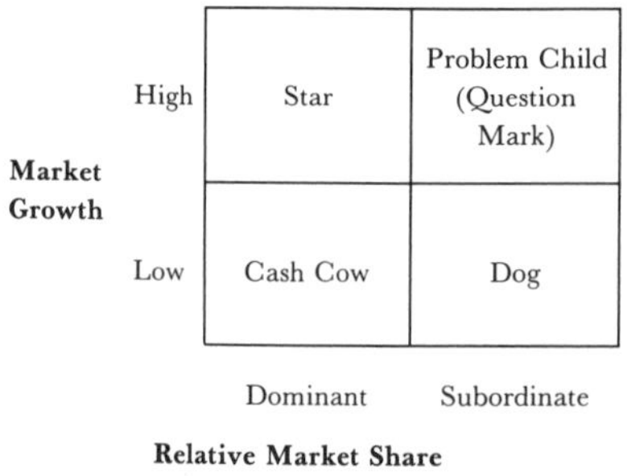

Market Growth		Dominant	Subordinate
	High	Star	Problem Child (Question Mark)
	Low	Cash Cow	Dog

Relative Market Share

These quadrants include **cash cow**: likely to be profitable and net cash generators, as low growth demands less cash and the business is relatively profitable; **star**: strong market share position, but in a rapidly growing market; profitable, but likely to be net cash user; **problem child (question mark)**: have a large appetite for cash; **dog**: small relative share in low growth market, generates moderate amount of cash, but uses most if not all the cash generated in maintaining operations and share position. (See also **portfolio analysis**.) [GSD]

GRP See **gross rating point**

guarantee The assurance, expressed or implied, of the quality of goods offered for sale. Expressed guarantee, with definite promise of money back or other specific assurance, is often used as a sales aid, especially in nonstore retailing. (See also **expressed warranty** and **warranty**.) [WRD]

guaranty See **guarantee**

guidance See **goal** and **objective**

Guttman scale A general procedure to determine whether or not the responses of subjects to a set of items form a scale. If the items form a scale, only a limited number of response patterns are possible, and relative nonoccurrence of deviant patterns allows the recovery of the order of the individuals and category boundaries of the items from the observed data. (See also **comparative rating scale, constant sum method, graphic-rating scale, interval scale, itemized rating scale, nominal scale, ordinal scale, ratio scale, Stapel scale,** and **summated rating**.) [GAC]

habit A learned response to a stimulus that has become automatic and routine, requiring little or no cognitive effort. (See also **habitual decision making** and **routinized response behavior**.) [HHK/MCC]

habit formation The process of learning a specific behavior often requiring practice or rehearsal of the response. There is considerable controversy, however, on just how much repetition or how many trials are necessary for learning to occur. It probably differs between cognitive problem solving and simple physiological or muscular reactions. [HHK/MCC]

habitual decision making The choices or decisions made out of "habit" without much deliberation or product comparison. (See also **extensive problem solving**.) [HHK/MCC]

halo effect A problem that arises in data collection when there is carry-over from one judgment to another. [GAC]

hand marking The use of grease pencils, ink stamps, and pens to directly mark, package, label, tag, or ticket merchandise. [WRD]

hand-to-mouth buying The purchase by a business in the smallest feasible quantities for immediate requirements. [WRD]

handbill The term commonly used to identify a promotion piece that is either handed out to shoppers at the store or distributed door-to-door by a messenger. [WRD]

hard goods As compared with soft goods, which have a textiles base, these goods mainly comprise hardware, home furnishings, and furniture and appliances. These goods are usually also durable goods. [WRD]

hard-sell See **high-pressure selling**

Harmonized Tariff System (HTS) This replaced the Brussels Nomenclature in January 1989 and incorporates a common classification system for all products. [WJK]

Hart-Scott-Rodino Antitrust Improvement Act (1976) This act requires that mergers involving corporations of a certain size must be reported in advance to the enforcement agencies. It also permits state attorneys general to bring *parens patriae* suits on behalf of those injured by violations of the Sherman Antitrust Act. [DC]

harvest market position See **investment strategy**

harvesting strategy The maximization of short-run cash flow from a business in expectation of a deterioration of market share and eventual withdrawal from the market. The cash flow raised is directed toward other areas of business where it is needed. (See also **divest strategy, investment strategy**, and **portfolio analysis**.) [GSD]

headline The part of the written component of print advertising that is meant to help attract the reader's attention to the ad. (See also **subhead**.) [JE]

health care marketing Marketing designed to influence the behavior of target audiences in which the benefits would accrue to the target audience's physical and/or mental health. Comment: Health care marketing may be carried out by individuals, by hospitals or clinics, or by national agencies such as the National Cancer Institute. [ARA]

heavy equipment Products that are typically capital goods, normally purchased by end user customers. They are treated as an asset by the purchasing firm and depreciated for tax purposes. Examples are lathes, drilling machines, and grinders. (See also **installations**.) [GLL/DTW]

hedging The sale or purchase of a currency in forward markets for future delivery to satisfy a future obligation or obtain a future payment. The purpose of hedging is to reduce risks. [WJK]

hedonistic consumption A focus on the sensory pleasures or hedonic benefits provided by interaction with products or services. (See also **conspicuous consumption**.) [HHK/MCC]

Hendry model A model representing the amount of switching among the brands in a product category. The model postulates that, for directly competing brands (i.e., brands within the same market partition), the level of switching among those brands should be proportional to the product of their market shares. The exact level of switching (i.e., the proportionality constant) is assumed to be the value that maximizes the entropy (i.e., randomness or lack of information) in this probabilistic system. (The Hendry Corporation 1970, 1971; Kalwani and Morrison 1977; Rubinson, Vanhonacker, and Bass 1980.) (See also **brand choice models**.) [DCS/YJW]

heuristic 1. (consumer behavior definition) A proposition that connects an event with an action. Heuristics usually simplify decision making. For example, "buy the cheapest brand" is a choice heuristic that would simplify purchase. [JPP/JCO] 2. (consumer behavior definition) The simplified "rules of thumb" by which decisions are made. [HHK/MCC]

hiatus See **flighting**

hierarchical business structure See **bureaucratic organization**

hierarchical choice model See **Elimination-By-Aspects model**

Hierarchical Elimination Model See **Elimination-By-Aspects model**

hierarchical organization A classic form of organization which, during the 19th century, was adapted by business from centuries-old religious and military organizations. In this type of organization, authority flows from the person in charge through various levels of supervision (called "chain of command" by the military). Conversely, information and requests for guidance and decisions travel upward through the same channels. Few, if any, modern business organizations follow this strict organizational structure. Rather, they delegate much decision making to lower levels of management. When top management needs to be involved, modern techniques for information processing enable top and lower levels of management to communicate quickly. Decisions are often made during discussions via telecommunications. Comment: Some business media continue to describe business organizations as if they operated in the outdated classical hierarchical manner. It is true that business organization charts often follow the hierarchical pyramid design even though they operate in the less formal manner described above. The formal organization chart shows the corporate management structure that is responsible to government and stockholders for fiduciary, fiscal, and legal requirements. The line of authority from the top down enables top management to ensure that its legal and ethical policies are promulgated and followed. (See also **bureaucratic organization; centralized management; decentralized management; divisional organization; flat organization; functional organization; geographic organization; market management organization; marketing organization, forms of; matrix organization; multibusiness organization; nonbusiness marketing organization;** and **product management organization.**) [VPB]

hierarchical pyramid design See **hierarchical organization**

hierarchy of effects model 1. A concept related to the manner in which advertising supposedly works; it is based on the premise that advertising moves individuals systematically through a series of psychological stages such as awareness, interest, desire, conviction, and action. (See also **AIDA.**) 2. An early model that depicted consumer purchasing as a series of stages including awareness, knowledge, liking, preference, conviction, and purchase. (See also **low involvement hierarchy.**) [JPP/JCO]

hierarchy of merchandising information The strategic placement of in-store messages that lead the customers through the shopping and buying process beginning with the customers entering the store and ending with them looking at specific merchandise. [WRD]

hierarchy of needs A theory proposed by Maslow (1943) concerning the specific order of the development of needs. He proposed that needs develop in an individual in a sequential order from lower to higher needs, ranging from physiological needs to safety needs (security, order) to belongingness and love needs. Then esteem needs (prestige, respect) and self-actualization (self- fulfillment) follow. Higher order needs emerge as lower order ones are more or less satisfied. [HHK/MCC]

high income countries Countries whose income per capita are high compared to the rest of the world. (See also **low income countries** and **middle income countries**.) [WJK]

high involvement See **involvement**

high-pressure selling A selling approach in which the salesperson attempts to control the sales interaction and pressure the customer to make a purchase. (See also **approach, sales; balance sheet method; benefit approach; compliment approach; consultative selling; customer orientation; formula selling; multilevel selling; problem solution approach; soft sell;** and **systems selling**.) [BAW]

hired hand A salesperson who receives relatively little support or latitude from his or her sales manager. Hired hands tend to perform basically those tasks that are enumerated in the job description, as their managers perceive them as being unable or unwilling to take on additional responsibilities. Hired hands are the opposite of cadre salespeople. [AJD]

hit rate The percentage of the desired number of outcomes received by a salesperson relative to the total activity level. For example, it is the number of sales as a percentage of the number of calls. It also is called batting average and conversion rate. [BAW]

hold strategy See **portfolio analysis**

home improvement center A store category specialist combining the traditional hardware store and lumber yard. [WRD]

homemade diversification theorem A theorem that states that (in the absence of synergy) diversification by a firm is not valuable to shareholders because they can diversify their own portfolios more cheaply by purchasing shares of stocks in the market. [PFA]

homeostasis A state of physiological balance within the individual. For example, lack of water leads to the uncomfortable sensation of thirst. The individual seeks products, such as soft drinks, that reduce the ensuing tension to return to a state of physiological balance or homeostasis.[HHK/MCC]

horizontal buy A purchase that is made from a direct competitor. For example, a west coast chemical company may buy a chemical compound from an east coast competitor because of a geographic supply and/or demand imbalance. [GLL/DTW]

horizontal competition The rivalry to gain customer preference among entities at the same level, such as competition among competing wholesalers or competing retailers. [WL/MBC]

horizontal cooperative advertising An advertising partnership in which several retailers share the cost of a promotion. (See also **vertical cooperative advertising**.) [WRD]

horizontal diversification See **diversification**

horizontal expansion See **horizontal integration**

horizontal integration 1. (environments definition) The expansion of a business by acquiring or developing businesses engaged in the same stage of marketing or distribution. The most common approach is to buy out competitors. It is also known as horizontal expansion. [WL/MBC] 2. (channels of distribution definition) The combination of two or more separate enterprises at the same stage in the channel through ownership, including mergers or acquisitions. (See also **integration.**) [GLF]

horizontal merger The joining together or combination of companies in the same industry. The merger may be deemed illegal if it tends to reduce competition substantially. [WL/MBC]

horizontal organization See **flat organization**

horizontal price-fixing A conspiracy among competitors at the same level in the channel to set prices for a product. (See also **vertical price-fixing.**) [DLS]

horizontal structure of the sales organization A sales organization may incorporate an internal company sales force or outside agents. When a company sales force is used, alternative approaches to sales organization include: (1) geographical organization; (2) organization by type of product; (3) organization by type of customer; and (4) organization by selling function. (See also **sales force organization** and **vertical structure of the sales organization.**) [AJD]

hot money See **discretionary buying power**

house account An account, usually large, not assigned to a field salesperson, but handled directly by executives or home-office personnel. (See also **key account** and **national account.**) [BAW]

house agency An advertising agency that is owned and operated by an advertiser. It is also called an in-house agency. [JE]

house brand A private brand, usually associated with retailers. (See also **brand.**) [DW]

house publication An internally developed or produced magazine or brochure designed to communicate the views of the organization to a selected audience without outside editorial restraints. [DES/BEB]

house-to-house salesperson A salesperson who is primarily engaged in making sales direct to ultimate consumers in their homes. [WRD]

Household Goods Carrier Operations Act (1980) This act specifies that carriers of household goods may, upon request, provide the shipper with an estimate of charges for transportation of household goods; proposed service charges for such estimates are subject to antitrust laws. [DC]

households using television See **sets in use**

HTS See **Harmonized Tariff System**

human ecology The application of the concepts of plant and animal ecology to human collective life to seek knowledge about the structure of social systems and the way in which structures develop, paying attention to spatial configurations. It is the human population's adaptation to the natural environment. [WL/MBC]

HUT See **sets in use**

hypermarket An unusually large, limited service combination discount store, supermarket, and warehouse under a single roof. Typically it sells both food and nonfood items at 10 to 15 percent below normal retail prices and stacks much reserve stock merchandise in the sales area. The hypermarket is an innovation of European origin. [WRD]

hypothesis A statement that specifies how two or more measurable variables are related. [GAC]

IBRD See **International Bank for Reconstruction and Development**

ICC See **Interstate Commerce Commission**

ICS See **Consumer Sentiment Index**

id The part of the personality, according to Freudian theory, that reflects the basic physiological and sexual drives (libido) of an individual demanding immediate gratification. (See also **ego** and **ego defenses**.) [HHK/MCC]

IDA See **International Development Association**

idea generation That stage of the new product development cycle in which ideas are sought for new products. These ideas may be created in-house or sought from outsiders. This stage is often called concept generation rather than idea generation, because the new product is but a concept at this time. The activity of generation often follows some stated or implied strategic focus, and it precedes the concept evaluation stage. [DW]

idea screening See **screening of ideas**

ideal self concept The knowledge, attitudes, and perceptions people have about the self they would be like if they were perfect or ideal. (See also **real self concept** and **self concept**.) [JPP/JCO]

identification See **ego defenses**

IIA See **Elimination-By-Aspects model** and **Luce's Choice Axiom**

image The consumer perception of a product, institution, brand, business, or person that may or may not correspond with "reality" or "actuality." For marketing purposes the "image of what is" may be more important than "what actually is." [WL/MBC]

IMF See **International Monetary Fund**

imitation effect See **diffusion model**

imitative strategy An imitative strategy relies on the designs of other companies in creating its designs. The imitative company also may base its accompanying product marketing strategy on the strategy of the market leader or pioneer. Imitative strategies frequently are used in the fashion goods, furniture, entertainment, and food products industries. (See also **innovative imitation, pioneering innovativeness,** and **product adaptation.**) [DW]

impact evaluation In social marketing, the evaluation of program outcomes in terms of original objectives. This also is known as outcome evaluation and summative evaluation. [ARA]

imperfect competition 1. (economic definition) A market situation in which many sellers, each of whom has a relatively small market share, compete for consumer patronage. The term originated with English economist Joan Robinson in the 1930s. (See also **duopoly, monopolistic competition, monopoly, monopsony, oligopolistic competition, oligopolistic environment, oligopoly, oligopsony, perfect**

competition, pure competition, and **workable competition.**) [DLS] 2. (environments definition) The market conditions in which firms have some control, but not necessarily absolute control, over price, by such techniques as differentiating products and limiting supply. Monopoly, oligopoly, and monopolistic competition are examples of imperfect competition. (See also **competition.**) [WL/MBC]

implementation The stage in the strategic market planning process in which an action program is designed to meet the strategic objective(s) using the available resources and given the existing constraints. The action program is intended to be both a translation of a strategic plan into operational terms as well as a means by which the strategic performance may be monitored and controlled. The action plan has three major components: (1) *specific tasks*—what will be done including the specification of the marketing mix to be employed; (2) *time horizon*—when it will be done; and (3) *resource allocation and budgeting*—attaching a dollar figures to each income- and expense-related activity and allocating capital funds. (See also **adaptive planning** and **tactics.**) [GSD]

implementation of the sales program See **sales management**

implications See **SPIN**

implicit alternative An alternative answer to a question that is not expressed in the options. [GAC]

implicit cost The use value of an economic resource that is not explicitly charged on accounting records of a firm—e.g., interest on owner's capital investment. [WRD]

implicit price index (IPI) A relative measure of changes in the general price level of goods and services produced by an economy during a given time period. [DLS]

implied warranty A warranty (promise of performance) that is extended to the customer but unstated. It usually is assumed from common practice in the trade, or suggested by statements made about the product by the seller. (See also **expressed warranty.**) [DW]

import agent A manufacturers' agent who specializes in the import trade. (See also **export agent.**) [DLS]

import broker A broker who specializes in international marketing. (See also **export agent.**) [DLS]

import commission house A broker who specializes in international marketing. (See also **export agent.**) [DLS]

import license An instrument of government control that regulates access to foreign exchange and the quantity and/or value of imports. [WJK]

improved product introduction See **consumer sales promotion**

impulse buying A purchase behavior that is assumed to be made without prior planning or thought. Often, it is claimed, impulse buying involves an emotional reaction to the stimulus object (product, packaging, point-of-purchase display, or whatever) in addition to the simple acquisition act. (See also **planned buying vs. unplanned buying.**) [HHK/MCC]

impulse product A convenience product (good or service) that is bought on the spur of the moment, without advance planning or serious consideration at the time, and often by the stimulus of point-of-sale promotion or observation. (See also **consumer product, emergency product, shopping product, specialty product,** and **staple good.**) [DW]

impulse purchase 1. (consumer behavior definition) A purchase typically made in-store with little or no decision making effort. [JPP/JCO] 2. (retailing definition) An unplanned purchase by a customer. [WRD]

impulse-intercept merchandise Merchandise purchased on impulse, when the customer happens to see it in the store, prior to which the customer had no perceived need. [WRD]

in supplier A firm currently supplying the company or currently on its approved vendor list. [GLL/DTW]

in transit A condition that exists when merchandise has been shipped from the vendor and has not yet arrived at the buyer's receiving dock. [WRD]

in-flow See **cash flow**

in-house agency See **house agency**

in-pack premium A small, often low value, gift placed inside a product package to encourage purchase or reward the purchaser. (See also **near-pack premium, on-pack premium,** and **premium**.) [DES/BEB]

in-store coupon A certificate redeemable only at one specific retail store or chain. The coupon generally is distributed through newspaper advertisements, flyers, or within the store. (See also **solo coupon** and **specialty distributed coupon**.) [DES/BEB]

in-store marketing The marketing dollars spent inside the store in the form of store design, merchandising, visual displays, or in-store promotions. [WRD]

incentive An inducement (money, premiums, prizes) offered by sellers to reward or motivate salespeople, channel members, and/or consumers to sell/purchase their products or services. (See also **bonus, buy-back allowance, consumer sales promotion, demand creation, free merchandise, frequent shopper program, incentive plan, pass-along deal, pass-through rate, premium, push money, sales contest, sales promotion,** and **trade sales promotion**.) [DES/BEB]

incentive compensation Sales compensation based on performance. (See also **bonus, combination compensation plan, commission,** and **salary.**) [BAW]

incentive pay Any compensation plan other than straight salary wherein the salesperson is given encouragement to sell more. Examples are straight commission (the strongest incentive); a salary plus a small percentage of net sales, etc. [WRD]

incentive plan An event offering rewards or inducements to stimulate the salesforce or channel members to achieve predetermined sales, profit, distribution, or other goals. (See also **trade sales promotion.**) [DES/BEB]

incentive travel A form of sales promotional activity in which large companies reward their salespeople, agents, distributors, or dealers with trips to interesting places for attaining a specific objective, usually sales volume (or purchase commitments) in excess of some predetermined quota. [WRD]

incidence A percentage of the population or group that qualifies for inclusion in the sample using some criteria. [GAC]

incidence of taxation The final resting place of the burden of the tax. The incidence may be on the person who originally pays the tax, or on someone else to whom the tax may be shifted. [DLS]

income A flow of money, goods, and benefits to a person or an organization. [DLS]

income differential The difference in income levels among people of various categories, such as different jobs, geographic areas, age classes, sexes, races, and the like. [WL/MBC]

income effect 1. (economic definition) The change in patterns of consumption for a product given consumers have an increase in real income. [DLS] 2. (environments definition) The increase or decrease in a consumer's real income as a result of the change in the price of a good or service. [WL/MBC]

income maintenance The policies designed to raise or maintain the income levels of designated groups of individuals. [WL/MBC]

income sensitivity of demand The relationship between a real increase in disposable personal income and the corresponding change in consumption. [WL/MBC]

incomplete assortment See **close-out**

incomplete stock See **close-out**

inconsistent stimulus See **selective perception**

increasing entry costs See **market defense**

increasing investments See **market defense**

increasing usage by present users See **market development**

incremental productivity method A method of determining sales force size by adding sales representatives as long as the incremental profit produced by their addition exceeds the incremental costs. The method recognizes that there will probably be diminishing returns with the addition of salespeople. (See also **equalized workload method.**) [AJD]

incremental sales Units of the product sold to retailers or consumers through a sales promotion effort over and above the amount that would have been sold in the absence of the promotional deal. [DES/BEB]

incrementalism The notion that strategies are the outcome of a series of piecemeal and minor tactical decisions in response to problems and opportunities rather than through systematic, formal, prepared plans. Incrementalism holds that organizations are more reactive than proactive. [GSD]

independence from irrelevant alternatives See **Elimination-By-Aspects model** and **Luce's Choice Axiom**

independent carrier An owner-operator or individual trucker who provides line-haul service for others. Under current transportation regulations, an independent carrier can make business arrangements with common carriers, contract carriers, exempt carriers, and private carriers. [DJB/BJL]

independent sector Collectively, all private nonprofit marketers. (See also **private nonprofit marketer** and **third sector.**) [ARA]

independent store A retail outlet owned individually; not a chain store or branch store. [WRD]

Index of Consumer Sentiment See **Consumer Sentiment Index**

index of retail saturation A technique normally used in larger areas to aid retailers' choice among possibilities for location of new outlets. It offers better insight into location possibilities than a simple descriptive analysis of market potential because it reflects both the demand side and the supply side; i.e., the number of existing outlets in the area and the number and/or income of consumers. [WRD]

indirect channel A channel whereby

goods and services are sold indirectly from producer through independent middlemen to final users. (See also **direct channel.**) [GLF]

indirect costs See **contribution**

indirect denial A method used by salespeople to respond to prospect objections by denying the validity of the objection but attempting to soften the response by first agreeing that the issue raised in the objection is important. (See also **boomerang method, direct denial, feel-felt-found method, pass up method** and **postpone method.**) [BAW]

indirect exporting Sales to export intermediaries who in turn sell to overseas customers. The indirect exporter has no direct contact with overseas customers. (See also **direct exporting.**) [WJK]

indirect traceable costs Costs that are not incurred solely for a particular activity but, through reasonably objective means, can be traced, in part, to the activity for which they are incurred. (See also **average fixed cost; average total cost, average variable cost, buyers' costs, common costs, cost, direct costs, direct fixed costs,** and **direct variable costs.**) [KM]

individual brand The brand identity given to an individual product, as separate from other products in the market and from other items in the product's own line. A trademark. (See also **brand extension; branding, individual; family brand; generic brand;** and **product life cycle.**) [DW]

individual preference models See **POSSE**

industrial advertising See **business-to-business advertising**

industrial buying behavior See **organizational buying behavior**

industrial buying influences See **buying influence**

industrial demand See **demand, industrial**

industrial distributor A wholesaler who sells primarily to business or institutional customers who purchase items for business use rather than for resale. [WRD]

industrial market The industrial market (also called the producer market or business market) is the set of all individuals and organizations that acquire goods and services that enter into the production of other products or services that are sold, rented, or supplied to others. The major types of industries making up the industrial market (business market) are agriculture, forestry, and fisheries; mining; manufacturing; construction and transportation; communication and public utilities; banking, finance, and insurance; and services. (See also **organizational market.**) [GLL/DTW]

industrial market segmentation The process of separating an industrial market (business market) into groups of customers or prospects such that the members of each resulting group are more like the other members of that group than they are like members of other segments. [GLL/DTW]

industrial marketing The marketing of goods and services to industrial markets (business markets). [GLL/DTW]

industrial products Goods that are destined to be sold primarily for use in producing other goods or rendering services as contrasted with goods destined to be sold primarily to the ultimate consumer. They include accessory equipment; installations; component parts; maintenance, repair, and operating items and supplies; raw materials; and fabricating materials. The distinguishing characteristic of industrial goods is the purpose for which they are to be used, i.e., in carrying on business or industrial activities rather than for consumption by individual ultimate consumers or resale to them. The category also includes merchandise destined for use in carrying on various types of institutional enterprises. Relatively few goods are exclusively industrial products. The same article may, under one set of circumstances, be an industrial good, and under other conditions, a consumer good. (See also **business services, installations, parts, semimanufactured goods,** and **supplies.**) [GLL/DTW]

industrial salesperson A salesperson who is primarily responsible for making sales of goods and services to businesses and institutions such as hospitals. [BAW]

industrial user See **buying roles**

industrialized country A country whose 1987 GNP per capita ranged from $2,500 to $8,499. The industrialized country displays the following characteristics: (1) degree of urbanization increases, literacy levels are very high, often exceeding 85 percent, and the population engaged in agriculture drops substantially; (2) wage levels rise sharply, and ownership of every type of consumer durable, transportation, leisure time, and housing products, rises sharply; and (3) the need for labor saving methods creates new industrial product markets in existing industries and development creates entirely new industries. (See also **developing country, postindustrialized country, preindustrialized country,** and **underdeveloped country.**) [WJK]

industry A set of companies that vie for market share of a given product. [DLS]

industry attractiveness See **market attractiveness**

industry life cycle See **market evolution**

inelastic demand 1. A situation in which a cut in price yields such a small increase in quantity taken by the market that total revenue decreases. 2. A situation in which the percentage of quantity taken in the market "stretches" less than the percentage drop in price. (See also **elastic demand** and **elasticity coefficient.**) [DLS]

inelastic supply 1. A situation in which the quantity offered to the market increases less than proportionately to an increase in price. 2. A situation in which the percentage of goods offered to the market "stretches" less than the percentage increase in price. (See also **elastic supply.**) [DLS]

infant industry An industry that justifies a national policy of protection from global competition on the grounds that it needs time to get established. Infant industry protection is always temporary. [WJK]

inferences The beliefs consumers form to represent relationships that are not explicit in the environment; inferences are largely influenced by prior knowledge in memory. [JPP/JCO]

inferior goods The less expensive substitutes for products that consumers prefer. [DLS]

inflation 1. (economic definition) An economic condition characterized by a continuous upward movement of the general price level. (See also **deflation** and **stagflation.**) [DLS] 2. (global marketing definition) An increase in prices in a country that results in a decline in the purchasing power of consumers. [WJK]

influence, interpersonal, in the buying center The influence of one individual member of the buying center on another is the change in behavioral and/ or psychological states of other buying center members brought about by the perception of each other's power in an organizational buying situation. (See also **buying influence.**) [GLL/ DTW]

influence strategy A means of communication used by a channel member's personnel in applying its power in specific channel relationships. (See also **coercive influence strategy** and **noncoercive influence strategy.**) [GLF]

influencer See **buying roles**

influences, buying center See **influence, interpersonal, in the buying center**

infomercial The use of a program-length time period to advertise products and services. This approach often includes a direct response offer to sell the advertised items directly to the public. (See also **direct response advertising.**) [JE]

informal group The interpersonal and intergroup relationships that develop within a formal group or organization. This might include cliques, "coffee-colleagues" or friendship circles. An informal group tends to form when the formal organization fails to satisfy important needs of the members. [HHK/MCC]

information control A term applied to studies using questionnaires and concerning the amount and accuracy of the information that can be obtained from respondents. [GAC]

information processing See **consumer information processing**

information processing theory See **piecemeal processing**

information search 1. (industrial definition) The process by which a buyer seeks to identify the most appropriate supplier(s) once a need has been recognized. The information search process may vary based upon variables such as organizational size and buying situation. (See also **buyclasses** and **buying center.**) [GLL/DTW] 2. (consumer behavior definition) Intentional exposure to information. Before buying a camera, for example, the consumer might be attracted to and seek out advertisements for cameras, read articles in photography magazines, and turn to *Consumers' Reports*. Seeking the advice of an expert, knowledgeable acquaintance, or salesperson can be involved. [HHK/MCC]

information seeking See **information search**

informational advertising Advertising that presents factual, usually verifiable, information about the product or product usage. (See also **transformational advertising.**) [HHK/MCC]

informative label See **descriptive labeling**

informed stage See **buyer readiness stage**

infrastructure A nation's systems, facilities, and installations such as road and highway networks for transportation and distribution. [WL/MBC]

initial markon See **initial markup**

initial markup The difference between the merchandise cost and the original retail price placed on the goods; expressed as a percentage of the retail value. (See also **markup** and **retail inventory method of accounting.**) [WRD]

initiating structure A leadership style wherein sales managers closely direct their sales personnel; clarify their roles for them; and plan, coordinate, problem solve, criticize, and pressure them to perform. A sales manager using this leadership style tends to exhibit task-oriented behavior. (See also **consideration, contingent reward leadership, laissez faire leadership, management-by-exception leadership,** and **transformational leadership.**) [AJD]

initiator See **buying roles**

inner-directedness A system of values prevalent in production-oriented societies in which members of the society are taught specific value systems dependent on self-sufficiency and inner values. This was first developed by David Riesman in his monograph *The Lonely Crowd* and later adapted by Stanford Research Institute in its VALS program. (See also **other- directedness** and **social character.**) [HHK/MCC]

innovation In the marketing literature, innovation implies the introduction of a new product, idea, or service into the market place. According to Robertson, it involves a new product that is very different from the established products or at least perceived to be different by consumers in the relevant market segment. New products can be referred to as continuous innovations such as Crest spearmint toothpaste or Michelob light beer. Or they can be discontinuous innovations, a completely new product such as the electric light bulb or perhaps the computer. (See also **diffusion of innovation** and **supply-pushed innovation.**) [HHK/MCC]

innovation effect See **diffusion model**

innovation stage See **retail life cycle**

innovative imitation The strategy or practice whereby a firm's new products are emulative of others already on the market but are significantly different in at least one aspect. The product differs from pure imitation, in which the new item is a "me-too" product or a total copy, and from an emulative product because the difference here is significant. (See also **adaptive product** and **imitative strategy.**) [DW]

innovativeness 1. (product development definition) When applied to a buyer, the extent to which that person or firm is willing to accept the risks of early purchase of an innovation. [DW] 2. (consumer behavior definition) A personality trait designed to account for the degree to which a consumer accepts and purchases new products and services. [JPP/JCA]

innovators Firms or persons that are innovative. The term is often applied (1) to those who are the first to create a new type of product, or (2) to those who are the first to adopt a new product that has been introduced into the marketplace. Innovators are often thought to be opinion leaders. (See also **adopter categories, adoption process, early adopters, early majority, laggards, late majority,** and **product adoption process.**) [DW]

input evaluation measure An objective measure of the amount of effort or resources expended by the sales force, including the number of sales calls; amount of time and time utilization; expenses; and nonselling activities such as letters written, number of phone calls made, and number of customer complaints received. (See also **output evaluation measure, ratio of output and/or input measures,** and **sales force evaluation.**) [AJD]

input-output models See **forecasting models**

inquiry A customer's request for additional information about a product or service. Comment: Inquiries are often generated through advertising in which a customer can request additional information by mailing a card or coupon. (See also **lead, sales**) [BAW]

inquiry test A method of testing the effectiveness of an advertising message and/or media vehicles based on the number of customer inquiries that can be directly attributed to the message by means of coupons attached to the ads or special telephone numbers or code numbers used in ads or commercials. (See also **advertising effectiveness.**) [JE]

inside salesperson A salesperson who performs selling activities over the telephone at the employer's location. Comment: An inside salesperson typically answers questions and takes orders; however, there is a growing trend for an inside salesperson to actively solicit orders. (See also **field salesperson** and **telephone selling.**) [BAW]

installation costs See **buyers' costs**

installations These are non-portable major industrial products such as furnaces and assembly lines that are bought, installed, and used to produce other goods or services. They are often grouped with accessory equipment to comprise capital goods. They also are called heavy equipment. [DW]

installed base The number of units of a durable product in use at the customers' premises. The term is used for equipment such as computers and copiers. [GLL/DTW]

installment account The resulting charge account of a customer who has purchased on an installment-credit plan; i.e., pays a down payment and specified amount per month including a service charge. The customer has the use of the merchandise during the life of the installment account. (See also **installment sale** and **revolving credit.**) [WRD]

installment sale A sale of real or personal property for which a series of equal payments is made over a period of weeks or months. (See also **installment account** and **installment- credit plan.**) [WRD]

installment-credit plan A plan enabling consumers to pay their total purchase price (less down payment) in equal installment payments over a specified time period. (See also **installment account** and **installment sale.**) [WRD]

institutional advertising An advertising message or advertising campaign that has the primary purpose of promoting the name, image, personnel, or reputation of a company, organization, or industry. When employed by a company or corporation it is sometimes called corporate advertising. (See also **advocacy advertising.**) [JE]

institutional boundary A market area that is defined by governments (e.g., tariffs, post office districts) or by firms in order to restrict spatial competition (e.g., dealerships). [DLH]

institutional market The market consisting of churches, museums, private hospitals, schools and colleges, clubs, and many other organizations that have objectives that differ basically from those of traditional business organizations. (See also **institutional marketing.**) [GLL/DTW]

institutional marketing The marketing of goods and services to the institutional market. [GLL/DTW]

institutional signage The signage that describes the merchandising mission, customer service policies, and other messages on behalf of the retail institution. [WRD]

institutionalization In social marketing, creating the conditions under which a behavior-change program is continued beyond its initial campaign. Comment: Institutionalization is of major concern to agencies funding social marketing programs in developing countries that wish to terminate program support but see the effects continue. [ARA]

instrument variation Any and all changes in the measuring device used in an experiment that might account for differences in two or more measurements. (See also **equivalence** and **method variance.**) [GAC]

instrumental conditioning See **operant conditioning**

instrumental function of attitudes A function of attitudes that provides the maximum benefits and the minimum costs to the individual. Instrumental attitudes are those that provide the individual with more rewards than punishments. These attitudes are usually based on attributes of the attitude object and thus the instrumental function is highly similar to Fishbein's learning theory of attitudes. It also is referred to as utilitarian function of attitudes or adjustive function of attitudes. (See also **ego-defensive function of attitudes, functional theory of attitudes, knowledge function of attitudes, multiattribute models of attitudes,** and **value-expressive function of attitudes.**) [HHK/MCC]

instrumental values One of two major types of values proposed by Milton Rokeach. Instrumental values represent preferred modes of conduct or preferred patterns of behavior. (See also **terminal values.**) [JPP/JCO]

instrumentality A salesperson's estimate of the likelihood that higher levels of performance will lead to his or her receiving greater rewards. In essence, it is the linkage between salesperson performance and attainment of various rewards. For example, a salesperson might estimate that there is a 25 percent probability (instrumentality) of his or her receiving a pay raise if he or she achieves quota. Instrumentalities can influence a salesperson's level of motivation. (See also **expectancy, salesperson motivation,** and **valence.**) [AJD]

integer programming See **mathematical programming, product line optimization,** and **sales force models.**

integrated development A process of combining diverse organizational talents and functional groups to support a new product's development. Also called cross-functional integration, integrated development requires regular, high-quality communication and problem- solving among the different contributors to the new product development process. [DW]

integrated division This division contains both marketing and production functions, thereby providing the division manager coordination and control of the principal factors affecting profits. (See also **divisional organization** and **partially integrated division.**) [VPB]

integrated marketing communications A planning process designed to assure that all brand contacts received by a customer or prospect for a product, service, or organization are relevant to that person and consistent over time. [DES/BEB]

integrated service provider A for-hire firm that performs a range of logistics service activities such as warehousing, transportation, and other functional activities that constitute a total service package. The majority of these firms customize the service package to meet individual customer needs. (See also **third party provider.**) [DJB/BJL]

integration The acquisition or development of businesses that are related to the company's current businesses as a means of increasing sales and/or profit and gaining greater control. There are three forms of integration: (1) **backward integration**—in which the company acquires one or more of its suppliers or develops its own supply capability in order to gain more profit and/or control; (2) **forward integration**—in which the company acquires one or more of its buyers (e.g., wholesalers or retailers when the buyer is not the "ultimate buyer"); and (3) **horizontal integration**—in which the company acquires one or more of its competitors. (See also **diversification, horizontal integration,** and **merger**.) [GSD]

intellectual property Abstract forms of "property" such as patents, copyrights, and trademarks, as distinct from the concrete form of real property. [DC]

intelligence gathering and analysis See **public affairs**

intending to buy stage See **buyer readiness stage**

intensive distribution A form of market coverage in which a product is distributed through all available wholesalers or retailers who stock and sell the product in a given market area. (See also **exclusive distribution** and **selective distribution.**) [GLF]

intention 1. (marketing research definition) Anticipated or planned future behavior. [GAC] 2. (industrial definition) The decision to acquire specific goods and/or services under given terms and conditions. (See also **buyer intention.**) [GLL/DTW]

interaction with consumer groups See **consumer relations**

interbusiness alliance See **keiretsu**

intercept merchandise The merchandise that customers do not specifically go to a store to buy, but buy because the retailer intercepts them in the course of their store visit activities. [WRD]

intercept store A store that intercepts consumers passing by it. [WRD]

interdepartmental merchandise transfer See **transfer (interdepartmental merchandise)**

interest See **AIDA, AIO, hierarchy of effects model,** and **life style**

interested stage See **buyer readiness stage**

interindustry competition The rivalry among sellers in different industries to achieve such objectives as gaining a larger share of the market, increasing profits, or increasing sales, by urging consumers to substitute a seller's products or services for their current choices. Examples are substituting cotton clothing for synthetics, or fish for steaks. (See also **intraindustry competition.**) [WL/MBC]

intermediary See **middleman**

intermodal transportation The movement of goods that combines two or more modes of transportation such as truck and rail to maximize the benefits of both modes while minimizing their drawbacks. For example, the combination of rail and motor carriage utilizes the flexibility of motor carriers and the low line-haul cost of rail. (See also **container-on-flatcar, piggyback,** and **trailer-on-flatcar.**) [DJB/BJL]

internal communication See **public affairs**

internal data The data that originate within the organization for which the research is being done. (See also **external data.**) [GAC]

internal factors See **situation analysis**

internal marketing Marketing to employees of an organization to ensure that they are effectively carrying out desired programs and policies. [ARA]

internal stimulus See **external stimulus**

internal validity One criterion by which an experiment is evaluated; the criterion focuses on obtaining evidence demonstrating that the variation in the criterion variable was the result of exposure to the treatment or experimental variable. (See also **construct validation, content validity, convergent validity, discriminant validity, external validity, pragmatic validity,** and **validity.**) [GAC]

internal vulnerabilities See **risk analysis**

international advertising The advertising phenomenon that involves the transfer of advertising appeals, messages, art, copy, photographs, stores, and video and film segments (or spots) from one country to another. (See also **global advertising.**) [WJK]

International Bank for Reconstruction and Development (IBRD) A bank set up under the Bretton Woods Agreement in December 1945 for two purposes: (1) to help finance the rebuilding of war-devastated areas and to aid in the advancement of less developed countries; and (2) to provide technical advice to governments or other borrowers, including general economic surveys for governments wishing to study resources and to plan long-range programs of development. (See also **International Development Association.**) [WJK]

international channel of distribution The structure of intracompany organization units and extracompany agents and dealers, wholesale and retail, through which a commodity, product, or service is marketed in international markets. [WJK]

international corporation An early stage in the development of a global/transnational corporation. An international corporation may operate in many countries, but it does not have a global vision or strategy. (See also **multinational corporation.**) [WJK]

International Court of Justice The principal judicial organ of the United Nations. It settles disputes between the sovereign nations of the world but not between private citizens. (See also **international law.**) [WJK]

International Development Association (IDA) An affiliate of the International Bank for Reconstruction and Development formed in 1960 to help developing countries by extending financial aid on subsidized terms. It helps countries whose credit standing does not enable them to borrow from the bank, and it is prepared to finance a wide variety of projects. [WJK]

international law The set of rules and principles that states and nations consider binding upon themselves. (See also **International Court of Justice.**) [WJK]

International Monetary Fund (IMF) A multinational organization whose objective is to promote international financial cooperation and to coordinate the stabilization of exchange rates and the establishment of freely convertible currencies. [WJK]

international product cycle A model developed by Professor Raymond Vernon that shows the relationship of production, consumption, and trade over the life cycle of a product. Based on empirical data for the pre-1967 era, the model showed how the location of production shifted from the United States to other advanced countries and then to less developed countries. (See also **international trade product life cycle** and **product trade life cycle.**) [WJK]

international retailing Retailing activity by an organization that reaches across national boundaries. (See also **global retailing.**) [WJK]

international trade product life cycle A trade cycle model that suggests that many products go through a cycle in which high income, mass consumption countries are initially exporters, then lose their export markets, and finally become importers of the product. (See also **international product cycle** and **product trade life cycle.**) [WJK]

interpersonal factors Those influences or forces on the consumer due to other individuals within the individual's life space or sphere of activity. Wearing a tie when others are doing so would be an example, as would a person purchasing perfume to impress someone else. [HHK/MCC]

Interstate Commerce Commission (ICC) (1887) The first independent regulatory agency established, the ICC is required to "foster the preservation and development of a national transportation system adequate to meet the needs of the commerce of the United States, of the postal service, and of the national defense." [DC]

intertype competition The competition between different types of firms selling the same product. For example, automobile tires may be sold through discount stores; gasoline service stations; department stores; tire, battery, and accessory dealers; and independent garages. (See also **intratype competition.**) [WRD]

interurbia A large urban area resulting from the mingling and eventual uniting of close market areas into one large market area. [WRD]

interval scale A measurement in which the numbers assigned to the attributes of the objects or classes of objects legitimately allow comparison of the size of the differences among and between objects. (See also **comparative rating scale, constant sum method, graphic-rating scale, Guttman scale, itemized rating scale, nominal scale, ordinal scale, ratio scale, Stapel scale,** and **summated rating.**) [GAC]

inter-selling The process of selling between and among departments to facilitate larger transactions and to make it more convenient for the customer to accessorize. (See also **cross selling.**) [WRD]

intraindustry competition The rivalry among sellers of the same product or service to achieve such objectives as increasing sales, market share, or profits. (See also **interindustry competition.**) [WL/MBC]

intransit storage A facility for storing, transferring, or modifying shipments enroute to their final destination, often used for break-bulk or consolidation purposes. [DJB/BJL]

intrapreneurship The practice of entrepreneurship within a large firm. Intrapreneurship is a style of management thought to be independent, risk-taking, innovative, daring, and typical of the style used in successful start-up firms. In some situations intrapreneurship requires that the entrepreneurial unit be segregated or isolated from the other units, thus permitting the unique style of management. [DW]

intratype competition The conflict (or competition) between firms of the same type—e.g., a department store competes with another department store; a supermarket competes with another supermarket. (See also **intertype competition.**) [WRD]

intrinsic reward A reward that comes from within the individual rather than externally. Practicing the piano for the sheer joy of learning and creating music rather than for a cash reward is an example. (See also **extrinsic reward.**) [HHK/MCC]

introduction approach A method for approaching prospects in which salespeople simply state their name and the name of their company. (See also **center of influence method, cold-canvassing, curiosity approach, endless chain method, product approach,** and **referral approach.**) [BAW]

introduction stage See **product life cycle**

introductory stage of product life cycle The first stage of the product life cycle. The new product is introduced to the market, sales are slow, promotion is usually heavy, costs are accumulated, profits are frequently negative, and expectation is focused on determining when and if the product will soon enter the second (growth) stage of the cycle. [DW]

invention A new device, process, etc., that has been created. The invention can be in either physical or conceptual form. Preexisting knowledge is combined in a new way to yield something that did not heretofore exist. It is not to be confused with a product innovation, which is an invention that has been converted by future management and process development into a marketable product. Invention is thought to require both engineering science and art, but scientific findings and artistic creations, alone, though they may be original, may not constitute inventions. [DW]

invention pricing policy A pricing policy in which the company neither fixes a single price worldwide nor remains aloof from subsidiary pricing decisions, but strikes an intermediate position. (See also **adaptation pricing policy** and **extension pricing policy.**) [WJK]

inventory 1. Goods or merchandise available for resale. 2. The value of merchandise on hand at cost or retail. [WRD]

inventory control The procedures used to ensure that desired inventory levels are maintained. Most procedures are based on either perpetual or periodic review. (See also **stock or inventory control.**) [DJB/BJL]

inventory control-based promotion models See **promotion models**

inventory cushion The allowance in the inventory made for uncertainties in sales or deliveries, often added to the basic low stock to provide for conditions neither controllable nor accurately predictable. [WRD]

inventory management The process of acquiring and maintaining a proper assortment of merchandise while keeping ordering, shipping, handling, and other related costs in check. [WRD]

inventory overage The value of physical inventory in excess of the book value. [WRD]

inventory policy A firm's standard practice regarding the level of inventory to be maintained. For example, it may be customary to hold a 60- or 90-day supply. [DJB/BJL]

inventory stock shortage The value of the book inventory in excess of the actual physical inventory, often expressed as a percentage of net sales. It is the amount of theft, breakage, sales in excess of amounts charged customers, and errors in record keeping. It may be either clerical (caused by miscalculation), or physical (caused by misappropriation of goods). [WRD]

inventory turnover 1. (physical distribution definition) The number of times average inventory is sold during a specified time period (usually one year). (See also **stock turnover.**) [DJB/BJL] 2. (retailing definition) The number of times per year the retailer sells its average inventory. (See also **stock turnover.**) [WRD]

investment Any outlay of cash flow in the near term that is expected to generate cash inflows in future periods. Typically some or all of the cash outlay is capitalized on the balance sheet of the firm. [PFA]

investment strategy A strategy that specifies (1) the requirements for funds needed to achieve the competitive advantage, and (2) the outcomes expected from the allocation of these funds. The broad investment choices are build, defend, or harvest market position. (See also **divest strategy, harvesting strategy, market defense,** and **portfolio analysis.**) [GSD]

invisible assets Assets that are hard to copy, very time-consuming to develop, capable of many uses, and unattainable with money alone. Invisible assets are mainly embodied in factors such as the superior skills of people, corporate culture, advanced technical design and production skills, and mastery of the dominant technologies. These assets may be acquired through first-mover advantages, accumulated experience, continued investment in training, and insightful nurturing of strengths. (See also **sustainable competitive advantage.**) [GSD]

involvement The degree of personal relevance a consumer perceives a product, brand, object, or behavior to have. High involvement products are seen as having important personal consequences or as useful for achieving important personal goals. Low involvement products are not linked to important consequences or goals. [JPP/JCO]

IPI See **implicit price index**

irrational appeals See **rational appeals**

irregular goods See **as is**

item merchandising The special planning and control effort employed to discover and take advantage of the sales opportunities afforded by items that are in greater consumer demand. [WRD]

item nonresponse A source of nonsampling error that arises when a respondent agrees to an interview but refuses or is unable to answer specific questions. (See also **noncoverage error, nonobservation error, nonresponse error, not-at-home, observation error, office error, overcoverage error,** and **refusals.**) [GAC]

itemized rating scale A scale distinguished by the fact that individuals must indicate their ratings of an attribute or object by selecting one from among a limited number of categories that best describe their position on the attribute or object. (See also **comparative rating scale, constant sum method, graphic-rating scale, Guttman scale, interval scale, nominal scale, ordinal scale, ratio scale, Stapel scale,** and **summated rating.**) [GAC]

JIT See **just-in-time**

JIT II See **just-in-time II**

job description See **position description**

job lot A promotional grouping of merchandise through which some vendors dispose of end-of-season surpluses and incomplete assortments. For example, a blouse manufacturer may offer, in minimum units of three dozen garments, a miscellaneous selection of different sizes and styles at one-half the original or early season wholesale price. [WRD]

jobber Earlier, a dealer in odd lots or job lots; now, a middleman who buys from manufacturers (or importers) and sells to retailers; a wholesaler. (See also **supply house.**) [WRD]

joint rate A form of transportation pricing in which more than one carrier is involved in the movement of freight. A joint rate means that freight moves on a through bill of lading even though multiple carriers are involved in the transport. [DJB/BJL]

joint venture A form of participation in foreign markets by means of alliance with a local partner. (See also **venture.**) [WJK]

joint venturing A linkage between two companies in order to facilitate the supply and/or sale of products to a market or market segment. A joint venture arrangement might be set up between two or more companies in order to enter a new market (e.g., a foreign market), or between two or more companies in the value chain as when the child of two corporate parents develops a new distribution or builds a supplying plant. Joint ventures can be informal sharing agreements or formal equity-sharing arrangements. [GSD]

judgment sample A nonprobability sample that is often called a purposive sample because the sample elements are handpicked because they are expected to serve the research purpose. (See also **convenience sample, quota sample, sequential sample,** and **snowball sample.**) [GAC]

judgmental models See **forecasting models**

junket A publicity device in which members of the media are brought to a company to observe the product being made, research facilities, and the like. [DES/BEB]

jury of executive opinion A method of developing a sales forecast in which the executives of the company are polled for their assessment of likely sales. It is also known as the jury of expert opinion method. [GAC]

jury of expert opinion See **jury of executive opinion**

just-in-time (JIT) An inventory management system based upon the philosophy that well- run manufacturing plants do not require the stockpiling of parts and components. Instead, they rely upon receiving necessary inventory in the exact quantity and at a specified time to support manufacturing schedules. [DJB/BJL]

just-in-time II (JIT II) A supply management system that builds on JIT to include close working relationships between suppliers and manufacturers. Suppliers actually work in the manufacturer's facility to coordinate production scheduling, delivery, and participate in early product design. No traditional buyer/supplier representatives exist in such a relationship. DJB/BJL]

just-in-time inventory management system See **quick-response delivery system**

keiretsu A Japanese interbusiness alliance or enterprise group. [WJK]

kerning The degree of tightness in the space between type characters such as the individual letters in headlines, subheads, and body copy. Art directors frequently adjust the degree of closeness between type characters to give the appearance of more natural (and more readable) character and word spacing. [JE]

key account A large account, usually generating more than a prespecified annual sales level, that receives special treatment from salespeople. (See also **house account** and **national account.**) [BAW]

key items The items that are in the greatest consumer demand. They are also referred to as best sellers. (See also **never-out list.**) [WRD]

key success factors Those factors that are a necessary condition for success in a given market. That is, a company that does poorly on one of the factors critical to success in its market is certain to fail. [GSD]

keystone markup A markup in which the cost price is doubled or a markup of 50 percent of retail is obtained. For example, if an item is retailed at $20 and cost the retailer $10, then the keystone markup has been applied. [WRD]

kickback A payment made by a salesperson to a buyer based on the size or number of orders placed by the buyer for the salesperson's products or services. [BAW]

knowledge Consumers' meanings or beliefs about products, brands, stores, etc., that are stored in memory. (See also **adoption process, AIDA, hierarchy of effects model,** and **opinion.**) [JPP/JCO]

knowledge function of attitudes A function of attitudes that serves the individual in understanding the environment. The knowledge function aids the individual in organizing information into an understandable or cohesive whole. It is one of the functions of attitudes proposed by the functional theory of attitudes. (See also **ego-defensive function of attitudes, instrumental function of attitudes,** and **value-expressive function of attitudes.**) [HHK/MCC]

Koyck transformation See **carry over models**

label The information attached to or on a product for the purpose of naming it and describing its use, its dangers, its ingredients, its manufacturer, and the like. A label is usually thought of as printed material, but labeling in the broader sense has been ruled to include spoken information and separate promotional pieces, if they serve the information purpose and are closely allied to the product. (See also **descriptive labeling** and **proof-of-purchase.**) [DW]

labeling See **label**

labor intensive A product or an industry in which labor requirements are large relative to requirements for capital goods. [DLS]

laboratory experiment A research investigation in which investigators create a situation with exact conditions so as to control some variables and manipulate others. [GAC]

laddering A technique to discover the associations consumers have between specific product attributes and more general end states or consequences. (See also **projective technique.**) [HHK/MCC]

laggards The fifth, and last, group of users to adopt an innovation. (See also **adopter categories, adoption process, early adopters, early majority, innovators, late majority,** and **product adoption process.**) [DW]

lagged effect See **carry over models** and **Vidale-Wolfe model**

laissez faire leadership A leadership style wherein sales managers supervise their sales personnel minimally and thus have a low degree of active involvement with them. Using this sales management leadership style usually requires sales personnel to resort to their own devices to execute their job tasks. (See also **consideration, contingent reward leadership, initiating structure, management-by-exception leadership,** and **transformational leadership.**) [AJD]

landed cost price The quoted or invoiced price of a commodity, plus any inbound transportation charges. [WRD]

language system See **dialog system**

Lanham Trademark Act (1946) This act provides for the registration and protection of trademarks. [DC]

late majority The fourth (and large) group of users to adopt an innovation. (See also **adopter categories, adoption process, early adopters, early majority, innovators, laggards,** and **product adoption process.** [DW]

latent conflict The existence of antecedent conditions of other states of conflict. (See also **affective conflict, manifest conflict,** and **perceived conflict.**) [GLF]

lateral diversification See **diversification**

launch control The process by which a management plans for and supervises the introduction of a new product; the product's progress is monitored against preestablished norms, variances are detected, and corrections made such that the original goals set for the product are achieved. [DW]

law of comparative advantage This law states that a country tends to export those economic goods in the production of which it has a comparative advantage and to import those economic goods in the production of which it has a comparative disadvantage. If a country has no comparative advantage, then it should tend to produce those products for which it has the least comparative disadvantage. [DLS]

law of demand 1. (popular definition) The law that, other things being equal, consumers will buy more of a product at a low price than at a high price. 2. (economic definition) The law that, under the same conditions of demand, the amount of product taken by a market varies inversely with its price. [DLS]

law of diminishing marginal utility A situation in which consumption of an additional unit of a good adds less to total satisfaction than the preceding unit. (See also **diminishing marginal utility, diminishing utility,** and **marginal utility.**) [DLS]

law of diminishing return After a certain point has been reached, each successive application of a factor of production will add less to total output than before (See also **diminishing return, point of diminishing return,** and **point of negative return.**) [DLS]

law of effect A technical term from learning theory in psychology often credited to Thorndike. Of the several responses made to the same situation, that which is accompanied or closely followed by satisfaction, other things being equal, will more likely be repeated, and the connections learned. Those responses that are followed by punishment will be extinguished. For example, the consumer's probability of repeating purchase of a brand would increase if he/she were satisfied with the purchase and decrease if he/she were dissatisfied. However, whether rewards and punishment are essential for learning to occur is controversial in that many learning theorists claim that reinforcement is unnecessary. (See also **reinforcement.**) [HHK/MCC]

lay-away The purchase of an article with a down payment, but the store retains the article until full payment is made, often in a series of installments. [WRD]

layout The format of a print advertisement that indicates where the component parts (artwork, body copy, headline, subhead, trademark, and other graphic elements) are to be placed on the page. (See also **comprehensive layout, dummy, mechanical, rough, storyboard,** and **thumbnail.**) [JE]

LCL See **less-than-carload-lot**

LCV See **longer combination vehicle**

LDC See **United Nations Conference on Trade and Development**

lead, sales An inquiry or referral about an individual or organization that is a potential customer. [BAW]

lead users 1. (product development definition) A small group of potential product users who need new products before the general market recognizes the need. If this need can be satisfied, the lead user expects significant benefits. Because lead users have a specific problem to be solved in their own organizations, they can provide valuable information and assistance to a product developing organization [DW] 2. (industrial definition) The buying organizations that consistently are early adopters of new technologies. Lead users have needs that will become general in the marketplace later on, benefit significantly by obtaining a solution to those needs, and often largely influence other firms' buying decisions. For example, Intel has been a lead user of micro chip production equipment. [GLL/DTW]

leader pricing The practice of knowingly and intentionally marking a part of the stock at prices that will not yield the maximum profit return on these particular goods. The article so selected for special price emphasis is identified as a leader. (See also **loss leader.**) [WRD]

leadership substitute A nonsupervisory source of direction, guidance, support, and encouragement for salespeople. Examples of leadership substitutes include closely-knit, cohesive work groups; advisory and staff personnel; formalized and detailed job descriptions; quotas; sales force compensation plans; and expense plans. Use of leadership substitutes can provide direction and guidance to sales personnel in the absence of a sales manager and may afford a sales manager additional time to attend to particularly important supervisory duties. [AJD]

leading The amount of space between lines of text on a printed page. [JE]

leading economic indicators Those economic indicators that reach peaks or troughs before aggregate economic activity. [DLS]

leading question A question framed so as to give the respondent a clue as to how he or she should answer. [GAC]

leadtime 1. (retailing definition) The amount of time determined by a merchandiser to be necessary to add on to the purchasing period in order to assure that sufficient merchandise will be on hand until the particular order is received. If delivery time is long, or if raw materials are in short supply, leadtime may be longer than when conditions are normal. [WRD] 2. (physical distribution definition) The time required to receive inventory once an order is placed. It is also called replenishment time. [DJB/BJL]

leapfrog routing A method for scheduling calls that requires salespeople to call on a cluster of customers that are in close geographic proximity, "leaping" over single customers in isolated areas. The objective of the method is to minimize travel time. (See also **call frequency, circular routing, routine call pattern, routing,** and **zoning.**) [BAW]

learned reaction See **cognition**

learning According to Hilgard, learning refers to more or less permanent change in behavior that occurs as a result of practice. It is a process by which an activity originates or is changed through reacting to an encountered situation, but does not include those changes induced by maturation, genetic response tendencies, or temporary situations such as fatigue or drug influence. It includes such activities as the learning of facts and skills, brands, jingles, purchase behavior, beliefs, and attitudes. (See also **classical conditioning, cue, experience curve effect, habit formation, law of effect, reinforcement, theory of reasoned action,** and **trial.**) [HHK/MCC]

learning curve Typically, this is a graph of the amount of material learned, plotted against time or number of trials. Many learning situations lead to an S-shaped curve. [HHK/MCC]

learning decay The fading of memory of a specific learned response. Because forgetting is a controversial issue among learning theorists—some claiming that nothing is ever forgotten—the terms decay of advertising effects or decay of a learned response are more accurate for the process of forgetting. [HHK/MCC]

leased department A section of a retail business managed and operated by an outside person or organization rather than by the store or which it is a physical part, whether conducted by an individual or a chain. [WRD]

leasing A contract through which the asset owner (lessor) extends the right to use the asset to another party (lessee) in return for periodic payment of rent over a specific period. It is divided into financial leases and operating leases. [GLL/DTW]

least squares regression See **Multiplicative Competitive Interaction model**

legal Something that is permitted, authorized, or sanctioned by law, not forbidden by law. [DC]

less-than-carload-lot (LCL) The shipping rate that applies to less than full carload shipments. [WRD]

less-than-truckload (LTL) A small freight shipment typically less than 10,000 pounds transported by common carriers. [DJB/BJL]

letter of credit A letter by which a bank substitutes its creditworthiness for that of the buyer. It is a conditional guarantee issued by the bank on behalf of the buyer to a seller assuring payment if the seller complies with the terms set forth in the letter of credit. [WJK]

letters to the editor A newspaper section used to air public opinion. When used as a publicity device, letters to the editor can help a company make known its position on various topics of community interest. [DES/BEB]

leverage The degree to which a change in sales volume leads to a subsequent change in operating profits and financial performance of a company. [KM]

lexicographic rule Unlike the conjunctive rule or disjunctive rule, the lexicographic rule, or heuristic, assumes that attributes of products can be ordered in terms of importance. In making a choice, alternative brands are first compared with respect to the most important attribute. If one alternative is preferred over all others for this attribute, then that alternative is chosen regardless of the values the alternatives have on the other attributes. If two brands are equal on the most important attribute, the second attribute is considered, then the third, and so on. (See also **choice rule, expectancy-value model, noncompensatory rules,** and **piecemeal processing.**) [HHK/MCC]

LEXIS An on-line database that indexes articles and casework related to legal matters. (See also **NEXIS.**) [DES/BEB]

libido see **id**

licensing 1. (strategic marketing definition) A relatively simple, low risk linkage that allows a manufacturer to "enter" new markets (typically foreign markets). It is an arrangement in which a licensee in a new market is given the right to use a process, trademark, patent, or other proprietary item for a fee or royalty. [GSD] 2. (global marketing definition) An agreement between two companies in which the licenser grants the right to the licensee to sell a patented product in specified markets for an agreed-upon fee. It is a tool for participating in foreign markets without large capital outlays. When capital is scarce, when import restrictions forbid any means of entry, when a country is sensitive to foreign ownership, or when it is necessary to protect trademarks and patents against cancellation for non-use, licensing is a legitimate means of capitalizing on a foreign market. [WJK]

life style 1. (consumer behavior definition) In general, this is the manner in which the individual copes and deals with his/her psychological and physical environment on a day-to-day basis. More specifically, it is used by some theorists as a phrase describing the values, attitudes, opinions, and behavior patterns of the consumer. [HHK/MCC] 2. (consumer behavior definition) The manner in which people conduct their lives, including their activities, interests, and opinions. (See also **AIO, psychographic analysis,** and **psychographic segmentation.**) [JPP/JCO]

life style analysis See **psychographic analysis**

life-cycle costs The costs of a durable good over its entire operating life. Comment: Life-cycle costs are often introduced to show that products with higher initial costs (e.g., because they are built better) really have lower costs over their effective lives. (e.g., because they need fewer repairs). [ARA]

light equipment The industrial product (business product) classification that includes items such as portable power tools such as drills, saws, grinders, measuring instruments, typewriters, calculators, etc. (See also **equipment.**) [GLL/DTW]

light factory equipment See **equipment**

Likert scale See **summated rating**

liking See **AIDA** and **hierarchy of effects model**

limen See **subliminal perception**

limited price variety store See **variety store**

limited problem solving (or decision making) A choice process involving a moderate degree of cognitive and behavioral effort. (See also **extensive problem solving** and **routinized choice behavior.**) [JPP/JCO]

limited promise See **warranty**

limited service See **full-service (of retailing)**

limited-function wholesaler The term applied to a variety of types of wholesalers that have placed emphasis upon reducing, eliminating, or modifying certain well-established functions ordinarily performed by regular wholesalers. [WRD]

limited-service advertising agency An advertising agency that specializes on a particular function such as the development of advertising messages, media planning, or media buying. (See also **creative boutique** and **media buying service.**) [JE]

line authority The authority managers need to manage the people assigned to them in order to achieve the goals for which they are held responsible by higher management. It generally encompasses the authority to hire, assign, direct, reward, demote, and fire, although company policy may require that some of these actions have the approval of higher line managers or managers with functional authority. [VPB]

line extension A new product marketed by an organization that already has at least one other product being sold in that product/market area. Line extensions are usually new flavors, sizes, models, applications, strengths, etc. Sometimes the distinction is made between near line extensions (very little difference) and distant line extensions (almost completely new entries). (See also **brand ex-**

tension, fighting brand, flanker brand, and **product modification.**) [DW]

line-haul rate The transportation rate commonly charged by common carriers (motor carriers). There are three basic types of line-haul rate: class rate, exception rate, and commodity rate. [DJB/BJL]

linear learning model A brand choice model that views the probability of choosing a particular brand on the current choice occasion as linearly related to the consumer's probability for choosing that brand on the previous occasion. The particular linear function applied to the previous period's choice probability depends on whether the brand of interest was actually chosen last time (in which case the "acceptance operator" is applied) or not chosen last time (causing the "rejection operator" to be applied) (Kuehn 1962). In this model, the consumer's probability of selecting a particular brand on the current choice occasion is affected by the entire sequence of previous choices—hence the term learning model is appropriate. [DCS/YJW]

linear programming See **advertising models, mathematical programming,** and **sales force models.**

list of key items See **never-out list**

list price The selling price for an item before any discount or reductions in price. [KM]

listening See **active listening**

literature search A search of statistics, trade journal articles, other articles, magazines, newspapers, and books for data or insight into the problem at hand. [GAC]

LITMUS A model for predicting the sales over time of a new (typically frequently purchased) consumer product using pretest market data. The approach views a potential customer as moving through the stages of awareness-trial-repeat. It incorporates explicitly the effect of advertising and promotion on awareness and trial of the product. The model's parameters are calibrated using a laboratory-test-market coupled with a follow-up telephone interview (Blackburn and Clancy 1982). LITMUS II adds monthly or quarterly projections, sensitivity analysis, and profit analysis. (See also **advertising models, ASSESSOR, new product forecasting models, Newprod, NEWS, promotion models, SPRINTER Mod III, STEAM,** and **Tracker.**) [DCS/YJW]

live rack A storage rack designed so product automatically flows forward to the desired selection position. The typical live rack contains roller conveyors and is constructed for rear loading. The rear of the rack is elevated; gravity causes the product to flow forward. [DJB/BJL]

living conditions See **census tract**

living standard A measure of the possession and distribution of the material goods among members of a society. [DLS]

lobbying A person or group of persons seeking to influence the proceeding of legislative bodies through personal intervention. (See also **political marketing.**) [DC]

local advertising Any advertising placed by a company, organization, or individual operating in a limited geographical area such as a city or within a state. Local advertising does not include advertising placed directly with media in local markets by nationwide advertisers, or regional advertising activities that encompass multistate geographic areas. [JE]

local brand 1. (product development definition) A brand of product that is marketed (distributed and promoted) in a relatively small and restricted geographical area. It may be called a regional brand if the area encompasses more than one metropolitan market. (See also **national brand** and **private brand.**) [DW] 2. (global marketing definition) A brand that is developed for a specific national market. (See also **global brand.**) [WJK]

local rate The price charged local advertisers for space and time in local advertising media. Traditionally, newspapers, radio, and television stations have charged lower rates for local advertising than for national advertising. [JE]

location affinities The clustering of similar or complementary kinds of retail stores. (See also **affinities.**) [WRD]

logistical cost The costs associated with providing purchasing, manufacturing support, and physical distribution services. [DJB/BJL]

logistical resource planning (LRP) A formal plan for controlling and monitoring overall materials logistics process. Emphasis is placed on integrating the overall objectives of the enterprise with logistical requirements. [DJB/BJL]

logistics A single logic to guide the process of planning, allocating, and controlling financial and human resources committed to physical distribution, manufacturing support, and purchasing operations. The Council of Logistics Management (formerly NCPDM) offers the following definition: "Logistics management is the term describing the integration of two or more activities for the purpose of planning, implementing and controlling the efficient flow of raw materials, in-process inventory and finished goods from point of origin to point of consumption. These activities may include, but are not limited to, customer service, demand forecasting, distribution communications, inventory control, materials handling, order processing, parts and service support, plant and warehouse site selection, procurement, packaging, return goods handling, salvage and scrap disposal, traffic and transportation and warehousing and storage." [DJB/BJL]

logistics manager See **physical distribution manager**

logistics model See **distribution models**

logistics-related optimization model See **distribution models**

logit model A probabilistic model for representing the discrete brand choice behavior of individuals. On any choice occasion the individual is assumed to choose the item for which he/she has the highest preference. Over repeated choice occasions preferences are assumed to have a probabilistic component. For the logit model this random component of preference is taken to have the double exponential distribution (i.e., the type I Fisher-Tippett extreme value distribution). The model can be used to predict choice probabilities based on attributes of the items being chosen (Corstjens and Gautschi 1983; Yellott 1977). This model is a substitute for discriminant analysis that in addition provides approximate standard errors of estimated model parameters. It is an alternate to regression analysis when the dependent variable is categorical as opposed to continuous. Unlike the probit model or the nested logit model or the Elimination-By-Aspects model, logit assumes that Luce's Choice Axiom holds, which is sometimes seen as a drawback to the use of this model. (See also **brand choice models, discriminant analysis,** and **regression analysis.**) [DCS/YJW]

logo 1. (product development definition) A clipped or shortened form of *logotype.* A logo is a word or phrase that serves to identify an organization. It is similar to a trade name. [DW] 2. (advertising definition) A graphic design that is used as a continuing symbol for a company, organization, or brand. It is often in the form of an adaptation of the company name or brand name or used in conjunction with the name. [JE]

long-range planning See **planning**

longer combination vehicle (LCV) A truck tractor pulling two or more trailers that exceed standard length. LCVs are restricted to certain states and highways in the United States. Considerable debate exists regarding the safety and environmental impact of LCVs. [DJB/BJL]

longitudinal study An investigation involving a sample of elements that is measured repeatedly through time. (See also **cross-sectional study.**) [GAC]

loop layout A type of store layout that provides a major customer aisle that begins at the entrance, loops through the store, usually in the shape of a circle, square, or rectangle, and then returns the customer to the front of the store. It is also referred to as a racetrack layout. (See also **block plan, boutique store layout, bubble plan, free-flow patterns, free-form,** and **gridiron pattern.**) [WRD]

loose money See **discretionary buying power**

loss leader An item that is sold at a "loss" of markup that would normally be obtained on the particular item, for the express purpose of increasing store traffic. (See also **leader pricing.**) [WRD]

loss leader pricing The featuring of items priced below cost or at relatively low prices to attract customers to the seller's place of business. [KM]

loss prevention department or function See **protection department**

love needs See **hierarchy of needs** and **Maslow's need hierarchy**

low income countries Countries with the lowest income per capita compared with the rest of the world. Normally the bottom decile to bottom quartile are considered low income. (See also **high income countries** and **middle income countries.**) [WJK]

low involvement consumer behavior Consumer decision making in which very little cognitive activity is involved. It includes those situations in which the consumer simply does not care and is not concerned about brands or choices and makes the decision in the most cognitively miserly manner possible. Most likely, low involvement is situation-based and the degree of importance and involvement may vary with the individual and with the situation. [HHK/MCC]

low involvement hierarchy In the hierarchy of effects model, the order consists of acquiring information, leading to formation of positive attitudes and then to the behavioral act of purchase or trial. Under low involvement conditions, the process is reversed such that it is after purchase, if at all, that interest and attitudes emerge. [HHK/MCC]

low-balling A negotiation strategy in which the salesperson agrees to a low price and later raises the price claiming that circumstances changed after agreeing on the price, but before the order was placed. (See also **good guy-bad guy routine** and **win-win negotiation.**) [BAW]

lower-class See **social class**

LRP See **logistical resource planning**

LTL See **less-than-truckload**

Luce's Choice Axiom A statement that the relative odds of an individual's choosing one particular item (e.g., brand A) over another (e.g., brand B) are unaffected by the presence or absence of other items (e.g., brand C, brand D, etc.) as potential choices. The property is also known as independence from irrelevant alternatives or IIA (Luce 1977; Yellott 1977). The logit model possesses this property (which is sometimes seen as a liability), while the probit model and other brand choice models can avoid it. (See also **brand choice models** and **Elimination-By-Aspects model.**) [DCS/YJW]

macro/micro segmentation A multi-step, nested approach to industrial market segmentation, in which one moves from general macro criteria at the level of the organization, such as SIC code and size of the buying firm, through criteria at the level of the order or application, such as order size and urgency, to specific micro criteria at the level of the buying center, such as risk perception and attitude toward the vendor. [GLL/DTW]

macroenvironment The collection of uncontrollable forces and conditions facing a person or a company, including demographic, economic, natural, technological, political, and cultural forces (See also **microenvironment.**) [WL/MBC]

macromarketing The study of marketing processes, activities, institutions, and results from a broad perspective such as a nation, in which cultural, political, and social, as well as economic interaction are investigated. It is marketing in a larger context than any one firm. (See also **micromarketing.**) [WL/MBC]

magazine See **house publication**

magazine supplement See **supplement**

Magnuson-Moss Warranty-Federal Trade Commission Improvement Act (1975) This act requires the seller of a consumer product who provides a written warranty to indicate clearly and conspicuously whether the warranty is a "full" or "limited" warranty. The FTC was given responsibility for administering the act as well as additional powers including the authority to promulgate trade regulation rules that specifically define "unfair or deceptive acts or practices." (See also **consumer protection legislation.**) [DC]

mail questionnaire A questionnaire administered by mail to designated respondents under an accompanying cover letter and its return, by mail, by the respondent to the research organization. [GAC]

mail-order house An establishment primarily engaged in distributing merchandise through the mail as a result of mail or telephone orders received. (See also **category killer.**) [WRD]

main brand See **fighting brand** and **line extension**

maintained item A specific item that is continuously maintained in assortments. [WRD]

maintained markon See **maintained markup**

maintained markup 1. The amount of markup that the retailer wishes to be maintained on a particular category of merchandise after allowing for markdowns or other reductions. It is net sales minus cost of goods sold. 2. The differential between the cost of goods sold and net sales. (See also **gross cost of merchandise sold, markup,** and **retail inventory method of accounting.**) [WRD]

maintenance and repair services Business services aimed at keeping the plant and equipment in good operating condition or repairing inoperable equipment. They are usually available from the original equipment manufacturer, but in many industries specialized organizations perform this function as well. Examples are window cleaning and air conditioning system repairs. [GLL/DTW]

maintenance items See **maintenance, repair, and operating items and supplies**

maintenance, repair, and operating items and supplies (MRO) Maintenance items are the supplies used to preserve the plant and equipment in good working condition such as paint, mops, and brooms. Repair items are the materials or replacement items used to keep equipment in good operating condition or to repair inoperable equipment such as light bulbs, new switches, new valves. Operating items are the supplies used to operate the equipment such as fuel oil, typing paper. (See also **industrial products** and **supplies.**) [GLL/DTW]

maintenance stage See **salesperson career cycle**

majority fallacy A marketing strategy that directs a new product to an entire market, or to the largest segment in it, solely because of its size. Today, this "shotgun" approach is felt to be almost always inferior to the alternative strategy of targeting to smaller segments. [DW]

makegood The rescheduling of an ad or commercial by an advertising media operator when it has been incorrectly printed, broadcast, or distributed or when unavoidably canceled or preempted. [JE]

mall intercept A method of data collection in which interviewers in a shopping mall stop or intercept a sample of those passing by to ask them if they would be willing to participate in a research study; those who agree are typically taken to an interviewing facility that has been set up in the mall where the interview is conducted. [GAC]

mall-type shopping center A grouping of stores near the center of a shopping center plot with parking area surrounding the store concentration on all sides. All or most of the stores face a mall or pedestrian shopping area. (See also **arcade shopping center, community shopping center, factory outlet center, neighborhood shopping center, off-price shopping center, regional shopping center, strip-type shopping center,** and **super regional shopping center.**) [WRD]

management information system (MIS) A set of procedures and methods for the regular, planned collection, analysis, and presentation of information for use in making management decisions. (See also **marketing information system.**) [GAC]

management of marketing See **marketing management**

management of products See **product manager** and **product planning manager**

management of sales force See **sales management**

management-by-exception leadership A leadership style wherein sales managers intervene only when their salespeople have failed to meet their performance standards (e.g., a sales quota). If sales personnel are performing as expected, the sales manager will take no action. (See also **consideration, contingent reward leadership, initiating structure, laissez faire leadership,** and **transformational leadership.**) [AJD]

manifest conflict Overt behaviors, such as disagreements or blocking behaviors, that arise as a result of the earlier states of conflict. (See also **affective conflict, latent conflict,** and **perceived conflict.**) [GLF]

manipulation check A measurement that is taken in an experiment to make sure that subjects accurately perceived the actual changes in the treatment variable. [GAC]

manufacturer's agent An independent business person who is paid a commission to sell a manufacturer's products or services but does not take title to the products. [BAW]

manufacturer's branch house See **branch house**

manufacturer's brand A brand owned by a manufacturer, as distinguished from a brand owned by a reseller. (See also **national brand** and **private brand.**) [DW]

manufacturer's export representative Combination export management firms often refer to themselves as manufacturer's export representatives whether they act as export distributors or export commission representatives. [WJK]

manufacturer's sales branches and sales offices The captive wholesaling operations owned and operated by manufacturers. Sales branches carry inventory, whereas sales offices do not. [GLF]

manufacturer's sales offices See **manufacturer's sales branches and sales offices**

manufacturers' agent An agent who generally operates on an extended contractual basis; often sells within an exclusive territory; handles noncompeting but related lines of goods; and possesses limited authority with regard to prices and terms of sale. (See also **sales agent.**) [WRD]

manufacturing resource planning (MRP-II) An extension of standard MRP (materials requirements planning) to include planning and feedback in the manufacturing system. It also integrates the manufacturing plan into the financial business plan of the firm. It is sometimes referred to as "closed-loop" MRP. [DJB/BJL]

mapping approach See **analog approach**

margin The difference between the selling price and total unit costs for an item. [KM]

marginal analysis A technique of explanation that focuses on the impact of producing, marketing, or consuming one more unit. [DLS]

marginal cost (MC) The net change in total cost that results from producing and marketing one additional unit. [DLS]

marginal efficiency of capital The rate of discount that, when applied to the whole series of future incomes from a capital good, will bring the sum of their present values equal to the cost or supply price of the capital good. [DLS]

marginal propensity to consume The fraction of each extra dollar that consumers will spend on consumption, given an extra dollar of real income. (See also **propensity to consume.**) [DLS]

marginal propensity to save The fraction of each extra dollar that consumers will save, given an extra dollar of real income. [DLS]

marginal revenue (MR) The net change in total revenue that results from producing and marketing one additional unit. (See also **average revenue.**) [DLS]

marginal unit The last unit, i.e., that unit whose acquisition or loss is under consideration. [DLS]

marginal utility The change in total utility due to purchasing or consuming one additional unit of a product. (See also **diminishing marginal utility** and **law of diminishing marginal utility.**) [DLS]

markdown 1. (pricing definition) The amount of a reduction from the selling price. [KM] 2. (retailing definition) A reduction in the original or previous retail price of a piece of merchandise. For management purposes, a markdown is stated as a percentage of net sales in contrast with off-retail percentage. (See also **gross markdown** and **markdown cancellation.**) [WRD]

markdown cancellation An upward price adjustment that is offset against a former markdown. The most common example is the restoration of a price to original retail after the goods have been marked down temporarily for purposes of a special sales event. (See also **gross markdown** and **markdown control.**) [WRD]

markdown control Any system ensuring that every markdown taken is accounted for, so that book retail inventory may be kept in line with the actual physical inventory. [WRD]

markdown money The funds provided by a vendor to a retailer to cover decreased gross margin from markdowns and other merchandising issues. [WRD]

market area See **trade area**

market attractiveness A measure of the profit potential inherent in the structure of a market or industry. There are a multitude of factors contributing to (and which can be used to measure) market attractiveness. The major categories and some examples from each of the categories are provided in the following: (1) *market factors*—market growth rate, market size, and life cycle stage; (2) *economic and technological factors*—investment intensity, industry capacity, barriers to entry or barriers to exit, and access to raw materials; (3) *competitive forces*—types of direct rivals, structure of competition and substitution threats, bargaining power of buyers and suppliers; and (4) *environmental factors*—regulatory climate, degree of social acceptance, and human factors. [GSD]

market attractiveness-competitive position matrix In this matrix, each business unit or product is classified jointly by market attractiveness and the strength of the competitive position. The market attractiveness-competitive position matrix is a multifactor portfolio model developed jointly by McKinsey and General Electric (GE), with each dimension of the matrix being based on multiple factors. It is sometimes called a nine-block matrix because each of the two dimensions is divided into three levels. (See also **portfolio analysis.**) [GSD]

market concentration The degree to which relatively few firms account for a large proportion of the market such as in an oligopolistic situation. It is also known as the concentration ratio. [WL/MBC]

market coverage The number of available outlets in a given line of retail or wholesale trade, relative to a saturation level, that are selling a manufacturer's brand in a given market area. Manufacturers typically follow one of three forms of market coverage: exclusive distribution, intensive distribution, or selective distribution. (See also **market segmentation strategies.**) [GLF]

market coverage strategies Alternative approaches that a company can use to select and target markets. Five common market coverage strategies are: (1) **single market concentration,** focusing on one part of the market; (2) **product specialization,** making one product for all markets; (3) **market specialization,** making all products for one market; (4) **selective specialization,** making products for multiple niches; and (5) **full coverage,** making a product for every customer. [GLL/DTW]

market crystallization A market development stage that refers to the effort needed to identify a latent market (i.e., organizations that share a similar need or want for something that does not yet exist) and to work to crystallize that need. The result is a new method or service that can satisfy all or part of the market. For example, the videotext market is in the market crystallization phase. It appears to have some market benefits, but those benefits have not been fully developed. [GLL/DTW]

market defense The strategic moves that attempt to minimize or deter threatening actions by existing or potential competitors. Strategic moves can deter all or some of the prospective challengers by making the profit prospects so unattractive and risky that market share gains are not worth pursuing. Deterrence strategies include the following: (1) signaling intentions to defend, (2) foreclosing avenues for attack by building barriers to entry or mobility, (3) increasing entry costs or investments, and (4) reducing market attractiveness by lowering prices. If challengers cannot be deterred, then the purpose of market defense is to contain challengers' moves and minimize the damage (See also **investment strategy.**) [GSD]

market demand The total volume of a given product or service bought by a specific group of customers in a specified market area, during a specific time period. [WL/MBC]

market development The expansion of the total market served by a business, achieved by (1) *entering new segments*—by expanding the geographic base of the business or by using new channels to reach unserved customers; (2) *conversion of nonusers*—by lower prices or increased (or specially designed) promotion; and (3) *increasing usage by present users*—by developing and promoting new uses for the product. [GSD]

market economy 1. (environments definition) An economic system in which decisions concerning production and consumption are made by individuals and organizations without intervention by a central planning authority. The economic "laws of supply and demand" operate relatively unrestrained by governmental direction, as contrasted with a planned economy. [WL/MBC] 2. (economic definition) An economy in which decisions about what and how much to be produced and marketed are made by the collective action of competitors vying for consumer patronage. (See also **planned economy.**) [DLS]

market evolution The market (or industry) life cycles describe the evolution of the market. These cycles have a similar shape to the product life cycle and similarly, have a number of distinct stages: (1) *embryonic*—the product class and industry definitions are virtually synonymous, diffusion rates are gradual, and there is considerable uncertainty about the product; (2) *growth*—the industry structure develops, the introduction of new product classes becomes easier as consumers become more knowledgeable, and the channels facilitate the marketing of new product classes established; and (3) *maturity*—an established infrastructure facilitates rapid introduction and diffusion of new product variants or product classes, competitors jockey for position, and older products have to make adjustments to protect their declining position. [GSD]

market expansion potential (MEP) A term used in trade area analysis to estimate an area's potential for creating new demand. [WRD]

market extension strategies A strategy of "extending" i.e., using a country strategy from one country to another country. [WJK]

market factor A feature or characteristic in a market that is related to the demand for the product, e.g., number of households in the market is related to the demand for many products. (See also **market index.**) [GAC]

market factors See **market attractiveness**

market fragmentation The emergence of new market segments with distinct needs and requirements out of previously homogenous segments. These new segments limit the usefulness of mass marketing and erode brand loyalty. [GSD]

market index A mathematical expression that combines two or more market factors into a numerical index, typically by forming a linear combination of the factors in which the weights assigned each factor reflect their relative importance in affecting demand for a product or products. [GAC]

market life cycle See **market evolution**

market management organization An organization in which market managers are responsible for developing marketing plans, implementing the plans (or coordinating their implementation by functional departments), and monitoring performance for their assigned market. The market manager may be a staff position for planning and for providing authoritative market information to the functional departments that implement plans. Or it may be a line position with its own (for example) sales and advertising personnel. Market managers may report directly to the marketing manager or (if numerous) to an intervening level of management such as a group marketing manager. Or market managers may report to a product manager of a major product line that is sold to different markets. Comment: The market management form of organization may be appropriate when company products are sold to different markets through different channels of distribution. This is often the case with industrial goods companies that sell the same or similar products to different industries (i.e., markets) and when knowledge of industry product application is essential to successful market penetration. With expert knowledge of the needs and practices of a particular market, the market manager provides feedback from customers for the guidance of research and development, sales engineers, and technical service personnel. (See also **bureaucratic organization; centralized management; decentralized management; divisional organization; flat organization; functional organization; geographic organization; hierarchical organization; marketing organization, forms of; matrix organization; multibusiness organization; nonbusiness marketing organization;** and **product management organization.**) [VPB]

market manager Within an organization, a person assigned responsibility for overseeing all functional activities (e.g., manufacturing, pricing, service) that relate to a particular market (customer group or product application). The market manager is to a market what a product manager is to a product, and delineating their respective roles in industrial firms is difficult. [DW]

market models See **advertising models**

market niche strategies See **niche strategies**

market opportunity See **situation analysis**

market opportunity analysis The analysis and evaluation of probable future situations by a variety of techniques to identify market opportunities that a company can profitably cultivate. It is part of the strategic analysis of the company's strengths, weaknesses, opportunities, and threats. [WL/MBC]

market opportunity index The use of relevant criteria by a company to rank future opportunities that have been identified and facilitate the selection of the most promising opportunities. [WL/MBC]

market penetration A growth strategy designed to enhance competitive advantage by developing low-risk improvement or revisions to the present product range. These are either *proactive* moves designed to identify and target changing customer requirements, or *reactive* moves for market defense triggered by competitive actions. [GSD]

market penetration strategy A move by management to increase its market share held by current products in currently serviced markets. Market share may be increased by some combination of (1) attracting users of competitive brands, (2) persuading current users to increase usage, or (3) attracting nonusers of the product category. [GSD]

market position See **competitive position**

market positioning Positioning refers to the customer's perceptions of the place a product or brand occupies in a market segment. In some markets, a position is achieved by associating the benefits of a brand with the needs or life style of the segments. More often, positioning involves the differentiation of the company's offering from the competition by making or implying a comparison in terms of specific attributes. [GSD]

market potential An estimate of the maximum possible sales of a commodity, a group of commodities, or a service for an entire industry in a market during a stated period. (See also **sales potential.**) [GAC]

market profile A breakdown of a facility's market area according to income, demography, and life style. [DLH]

market research The systematic gathering, recording, and analyzing of data with respect to a particular market, where market refers to a specific customer group in a specific geographic area. [GAC]

market response function models See **promotion models**

market rollout The introduction of a new product into a market sequentially. The rollout may be by geographical areas, by applications or uses, or by individual customers. Over time, depending on the speed of the rollout, the entire market is covered. (See also **payback, product introduction,** and **test marketing.**) [DW]

market segment See **market fragmentation**

market segmentation The process of subdividing a market into distinct subsets of customers that behave in the same way or have similar needs. Each subset may conceivably be chosen as a market target to be reached with a distinct marketing strategy. The process begins with a basis of segmentation—a product-specific factor that reflects differences in customers' requirements or responsiveness to marketing variables (possibilities are purchase behavior, usage, benefits sought, intentions, preference, or loyalty). Segment descriptors are then chosen, based on their ability to identify segments, to account for variance in the segmentation basis, and to suggest competitive strategy implications (examples of descriptors are demographics, geography, psychographics, customer size, and industry). To be of strategic value, the resulting segments must be measurable, accessible, sufficiently different to justify a meaningful variation in strategy, substantial, and durable. [GSD]

market segmentation strategies Having segmented a market, the task is then to determine which segments are profitable to serve. The business can adopt one of three market segmentation strategies: (1) **undifferentiated marketing**—in which the business attempts to go after the whole market with a product and marketing strategy intended to have mass appeal; (2) **differentiated marketing**—in which the business operates in several segments of the market with offerings and market strategies tailored to each segment; (3) **concentrated marketing**—in which the business focuses on only one or a few segments with the intention of capturing a large share of these segments. [GSD]

market share 1. (geography definition) A proportion of total sales in a market obtained by a given facility or chain. [DLH] 2. (strategic marketing definition) The proportion of the total quantity or dollar sales in a market that is held by each of the competitors. The market can be defined as broadly as the industry, or all substitutes, or as narrowly as a specific market segment. The choice of market depends on which level gives the best insight into competitive position. [GSD]

market share model See **attraction model, decision calculus model, Multiplicative Competitive Interaction model, NEWPROD, NEWS, Parfitt-Collins model, probit model,** and **STRATPORT**

market specialization See **market coverage strategies**

market specialization coverage See **product-market grid**

market structure The pattern formed by the number, size, and distribution of buyers and sellers in a market. [DLS]

market test A controlled experiment, done in a limited but carefully selected sector of the marketplace, whose aim is to predict the sales or profit consequences, either in absolute or relative terms, of one or more proposed marketing actions. (See also **advertising effectiveness.**) [GAC]

market testing The phase of new product development in which the new item and its marketing plan are tested together. Prior testing, if any, involved separate components. A market test simulates the eventual marketing of the product and takes many different forms, only one of which bears the name test market. (See also **payback, product introduction, simulated test market,** and **test marketing.**) [DW]

market-driven innovation See **demand-pulled innovation**

marketing The process of planning and executing the conception, pricing, promotion, and distribution of ideas, goods, and services to create exchanges that satisfy individual and organizational goals. [AMA]

marketing and consumer satisfaction See **consumer satisfaction** and **post-purchase evaluation**

marketing channel A set of institutions necessary to transfer the title to goods and to move goods from the point of production to the point of consumption and, as such, which consists of all the institutions and all the marketing activities in the marketing process. [WRD]

marketing conduct A legal view of marketers' decisions on marketing mix variables and the process by which they make these decisions. [DLS]

marketing cost analysis An attempt to determine the actual costs incurred for marketing and distributing a product. [KM]

marketing decision variables See **decision variables, marketing**

marketing driven modified financial portfolio models See **product and business portfolio models.**

marketing ethics 1. (legislation definition) Standards of marketing decision-making based on "what is right" and "what is wrong," and emanating from our religious heritage and our traditions of social, political, and economic freedom. [DC] 2. (environments definition) The use of moral codes, values, and standards to determine whether marketing actions are good or evil, right or wrong. Often standards are based on professional or association codes of ethics. [WL/MBC]

marketing geography The field of study that analyzes the spatial characteristics of marketing activities: the consumers and the distribution network. [DLH]

marketing goals See **goal**

marketing information system (MkIS) A set of procedures and methods for the regular, planned collection, analysis, and presentation of information for use in making marketing decisions. (See also **management information system.**) [GAC]

marketing intelligence system The development of a system to gather, process, assess, and make available marketing data and information in a format that permits marketing managers and executives to function more effectively. Marketing data, when analyzed, may yield information that can then be processed and put into a format that gives intelligence for planning, policy making, and decision purposes. [WL/MBC]

marketing management The process of setting marketing goals for an organization (considering internal resources and market opportunities), the planning and execution of activities to meet these goals, and measuring progress toward their achievement. Comment: The process is ongoing and repetitive (as within a planning cycle) so that the organization may continuously adapt to internal and external changes that create new problems and opportunities. [VPB]

marketing manager The generic title for the line executive responsible for designated marketing functions (such as marketing research, product planning and market planning, pricing, distribution, the promotion mix, and customer services) and for coordinating with other departments that perform marketing related activities (such as packaging, warehousing, order filling, shipping, design of new and improved products, credit, billing, collections, accounting, legal, transportation, purchasing, product repair, warranty fulfillment, and technical assistance to customers). The marketing manager may have an officer title (such as vice president of marketing) and usually reports to the chief executive officer in a functionally organized company or to the division manager (president) in a divisionalized company. Comment: The above definition describes the marketing manager with full responsibility for marketing. However, the title is sometimes used for jobs of lesser scope; for example, in a multiproduct division a manager may be in charge of a line of products or a business segment and report to the division marketing manager. Also, it is not uncommon for the sales and marketing functions to report separately to a common supervisor such as the division manager. In such a case the marketing manager may be in charge of marketing functions other than personal selling. This dichotomy most often occurs in industrial or consumer durable goods businesses in which personal selling is the key aspect of promotion. (See also **category manager, divisional organization, functional organization, group product manager, marketing of services, new product manager, nonbusiness marketing organization, product manager, product planning manager,** and **promotion mix.**) [VPB]

marketing manager, corporate level executive Some large divisionalized companies have a corporate marketing vice president who performs a staff role designated by the corporate chief executive officer. In general, the principal role is to view marketing problems and opportunities from a broader perspective than that of division management. It may also include specific functions such as providing marketing counsel to corporate management, monitoring divisional marketing performance, critiquing divisional marketing plans, evaluating potential acquisitions, assisting with or directing the corporate strategic planning function, searching for new product and business opportunities outside of present division charters, assisting with setting research and development priorities, and administering the corporate advertising and/or corporate image programs. This position usually reports to the corporate chief executive. [VPB]

marketing mix The mix of controllable marketing variables that the firm uses to pursue the desired level of sales in the target market. The most common classification of these factors is the four-factor classification called the "Four Ps"—price, product, promotion, and place (or distribution). Optimization of the marketing mix is achieved by assigning the amount of the marketing budget to be spent on each element of the marketing mix so as to maximize the total contribution to the firm. Contribution may be measured in terms of sales or profits or in terms of any other organizational goals. [GSD]

marketing mix models The determination of an optimal marketing mix is often aided by models that take into account the market response to the various marketing mix elements and their interactions. These models include econometric market response models to the marketing mix variables of the firm (and its competitors) as well as specialized models such as Advisor and BRANDAID, microsimulation models, various optimization models, and customized applications of the analytic hierarchy process and other resource allocation models. (See also **adaptive experimentation, BRANDAID, carry over models, decision calculus models, decision support system, forecasting models,** and **SPRINTER Mod III.**) [DCS/YJW]

marketing objectives See **objective**

marketing of services The organizational structure for the marketing of intangible services is the same as, or similar to, the marketing of tangible products. The term *product* as used in the organizational definitions in this dictionary can be read to mean services as well. Also, the term *production* refers to manufacturing, assembly, or other means of creating a tangible product, while the term *operations* commonly refers to the functions that supply an intangible service. Hence, when substituting *service* for *product* in a definition, one can also substitute *operations* for *production.* Comment: *Service* has meanings in marketing other than product. This can be seen in the definition for *marketing services,* in which *service* refers to auxiliary functions that aid in the sale, distributions, and customer usage of a product. Another meaning of *service* can be seen in the definition for *marketing services department,* in which a centralized department supplies assistance (i.e., services) to division marketing departments in a divisionalized company. (See also **customer service, functional organization, marketing manager,** and **services.**) [VPB]

marketing (only) division This division contains the usual marketing functions, including sales, but its products are supplied by a centralized production operation that supplies two or more marketing divisions. When standardized products can be mass produced by a centralized facility, economies of scale are the usual result. (See also **divisional organization** and **functional organization.**) [VPB]

marketing organization, forms of No two companies are likely to have identical structures. Most utilize one or more of the classic structural forms with the choice at any one time having to do with the stage of company development. It should be noted that larger companies may be using different forms in different parts of the company at the same time. (See also **bureaucratic organization, centralized management, decentralized management, divisional organization, flat organization, functional organization, geographic organization, hierarchical organization, market management organization, matrix organization, multibusiness organization, nonbusiness marketing organization,** and **product management organization.**) [VPB]

marketing plan A document composed of an analysis of the current marketing situation, opportunities and threats analysis, marketing objectives, marketing strategy, action programs, and projected or pro-forma income (and other financial) statements. This plan may be the only statement of the strategic direction of a business, but it is more likely to apply only to a specific brand or product. In the latter situation, the marketing plan is an implementation device that is integrated within an overall strategic business plan. (See also **marketing planning.**) [GSD]

marketing planning The process that leads to the development of the marketing plan. [GSD]

,marketing public relations Publicity activities intended to encourage product purchase and consumer satisfaction. (See also **public relations.**) [DES/BEB]

marketing research The function that links the consumer, customer, and public to the marketer through information—information used to identify and define marketing opportunities and problems; generate, refine, and evaluate marketing actions; monitor marketing performance; and improve understanding of marketing as a process.

Marketing research specifies the information required to address these issues; designs the method for collecting information; manages and implements the data collection process; analyzes the results; and communicates the findings and their implications. [AMA]

marketing research manager This manager is responsible for providing professional research services to executives who require objective and timely market information to assist with planning, problem resolution, and decision making. Normally the marketing research manager reports to the marketing manager. In larger companies, however, there may be multiple marketing research managers reporting, for example, to the corporate marketing or strategic planning executive, to division managers, and to the research and development director. Comment: The types of research carried out will vary by type of company, industry, and the organizational unit to which the manager is assigned. With the growth of computerized data systems and the availability of outside marketing research organizations that report repetitive market data, the marketing research manager assembles the information needed for a particular problem and, when necessary, directs the development of information that must be obtained via special studies. The typical marketing research manager works with a small staff and uses outside research firms to carry out all or parts of field studies. [VPB]

marketing services Sometimes called customer services, this is an all-inclusive term that covers different sets of functions for different companies. Historically it has included some or all of the functions needed to service channel intermediaries and/or end customers, such as inventory planning and control; order processing, shipping, and delivery information; product installation, maintenance, repair, replacement, and warranty administration; and answering customer inquiries. Organizationally most of these services are provided by functional departments other than marketing. They may or may not be coordinated by a marketing service manager or customer service manager reporting to the marketing manager. Comment: While the above named services are basic to providing marketing services to channels of distribution and customers, another use of the term applies to a centralized department that provides in-house services to company divisions. (See also **customer service** and **marketing services department.**) [VPB]

marketing services department A unit in a multidivision company that performs marketing functions for divisions that can be performed better or at less cost when carried out centrally. Although the functions of this unit may vary by company, they may include some or all of the following: media planning, coordination of media buying, sales promotion planning and counselling, providing sales promotion materials, package design, control of advertising production costs, advertising research, creative services, and advertising claims substantiation. For small divisions with limited personnel, the marketing services department may serve as their advertising, sales promotion, product publicity, or marketing research department. (See also **marketing services** and **marketing services director.**) [VPB]

marketing services director This person manages the marketing services department and may report to a corporate executive, group executive, or to the manager of a major division. Irrespective of the reporting level, this manager provides the services for all divisions that require them. (See also **marketing services department.**) [VPB]

marketing strategy A statement (implicit or explicit) of how a brand or product line will achieve its objectives. The strategy provides decisions and direction regarding variables such as the segmentation of the market, identification of the target market, positioning, marketing mix elements, and expenditures. A marketing strategy is usually an integral part of a business strategy that provides broad direction to all functions. [GSD]

marketing tactics See **tactics**

markon See **cumulative markon** and **markup**

Markov model Brand switching matrices (from time $t - 1$ to t) are sometimes envisioned as arising from a stationary first-order Markov model. This model assumes that only the brand chosen in $t - 1$ affects brand choice at t. The transition probability matrix describes the brand choice. Higher order models (i.e., in which choice at t is dependent on several previous choices) with varying transition probabilities have also been proposed. For example, see Kahn, Kalwani, and Morrison (1986) and Lattin and McAlister (1985). (See also **brand choice models** and **elasticon.**) [DCS/YJW]

markup 1. (pricing definition) The amount of increase in price over total unit costs. [KM] 2. (retailing definition) The difference between merchandise cost and the retail price. It is also referred to as markon. 3. The increase in the retail price after the initial markup percentage has been applied, but before it is placed on the selling floor. (See also **additional markup, initial markup, maintained markup,** and **retail inventory method of accounting.**) [WRD]

markup percentage The difference between cost and retail, expressed either as a percentage of cost or, commonly, as a percentage of retail. (See also **markup, markup table,** and **markup wheel.**) [WRD]

markup table A tabulation giving markup percentages on cost price with the corresponding markup percentage on retail price. (See also **markup wheel.**) [WRD]

markup wheel See **markup table**

Maslow's need hierarchy A popular theory of human motivation developed by Abraham Maslow that suggests humans satisfy their needs in a sequential order beginning with physiological needs (food, water, sex), and ranging through safety needs (protection from harm), belongingness and love needs (companionship), esteem needs (prestige, respect of others), and finally, self-actualization needs (self-fulfillment). [JPP/JCO]

mass communications See **two step flow of communication**

mass media See **advertising media**

master carton A container that is used primarily for protective purposes in transportation and warehousing. It contains multiple, usually identical, products that may be individually packaged for resale. [DBL/BJL]

master production schedule A detailed listing of how many end items are to be produced and when they will be produced. A materials requirements planning system requires a valid and detailed master production schedule as critical first input in the system. [DJB/BJL]

materialism The evaluation of the self

in terms of how much is owned or how much can be consumed. The importance that people attach to worldly possessions. [HHK/MCC]

materials handling A term applied to the study of physical flow in a logistics system. It is usually used to describe a mechanical or electro-mechanical set of devices that facilitate the physical handling of products in a logistics environment. [DJB/BJL]

materials management Either an organizational component or an approach to managing the material flow process of the firm. A distinctive characteristic of the term is that it includes the purchasing function as an integral part of the material flow process. The term *materials manager* is also used to describe a related job function. [DJB/BJL]

materials manager See **materials management**

materials requirements planning (MRP) A production and inventory planning system that integrates product components, manufacturing and procurement schedules, leadtimes, and capacities against output requirements.

mathematical programming A set of optimization models whose aim is to find the maximum (or minimum) of an objective function subject to certain constraints. The most commonly used mathematical programming technique is linear programming (LP), a linear objective function subject to linear constraints. LP provides both the values of the decision variables for the optimal solution and the shadow prices for the constraints (i.e., the change in value of the objective function per unit change in the value of the constraint). Other mathematical programming techniques include integer programming (for integers as opposed to continuous values), nonlinear programming, quadratic programming, and dynamic programming. Dynamic programming is a general type of approach to solve multistage problems in continuous or discrete space under certainty or uncertainty. Uncertainty can be incorporated in linear programming as well as either stochastic programming (some of the parameters are random variables) or chance constrained programming (feasible solutions are allowed to have a small probability of violating the constraints). Mathematical programming has been used in marketing, especially in media selection and salesforce allocation problems. (See also **distribution models, resource allocation models** and **sales force models.**) [DCS/YJW]

matrix organization This organization attempts to combine functional and product forms of organization to obtain the advantages of each. Teams of functional personnel (e.g., manufacturing, research and development, finance, and sales) report to a manager with profit responsibility bearing a title such as business manager, category manager, or new product manager. The functional personnel also report to their functional bosses, who are responsible for maintaining the quality of functional performance. Comment: In this arrangement, functional personnel report to two bosses, which requires a high order of understanding and cooperation if it is to be effective. Matrix organization has met with mixed results and has both critics and champions. (See also **bureaucratic organization; centralized management; decentralized management, divisional organization; flat organization; functional organization; geographic organization, hierarchical organization; market management organization; marketing organization, forms of; multibusiness organization; nonbusiness marketing**

organization, and **product management organization.**) [VPB]

maturity market life cycle stage See **market evolution**

maturity stage See **product life cycle**

maturity stage of product life cycle The third stage of the product life cycle, in which initial rapid growth is over and sales level off (though there may be intermittent surges and declines over the years before final decline sets in). During the maturity stage price competition becomes very strong, similar products are made available by competition, the adoption process is mostly over, and profits fall. (See also **retail life cycle.**) [DW]

maximum acceptable price The highest price a buyer is willing to pay for a product or service. It is also called a reservation price. [KM]

maximum operating stock The largest quantity of inventory that should ever be on hand during normal operating conditions, usually at the stockkeeping unit level. It consists of merchandise to sell during the buying period, the cushion, and the basic low stock. [WRD]

maximum system of stock control The system of setting, for each item of staple merchandise carried, an amount large enough to take care of probable demands of customers, and of reordering, periodically, the difference between the actual stock and the maximum set. [WRD]

MC See **marginal cost**

McGuire-Keogh Fair Trade Enabling Act (1952) This act declared that exemption of resale price maintenance agreements from antitrust laws as provided under the Miller-Tydings Resale Price Maintenance Act would be extended to non-signer agreements (whereby all dealers are bound to the contract if only one signs) in states that have non-signer clauses in their fair trade statutes. (See also **Consumer Goods Pricing Act** and **resale price maintenance laws.**) [DC]

MCI model See **Multiplicative Competitive Interaction model**

McKinsey & Company See **market attractiveness-competitive position matrix**

meaning People's personal interpretation of information in the environment; it is essentially the same as beliefs and knowledge. [JPP/JCO]

means-ends chain A simple knowledge structure that organizes consumers' product knowledge by linking product attributes to the more abstract consequences and finally to high-level consumer values. [JPP/JCO]

measured value See **contingency contract** and **contingency pricing**

measurement A rule for assigning numbers to objects to represent quantities of attributes. [GAC]

Meat Inspection Acts (1906) These acts required inspection and approval of live stock, carcasses, and canned or packaged meat products as well as sanitary conditions in slaughterhouses. [DC]

mechanical The final photo-ready assembly of all of the elements of a print ad, brochure, or other printed material that is transmitted to the printer. This is also known as a paste-up. (See also **comprehensive layout, dummy, layout, rough, storyboard,** and **thumbnail.**) [JE]

media See **advertising media**

media buy The purchase of a specific amount of time or space in an advertising media vehicle. It is sometimes referred to as a buy. [JE]

media buying The advertising agency function that involves negotiating with the salespeople of various advertising media in order to obtain needed time and space for advertising agency clients at the most favorable prices. (See also **media buying service**.) [JE]

media buying service An organization that specializes in buying media time and space for advertisers. Some media buying services also engage in media planning activities for their clients. (See also **limited-service advertising agency** and **media buying.**) [JE]

media exposure patterns See **Beta binomial model** and **zero order model**

media kit A package of promotional materials relating to a specific advertising media vehicle, including the rate card, audience statistics, case studies showing success stories, and related materials. [JE]

media mix The specific combination of various advertising media (including network television, local television, magazines, newspapers, specialty advertising, etc.) used by a particular advertiser and the advertising budget to be allocated to each medium. [JE]

media model A mathematical formula (or computer algorithm) used in combination with audience data from specific media vehicles to estimate the reach, frequency, and exposure distribution of alternative media schedules. [JE]

media planning The advertising agency function that involves the determination of advertising objectives, advertising strategies, and advertising tactics relating to the advertising media to be used by specific clients. A media plan includes a statement of objectives, target market definition, types of advertising media to be used, and the amount of resources to be allocated to each (the media mix), and a specific time schedule for the use of each media vehicle. (See also **media buying service.**) [JE]

media relations The activities involved in working with the media to generate publicity for a product, service, or organization. This includes establishing contact with members of the media, providing publicity materials, and being available to answer any questions the media might have. [DES/BEB]

media rep See **media representative**

media representative A person or a company that specializes in selling space or time in advertising vehicles to advertisers and advertising agencies. [JE]

media schedule A specific schedule showing the media vehicles (including dates, positions in the publication or time of day, and size of ad space or duration of commercials) to be used during an advertising campaign. [JE]

media scheduling models See **advertising models** and **MEDIAC**

media selection models See **advertising models, mathematical programming,** and **MEDIAC**

media type See **advertising media**

media vehicle A specific newspaper, magazine, radio station, television program, outdoor advertising location, edition of Yellow Pages, etc., that can be employed to carry advertisements or commercials. For example, *The New Yorker* magazine is a media vehicle in the magazine category of advertising media. [JE]

media viewing pattern model See **Bernoulli process** and **probability mixture model**

media weight A measure of the amount

of advertising media used in an advertising campaign. It can be expressed in terms of dollar amounts, gross rating points, circulation data, or other means. [JE]

MEDIAC A model providing a decision support system for the advertising media selection and scheduling decision (Little and Lodish 1969). Little and Lodish (1966) describe the perspective adopted by the model: "The population is divided into 'market segments.' Each segment has its own sales potential and media habits. . . . A media schedule consists of insertions in 'media vehicles'. . . . An insertion brings about exposures in the various market segments. The exposures serve to increase what we shall call 'exposure value' in the market segments. However, people are subject to 'forgetting,' and so the retained exposure level decays with time in the absence of new exposures. The 'anticipated sales' to a market segment increases with exposure level but with diminishing returns." (See also **ADBUDG, ADMOD, advertising models** and **decision calculus models.**) [DCS/YJW]

medium See **advertising media**

membership group A small group of individuals in which the individual is phychologically and formally a member. A fraternity, the Rotary Club, or a bowling team are examples of membership groups. It is those groups in which the individual has direct, face-to-face psychological relations and interdependence with other members. [HHK/MCC]

memorandum purchase and dating This indicates that merchandise shipped to a buyer is returnable within a specified period of time. Payment for goods kept longer or sold need not be made until this time, though legal title usually transfers at the time of shipment. (See also **advance dating, dating, end of month dating, extra dating, future dating, ordinary dating, proximo dating, receipt-of-goods dating,** and **season dating.**) [WRD]

memorandum terms A special form of indefinite future dating under which the title of the merchandise passes to the buyer, and the buyer assumes all risk of ownership. [WRD]

MEP See **market expansion potential**

mercantile trade credit The credit one businessperson extends to another when selling goods on time for resale or commercial use. [WRD]

mercantilism A set of economic policies designed to give a country an advantage by developing a favorable balance of trade, encouraging agriculture and manufacturing, creating a merchant marine, and establishing foreign trading monopolies. [DLS]

merchandise budget A statement prepared by management containing planned dollar commitments for all the components of the merchandise plan (sales, reductions, stocks, margins, and purchases) for a seasonal period. [WRD]

merchandise classification A subdivision of a selling department; a dissection of a department's inventory, purchase, and/or sales figures for the purpose of closer control. (See also **classification, classification control,** and **dissection control.**) [WRD]

merchandise control The determination and direction of merchandising activities, both in terms of dollars (dollar control) and in terms of units (unit merchandise control). [WRD]

merchandise cost The billed cost of merchandise less any applicable trade discounts or quantity discounts, plus inbound transportation costs if paid by the purchaser. (See also **initial markup** and **markup.**) [WRD]

merchandise dissection See **merchandise classification**

merchandise in-transit Merchandise with its legal title passed to the retailer, but which has not been charged to a merchandise selling department. [WRD]

merchandise line A group of products closely related because they are intended for the same end use, are sold to the same customer group, or fall within a given price range. (See also **product line.**) [WRD]

merchandise management The analysis, planning, acquisition, promotion, and control of merchandise sold by a retailer. [WRD]

merchandise mix The breadth and depth of the merchandise inventory carried by retail establishments. [WRD]

merchandise performance analysis See **merchandise productivity analysis**

merchandise plan A plan, generally for department stores, for a six-month period, by months, in which the chief elements enter into gross profit. The essential are sales, markdowns, retail stocks at the first of each month, purchases, and markup percentages. Inventory shortages, cash discounts, and alteration costs may also be budgeted. [WRD]

merchandise productivity analysis A financial analysis of the productivity (performance) of various merchandise categories. [WRD]

merchandise shopping See **comparison shopping**

merchandising A term of many varied and not generally adopted meanings. It can (1) relate to the promotional activities of manufacturers that bring about in-store displays, or (2) identify the product and product line decisions of retailers. [DW]

merchant A business unit that buys, takes title to, and resells merchandise. [WRD]

merchant middleman A middleman who buys the goods outright and takes title to them. [WRD]

merchant wholesalers The wholesalers who take title to the products they sell. [GLF]

mere exposure effect The repeated exposure to an object resulting in a more positive attitude toward the object; the mere exposure to the object is believed to produce the more positive attitude. [HHK/MCC]

merger The joining together of two or more independent business organizations into a single entity. (See also **acquisition, alliances, conglomerate, consolidation, diversification, horizontal integration, integration, takeover, vertical integration,** and **vertical merger.**) [WL/MBC]

message See **Elaboration Likelihood Model**

message argument A statement of the customer benefit and the specific product performance characteristic that delivers that benefit. (See also **advertising strategy.**) [JE]

method variance The variation in scores attributable to the method of data collection. (See also **equivalence** and **instrument variation.**) [GAC]

metropolitan statistical area (MSA) A freestanding metropolitan area surrounded by nonmetropolitan counties, including a large central city or urbanized area of 50,000 or more people. (See also **census metropolitan area, consolidated metropolitan statistical area, primary metropolitan statistical area,** and **standard metropolitan statistical area.**) [DLS]

"me-too" product See **adaptive product** and **emulative product**

MFN See **Most Favored Nation Principle**

microenvironment The set of forces close to an organization that have direct impact on its ability to serve its customers. The microenvironment includes channel member organizations, competitors, customer markets, publics, and the capabilities of the organization itself. (See also **macroenvironment.**) [WL/MBC]

micromarketing The study of marketing activities of an organization. (See also **macromarketing.**) [DLS]

microsimulation models See **marketing mix models**

middle income countries Countries whose income per capita falls between the highest and the lowest group. (See also **high income countries** and **low income countries.**) [WJK]

middle-class See **social class**

middleman 1. (retailing definition) A business concern that specializes in performing operations or rendering services directly involved in the purchase and/or sale of goods in the process of their flow from producer to consumer. (See also **merchant middleman.**) [WRD] 2. (channels of distribution definition) An independent business concern that operates as a link between producers and ultimate consumers or industrial users. There are at least two levels of middlemen: wholesalers and retailers. [GLF]

military buying The purchase of goods and services by the Defense Department largely through the Defense Logistics Agency, the General Services Administration, and the three military departments: Army, Navy, and Air Force. [GLL/DTW]

military organization See **hierarchical organization** and **nonbusiness marketing organization**

Miller-Tydings Resale Price Maintenance Act (1937) In this act, resale price maintenance contracts prescribing minimum prices for name brand commodities were made exempt from the Sherman Antitrust and Federal Trade Commission Acts in those states having fair trade laws permitting such contracts. (See also **Consumer Goods Pricing Act, McGuire-Keogh Fair Trade Enabling Act,** and **resale price maintenance laws.**) [DC]

minimum and maximum system of stock control A system whereby for each item of staple merchandise carried, a minimum quantity of inventory is established which, when reached, indicates a need to reorder. Maximum stock consists of the minimum and the predetermined reorder quantity. [WRD]

minimum charge In most transportation tariffs, the minimum charge is the lowest price at which a carrier will accept a shipment for delivery. A minimum charge reflects the fixed cost component of the transportation carrier's cost of doing business and is often used as an incentive to encourage the shipper to consolidate multiple shipments. [DJB/BJL]

minimum order The smallest unit of sales permitted by a manufacturer or wholesaler. It may be expressed in units, as a dollar amount, or, sometimes, as a weight. [WRD]

MIS See **management information system**

misredemption The improper claiming of price savings, premiums, prizes, or other sales promotion rewards by not following the stated rules, after the specified time period, or by persons not eligible for the incentive. (See also **coupon fraud** and **coupon redemption.**) [DES/BEB]

mission See **corporate purpose**

mission statement An expression of a company's history, managerial preferences, environmental concerns, available resources, and distinctive competencies to serve selected publics. It is used to guide the company's decision making and strategic planning. [DES/BEB]

missionary salesperson A salesperson who is employed by a manufacturer to call on end-users with the objective of stimulating demand for the manufacturer's offerings even though the purchases will be made from other firms in the channel of distribution. (See also **detail salesperson.**) [BAW]

mixed bundling The practice of offering for sale two or more products or services either at individual prices or for one single price. The single price for the "bundle" is usually less than the sum of the individual prices. (See also **bundling, multiple-unit pricing** and **price bundling.**) [KM]

mixed-use development (MXD) The shopping centers that have various types of non- retail uses such as office towers, hotels, residential complexes, civic centers, and convention complexes on top of or attached to the shopping area. [WRD]

MkIS See **marketing information system**

MNC See **multinational corporation**

model stock approach to space allocation A method of determining space allocation for departments in a retail store. It is based upon an analysis of an ideal stock necessary to achieve projected sales volume, of how much stock should be displayed versus how much should be kept in reserve space, of how much physical space will be required to display the merchandise, and of how much physical space will be needed for any service requirements. [WRD]

model stock list An assortment of fashion merchandise indicating in very general terms (product lines, colors, and size distribution) what should be carried in a particular merchandise category. (See also **model stock plan.**) [WRD]

model stock plan An outline of the composition of an ideal stock in terms of general characteristics or assortment factors, usually with optimum quantities indicated in an amount that reflects balance in relation to expected sales. (See also **model stock list.**) [WRD]

model system The part of a decision support system that includes all the routines that allow the user to manipulate the data so as to conduct the kind of analysis the individual desires. [GAC]

modeling See **vicarious learning**

modified rebuy See **buyclasses** and **buygrid framework**

modified risk return models See **product and business portfolio models**

momentum strategy See **gap analysis**

monetary perceived risk See **perceived risk**

monetary policy The pursuit of a course of action by a government acting through its central bank to control money and credit. [DLS]

money income 1. (environments definition) The income received by an individual exclusive of certain items such as capital gains, social security and the like. It does not include non-cash benefits. [WL/MBC] 2. (economic definition) Income before the deduction of income taxes and social security taxes. Non-cash benefits are excluded. (See also **discretionary buying power, disposable personal income, national income, personal disposable income, personal income, poverty level,** and **real income.**) [DLS]

monopolistic competition 1. A market situation where many sellers, each with a relatively small market share and with slightly differentiated products, compete for consumer patronage. 2. A market situation where many sellers compete, often emphasizing marketing variables other than price. The term originated with Harvard economist Edward Chamberlain in the 1930s. (See also **duopoly, imperfect competition, monopoly, monopsony, oligopolistic competition, oligopolistic environment, oligopoly, oligopsony, perfect competition, pure competition,** and **workable competition.**) [DLS]

monopoly 1. (environments definition) A market situation where one firm markets all the goods or services and can influence price. [WL/MBC] 2. (economic definition) The complete control of an economic good for which there is no substitute. (See also **competition, duopoly, imperfect competition, monopolistic competition, monopsony, oligopolistic competition, oligopolistic environment, oligopoly, oligopsony, perfect competition, pure competition,** and **workable competition.**) [DLS]

monopsony A single buyer with monopoly buying power. (See also **duopoly, imperfect competition, monopolistic competition, monopoly, oligopolistic competition, oligopolistic environment, oligopoly, oligopsony, perfect competition, pure competition,** and **workable competition.**) [DLS]

mood An emotional state at a particular time. A mood felt by an individual at one point in time may be unrelated to emotions felt an another point in time. [HHK/MCC]

moral self See **ego**

mores The cultural norms that specify behavior of vital importance to society and embody its basic moral values. The prohibition against bigamy or child abandonment in some cultures are examples. Mores often are codified into law such that legal as well as social sanctions can be applied to assure conformity. In comparison, folkways are cultural norms that specify behavior not vital to the welfare of the groups and the means of enforcement are not clearly defined (according to Krench, Crutchfield and Ballachov). For example, folkways specify that a student shall wear specifically defined clothes on campus. If the student does not, the student may be considered a boor or a nerd, but this nonconformity is not regarded as having important consequences for the group. The punishment for nonconformity is informal, mild, and variable. (See also **norms.**) [HHK/MCC]

Most Favored Nation (MFN) Principle The principle whereby each country agrees to extend all countries the most favorable terms that it negotiates with any country. [WJK]

motivation The positive or negative needs, goals, desires, and forces that impel an individual toward or away from certain actions, activities, objects, or conditions. It is the needs and wants of the individual, the driving force, guided by cognitions, behind the behavior to purchase, approach, or avoid products and ideas and things. (See also **Elaboration Likelihood Model, expectancy-value model,** and **objective.**) [HHK/MCC]

motivational approach to attitudes See **functional theory of attitudes**

motivationally neutral See **belief**

motor carrier See **common carrier**

Motor Carrier Act (1980) This act was designed to reduce unnecessary regulation by the federal government in the trucking industry; however, it introduced new and complex regulations. [DC]

moving averages models See **forecasting models**

MR See **marginal revenue**

MRO See **maintenance, repair, and operating items and supplies**

MRP See **materials requirements planning**

MRP-II See **manufacturing resource planning**

MSA See **census tract** and **metropolitan statistical area**

multi-market firm See **conglomerate**

multiattribute attitude models These models are designed to predict attitudes toward objects (such as brands) based on consumers' evaluations of product attributes or expected consequences. [JPP/JCO]

multiattribute models of attitudes The several theories of attitudes, such as Fishbein's learning theory of attitudes, with the basic assumption that attitudes are based upon the individual's perceptions of the attributes of the choice alternatives. These models usually include the idea that the individual assigns importance weights to each attribute and arrives at an overall evaluation on the basis of these weighted attributes. (See also **instrumental function of attitudes.**) [HHK/MCC]

multibrand strategy In this strategy, the company has more than one brand of product, competing with each other, in a given market. This contrasts with the strategy of family brands where the separate items are given a common line identity and are usually each directed to one segment within the market. Under multibrand strategy there may not even be manufacturer identification, unless required by law. [GSD]

multibusiness organization This is a corporation engaged in more than one class of business. Each business may be organized as a division of the corporation or as a subsidiary company. Comment: Organizationally there may be no difference in the way a division and a subsidiary are viewed by corporate management even though the subsidiary is a separate legal entity controlled by the parent corporation through majority ownership or full ownership. (See also **bureaucratic organization; centralized management, decentralized management; divisional organization; flat organization; functional organization; geographic organization; hierarchical organization; market management organization; marketing organization, forms of; matrix organization; nonbusiness marketing organization;** and **product management organization.** [VPB]

multichotomous question A fixed-alternative question containing three or more alternatives in which respondents are asked to choose the alternative that most closely corresponds to their position on the subject. (See also **dichotomous question.**) [GAC]

multidimensional scaling An approach to measurement in which people's perceptions of the similarity of objects and their preferences among the objects are measured, and these relationships are plotted in a multidimensional space. (See also **product design models.**) [GAC]

multidomestic strategy A strategy that enables individual subsidiaries of a multinational firm to compete independently in different domestic markets. The multinational headquarters coordinates financial controls and some marketing policy, and may centralize some R&D and component production. Each subsidiary behaves like a strategic business unit that is expected to contribute earnings and growth proportionate to the market opportunity. (See also **global strategy.**) [GSD]

multifactor productivity See **productivity**

multilevel selling 1. A sales approach that involves using company employees at multiple levels in the firm's hierarchy to call on similar levels in the account. For example, the Vice President of Sales would call on the Vice President of Purchasing. 2. A strategy used by direct selling companies to have independent agents serve as distributors and resell merchandise to other agents who eventually make sales to consumers. (See also **approach, sales; balance sheet method; benefit approach; compliment approach; consultative selling; customer orientation; formula selling; high-pressure selling; problem solution approach;** and **systems selling.**) [BAW]

multinational corporation (MNC) A stage in the development of the global/transnational corporation. (See also **international corporation.**) [WJK]

multinomial distribution See **Dirichlet multinomial model**

multipage insert See **preprint advertising**

multiple basing-point pricing system In a multiple basing-point pricing system, several locations are designated as basing points. The choice of a basing point is the point that yields the lowest delivered cost to the buyer. (See also **basing-point pricing.**) [KM]

multiple channels The use of a combination of channels in selling a product or service to reach different and isolated target markets with different demands for service outputs. [GLF]

multiple packaging This usually refers to multiple-unit packaging, but it also refers to situations in which a product has a primary package such as foil, bottle, or polyurethane, a secondary package such as a paper carton, and a tertiary package such as a corrugated shipping carton. (See also **factory pack** and **package.**) [DW]

multiple product purchase See **consumer sales promotion**

multiple purchasing The strategy of dividing annual purchasing requirements of a good or service among more than one supplier. This is done to create a more competitive environment among suppliers and to reduce the buying firm's dependence on a single source of supply. This is also called multiple sourcing. [GLL/DTW]

multiple purpose trip A key concept in central place theory that argues that consumers prefer to visit more than one store per trip, generating positive externalities for neighboring stores. [DLH]

multiple sourcing See **multiple purchasing** and **sourcing**

multiple-unit packaging The practice of putting two or more finished packages of a product into a larger packaged unit (such as a six-pack of soda). The new wrap may vary from a band to a larger completely closed container. Multiple packaging may be temporary, related to a promotional program. [DW]

multiple-unit pricing 1. (retailing definition) The combination of several like products as a unit of one, involving at least a slightly different markup than is obtained when the items are sold separately. [WRD] 2. (pricing definition) The practice of pricing several items as a single unit. (See also **bundling, mixed bundling** and **price bundling.**) [KM]

multiple-zone pricing system In a multiple-zone pricing system, delivered prices are uniform within two or more zones. (See also **single-zone pricing.**) [KM]

Multiplicative Competitive Interaction (MCI) model An attraction model for explaining and predicting market share. In an MCI model each brand's attractiveness is modeled as a multiplicative function of some explanatory variables (e.g., brand attributes). Nakanishi and Cooper (1974) show how such a nonlinear model can be estimated by least squares regression techniques. (See also **attraction model** and **distribution models.**) [DCS/YJW]

multiunit establishment One of two or more establishments in the same general kind of business operated by the same firm. It is sometimes referred to as a chain store. (See also **chain store system.**) [WRD]

multivariate normal distribution See **probit model**

municipal market See **public market**

MXD See **mixed-use development**

NAAG See **National Association of Attorneys General**

NAD See **National Advertising Division**

NAFTA See **North American Free Trade Agreement**

naive theory of causality See **attribution theory**

NARB See **National Advertising Review Board**

narrow class See **product class**

Nash Equilibrium See **game theoretic models**

national account A prospect or customer with locations in several sales territories that are sold, using a coordinated national strategy rather than strategies that focus on specific locations. A national account with an international scope is referred to as a global account. (See also **house account** and **key account.**) [BAW]

national account manager An account executive responsible for coordinating the sales effort directed toward a national account. [BAW]

national advertising Any advertising that is placed by a company, organization, or individual that operates on a national or regional (multistate) basis. Some of the advertising may be placed directly with local advertising media, but it is likely that this advertising would be part of the nationwide advertising effort of the company, organization, or individual. [JE]

National Advertising Division (NAD) A division of the Council of Better Business Bureaus that assists advertisers in resolving disputes about the content of advertising messages. The NAD serves as a third party that can help resolve complaints by advertisers and members of the public. If complaints are not resolved by the NAD staff members they are referred to the National Advertising Review Board. [JE]

National Advertising Review Board (NARB) A group of advertising industry executives, advertising executives from corporations, and members of the public who work in conjunction with the National Advertising Division of the Council of Better Business Bureaus. Members of this board attempt to resolve complaints forwarded to the board by the staff of the National Advertising Division. [JE]

National Association of Attorneys General (NAAG) An organization formed by the attorneys general of all fifty states and five territories in an effort to coordinate their activities and provide some uniformity in regulatory control. NAAG has no law enforcement authority, but can express the opinions of its members, adopt policy resolutions, and participate in litigation. [DC]

national brand A brand that is marketed throughout a national market. It contrasts with regional brand and local brand. It usually is advertised and usually is owned by a manufacturer, though neither is necessary for the definition because Kmart's brands, for example, are obviously national, even international. (See also **manufacturer's brand** and **private brand.**) [DW]

national character The values, beliefs, and personality characteristics that describe the people of a country in general terms. (See also **social character.**) [HHK/MCC]

National Environmental Policy Act (NEPA) (1969) The act in which Congress applied at the national level an across-the-board policy of environmental protection for the federal government and all its agencies. Environmental quality under the NEPA has become a major factor in agency decision making. [DC]

national income (NI) 1. (environments definition) The aggregate of labor and property earnings from the current production of goods and services. It comprises employee compensation, proprietors' income, rental income, profits, and net interest. [WL/MBC] 2. (economic definition) The sum of money incomes that individuals and firms receive for supplying units of the productive agents during a given period. It is equal to net national product less indirect business taxes, business transfer payments, and current surpluses of government enterprises plus government subsidies to business firms. (See also **discretionary buying power, disposable personal income, personal disposable income, personal income,** and **real income.**) [DLS]

national rate The price charged national advertisers for space and time in local advertising media. Traditionally, newspapers, radio, and television stations have charged higher rates for national advertising than for local advertising. [JE]

National Traffic and Motor Vehicle Safety Act (1966) An act designed to improve the safety of automobiles, roads, and tires, delegating the responsibility for implementing standards to the Department of Transportation. [DC]

nationalism A national spirit that emphasizes the interests of one's own nation above all else. [DLS]

natural environment The physical forces in nature including climate, weather, and natural resources that affect a firm's market or its ability to carry out it marketing activities. (See also **cultural environment, demographic environment, economic environment,** and **political environment.**) [WL/MBC]

natural selection theory A theory of retail institutional change that states that retailing institutions that can most effectively adapt to environmental changes are the ones most likely to prosper or survive. (See also **central place theory, concentric zone theory, dialectic process, gravity model, retail accordion theory, retail life cycle,** and **wheel of retailing theory.**) [WRD]

NBD model See **Negative Binomial Distribution model**

near line extension See **line extension**

near-pack premium A gift or other item generally too large to be included with or in the product package that is offered as an inducement to purchase. Commonly, the premium is placed near the product's in-store location. (See also **in-pack premium, on-pack premium,** and **premium.**) [DES/BEB]

need See **cognition**

need definition See **buygrid framework**

need description See **buygrid framework**

need payoff See **SPIN**

need recognition See **buygrid framework**

need satisfaction selling A type of customized sales presentation in which the salesperson first identifies the prospective customer's needs and then tries to offer a solution that satisfies those needs. (See also **canned sales presentation; outlined presentation; presentation, sales;** and **stimulus response sales approach.**) [BAW]

needs and wants See **motivation**

negative advertising The use of advertising messages that concentrate on pointing out undesirable aspects of competing products, services, organizations, or ideas. This technique is frequently used in political advertising to attack opposing politicians and political ideas. [JE]

negative appeal See **negative advertising**

negative authorization A verification system in which only poor credit risks are noted in the credit check. Any credit not negatively reported is assumed to be verified. [WRD]

Negative Binomial Distribution (NBD) model A probability mixture model representing the frequency and timing of product purchases, primarily applied to frequently purchased consumer goods. It assumes that sequential purchases made by an individual occur randomly in time, and also assumes that purchase rates have a gamma distribution across individuals (Ehrenberg 1972; Greene 1982). With these two assumptions the distribution for the number of purchases made by a randomly chosen set of customers in a fixed time period has the negative binomial distribution. The model can be used to predict future purchase patterns for customers with a given purchase history (Morrison and Schmittlein 1981). (See also **brand choice models**.) [DCS/YJW]

negative disconfirmation See **disconfirmation**

negative reference group See **reference group**

negative valance See **attitude**

negligence See **strict liability**

negotiation The process of trying to find mutually agreeable terms in an exchange situation. Negotiation leads either to mutually acceptable terms (agreement) or a decision not to transact (disagreement). (See also **channel flows**.) [GLL/DTW]

neighborhood shopping center 1. (geography definition) The smallest type of shopping center, comprising 30,000 to 100,000 square feet. It provides for the sale of convenience goods (food, drugs, and sundries) and personal services that meet the daily needs of an immediate neighborhood trade area. A supermarket is the principal tenant. [DLH] 2. (retailing definition) One of several standard classes of shopping centers recognized by the Urban Land Institute. The neighborhood shopping center provides for the sale of convenience goods and personal services. It typically has about 50,000 square feet of store area but ranges from about 30,000 square feet to 100,000 square feet. (See also **arcade shopping center, community shopping center, factory outlet center, mall-type shopping center, off-price shopping center, regional shopping center, strip-type shopping center,** and **super regional shopping center.**) [WRD]

NEPA See **National Environmental Policy Act**

nested logit model A probabilistic model for representing the discrete choice/behavior of individuals. On any choice occasion the individual is assumed to behave as though choice alternatives were considered in a hierarchical manner. At each stage of the hierarchy the choice to eliminate a set of items from consideration is made according to the logit model (McFadden 1986). The nested logit model arises as a random utility model in which the random component of utility has the generalized extreme value distribution. Guandagni (1983) used this model to represent jointly brand choice and purchase incidence decisions, and Dubin (1986) employed the model to represent consumers' choice of home water heating fuel (gas, oil, or electricity) given the type of space heating system in the home. (See also **brand choice models.**) [DCS/YJW]

net audience See **reach**

net investment Gross investment minus allowances for capital consumption. [DLS]

net markdown See **gross markdown, markdown,** and **markdown cancellation**

net national product (NNP) Gross national product less capital consumption allowance, i.e., depreciation on capital goods plus capital goods destroyed or damaged plus depreciation on minor capital goods. (See also **national income.**) [DLS]

net operating income Net sales less net cost of goods sold less operating expenses. [WRD]

net present value (NPV) technique The method of choice in financial economics for analyzing an investment project. Comment: Net Present Value (NPV) is calculated as follows:

$$NPV = \sum_{i=0}^{n} \frac{A_i}{(1+k)^1}$$

where A_1 equals the net after-tax cash flow in year i, n is the expected life of the project in years, and k is the risk-adjusted, after-tax required rate of return on the investment. [PFA]

net reach See **reach**

net terms Terms calling for the billed amount of the invoice. No cash discount is allowed. [WRD]

net unduplicated audience See **reach**

network broadcast See **spot broadcast**

neutral stimulus See **classical conditioning**

never-out list Key items or best sellers listed separately from a model stock plan or basic stock list, or that are especially identified on the basic stock list by colored stars or other suitable means. It is sometimes referred to as a list of key items, checking-list item, or best-seller list. [WRD]

new package introduction See **consumer sales promotion**

new product committee Made up of high level executives, the committee sets new product policies, establishes priorities, reviews progress, eliminates logjams, decides whether to abandon or commercialize a new product, and provides impetus to the overall new product program. Members typically include the chief executive, director of the new products department, and the managers of major functional departments. Comment: Usually the new product committee will be in addition to one or more other forms of new product organization listed under **new product organization, forms of.** While the committee does not actually manage the new product program, it serves to spotlight the performance of the committee members whose departments are responsible for carrying out parts of new product development projects. [VPB]

new product development The overall process of strategy, organization, concept generation, concept and marketing plan evaluation, and commercialization of a new product. It occasionally is restricted in meaning to that part of the process done by technical (research and development) departments. New product development concerns activity within an organization, in contrast to the acquisition of finished new products from outside. [DW]

new product director See **new product department**

new product failure A new product that does not meet the objectives of its developers. Depending on what those objectives are, a profitable new product can be a failure, and an unprofitable new product can be a success. (See also **abandonment.**) [DW]

new product forecasting models These models for forecasting the performance (e.g., trial, repeat, sales, share) of new products and services include three major types of models: 1) those based on management subjective estimates; 2) those based on analogy to a similar product that had been previously introduced to the market; and 3) those based on consumer studies. There are four types of consumer based models: 1) concept test-based forecasting models, including models such as POSSE; 2) pretest market-based models, especially those categorized as simulated test market models such as LITMUS; 3) test market-based forecasting models such as NEWS and Tracker; and 4) early sales-based forecasting models, which include the various diffusion models. For a review of these models, see Wind, Mahajan, and Cardozo (1981). (See also **diffusion model, NEWPROD, Parfit-Collins model, SPRINTER Mod III,** and **STEAM.**) [DCS/YJW]

new product introduction See **consumer sales promotion**

new product manager This manager is responsible for identifying new product needs, developing new product concepts, and testing the concepts with groups of consumers before turning to research and development for technical development. If a satisfactory product evolves from research and development, the new product manager arranges for consumer product and package testing; and, if these are successful, prepares market introduction plans. When ready for commercialization the new product usually is assigned to a product manager or category manager. The new product manager reports to the marketing manager or division manager. This position is most likely to be found in consumer packaged goods companies producing low technology products. (See also **matrix organization; new product organization, forms of;** and **product planning manager.**) [VPB]

new product organization, forms of New product organization provides for the planning, scheduling, coordination, and control of the new product process from idea to commercialization (or abandonment along the way), as well as getting participation from the internal functional departments and external agencies that must do the work. Comment: Internal participation is required of top management (corporate and/or divisional), major functional departments such as marketing, research and development, production, engineering, finance, and physical distribution (logistics). External participation may involve, for example, advertising agencies, industrial design firms, independent laboratories, market research agencies, new product consultants, and new product development companies. (See also **new product committee; new product manager; new**

products department; product manager; task force, in new product development; and **venture team, in new product development.**) [VPB]

new product strategy The goals a product is expected to achieve in a market. A product's strategy supports and complements the overall marketing strategy. Some products are used to introduce or pioneer new technologies while others are expected to balance current market offerings in terms of product price, product format, style, and features. [DW]

new products department This department is responsible for planning and coordinating the new product program for the company. The director has the functional authority to obtain the participation of other company departments and the line authority to hire outside agencies as needed. The director may have a staff of market research and technical people for conducting preliminary investigations before deciding to involve functional departments in full scale development. The director reports to the corporate chief executive. This provides an avenue for the chief executive to be directly involved in the new product program and provides the director with top management backing when needed to get action from functional managers. (See also **new product organization, forms of** and **new product committee.**) [VPB]

new task purchase See **buyclasses** and **buygrid framework**

newly married stage See **family life cycle**

NEWPROD A model for predicting market share of a new product using test market data. The approach views potential customers as progressing through the stages of awareness-trial-repeat purchase. It considers the effect of advertising and promotion on awareness and trial, and the effect of the level of distribution on trial and repeat purchase (Assmus 1975). (See also **advertising models, ASSESSOR, distribution models, LITMUS, new product forecasting models, NEWS, promotion models, SPRINTER Mod III, STEAM,** and **Tracker.**) [DCS/YJW]

NEWS A model used to predict the level of awareness-trial-repeat purchase, and market share over time for a new frequently purchased consumer product. It considers explicitly the effect of advertising and promotion on brand awareness and product trial, and also incorporates the effect of the level of distribution on trial and repeat purchases. For any particular new product, the model's parameters can be calibrated either using pretest market data (i.e., a telephone survey, advertising copy test, concept test, and in-home product-use test) in the NEWS/Planner version, or using test market data in the NEWS/Market version (Pringle, Wilson, and Brody 1982). (See also **advertising models, ASSESSOR, distribution models, LITMUS, new product forecasting models, NEWPROD, promotion models, SPRINTER Mod III, STEAM,** and **Tracker.**) [DCS/YJW]

news clip A type of film presentation in which editorial content is controlled by the sponsor. It is provided to broadcast media for their use as deemed appropriate. (See also **video news release.**) [DES/BEB]

news peg The main point of a news release that justifies the value of using the story to the media. A news peg should indicate how the story material will affect the media audience. [DES/BEB]

news release Information of timely value distributed by an organization to promote its views or product/services.

The news release is used to influence the media to communicate favorably about the material discussed. (See also **event creation, feature story, news peg,** and **video news release.**) [DES/BEB]

news story See **content analysis**

newsletter A brief digest of important or noteworthy information. A newsletter may be developed by individuals for sale or distributed free by associations, professional societies, and companies as a method of reaching various publics quickly. [DES/BEB]

newspaper distributed magazine See **supplement**

NEXIS A database service that includes over 200 full-text sources. It is used by public relations firms to track publicity for their own and competitors' products and services. (See also **LEXIS.**) [DES/BEB]

NGO See **nongovernmental organization**

NI See **national income**

niche strategy A game plan employed by a firm that specializes in serving particular market segments in order to avoid clashing with the major competitors in the market. "Nichers" pursue market segments that are of sufficient size to be profitable while at the same time are of less interest to the major competitors. [GSD]

nine-block matrix See **market attractiveness–competitive position market**

NNP See **net national product**

nominal credit terms The terms applied to the date on which full payment of the account is due. For vendors that bill customers on a monthly basis, full payment is usually due by the tenth day after billing. [WRD]

nominal scale A measurement in which numbers are assigned to attributes of objects or classes of objects solely for the purpose of identifying the objects. (See also **comparative rating scale, constant sum method, graphic-rating scale, Guttman scale, interval scale, itemized rating scale, ordinal scale, ratio scale, Stapel scale,** and **summated rating.**) [GAC]

non tariff barriers (NTBs) 1. The ongoing administrative, discriminatory, and ad hoc safeguard actions and practices to protect home industries. Typical NTBs include exclusion orders, standards (requiring, for example, that products admitted to the country meet exact specifications that either cannot be met in the case of some natural products or that are very expensive to meet in case of manufactured products), exclusionary distribution, and administrative delays (for example, when the French decided that the imports of Japanese VCRs were excessive, they simply applied the rules and gave each VCR a complete inspection. The number of VCRs entering the country dropped from thousands to six per day). 2. Any measure, public or private, that causes internationally traded goods and services to be allocated in such a way as to reduce potential real world income. [WJK]

non commercialized product concept statement See **concept statement, commercialized**

non-price competition The competition among firms on the basis of variables other than price, such as quality, brand, assortment, or services. It implies that a company can influence demand by its marketing activities. (See also **price competition.**) [WL/MBC]

nonprofit organization See **public service announcement**

non-signer clause A clause in state fair

trade laws permitting the enforcement of resale price maintenance contracts against all dealers in a state when such a contract had been signed by any one of them. [DC]

nonbusiness marketing organization Nonbusiness entities are usually nonprofit institutions that can and do borrow marketing methods and organization structures from business. There is growing acceptance of the concept that nonprofit institutions, as well as for-profit businesses, serve markets (i.e., customers) and that their success depends on how well they understand and cater to the needs and wants of these markets. Nonbusiness organizations often set marketing goals that are similar to those of business except for the absence of the profit goal. Examples drawn from nonprofit colleges and hospitals and from military organizations will illustrate this point. A major marketing goal of a nonprofit college or hospital is to bring in the income needed to operate the institution. A supportive marketing goal is to attract the number of college students or hospital patients that will fully utilize the institution's facilities. Another supportive marketing goal is to raise specific amounts of money from contributors for capital projects. A military organization is funded by the government and does not raise money. A major marketing goal of the military is to meet recruiting quotas in terms of the quantity and quality of personnel needed to perform its mission. Like companies, nonbusiness institutions can use marketing functions to help in setting their goals such as market research, personal selling, advertising, sales promotion, and product planning and development. Comment: Some nonbusiness organizations are reluctant to use marketing terms for fear of appearing too commercial, although the term marketing is often used. But a salesperson may be called "college representative"; advertising may be called "communications." (See also **bureaucratic organization; centralized management, decentralized management; divisional organization; flat organization; functional organization; geographic organization; hierarchical organization; market management organization; marketing organization, forms of; matrix organization; multibusiness organization;** and **product management organization.**) [VPB]

noncoercive influence strategy A means of communication that focuses on the beliefs and attitudes of the target about general business issues. (See also **coercive influence strategy** and **influence strategy.**) [GLF]

noncompensatory rules In evaluating alternatives, noncompensatory rules suggest that positive and negative consequences of alternatives do not compensate for each other. The types of noncompensatory rules include the conjunctive rule, the disjunctive rule, and the lexicographic rule. The conjunctive rules suggests that consumers establish a minimum acceptable level for each choice criterion and accept an alternative only if it equals or exceeds the minimum cutoff level for every criterion. The disjunctive rule suggests that consumers establish acceptable standards for each criterion and accept an alternative if it exceeds the standard on at least one criterion. The lexicographic rule suggests that consumers rank choice criteria from most to least important and choose the best alternative on the most important criterion. (See also **choice rule, expectancy-value model,** and **piecemeal processing.**) [JPP/JCO]

noncooperative game theory See **game theoretic models**

noncoverage error A nonsampling error that arises because of a failure to include some units, or entire sections, of the defined survey population in the actual sampling frame. (See also **item nonresponse, nonobservation error, nonresponse error, not-at-home, observation error, office error, overcoverage error,** and **refusals.**) [GAC]

noncumulative quantity discount A discount granted for volume purchased (measured either in units or dollars) at a single point in time. (See also **quantity discount.**) [KM]

nondurable good A good that is (1) made from materials other than metals, hard plastics, and wood, (2) is rather quickly consumed or worn out, or (3) becomes dated, unfashionable, or in some other way no longer popular. This is an awkward term that includes a highly varied set of goods and is useful primarily as a contrast with durable goods. (See also **soft goods.**) [DW]

nongovernmental organization (NGO) An organization that is not a governmental agency seeking solutions to social problems. (See also **private nonprofit organization.**) [ARA]

nonlinear model See **Multiplicative Competitive Interaction model**

nonlinear programming See **advertising models** and **mathematical programming**

nonmonetary transaction A marketing exchange in which the costs paid by the target audience do not include a transfer of economic assets. [ARA]

nonobservation error A nonsampling error that arises because of nonresponse from some elements designated for inclusion in the sample. (See also **item nonresponse, noncoverage error, nonresponse error, not-at-home, observation error, office error, overcoverage error,** and **refusals.**)]GAC]

nonprice competition The act of vying for sales through better products, promotion, service, and convenience with only minor emphasis on price. [DLS]

nonprobability sample A sample that relies on personal judgment somewhere in the element selection process and therefore prohibits estimating the probability that any population element will be included in the sample. (See also **probability sample.**) [GAC]

nonprofit marketer An individual or organization conducting nonprofit marketing. [ARA]

nonprofit marketing The marketing of a product or service in which the offer itself is not intended to make a monetary profit for the marketer. Comment: Nonprofit marketing may be carried out by any organization or individual and may or may not be designed to have a positive social impact. A nonprofit marketer may undertake specific ventures that are for-profit, as when a museum markets reproductions or offers food and beverages at a profit; however, its overall objective does not involve making profit. A nonprofit marketer may be incorporated privately or may be a governmental (public) agency. [ARA]

nonresponse error A nonsampling error that represents a failure to obtain information from some elements of the population that were selected and designated for the sample. (See also **item nonresponse, noncoverage error, nonobservation error, not-at-home, observation error, office error, overcoverage error,** and **refusals.**) [GAC]

nonsampling error An error that arises in research that is not due to sampling;

nonsampling error can occur because of errors in conception, logic, misinterpretation of replies, statistics, arithmetic, and errors in tabulating or coding, or in reporting the results. (See also **item nonresponse, noncoverage error, nonobservation error, nonresponse error, not-at-home, observation error, office error, overcoverage error, refusals,** and **sampling error.**) [GAC]

nonselling area The floor space, other than selling area, used in the conduct of business in a store building or in remote service or warehouse buildings, including entrances, show windows, vertical transportation facilities, offices, air conditioning systems, alteration rooms, workrooms, repair shops, receiving and marking rooms, and stockrooms. [WRD]

nonselling department Any department of a store engaged in work other than direct selling of merchandise—e.g., receiving department. [WRD]

nonstore retailing A form of retailing in which consumer contact occurs outside the confines of the retail store, such as vending machines and electronic shopping, at home personal selling, and catalog buying. (See also **direct marketing, direct selling, direct selling establishment,** and **direct selling organization.**) [WRD]

nonverbal communications The nonspoken forms of expression communicating thought and emotions including body language, space between the communicators, speech, and appearance. [BAW]

norms The rules of behavior that are part of the ideology of the group. Norms tend to reflect the values of the group and specify those actions that are proper and those that are inappropriate, as well as the rewards for adherence and the punishment for nonconformity. (See also **culture** and **mores.**) [HHK/MCC]

North American Free Trade Agreement (NAFTA) An agreement between the U.S., Canada, and Mexico to remove barriers to the movement of goods and service. [WJK]

not-at-home A source of nonsampling error that arises when replies are not secured from some designated sampling units because the respondents are not at home when the interviewer calls. (See also **item nonresponse, noncoverage error, nonobservation error, nonresponse error, observation error, office error, overcoverage error,** and **refusals.**) [GAC]

NPV See **net present value technique**

NTBs See **non tariff barriers**

Nutrition Labeling and Education Act (1990) A federal act that seeks to make nutrition information more precise and understandable. (See also **consumer protection legislation** and **Food and Drug Administration.**) [DC]

objection A concern or question raised by a prospect to a salesperson. (See also **boomerang method, direct denial, feel-felt-found method, indirect denial, overcoming objections, pass up method,** and **postpone method.**) [BAW]

objective The desired or needed result to be achieved by a specific time. An objective is broader than a goal, and one objective can be broken down into a number of specific goals. Like goals, objectives serve to provide guidance, motivation, evaluation, and control. (See also **profit maximization objective.**) [GSD]

objective method See **objective-and-task budgeting**

objective-and-task budgeting An advertising budget method in which advertising expenditures are determined on the basis of a specific audit of the resources needed to achieve the specific objectives and tasks outlined in the advertiser's media plan. (See also **adaptive control budgeting, all-you-can-afford budgeting, competitive parity budgeting, payout budgeting,** and **percent-of-sales budgeting.**) [JE]

observation A method of data collection in which the situation of interest is watched and the relevant facts, actions, or behaviors recorded. [GAC]

observation error A nonsampling error that arises because inaccurate information is secured from the sample elements or because errors are introduced in the processing of the data or in reporting the findings. (See also **item nonresponse, noncoverage error, nonobservation errors, nonresponse error, not-at-home, office error, overcoverage error,** and **refusals.**) [GAC]

obsolescence The act or process of a product's becoming out-of-date, discarded, no longer in use. The rejection is for some reason other than being worn out or inoperable. It may apply to an individual item or to all of the items in a given class or group. The active verb form, less widely acceptable, is to obsolete or to make obsolete. (See also **planned obsolescence** and **shelf life.**) [DW]

occupancy functional expense See **functional expense classification**

OCR-A See **optical character recognition** and **universal product code**

odd lot Dealing with broken lots or unbalanced assortments reduced in price for quick turnover. [WRD]

odd price A price ending in an odd number (such as 57 cents or 63 cents), or a price just under some round number (such as $98 instead of $100). (See also **odd-even pricing.**) [WRD]

odd-even pricing A form of psychological pricing that suggests buyers are more sensitive to certain ending digits. Odd price refers to a price ending in an odd number (e.g., 1,3,5,7,9), or to a price just under a round number (e.g., $0.89, $3.99, $44.98). Even price refers to a price ending in a whole number or in tenths (e.g., $0.50, $5.00, $8.10, $75.00). [KM]

OECD See **Organization of Economic Cooperation and Development**

OEM See **original equipment manufacturer**

off-invoice allowance A type of trade sales promotion in which the manufacturer offers the retailer a price reduction on the product price at the time of billing, generally for a limited period of time. [DES/BEB]

off-price shopping center A shopping center specializing in off-price retail tenants such as T.J. Maxx or Burlington Coat Factory. (See also **arcade shopping center, community shopping center, factory outlet center, mall-type shopping center, neighborhood shopping center, regional shopping center, strip-type shopping center,** and **super regional shopping center.**) [WRD]

off-retail percentage The markdown as a percentage of the original price. For example, an item originally retails for $10 and is marked down to $5; the off-retail percentage is 50%. [WRD]

offer The terms and conditions (price, quantity, delivery date, shipping costs, guarantee, etc.) under which a product or service is presented for sale to potential customers in direct response advertising. (See also **infomercial.**) [JE]

office equipment See **equipment**

office error A nonsampling error that arises in the processing of data because of errors in editing, coding, tabulation, or in some other part of the analysis. (See also **item nonresponse, noncoverage error, nonobservation error, nonresponse error, not-at-home, observation error, overcoverage error,** and **refusals.**) [GAC]

oligopolistic competition A market condition in which only a few large sellers vie and collectively account for a relatively large market share. (See also **duopoly, imperfect competition, monopolistic competition, monopoly, monopsony, oligopolistic environment, oligopoly, oligopsony, perfect competition, pure competition,** and **workable competition.**) [DLS]

oligopolistic environment A market situation in which only a few large firms compete in either buying or selling in the market. (See also **duopoly, imperfect competition, monopolistic competition, monopoly, monopsony, oligopolistic competition, oligopoly, oligopsony, perfect competition, pure competition,** and **workable competition.**) [DLS]

oligopoly A market situation in which there are so few sellers that each anticipates the impact of its marketing actions on all competitors. The products can be either differentiated or undifferentiated. (See also **differentiated oligopoly, duopoly, imperfect competition, monopolistic competition, monopoly, monopsony, oligopolistic competition, oligopolistic environment, oligopsony, perfect competition, pure competition, undifferentiated oligopoly,** and **workable competition.**) [DLS]

oligopsony A market situation in which there are so few buyers that each anticipates the impact of its marketing actions on the others. (See also **duopoly, imperfect competition, monopolistic competition, monopoly, monopsony, oligopolistic competition, oligopolistic environment, oligopoly, perfect competition, pure competition,** and **workable competition.**) [DLS]

omnibus panel See **panel (omnibus)**

on order When the retailer has ordered merchandise and it has not been received, it is considered to be on order and thus a commitment against a planned purchase figure. Thus, the open-to-buy figure is affected by the amount of the on order dollars [WRD]

on-pack premium A gift attached to the product or product package in some way such as banding, taping, or other adhesive. It is used to influence product purchase or reward the purchaser. (See also **in-pack premium, near-pack premium,** and **premium.**) [DES/BEB]

on-percentage The result of multiplying together the complements of a given series of discount percentages. To find the net merchandise price, the list price is multiplied by the on-percentage. (See also **chain discount.**) [WRD]

one hundred percent location The retail site in a major business district that has the greatest exposure to a retail store's target market customers. [WRD]

one price policy A policy that, at a given time, all customers pay the same price for any given item of merchandise. (See also **single price policy/store** and **variable price policy.**) [WRD]

one price retailer A store that offers all merchandise at a fixed price, the same to all customers, as opposed to bargaining or negotiating a price. [WRD]

one-stage area sampling See **area sampling**

one-stage cluster sampling See **cluster sample**

OPEC See **Organization of Petroleum Exporting Countries**

open account The sale of goods on credit. The seller gives the buyer no written evidence of indebtedness; instead the seller debits the buyer's account; open credit. [WRD]

open bid See **bidding**

open credit See **open account**

open dating The practice of putting onto a product information that reveals the date beyond which it should no longer be sold or used. This applies primarily to perishable products, those that lose some important attribute over time while awaiting sale in the channel between maker and user. Open dating is common to certain industries (for example, dairy products and pharmaceuticals) and is sometimes mandated by law. [DW]

open order An order sent by a store to a market representative to be placed with whatever vendor the latter finds can best fill it. In department store buying, it is the authority granted to a resident buyer to purchase merchandise required by the store. [WRD]

open rate The highest rate charged for space or time by an advertising vehicle. (See also **flat rate.**) [JE]

open stock The items kept on hand in retail stores and sold either in complete sets or in separate pieces—e.g., china, glassware. (See also **closed stock.**) [WRD]

open-code dating A date marked on food products to indicate the last day that the food can be sold in the store. It sometimes indicates use dates. (See also **open-date labeling.**) [WRD]

open-date labeling A date marked on food products to indicate the last day that the food can be sold in the store. (See also **open-code dating.**) [WRD]

open-ended question A question characterized by the condition that respondents are free to reply in their own words rather than being limited to choosing from among a set of alternatives. (See also **fixed-alternative question.**) [GAC]

open-to-buy (OTB) The residual balance of current purchase allotments; total planned purchases for a period, less receipts and merchandise on order. [WRD]

open-to-buy report A statement of existing or expected relations between dollar inventory and sales, used to calculate open-to-buy amounts. [WRD]

operant conditioning The process of altering the probability of a behavior being emitted by changing the consequences of the behavior. [JPP/JCO]

operating items See **maintenance, repair, and operating items and supplies**

operating leases See **leasing**

operational definition A definition of a construct that describes the operations to be carried out in order for the construct to be measured empirically. (See also **constitutive definition.**) [GAC]

opinion A belief or emotionally neutral cognition the individual holds about some aspect or object in the environment. Those things he/she "knows" to be true have been defined as knowledge and those things he/she "thinks" are true or he/she is "pretty sure are true" are defined as opinions. [HHK/MCC]

opinion leader Not all individuals in a group or all consumers in a society wield equal personal influence on the attitudes, opinions, and behavior of others. The most influential are termed the opinion leaders; the ones to whom others turn for advice and information. (See also **early adopters, innovators, personal influence,** and **two step flow of communication.**) [HKK/MCC]

opinions See **AIO** and **life style**

opportunities and threats analysis See **situation analysis**

opportunity cost The cost attributable to doing a thing caused by foregone opportunities that are sacrificed in order to do this one thing. [DLS]

optical character recognition (OCR-A) An industry-wide classification system for coding information onto merchandise. It enables retailers to record information on each SKU, when it is sold, and transmit the information to a computer. [WRD]

optimization models See **distribution models, marketing mix models, mathematical programming, POSSE,** and **sales force models**

option A contract that allows the holder to buy or sell a specific stock at a fixed price at or before a stated maturity date. [PFA]

options pricing models A class of models designed to calculate the value of an option. Comment: The empirical adequacy of these models is an unresolved issue in financial economics. [PFA]

order entry The order entry phase is the beginning phase of the order cycle process. Order entry refers to the process of actually entering an order into the seller's order processing system. This may be done by a salesperson writing an order, a customer ordering by phone, a telemarketing solicitation, or by the buyer's computer communicating directly with the seller's computer, as in an electronic data interchange (EDI) system. [DJB/BJL]

order needs See **hierarchy of needs**

order processing The system of the firm that generally refers to the way orders are recorded by the firm and how this information is used to provide customer service and manage various functional elements of the business. It includes the management of the order entry process as well as the information flows that surround and support the order fulfillment objectives of the firm. [DJB/BJL]

order register A form or computerized record of orders placed with vendors. It includes the date of each order, the name of the vendor, the total amount of each order, the month in which shipment is to be made, the amount to be delivered each month, and a serial number. [WRD]

order-shipping-billing cycle This describes the paperwork or information cycle of the order processing system. [DJB/BJL]

ordering See **channel flows**

ordering procedures See **buygrid framework**

ordinal scale A measurement in which numbers are assigned to attributes of objects or classes of objects to reflect the order (for example, more than, greater than) of the objects. (See also **comparative rating scale, constant sum method, graphic-rating scale, Guttman scale, interval scale, itemized rating scale, nominal scale, ratio scale, Stapel scale,** and **summated rating.**) [GAC]

ordinary dating This is illustrated by such terms as "1/10, net 30" of "2/10, net 60." The two specified time elements are the cash discount and the net credit period. The cash discount may be deducted if the bill is paid within the discount period (10 days in both examples); otherwise, the full amount is due at the end of the credit period (30 and 60 days in the examples given). Both the cash discount and the net credit periods are usually counted from the date of the invoice. (See also **advance dating, dating, end of month dating, extra dating, future dating, memorandum purchase and dating, proximo dating, receipt-of-goods dating,** and **season dating.**) [WRD]

organization When used as a noun, organization implies the framework or structure within which people are assigned to positions and their work coordinated in order to carry out plans and achieve goals. [VPB]

organization by selling function See **horizontal structure of the sales organization**

organization by type of customer See **horizontal structure of the sales organization**

organization by type of product See **horizontal structure of the sales organization**

organization chart A visual representation of an organization structure. It identifies the organizational unit and portrays each position in relation to others. Positions are usually represented by squares or rectangles (although circles or ovals are sometimes used) that contain the position title; they may show the name of the incumbent as well. Each position is connected by a solid line running to the immediate supervisor and to positions supervised, if any. Broken or dotted lines may be used to show other than line relationships (e.g., advisory or functional). Comment: Some managers eschew organization charts because they like open and informal relationships among persons of different rank. They believe that an organization charts is inhibiting in this respect. Others believe it is the manager's style and not the organization chart that determines the degree of open and informal relationships. They see the organization chart as a useful device for assisting employees in understanding the organization and their role in it. [VPB]

Organization of Economic Cooperation and Development (OECD) An organization that came into being on September 30, 1961, succeeding the OEEC with the objectives to promote policies designed to achieve the highest sustainable economic growth and employment and a rising standard of living in member countries while maintaining financial stability. [WJK]

Organization of Petroleum Exporting Countries (OPEC) An association of countries formed in 1960 for the purpose of promoting the interests of the oil exporting countries. Member countries include Algeria, Bahrain, Brunei, Ecuador, Gabon, Indonesia, Iran, Iraq, Kuwait, Libya, Nigeria, Oman, Qatar, Saudi Arabia, Trinidad and Tobago, United Arab Emirates, and Venezuela. [WJK]

organization structure The formal and informal framework within which people work to achieve organization objectives. It includes the establishment of positions along with descriptions of their duties, responsibilities, authority, reporting relationships, and assignment to groups. Organization charts are used to show where positions fit within the structure. (See also **position description.**) [VPB]

organizational behavior The management theory and practice relating to how and why people behave as they do within organization structures and how managers can bring about improvements in individual and group performance. [VPB]

organizational buyer behavior See **buyer behavior**

organizational buying behavior The buying decision-making process of an organization rather than by an individual customer. Organizational buying behavior differs from consumer buying behavior in that (a) normally, multiple individuals are involved, (b) buying decision rules or standards may be applicable, and (c) purchases occur as a result of derived demand. [GLL/DTW]

organizational buying sales promotion See **sales promotion, in organizational buying**

organizational climate The general internal organizational environment that is determined by the organization's structure, leadership, philosophy, technology, people, and culture. [WL/MBC]

organizational market This market consists of industrial markets, reseller markets, and government markets. Industrial buyers buy goods and services to aid them in producing other goods and services (derived demand). Resellers buy goods and services to resell them at a profit. Government agencies buy goods and services to carry out mandated governmental functions. [GLL/DTW]

organized market A group of traders operating under recognized rules in buying and selling a single commodity or related commodities; a commodity exchange. [WRD]

original equipment See **parts**

original equipment manufacturer (OEM) This organization purchases industrial goods in order to incorporate them into other products that are sold in the industrial market (business market) or ultimate consumer market. For example, IBM, acting as an OEM, buys microprocessors for its personal computers from Intel. [GLL/DTW]

original retail The first price at which merchandise is offered for sale, accounted for as the retail value of receipts. [WRD]

OSD See **over, short, and damage**

OTB See **open-to-buy**

other-directedness A mode of conformity to the culture in which one draws values and beliefs from the peer group rather than from the family group. Tradition-directedness, inner-directedness, and other-directedness are part of the conceptualization of David Riesman in his monograph *The Lonely Crowd.* (See also **social character** and **VALS.**) [HHK/MCC]

out sizes The sizes that are either very large or very small and, if offered at all, are offered in very limited depth because of the thin market demand for them. Some stores specialize in fringe sizes or out sizes—e.g., tall women's shops, petite size shops. (See also **end sizes.**) [WRD]

out supplier A firm not currently supplying the company nor currently on its approved vendor list. [GLL/DTW]

out-flow See **cash flow**

out-of-stock costs The costs that can be directly or indirectly attributed to not having a product available when the buyer wants to purchase the product. They may include cost of lost future sales. (DJB/BJL]

outcome evaluation See **impact evaluation**

outlet store 1. A store specializing in job lots and clearance merchandise. 2. A store controlled by a vendor to dispose of surplus stocks or for other reasons to be in the retail business. (See also **factory outlet center.**) [WRD]

outlier An observation so different in magnitude from the rest of the observations that the analyst chooses to treat it as a special case. [GAC]

outlined presentation A systematic sales presentation that lists the most important sales points that a salesperson needs to make. (See also **canned sales presentation; customized sales presentation; need satisfaction selling; presentation, sales;** and **stimulus response sales approach.**) [BAW]

output evaluation measure An objective measure of sales force performance including number of orders; average size of orders; number of canceled orders; and number of active, new, lost, overdue, and prospective accounts. (See also **unput evaluation measure, ratio of output and/or input measures,** and **sales force evaluation.**) [AJD]

outshopping A practice whereby residents of smaller communities travel to larger communities to shop when prices become too high or assortments are not available in the smaller communities. A situation in which customers are shopping in other areas because their needs are not being met locally. [WRD]

outside salesperson See **field salesperson**

over, short, and damage (OSD) A traditional term used in transportation and warehousing to describe an inventory situation. After a physical inventory, it is possible to be "over" (have too much in inventory), be "short" (have a shortage of inventory), or have damaged inventory that is not usable. The same term may be applied to a shipment received by the buyer or an intermediary. It may be an accounting adjustment in some systems. [DJB/BJL]

over-the-counter remedies See **proprietary drugs**

overage The amount by which a physical inventory exceeds the book inventory figures, as opposed to shortage. It also may refer to cash excess. [WRD]

overbought 1. A condition in which a buyer has become committed to purchases in excess of planned purchase allotment for a merchandising period. 2. The purchase of merchandise in excess of demand. [WRD]

overcoming objections The process of successfully handling reasons given by prospects for not buying the salesperson's offering. (See also **boomerang method, direct denial, feel-felt- found method, indirect denial, objection, pass up method,** and **postpone method.**) [BAW]

overcoverage error A nonsampling error that arises because of the duplication of elements in the list of sampling units. (See also **item nonresponse, noncoverage error, nonobservation error, nonresponse error, not-at-home, observation error, office error,** and **refusals.** [GAC]

overhead costs See **common costs**

overprivileged family A family in a social class that has more than enough money to purchase the necessities, i.e., shelter, clothing, and transportation, appropriate for its class status. An overprivileged family is able to acquire luxuries above and beyond daily living expenses and usually is defined as having 25 to 30 percent greater income than the median for the social class. (See also **underprivileged family.**) [HHK/MCC]

overstored A market condition that exists when a geographic market area has too many stores to yield a fair return on investment for many of them. (See also **understored.**) [WRD]

ownership See **channel flows**

ownership utility See **possession utility**

package The container used to protect, promote, transport, and/or identify a product. The package may vary from a plastic band wrap to a steel or wooden box or drum. It may be primary (contains the product), secondary (contains one or more primary packages), or tertiary (contains one or more secondary packages). (See also **bonus pack, bounce back offer, flagging, in-pack premium, multiple packaging, multiple-unit packaging, near-pack premium, on-pack premium, price off, proof-of-purchase,** and **reusable container.**) [DW]

package delivery service A transportation service offering that requires packages to conform to specified size and weight restrictions. The packages may be moved by ground or air transportation, within a variety of delivery schedules. Prominent package delivery service carriers include Federal Express (FedEx), United Parcel Service (UPS), and the U.S. Postal Service. [DJB/BJL]

packaged good A good that is usually sold in smaller packages, carries a low unit price, is distributed through food and drug stores, is heavily promoted (usually in mass media), and is bought and consumed frequently. [DW]

packaging The process by which packages are created. Occasionally, it is used as synonymous with package. [DW]

paid circulation See **circulation**

pallet A platform usually made out of wood, but also made out of other materials, upon which product is stacked to provide a unit load in the transportation and distribution system. [DJB/BJL]

palming off A practice in which a retailer represents merchandise as being made by a firm other than the true manufacturer. [WRD]

panel (omnibus) A sample of respondents who are measured repeatedly over time but on variables that change from measurement to measurement. [GAC]

panel (true) A sample of respondents who are measured repeatedly over time with respect to the same variables. [GAC]

PAR ROI A regression model based on the PIMS program data that relates ROI (return on investment) to a set of independent variables. PAR ROI specifies the ROI and associated cash flow that could be expected for a business with a given market position, competitive conditions, and other specified conditions. In addition to allowing a comparison of PAR (based on the businesses in the PIMS program sample used for analysis) and actual ROI, the model allows the identification of the impact on ROI that various factors (such as attractiveness of the business environment, strength of competitive position, effectiveness of use of investment, etc.) will have (Day 1986, pp. 115–166). [DCS/YJW]

parallel barter See **counterpurchase**

parallel pricing The practice of following the pricing practices of other organizations, particularly competitors. [KM]

parallel trading See **counterpurchase**

parasite store A store that lives on existing traffic flow that originates from circumstances other than its own promotional effort, store personality, merchandising effort, or customer service. [WRD]

Parfitt-Collins model A model for predicting the market share of a new product, based on early panel data sales results. The model views market share as the product of three quantities: the brand's penetration level (i.e., proportion of buyers of this product class who try this brand), the brand's repeat purchase rate (i.e., the proportion of repurchases going to this brand by consumers who once purchased this brand), and the buying-rate index of repeat purchasers of this brand (where the average rate across consumers = 1.0. This index shows the extent to which the consumer is a relatively heavy buyer (rate > 1.0) or light buyer (rate < 1.0) of the product category). (Parfitt and Collins 1968). Panel data are used to make a projection over time for each of these quantities, from which the ultimate market share is calculated. (See also **new product forecasting models.**) [DCS/YJW]

partially integrated division This division contains production and marketing functions except for sales. Personal selling is provided by a centralized sales organization selling the products of two or more divisions. A centralized sales organization can be more cost effective when the divisions produce products that are sold to similar markets through the same channels of distribution. (See also **centralized sales organization; decentralized sales organization**; **full-line sales organization**; **sales organization, forms of**; **sales organization specialized by account**; **sales organization specialized by market**; and **sales organization specialized by product.**) [VPB]

parts Manufactured products such as bicycle sprockets and lenses that are bought as components of other goods being produced. Parts are often sold simultaneously in industrial channels (original equipment) and in consumer channels for replacement purposes. (See also **industrial products** and **semimanufactured goods.**) [DW]

parts, component See **component parts**

party selling 1. A direct selling approach that involves demonstrating and selling products to a group of consumers attending a party at a neighbor's or friend's house. [BAW] 2. A practice in which salespeople arrange to have a party in a home, at which merchandise is demonstrated to a group of the host's or hostess' friends. [WRD]

pass strategy A public relations strategy designed to move past government policy makers, public interest groups, and other special interest gatekeepers in order to communicate directly with the public at large. [DES/BEB]

pass up method A method used by salespeople to respond to a prospect objection by letting the prospect talk, acknowledging that the concern was heard, and then moving on to another topic without trying to resolve the concern. (See also **boomerang method, direct denial**, **feel-felt-found method, indirect denial,** and **postpone method.**) [BAW]

pass-along deal A seller's offer in which an item of value such as a price reduction, gift, premium, coupon, etc., is offered to the intermediary channel member with the intent that the incentive be re-offered to others in the channel. (See also **trade sales promotion**.) [DES/BEB]

pass-along readers The members of the audience of a print media vehicle who do not subscribe to the publication but obtain their copies from people who do subscribe. They are also called secondary readers in contrast to subscribers, who are called primary readers. [JE]

pass-through rate The number or percentage of sales promotion incentives offered to wholesalers or retailers by manufacturers that are extended to consumers by those channel members. (See also **trade sales promotion.**) [DES/BEB]

paste-up See **mechanical**

patent 1. (product development definition) The legal right of exclusive use and license granted by a government to the person who invents something. An invention is patentable if it is a useful, novel, and nonobvious process, machine, manufacture, or composition of matter. [DW] 2. (legislative definition) Patents (and patent laws) provide the owner the exclusive right to produce and sell the invention for a period of seventeen years. Patents are considered incentives to inventors, and the law recognizes the inherent inconsistency between antitrust laws, which are designed to foster competition, and patent laws, which restrict competition. [DC]

patent medicines See **proprietary drugs**

patronage discount The offering of a price reduction based on previous customer relationship or preferred customer standing. Such a discount is usually offered because of an established relationship between the seller and buyer. (See also **cumulative quantity discount**.) [KM]

patronage dividend Any surplus accrued from the spread between prevailing market prices and cost of merchandise and store operation that is paid to members (of a cooperative) in proportion to their volume of purchases. [WRD]

patronage motives The motives that drive an individual toward selection of a particular outlet, retailer, or supplier of services. [HHK/MCC]

pay, of salespeople See **sales force compensation**

payback The time, usually in years, from the point of full scale market introduction of a new product until it has recovered its costs of development and marketing. The market testing stage is usually considered to be a part of the evaluation process (and not in the payback period), but if a market rollout is used, practice varies on when the payback period should begin. [DW]

payment See **channel flows**

payment time and conditions See **price structure**

payout budgeting An advertising budget method in which advertising expenses are treated as part of the investment required to establish a new product. (See also **adaptive control budgeting, all-you-can-afford budgeting, competitive parity budgeting, objective-and-task budgeting**, and **percent-of-sales budgeting**.) [JE]

penetration price policy A pricing policy that sets a low initial price in an attempt to increase market share rapidly. This policy is effective if demand is perceived to be fairly elastic. (See also **skimming price policy**.) [DLS]

penetration pricing The strategy of setting a product's price relatively low in order to generate a high sales volume. This strategy is commonly associated with pricing new products that do not have identifiable price-market segments. [KM]

peoplemeter A device used to measure when a TV is on, to what channel it is tuned, and who in the household is watching it; each member in a household is assigned a viewing number that the individual is supposed to enter into the peoplemeter whenever the set is turned on, the channel is switched, or the person enters or leaves the room. [GAC]

per capita income A nation's total income divided by the number of persons in its population. Gross national product is a popular, but technically incorrect, surrogate for total income. [DLS]

***per se* illegality** An act that is illegal by, of, for, or in itself. [DLS]

***per se* rules:** 1. (legislative definition) Rules that define clear cut business violations. For example, restraint upon price competition when sought to be effected by combination or conspiracy is *per se* unlawful. [DC] 2. (economic definition) A rule under which the prosecution needs to show only that the alleged act was performed. (See also **rule of reason**.) [DLS]

perceived conflict A situation in which one channel member perceives another channel member(s) to be engaged in behavior that is preventing or impeding the attainment of its goals. (See also **affective conflict, latent conflict,** and **manifest conflict**.) [GLF]

perceived equity The degree to which a salesperson believes that he or she is being rewarded fairly for his or her level of performance relative to his or her peers. [AJD]

perceived quality The amount of quality buyers believe a product or service has. Perceived quality is usually based on some information or cues about the product, e.g., its price, brand name, or country of origin. [KM]

perceived risk 1. (consumer behavior definition) The expected negative consequences of performing an action such as purchasing a product. [JPP/JCO] 2. (consumer behavior definition) Most, if not all, decisions contain some risk, be it monetary, physical, psychological, or social. The degree of risk that is perceived to exist by the individual making a purchase or behavioral decision has been termed perceived risk in the consumer behavior literature. [HHK/MCC]

perceived role accuracy The degree to which the salesperson's perception of role set member demands—particularly company superiors—is accurate. [AJD]

perceived role ambiguity The degree to which a salesperson feels he or she does not have the information necessary to perform the job adequately. The salesperson may be uncertain about what some role set members expect of him or her in certain situations, how he or she should go about satisfying those expectations, or how his or her performance will be evaluated and rewarded. [AJD]

perceived role conflict The degree to which a salesperson believes that the role demands of two or more members of his or her role set are incompatible. [AJD]

perceived role overload The degree to which a salesperson believes that he or she has more to accomplish than is possible given the time available. [AJD]

perceived-value pricing A method of pricing in which the seller attempts to set price at the level that the intended buyers value the product. It is also called value-in-use pricing or value-oriented pricing. (See also **demand-oriented pricing.**) [KM]

percent-of-sales budgeting An advertising budget method in which advertising expenses are established as a fixed percentage of past, current, or future sales levels. (See also **adaptive control budgeting, all-you-can-afford budgeting, competitive parity budgeting, objective-and-task budgeting**, and **payout budgeting.**) [JE]

perception Based on prior attitudes, beliefs, needs, stimulus factors, and situational determinants, individuals perceive objects, events, or people in the world about them. Perception is the cognitive impression that is formed of "reality" which in turn influences the individual's actions and behavior toward that object. (See also **cognition**.) [HHK/MCC]

perceptual threshold See **subliminal perception**

perfect competition A market model that assumes pure competition plus perfect knowledge, perfect freedom of movement, and perfect substitutability of the factors of production. (See also **duopoly, imperfect competition, monopolistic competition, monopoly, monopsony, oligopolistic competition, oligopolistic environment, oligopoly, oligopsony,** and **workable competition.**) [DLS]

performance monitoring See **planning**

performance objectives See **planning**

performance review See **buygrid framework**

periodic inventory system An inventory system in which orders are placed at scheduled intervals (e.g., first day of month) but the amount of product ordered will be variable. [DJB/BJL]

peripheral route to persuasion One of two types of cognitive processes by which persuasion occurs. In the peripheral route, the consumer does not focus on the product message in an ad but on other stimuli such as attractive or well-known celebrities or popular music. The presence of these other stimuli may change the consumer's beliefs and attitudes about the product. (See also **central route to persuasion.**) [JPP/JCO]

perishable merchandise See **distress merchandise**

permanent income hypothesis A hypothesis that postulates that consumption patterns are relatively stable over time, or that consumer expenditures are based on average income expectations over time. [WL/MBC]

perpetual inventory system A stock control system that is designed to keep continuous track of all additions and deletions to inventory. (See also **automatic reordering system** and **book inventory**.) [DJB/BJL]

person marketing Marketing designed to influence target audiences to behave in some positive manner with respect to the positions, products, or services associated with a specific person. Comment: Attempts by an individual or organization to educate target audiences or change their attitudes about a person are not marketing. (See also **public relations**.) [ARA]

personal consumption expenditure The aggregate amount spent each year by consumers to buy goods and services from the marketplace. [DLS]

personal disposable income Current

money income less all taxes and money spent for the purchase of necessities. (See also **discretionary buying power, disposable personal income, national income, personal income,** and **real income.**) [DLS]

personal finance company See **consumer finance company**

personal goal setting See **behavioral self-management**

personal income 1. The national income adjusted for corporate profits and government transfer payments. 2. The current income received by persons from all sources less contributions for social insurance—e.g., Social Security. (See also **discretionary buying power, disposable personal income, money income, personal disposable income,** and **real income.**) [DLS]

personal influence The influence of one individual upon another in face-to-face interactions. It is the informal social influence transmitted among peers. (See also **opinion leader** and **two step flow of communication.**) [HHK/MCC]

personal interview A direct, face-to-face conversation between a representative of the research organization (the interviewer) and a respondent or interviewee. (See also **depth interview** and **focus group interview.**) [GAC]

personal judgment See **screening of ideas**

personal relationships in organizational buying Personal relationships in business marketing have a strong influence on organizational buying behavior. Positive or negative relationships between members of the buying and selling organizations often represent the deciding factor in supplier's choice. [GLL/DTW]

personal savings 1. (environments definition) That part of disposable personal income that is not used for current consumption purposes. [WL/MBC] 2. (economic definition) That part of disposable personal income that is not spent on taxes or consumption. (See also **savings.**) [DLS]

personal selling Selling that involves a face-to-face interaction with the customer. (See also **promotion mix.**) [BAW]

personal selling activities See **promotional campaign**

personality An individual's consistency in coping with one's environment. Personality is the consistent pattern of responses to the stimuli from both internal and external sources. It is this consistency of response that allows us to type people as aggressive or submissive, as obnoxious or charismatic. The particular theory or philosophy of motivation and personality held by scholars in this field colors their views, research, and even definitions of the term. Nevertheless, "a consistent pattern of responses in coping with perceived reality" is a good working definition. [HHK/MCC]

persuading current users to increase usage See **market penetration strategy**

persuasion The changes in consumers' beliefs and attitudes caused by promotion communications. (See also **central route to persuasion** and **peripheral route to persuasion.**) [JPP/JCO]

phantom freight This occurs in basing-point pricing when the seller quotes a delivered price that includes a freight charge greater than the actual transportation costs. [KM]

pharmacy See **apothecary**

physical distribution A concept or approach to managing the finished goods inventory of the firm. Typically it includes transportation, warehousing, inventory, and order processing functions of the firm. [DJB/BJL]

physical distribution agency The third party provider that supports the physical distribution objectives of the firm. This may include transportation companies, public warehousing companies, and companies that manage information flows between buyer and seller as third party intermediaries. [DJB/BJL]

physical distribution manager This manager (increasingly referred to as logistics manager) plans the flow of materials in a manufacturing organization (beginning with raw materials and ending with delivery of finished products to channel intermediaries or end customers) and coordinates the work of departments involved in the process, such as procurement, transportation, manufacturing, finance, legal, and marketing. In the more limited marketing sense, physical distribution management is concerned with the efficient movement of finished product from the end of the production line to customers. This is usually a staff position, reporting to corporate or division management, with the functional authority needed to coordinate the execution of distribution plans by functional departments so as to provide good customer service at acceptable cost. [VPB]

physical inventory An inventory determined by actual count and evidenced by a listing of quantity, weight, or measure. It is usually compiled in dollars as well as units. [WRD]

physical perceived risk See **perceived risk**

physical possession See **channel flows**

physiological balance See **homeostasis**

physiological motives The needs that must be satisfied if the organism is to survive. These are the basic biological drives such as the need for food and air, relief of pain, bowel and bladder, and other basic physiological processes. The sex drive, although driven by hormones and other biological processes, is heavily overladen with social needs and drives and hence can be classified as either a physiological or a social drive. (See also **consumer motivation** and **hierarchy of needs.**) [HHK/MCC]

physiological needs See **Maslow's need hierarchy** and **physiological motives**

physiological reaction technique A method of assessing attitudes in which the researcher monitors the subject's response, by electrical or mechanical means, to the controlled introduction of some stimulus. [GAC]

piecemeal processing A cognitive process in which an individual considers each piece of information separately in order to arrive at an evaluation. This type of processing is fairly effortful and is based on the assumption that each piece of information has some subjective value and that the individual somehow combines the pieces of information to determine the overall value. Information Processing Theory approaches traditionally assume this type of processing. Piecemeal processing is an alternative to category-based processing. (See also **attitude, choice rule, conjunctive rule, disjunctive rule, lexicographic rule,** and **noncompensatory rules.**) [HHK/MCC]

piggyback The transportation of highway trailers or detachable trailer bodies on special rail cars designed for this service. This type of service usually involves a combination rail-highway movement of goods. (See also **con-**

tainer-on-flatcar, intermodal transportation, and **trailer-on-faltcar.**) [DJB/BJL]

piggyback marketing An arrangement whereby one manufacturer obtains distribution of products through another's distribution channels. [WJK]

pilferage The stealing of a store's merchandise. (See also **protection department, security,** and **shoplifting.**) [WRD]

PIMS Program Operated by The Strategic Planning Institute (SPI), the PIMS Program provides individual companies with a data base describing the financial and market performance of over 2,800 businesses. Each business can extract information about the experience of their strategic peers (i.e., businesses facing similar strategic positions but possibly in different industries). Three basic sets of variables have been found to account for 75 to 80 percent of the variance in profitability and cash flow in the sample of businesses: (1) the competitive position of the business, as measured by market share and relative product quality; (2) the production structure, including investment intensity and productivity of operations; and (3) the relative attractiveness of the served market, comprising the growth and customers' characteristics. [GSD]

pioneer selling Selling a new and different product, service, or idea. In this situation, it is often difficult for salespeople to establish a need in the buyer's mind. [BAW]

pioneering advantage See **first-mover advantage**

pioneering innovativeness A strategy of trying to be the first to market new types of products. The highest order of innovativeness (others are adapting, emulating, and imitating), it is often based on technical breakthroughs. [DW]

pioneering stage A nonspecific period early in the life cycle of a new type of product during which the pioneers are trying to build primary demand for the product type more than secondary demand for their particular brands. [DW]

pioneering strategy See **product adaptation**

pipeline A line of pipe connecting shipper and intermediate point or end user. Pipelines are used primarily for shipment of liquids such as oil and gas. [DJB/BJL]

place marketing Marketing designed to influence target audiences to behave in some positive manner with respect to the products or services associated with a specific place. Comment: Attempts by an individual or organization to educate target audiences or change their attitudes about a place are not marketing. (See also **public relations.**) [ARA]

place utility The increased usefulness created by marketing through making a product available at the place consumers want. (See also **possession utility** and **time utility.**) [DLS]

planned buying See **planned buying vs. unplanned buying**

planned buying vs. unplanned buying Planned buying is purchasing activity undertaken with a problem previously recognized and a buying intention previously formed. Most organizational buying is planned buying. Unplanned buying is buying activity that occurs as a result of exposure to an advertisement or a salesperson's visit. Trial of new supplies or consumable supplies may begin as unplanned buying. (See also **impulse buying.**) [GLL/DTW]

planned economy 1. (economic definition) An economy in which a governmental authority decides what, when, and how much is to be produced and distributed. (See also **market economy.**) [DLS] 2. (environments definition) An economy in which a central authority makes economic decisions, as contrasted with a market economy. [WL/MBC]

planned obsolescence A product strategy that seeks new products to make prior products obsolete. It usually is applied to a product category in which annual product changes make prior years' models less desirable. [DW]

planned stock The dollar amount of merchandise a buyer desires to have on hand at a given time in a certain department, merchandise classification, price line, or other control unit. [WRD]

planned urban development A totally conceived and supervised community including housing, retail, and business activity. [WRD]

planning See **adaptive planning**

planning horizon See **planning**

planogram A visual plan showing the physical allocation of product display space within a product grouping used for standardizing merchandise presentation. [WRD]

PLC See **product life cycle**

plus-one dialing A technique used in studies employing telephone interviews in which a single randomly determined digit is added to numbers selected from the telephone directory. (See also **random digit dialing.**) [GAC]

PMSA See **primary metropolitan statistical area**

point of diminishing return That point at which total production begins to increase at a decreasing rate with successive application of inputs. (See also **diminishing return, law of diminishing return,** and **point of negative return.**) [DLS]

point of negative return That point at which total production decreases absolutely with successive applications of inputs. (See also **diminishing return,** and **point of diminishing return.) [DLS]**

point of sale transfer Payment for retail purchases by using an electronic funds transfer card. [WL/MBC]

point size The unit of measure of printing type. One point is 1/72 of an inch. The most easily read body copy is presented in 10- or 12-point type. [JE]

point system See **sales volume quota**

point-of-purchase (POP) Promotional materials placed at the contact sales point designed to attract consumer interest or call attention to a special offer. [DES/BEB]

point-of-purchase advertising Advertising usually in the form of window and/or interior displays in establishments where a product is sold to the ultimate consumer. [WRD]

point-of-purchase display On- and off-shelf display material or product stocking generally at the retail level that is used to call special attention to the featured product. It is sometimes referred to as point-of-sale display. (See also **display.**) [DES/BEB]

point-of-sale (POS) A data collection system that electronically receives and stores bar code information derived from sales transactions. [DJB/BJL]

point-of-sale display See **display** and **point-of-purchase display**

Poisson process See **probability mixture model**

polarity of retail trade A trend in retailing that indicates that the predominant retailing institutions are on one hand (pole) mass distribution outlets and, on the other hand (pole), specialty, single-line, boutique type retail institutions. [WRD]

policy adjustment An exception to the usual complaint adjustment practice or policy that is made nevertheless for the purpose of retaining the customer's goodwill. [WRD]

political environment The government/business surroundings that affect and shape market opportunities, including government's role as both a controller through legislation and regulation and as a customer of business. (See also **cultural environment, demographic environment, economic environment,** and **natural environment**.) [WL/MBC]

political marketing Marketing designed to influence target audiences to vote for a particular person, party, or proposition. Attempts by an individual or organization only to educate or change attitudes are not political marketing. (See also **lobbying.**) [ARA]

political risk The risk of change in government policy that would adversely impact a company's ability to operate effectively and profitably. [WJK]

political unification See **political union**

political union The final stage in economic integration encompassing an economic union and political unification. [WJK]

pollution Befouling the pure state of the environment. A workable definition of pollution is dependent on the public's decision as to what use it wants to make of its environment. [DC]

polycentric orientation The unconscious bias or belief that it is necessary to adopt totally to local culture and practice. It is a host country orientation in management. (See also **ethnocentric orientation, geocentric orientation,** and **regiocentrism orientation.**) [WJK]

polycentric pricing policy See **adaptation pricing policy**

polygon A trade area whose boundaries conform to streets, political boundaries, and other physical characteristics rather than being concentric circles. [WRD]

pool A group of commercials for a product or service that an advertiser has ready for use as part of an advertising campaign. [JE]

pool-out A commercial written in a fashion similar to an earlier commercial in an advertising campaign. [JE]

pooled buying The practice of independent merchants informally pooling their orders. [WRD]

pooling A process of combining shipments that are consigned to the same destination. This service, often provided by a third party provider, improves physical distribution productivity in the handling of multi-unit shipments.[DJB/BJL]

population The totality of cases that conforms to some designated specifications. (See also **census.**) [GAC]

population characteristics See **census tract**

portfolio 1. (advertising definition) A collection of the best creative work done by an art director or copywriter, used in job interviews to demonstrate the individual's talent, skill, and experience. [JE] 2. (product development definition) A set of things that are developed and/or marketed in relationship to each other. It most often is applied to that group of projects currently active in a research laboratory, but may apply to all new projects underway. [DW]

portfolio analysis More diversified companies are more usefully considered as being composed of a portfolio of strategic business units (SBUs). Portfolio analysis is used to assess needs and to allocate resources in recognition of differences in the contributions of different SBUs to the achievement of corporate objectives for growth and profitability. Portfolio analyses are often performed using models that classify SBUs and product-markets within a two dimensional matrix in which one dimension represents the attractiveness of the market and the other dimension the strength of competitive position. The position of the SBU within the matrix has direct implications for the generic investment strategy of the business—that is, whether it is appropriate to have an investment strategy/build strategy, hold strategy, harvesting strategy, or divest strategy. Some of the best known models for portfolio analysis include the Boston Consulting Group's growth-share matrix and General Electric's market attractiveness-competitive position matrix. [GSD]

portfolio investment See **foreign direct investment**

portfolio management The arrangement of investments so as to achieve a balance of risks and rewards acceptable to the investor. The term can be applied to a global product portfolio. [WJK]

portfolio models See **product and business portfolio models**

POS See **point-of-sale**

position analysis The analysis of existing products including the manufacturing program of the present company and of the subsidiaries, analysis of competitors' market shares, a technical and economic evaluation of all products in comparison with competitors' products, assessment of manufacturing capacity, assessment of sales capacity in the field and in the home organization, appraisal of product knowledge within the group, analysis of custom duties and tariffs, and some study of innovations to be expected in the future. [WJK]

position description A written description that helps the incumbent of a position know what is expected of him or her. It includes the organizational unit, position title, purpose of the position, reporting relationships, duties and responsibilities, and authority (if any). (See also **organization structure.**) [VPB]

positioning See **product positioning**

positioning analysis See **market positioning**

positive disconfirmation See **disconfirmation**

positive reference group See **reference group**

positive valence See **attitude**

POSSE A decision support system for making product design decisions. The approach uses conjoint analysis to identify the relation between the attributes possessed by a product and the desirability of that product, for each of a set of potential customers. In a second step, the level of market demand for any potential product is estimated by aggregating the individual preference models across customers. An optimization routine then reveals the most desirable product (or products) in terms of some specific management objective (e.g., maximizing incremental market share). This objective may take into account the presence of specific other products in the market and/or any cannibalization effect of the new product on specific existing products. Finally, the market segment most attracted to this optimal new product is identified (Green, Carroll, and Goldberg 1981). (See also **decision support system, new product forecasting models,** and **product design models.**) [DCS/YJW]

possession utility The increased usefulness created by marketing through making it possible for a consumer to own, use, and consume a product. It is also called ownership utility. (See also **place utility** and **time utility.**) [DLS]

post exchange A retail store operated by the armed forces primarily for the convenience of military base personnel and their families. It is also called a PX. (See also **commissary store.**) [WRD]

post-purchase dissonance See **buyer's remorse**

post-purchase evaluation The evaluation of a product or service after consumption. This may involve remorse as well as the feeling of satisfaction or dissatisfaction. (See also **cognitive dissonance, consumer satisfaction,** and **satisfaction/dissatisfaction.**) [HHK/MCC]

post-sale service See **service(s)**

post-testing The testing of advertising effectiveness after the audience is exposed to the advertising in the marketplace. (See also **copy research.**) [JE]

postindustrial society A concept referring to the next stage in our societal evolution in which the production of knowledge will be our major activity and most of the employment opportunities will be in the service sector. [WL/MBC]

postindustrialized country Characteristics of this type of an economy are (1) the importance of the service sector is to the extent of more than 50 percent of the GNP; (2) the crucial importance of information processing and exchange; and (3) the ascendancy of knowledge over capital as the key strategic resource; of intellectual technology over machine technology; of scientists and professionals over engineers and semiskilled workers; and of theory and models over empiricism. (See also **developing country, industrialized country, preindustrialized country,** and **underdeveloped country.**) [WJK]

postpone method A method used by salespeople to respond to prospect objections by asking permission to address the prospect's concerns at a later time. (See also **boomerang method, direct denial, feel-felt-found method, indirect denial,** and **pass up method.**) [BAW]

postponement 1. (channels of distribution definition) This concept holds that changes in the form and identity of a product and inventory location should be shifted to the latest possible point in the marketing process in order to reduce the costs of the marketing system. (See also **speculation.**) [GLF] 2. (physical distribution definition) An economic term used to describe a strategy whereby the seller postpones any customization of the product until a firm demand is received from the buyer. A common example would be when the consumer buys paint that is custom mixed at the hardware store after the order is placed by the customer. [DJB/BJL]

postpurchase costs See **buyers' costs**

potential rating index for zip markets (PRIZM) A data base combining

Census data, nationwide consumer surveys, and interviews with hundreds of people across the country into a geodemographic segmentation system. [WRD]

poverty level The poverty level is based solely on money income and updated every year to reflect changes in the consumer price index; it reflects the consumption requirements of families based on their size and composition. It is used to classify families as being above or below the poverty level. [WL/MBC]

pragmatic validity An approach to validation of a measure based on the usefulness of the measuring instrument as a predictor of some other characteristic or behavior of the individual; it is sometimes called predictive validity or criterion related validity. (See also **construct validation, content validity, convergent validity, discriminant validity, external validity, internal validity,** and **validity.**) [GAC]

pre-sale service See **service(s)**

pre-test market-based models See **new product forecasting models**

preapproach The activities preceding the sales call that include prospecting, collecting information, and planning the sales presentation. [BAW]

predatory pricing The practice of selectively pricing a product below that of competition so as to eliminate competition, while pricing the product higher in markets where competition does not exist or is relatively weaker. [KM]

predictive validity See **pragmatic validity**

predisposed to buying stage See **buyer readiness stage**

preemptive pricing The practice of setting prices low so as to discourage competition from entering the market. [KM]

preference See **AIDA** and **hierarchy of effects model**

preferential tariff A reduced tariff rate applied to imports from certain countries. (See also **tariff system.**) [WJK]

preindustrialized country The characteristics exhibited by this group of countries are (1) low literacy rates and high percentage of employment in agriculture; (2) low population density and low degree of urbanization; (3) linguistic heterogeneity and a small percentage of working age population; (4) industrial sectors virtually nonexistent and undeveloped; and (5) heavy reliance upon foreign sources for all manufactures and principal engagement in agricultural endeavors. (See also **developing country, industrialized country, postindustrialized country,** and **underdeveloped country.**) [WJK]

premarking The price marking by the manufacturer or other supplier before goods are shipped to a retail store. It is also called prepricing. [WRD]

premium 1. (retailing definition) Merchandise offered at a lower price, or free, as an additional incentive for a customer to make a purchase. [WRD] 2. (sales promotion definition) An item of value, other than the product itself, given as an additional incentive to influence the purchase of a product. (See also **bounce back offer, consumer sales promotion, dealer loader, demand creation, fulfillment, gift, in-pack premium, misredemption, near-pack premium, on-pack premium, pass-along deal, reusable containers,** and **self-liquidator.**) [DES/BEB]

prepaid rate A transportation charge that is paid before a shipment is delivered, usually by the shipper or seller. [DJB/BJL]

prepricing See **premarking**

preprint An advertisement printed at the retailer's expense and distributed as a free standing insert with a newspaper. [WRD]

preprint advertising Any advertising material printed ahead of a publication's regular press run, often on a printing press other than the regular publication press. The preprint advertising is inserted into the publication during its regular printing and binding process. Preprint advertising includes a variety of approaches, including multipage inserts, free standing inserts, reply cards and reply envelopes, and ads printed on a paper stock that is different from the paper stock on which the publication is printed. (See also **run-of-press.**) [JE]

prepurchase expectations See **confirmation, disconfirmation,** and **dissatisfaction**

preretailing The practice of determining prices and placing them on a copy of the purchase order at the time that goods are bought (orders placed). [WRD]

presentation, sales The core of the personal selling process in which the salesperson transmits the information about the product and attempts to persuade the prospect to become a customer. (See also **canned sales presentation, customized sales presentation, need satisfaction selling, outlined presentation,** and **stimulus response sales approach.**) [BAW]

press clipping bureau A service organization that monitors a wide range of media sources (newspapers, magazines, television and radio talk shows and newscasts) in order to collect and log mentions of the publicist's product, service, or organization. [DES/BEB]

press conference The convening of representatives of the media by a person or organization to explain, announce, or expand on a particular subject. (See also **event creation.**) [DES/BEB]

press party The convening of representatives of the media at a social event to distribute information or material for possible future use or to influence their opinion of the sponsoring organization. (See also **event creation.**) [DES/BEB]

prestige needs See **hierarchy of needs**

pretest The use of a questionnaire (or observation form) on a trial basis in a small pilot study to determine how well the questionnaire (or observation form) works. [GAC]

pretesting The testing of the potential communication effectiveness of advertising messages before they are exposed to audiences as part of a regular media schedule. Advertisers often expose versions of advertising messages that are under development to small samples of audience members to examine the extent to which the intended message is likely to be conveyed. (See also **copy research.**) [JE]

price The formal ratio that indicates the quantities of money goods or services needed to acquire a given quantity of goods or services. [KM]

price awareness The degree to which buyers are knowledgable of the prices of alternative products and services that they are interested in buying. [KM]

price bundling The practice of offering two or more products or services for sale at one price. (See also **mixed bundling** and **multiple-unit pricing.**) [KM]

price code A symbol or code placed on a price ticket or bin ticket to indicate the cost price of an item. [WRD]

price competition The rivalry among firms seeking to attract customers on the basis of price, rather than by the use of other marketing factors. (See also **nonprice competition.**) [WL/MBC]

price consciousness The degree to which buyers are sensitive to differences in price between alternative choices. Generally, a price-conscious person seeks to minimize the price paid for an item. [KM]

price control A legal limitation placed on market prices by a government. [DLS]

price cutting The practice of reducing the prices of established products or services. [KM]

price discrimination The practice of charging different buyers different prices for the same quantity and quality of products or services. [KM]

price elasticity of demand A measure of the sensitivity of demand to changes in price. It is formally defined as the percentage change in quantity demanded relative to a given percentage change in price. (See also **elastic demand.**) [KM]

price fixing The practice of two or more sellers agreeing on the price to charge for similar products or services. [KM]

price guarantee The practice of vendors offering their customers guarantees against price declines. [WRD]

price guideline A suggested target for price levels directed at marketers by government officials. [DLS]

price leader 1. (pricing definition) In competitive situations, the seller who normally initiates price changes in the market. [KM] 2. (retailing definition) An item of merchandise priced abnormally low for the purpose of attracting customers. [WRD]

price leadership The practice in an industry of recognizing and adopting the price established by one or more members of the industry. [WRD]

price lining 1. (pricing definition) The offering of merchandise at a number of specific but predetermined prices. Once set, the prices may be held constant over a period of time, and changes in market conditions are adapted to by changing the quality of the merchandise. [KM] 2. (retailing definition) A limited number of predetermined price points at which merchandise will be offered for sale—e.g., $7.95, $10.95, $14.95. (See also **size lining.**) [WRD]

price maintenance The determination by the manufacturer of the price at which an identified item shall be resold by wholesalers and/or retailers. [WRD]

price model See **BRANDAID, elasticon,** and **promotion models**

price off A stated reduction in the price of a product generally offered by the manufacturer and printed directly on the product package. (See also **trade sales promotion.**) [DES/BEB]

price promotion The advertising of a price for a product or service. Usually, the price being promoted is a reduction from a previously established price and may take the form of a lower price, a coupon to be redeemed, or a rebate to be received. [KM]

price reduction See **coupon, deal, deal merchandise, demand creation, flagging, off-invoice allowance, pass-along deal, price off, promotional allowance,** and **solo coupon**

price sensitivity meter A research method for establishing the range of prices that buyers are willing to pay for a product or service. (See also **acceptable price range.**) [KM]

price structure A price structure includes the time and conditions of payment, the nature of discounts to be allowed the buyer, and where and when title is to be taken by the buyer. [KM]

price thresholds The lowest and highest prices that buyers are willing to pay for a particular good or service. (See also **acceptable price range** and **reservation price.**) [KM]

price-quality relationship The degree to which product or service quality covaries with price. [KM]

primary advertising An approach to the advertising message that emphasizes the basic attributes of the product category. This approach is usually employed by trade associations in an attempt to build demand for all the competing brands in the product category and to enhance the image of the industry involved. (See also **generic advertising.**) [JE]

primary buying motive The motive that induces an individual to buy a certain kind or general class of article or service, as opposed to the selection of brands within a class. (See also **physiological motives.**) [WRD]

primary data The information collected specifically for the purpose of the investigation at hand. (See also **secondary data.**) [GAC]

primary demand The demand for a general product category, as contrasted with the demand for a branded product marketed by a firm. (See also **selective demand.**) [DLS]

primary metropolitan statistical area (PMSA) An area of at least one million people that includes a large urbanized county or a group of counties that have strong economic and social ties to neighboring communities. (See also **consolidated metropolitan statistical area, metropolitan statistical area,** and **standard metropolitan statistical area.**) [DLS]

primary package See **multiple packaging** and **package**

primary readers See **pass-along readers**

primary trade zone See **analog approach**

principal A person or firm who empowers another person or firm to act as the person's or firm's representative or agent. (See also **agency cost** and **agency theory.**) [WRD]

private carrier A corporate-owned and corporate-managed transportation capability. Private carriage usually refers to trucking, but corporate ownership of other modes is also found in rail and water transportation. (See also **independent carrier.**) [DJB/BJL]

private label 1. (product development definition) A brand that is owned by the product's reseller rather than by its manufacturer. In rare instances, the reseller may be the manufacturer as well. The term is often associated with (1) advertised brand versus unadvertised brand (a private brand is most often unadvertised) and (2) national brand versus regional brand or local brand (a private brand is usually less than national). These distinctions have become clouded by large retail and wholesale organizations (e.g., Sears, Kroger, Kmart, Ace) who advertise their private brands and market them nationally and internationally. (See also **distributor's brand, house brand, manufacturer's brand, private label,** and **store brand.**) [DW] 2. (retailing definition) A brand name or label name attached to or used in the marketing of a product other than by the product manufacturers; usually by a retailer. [WRD]

private nonprofit marketer A nonprofit marketer incorporated privately. Comment: Nonprofit marketers collectively have been defined as the third sector or the independent sector. (See also **non-governmental organization.**) [ARA]

private sector The economic activities that are outside the so-called public sector, or those activities that are independent of government control. They are usually, but not exclusively, carried on for profit. [WL/MBC]

privity of contract See **strict liability**

prizes The reward structure of cash and/or merchandise offered in a contest, game, or sweepstakes sales promotion. (See also **incentive** and **misredemption.**) [DES/BEB]

PRIZM See **potential rating index for zip markets**

proactive moves See **market penetration**

proactive pricing The managerial practice of deliberately analyzing the factors that influence prices before setting prices. Normally, a proactive pricer establishes specific objectives to be accomplished by the prices and then proceeds in the development of specific prices. [KM]

probabilistic model See **Bernoulli process, logit model, nested logit model, probability mixture model, probit model, stochastic model,** and **zero order model**

probability mixture model A stochastic model for representing the behavior (e.g., brand choice or media viewing) of a set of individuals. This type of model is characterized by two components. First, a particular family of probabilistic models (such as a Poisson process) is selected to represent the behavior of any single individual (for example, the number of product purchases made by the individual). Second, there is an explicit realization that individuals differ from each other (heterogeneity). That is, a distribution is selected to represent the variation across individuals in the particular probabilistic model followed, within the family of models noted above. (For example, the Poisson purchase rate varies from individual to individual.) Probability mixture models have been used to predict brand choice, product purchase, and media viewing patterns over time (Greene 1982; Massy, Montgomery, and Morrison 1970). (See also **Beta binomial model, brand choice models, Dirichlet multinomial model,** and **Negative Binomial Distribution model.**) [DCS/YJW]

probability sample A sample in which each population element has a known, nonzero chance of being included in the sample. (See also **nonprobability sample.**) [GAC]

probe A question or verbal expression made by a salesperson to elicit information from a customer. [BAW]

probit model A probabilistic model for representing the brand choice behavior of individuals. On any choice occasion the individual is assumed to choose the item for which he or she has the highest preference. Over repeated choice occasions preferences are assumed to have a probabilistic component. For the probit model this random component of preference, for the set of items being considered, is taken to have the multivariate normal distribution (Thurston 1927). The model can be used to predict choice probabilities (or market share, as an average of these probabilities) based on the distribution of preference levels, and also to link average preference to attributes of the items being chosen (Currim 1982; Daganzo 1979). Unlike the logit model, probit does not require that Luce's Choice Axiom hold, which is sometimes seen as an appealing feature of probit. On the other hand, this feature comes at the cost of significant additional computational complexity and more parameters to estimate, relative to the logit model. (See also **analytic hierarchy process.**) [DCW/YJW]

problem child See **growth-share matrix**

problem recognition This occurs when consumers notice the current state of affairs is not the ideal or desired state, thus creating a motivation to achieve a goal. It is the beginning of consumer decision making. [JPP/JCO]

problem recognition, in organizational buying The recognition that the current product or service can be replaced by a better product or service or that a cheaper way to operate exists. It is followed by a search for information and evaluation of whether new purchases are justified. Problem recognition may be stimulated internally (by a value analysis or audit, for example) or externally (by exposure to an advertisement or by a salesperson's visit). (See also **buygrid framework**.) [GLL/DTW]

problem solution approach A selling approach in which the salesperson identifies the customer's problems and several alternative solutions, then analyzes the advantages and disadvantages of the solution and helps the customer select the best option. (See also **approach, sales; balance sheet method; benefit approach; compliment approach; consultative selling; customer orientation; formula selling; high-pressure selling; mutlilevel selling;** and **systems selling.**) [BAW]

problems See **SPIN**

process specifications See **research and development**

processed materials Manufactured materials that have been partially processed before reaching an ultimate producer. In contrast to component parts, they must be processed further before becoming part of a finished product. Examples are steel, cement, wire, and textiles. (See also **fabricating materials** and **semimanufactured goods.**) [GLL/DTW]

procurement The function in the material acquisition cycle from the time an item is requisitioned until it is delivered. It includes responsibility for selection of vendor, negotiation of price, and assurance of quality and delivery; it may also include responsibility for transportation, receiving, inspection, and inventory control. It is a function usually performed by the purchasing department. (See also **buyer** and **purchasing.**) [GLL/DTW]

producer market See **industrial market**

producer price index A monthly price index of about 2,800 commodities prepared by the U.S. Bureau of Labor Statistics, formerly known as the wholesale price index. [WL/MBC]

producers' goods See **accessory equipment** and **installations**

producers' cooperative marketing A type of cooperative marketing that primarily involves the sale of products of the membership. It may perform only an assembly or brokerage function, but in some cases, notably milk marketing and citrus fruits, it extends into processing and distribution of the members' output. [WRD]

product (1) A bundle of attributes (features, functions, benefits, and uses) capable of exchange or use; usually a mix of tangible and intangible forms. Thus a product may be an idea, a physical entity (a good), or a service, or any combination of the three. It exists for the purpose of exchange in the satisfaction of individual and organizational objectives. (2) Occasional usage today implies a definition of product as that bundle of attributes for which the exchange or use primarily concerns the physical or tangible form, in contrast to a service, in which the seller, buyer, or user is primarily interested in the intangible. Though to speak of "products" and "services" is convenient, it leaves us without a term to apply to the set of the two combined. The term for tangible products is *goods*, and it should be used with *services* to make the tangible/intangible pair, as subsets of the term *product*. (See also **bounce back offer.**) [DW]

product adaptation The strategy of developing new products by modifying or improving on the product innovations of others. This contrasts with the strategies of pioneering and imitation. (See also **adaptive product** and **imitative strategy.**) [DW]

product adoption process The sequence of stages that individuals and firms go through in the process of accepting new products. The stages vary greatly in usage, but tend to include (1) becoming aware of the new product, (2) seeking information about it, (3) developing favorable attitudes toward it, (4) trying it out in some direct or indirect way, (5) finding satisfaction in the trial, and (6) adopting the product into a standing usage or repurchase pattern. (See also **adopter categories, awareness-trial-repeat, early adopters, early majority, innovators, laggards,** and **late majority.**) [DW]

product and business portfolio models Portfolio models of products, market segments, or businesses, not unlike the financial portfolio models, are designed to help allocate resources among the portfolio units (e.g., stocks, products, businesses) and select an optimal portfolio. In marketing, product and business portfolios have included standardized portfolio models (e.g., BCG growth-share matrix, the McKinsey/GE market attractiveness-competitive position matrix, A. D. Little Business Profile Matrix, and Shell International Directional Policy Matrix), marketing driven modified financial portfolio models (e.g., modified risk return and stochastic dominance models), and customized portfolio models (e.g., conjoint analysis-based simulation models or an analytic hierarchy process-based approach). Whereas the standardized models offer no more than product or business classification systems, the customized models and more recent hybrid models (combining models from the three classes—the McKinsey/GE with stochastic dominance and analytic hierarchy process) can provide operational guidelines for resource allocations. (See also **resource allocation models.**) [DCS/YJW]

product approach A method used by salespeople to approach prospects in which salespeople demonstrate the product features and benefits as they walk up to the prospects. (See also **center of influence method, cold-canvassing, curiosity approach, endless chain method, introduction approach,** and **referral approach.**) [BAW]

product assortment The collection of products (items, families, lines) that comprise the offering of a given seller. Though sometimes thought to be only a collection of categories of products, more common usage makes the term similar to product mix. Product assortment is used more by resellers; product mix more by manufacturers. [DW]

product attributes The characteristics by which products are identified and differentiated. Product attributes usually comprise features, functions, benefits, and uses. [DW]

product benefit See **benefit, product**

product brand See **brand**

product champion A person who takes an inordinate interest in seeing that a particular process or product is fully developed and marketed. The role varies from situations calling for little more than stimulating awareness of the item to extreme cases in which the champion tries to force the item past the strongly entrenched internal resistance of company policy or that of objecting parties. [DW]

product class A group of products that are homogeneous or generally considered as substitutes for each other. The class is considered as narrow or broad depending on how substitutable the various products are. For example, a narrow product class of breakfast meats might be bacon, ham, and sausage. A broad class would include all other meat and meat substitutes even occasionally sold for breakfast use. (See also **product form, product hierarchy, product life cycle,** and **substitute products.**) [DW]

product concept A verbal or pictorial version of a proposed new product. The concept consists of (1) one or more benefits it will yield, (2) its general form, and (3) the technology used to achieve the form. A new product idea becomes a concept when it achieves at least one benefit and either the form or the technology. Further work in the new product development process gradually clarifies and confirms those two and adds the third. A concept becomes a product when it is sold successfully in the market place; prior to that, it is still undergoing development, even if marketed. (See also **concept statement** and **research and development.**) [DW]

product decision See **buying decisions**

product decision model See **decision calculus models**

product deletion See **abandonment**

product demonstration See **event creation**

product design models Optimal product design models are often based on consumers' perceptions and preferences data and have typically been formulated in the context of multidimensional scaling methods or conjoint analysis. In the latter case, simulation and various optimization programs have been used. (See also **POSSE.**) [DCS/YJW]

product development See **new product development**

product differentiation One or more product attributes that make one product different from another. The differentiation may or may not be favorable, and thus constitute a differential advantage. The difference may or may not be promoted to the consumer. (See also **barriers to competition.**) [DW]

product elimination See **abandonment**

product evolution The gradual change in a product, as it is modified by its seller, to keep it competitive or to permit it to enter new markets. It is similar to the patterns of evolution in nature. [DW]

product feature See **feature, product**

product form The physical shape or nature of a good or the sequential steps in a service. Form is provided by one or more technologies and yields benefits to the user; for example, many technologies are used to make a front-wheel drive form of an automobile. Products of the same form make up a group within a product class (e.g., all front-wheel drive automobiles). Differences in form of service separate discount stock brokers and full-service stock brokers. (See also **product hierarchy** and **product life cycle.**) [DW]

product hierarchy An organizational-chart type of array of the products offered in a given market, breaking first into product class, then product form, then variations on form, then brand. For the transportation market, the top layer is broken into cars, trucks, buses, etc. The second layer breaks cars by form (sedans, station wagons, convertibles), trucks by form (semi, heavy duty, pick-up), etc. The third layer breaks each of these class/form groupings one more time, for example showing automobile sedans as two-door, four-door, etc. The fourth layer breaks each of these smaller groups into brands (Ford, Chevrolet, etc.). There are various options within these product hierarchy dimensions, so that the array can be designed to fit the needs of the analyst. The hierarchy concept fits services as well as it does goods. [DW]

product idea See **product concept**

product innovation (1) The act of creating a new product or process. It includes invention as well as the work required to bring an idea or concept into final form. (2) A particular new product or process. An innovation may have various degrees of newness, from very little to highly discontinuous, but that must include at least some degree of newness to the market, not just to the firm. (See also **product planning.**) [DW]

product introduction The first stage of the product life cycle, during which the new item is announced to the market and offered for sale. Most methods of market testing are considered pre-introduction, but many marketers call the market rollout an introduction because of the commitment implied in the method. If successful during the introduction, the new product enters the second (growth) stage. [DW]

product liability 1. (legislation definition) Product liability is concerned with injuries caused by products that are defectively manufactured, processed, or distributed. Liability for such injuries attaches to all members of the distributive chain from manufacturers to retailers. [DC] 2. (product development definition) The obligation a seller incurs regarding the safety of a product. The liability may be implied by custom or common practice in the field, stated in the warranty, or decreed by law. If injury occurs, various defenses are prescribed by law and judicial precedent. Sellers are expected to offer adequate instructions and warnings about a product's use, and these, too, have precise legal bases. (See also **strict liability.**) [DW]

product life cycle 1. (product development definition) (from biology) The four stages that a new product is thought to go through from birth to death: introductory, growth, maturity, and decline. Controversy surrounds whether products do indeed go through such cycles in any systematic, predictable way. The product life cycle concept is primarily applicable to product forms, less to product classes, and very poorly to individual brands. (See also **fashion cycle, pioneering stage,** and **product introduction.**) [DW] 2. (strategic marketing definition) This describes the stages in the sales history of a product.

The product life cycle (PLC) has four premises: (1) that products have a limited life; (2) that product sales pass through distinct stages, each stage having different implications for the seller; (3) that profits from the product vary at different stages in the life cycle; and (4) that products require different strategies at different stages of the life cycle. The product life cycle has four stages: (1) **introduction**—the slow sales growth that follows the introduction of a new product; (2) **growth**—the rapid sales growth that accompanies product acceptance; (3) **maturity**—the plateauing of sales growth when the product has been accepted by most potential buyers; and (4) **decline**—the decline of sales that results as the product is replaced (by a substitute) or as it goes into disfavor. (See also **market evolution.**) [GSD]

product line A group of products marketed by an organization to one general market. The products have some characteristics, customers, and/or uses in common, and may also share technologies, distribution channels, prices, services, etc. There are often product lines within product lines. (See also **merchandise line** and **product mix.**) [DW]

product line optimization Models to establish the optimal product line (in terms of number of products and their specific characteristics and positioning) have been typically developed in the context of conjoint analysis and have taken two forms: (1) buyer's welfare models (how to maximize the buyer's utility, utilizing, for example, integer programming or search heuristics); and (2) seller's welfare models that involve the selection of the best set of products to maximize the profits of the firm, utilizing, for example, dynamic programming or search heuristics. For a review of these approaches and a particular example that has been applied, see Green and Krieger (1985). [DCS/YJW]

product management organization Product managers or brand managers are responsible for developing marketing plans, coordinating implementation of the plans by the functional departments, and monitoring performance of their assigned products. Product managers report to the marketing manager unless there are large numbers of them, in which case they report to an intervening level of supervision such as the group product manager or category manager. The terms *product management* and *product manager* are interchangeable with *brand management* and *brand manager.* Comment: The advantage of this form of organization is that each product receives the full attention of one person responsible for its success. The disadvantage is that the product manager has no authority over the functional departments that design, produce, finance, distribute, sell, and service the product. Yet the system works well enough that it is widely used by multiproduct companies. (See also **bureaucratic organization; centralized management; decentralized management; divisional organization; flat organization; functional organization; geographic organization; hierarchical organization; market management organization; marketing organization, forms of; matrix organization; multibusiness organization;** and **nonbusiness marketing organization.**) [VPB]

product manager 1. (organization definition) This manager is responsible for the planning, coordination, and monitoring of performance of a product in a multiproduct company or division. The product manager reports to the marketing manager or (if there are numerous product managers) to an intervening level of supervision such as group product manager or category manager. Some multibrand companies use the term brand manager rather than product manager to denote this position. Note: Because the product manager does not have line authority over the functional units that execute plans, this manager's success in achieving product goals (e.g. sales, profits, and market share) is largely dependent on his/her expert knowledge and persuasive ability. Types of functional units with which the product manager has working relationships include research and development, engineering, production, physical distribution, packaging, finance, marketing research, sales, advertising, and sales promotion. The product manager may be the principal point of contact between marketing management and the advertising agency. Although it is the exception rather than the rule, new product development may be an added responsibility of the product manager. If so, it is usually limited to product improvement or product line extension. (See also **category manager, divisional organization, new product manager,** and **product management organization.**) [VPB] 2. (product development definition) A person charged with one or more products or brands. Most often, a product manager is responsible for formulating and implementing the marketing goals and strategies for commercialized products. In some cases, however, a product manager also may be responsible for new product development. As a rule, a product manager must coordinate the efforts of various disciplinary specialists, e.g., manufacturing, sales and marketing research. (See also **market manager.**) [DW]

product mix The full set of products offered for sale by an organization. The product mix includes all product lines and categories. It may be defined more narrowly in specific cases to mean only that set of products in a particular product line or a particular market. (See also **product assortment.**) [DW]

product modification The altering of a current product so as to make it more appealing to the market place. This contrasts with creating a line extension and with repositioning a current product, both of which can be used to achieve the same purpose. [DW]

product performance tracking A process for tracking the performance of a commercialized product in the market. The specific factors that are tracked depend on the product's marketing strategy. Typically, these factors are measured: sales, share of the market, consumer awareness, advertising effectiveness, and customer satisfaction. [DW]

product planning A term of many meanings, but generally it is used to designate a staff position charged with part or all of the task of managing product innovation within an organization. In some firms, it also includes acquisition of products or processes. [DW]

product planning manager In a functionally organized department (with no product managers), the product planning manager represents the marketing manager in contacts with functional units within and outside the marketing department with respect to product line planning, development of new products, improvement of existing products, and pruning the product line. The product planning manager reports to the marketing manager and assists this executive with the development of overall product strategy. Comment: This position usually is not present in a product functions listed above are the responsibility of product managers or category managers, except for new product development, which is usually assigned to a new product manager. (See also **functional organization.**) [VPB]

product portfolio See **product mix**

product portfolio analysis See **portfolio analysis**

product portfolio decision See **product and business portfolio models**

product positioning (1) The way consumers, users, buyers, and others view competitive brands or types of products. As determined by market research techniques, the various products are plotted onto maps, using product attributes as dimensions. This use of product positioning is perceptual, not necessarily valid as based on measured product attributes. Historically, the competitive product positionings were based on sales rank in the market, but this limited perception has long since given way to the full range of product assessments, including psychological ones. (2) For new products, product positioning means how the innovator firm decides to compare the new item to its predecessors. For the new item, the mental slates of persons in the market place are blank; this is the only chance the innovator will have to make a first impression. Later, after the introduction is over, the earlier definition of positioning will take over, as persons make their own positioning decisions. (3) For both new and established products, a product's positioning may be combined with a target segment to integrate the marketing tool decisions. Its earlier use exclusively in advertising is no longer appropriate. [DW]

product proliferation A charge sometimes leveled against organizations for marketing so many new products that economic resources are wasted; the consumer becomes confused and mistakes are made in the purchase of products. [DW]

product publicity See **consumer relations**

product publicity manager The product publicity manager is responsible for obtaining favorable publicity for new, improved, or existing products through such means as news stories, pictures and captions in newspapers and magazines, product exposure in programs and movies, direct mail, videocassettes, promotional events in shopping malls, and satellite programs beamed to local TV stations. This manager may report to the marketing manager, advertising manager, or public relations manager. [VPB]

product purchase model See **probability mixture model**

product quality (1) The measure of any particular attribute a product has (what flavor, how much, how lasting). (2) The measure of the intended customer's reactions to that attribute, how it is liked, its affect. On manufactured goods, the quality assessment is most often made on the quality of the product's physical features as created by the manufacturing process; the judgments are made by managers using proprietary standards. (3) Product quality may also be related to price, in which any particular lower-price item might be said to have good quality for the money; this use equates product quality with product value. [DW]

product repositioning See **product modification**

product safety See **product liability**

product specialization See **market coverage strategies**

product specialization coverage See **product-market grid**

product specifications See **research and development**

product symbolism The sum total of what a product means to the consumer and what the consumer experiences in purchasing and using it. [JPP/JCO]

product trade life cycle An empirical cycle that recognizes the relationship between production, consumption, trade, and the product life cycle for certain countries at certain times in history. The model shows how production of mature products with stabilized technologies has relocated from the U.S. to the developing to the less developed countries of the world as companies take advantage of lower wage and other factor costs in various parts of the world. (See also **international product cycle** and **international trade product life cycle.**) [WJK]

product transformation This occurs when the same physical product ends up serving a different function or use than that for which it was originally designed or created. [WJK]

product trial See **consumer sales promotion**

product use test One of several key evaluation steps in the product development process. This involves giving a prototype or pilot plant product to persons or firms in the intended target market and asking them to use it for a time and report their reactions to it. The purposes of a product use test are (1) to see if the item developed by the organization has the attributes prescribed for it, (2) to learn whether it satisfies the market needs that were identified during the ideation process, and (3) to disclose information about how and by whom the item is used. [DW]

product value See **product quality**

product-line pricing The establishing of prices for all items in a product line. (See also **full-line pricing.**) [KM]

product-market concentration strategies See **PIMS Program**

product-market definition The boundaries of a market are defined by choices of distinct categories along four dimensions: (1) customer functions, or the pattern of benefits being provided to satisfy the needs of customers; (2) technology, which represents the various ways a particular function can be performed; (3) customer segments, which describes whose needs are being served and where they are geographically located; and (4) the sequence of stages of the value-added system. A product-market boundary is crossed when distinctly different competitive strategies are required. Within this market there may be submarkets composed of customers with similar patterns of uses or applications for the product. (See also **served market.**) [GSD]

product-market expansion grid A two-by-two matrix that allows the identification of expansion opportunities as follows: [GSD]

	Current Products	**New Products**
Current Markets	Market Penetration	Product Development
New Markets	Market Development	Diversification

product-market grid One method of segmenting the market to identify strategically important target markets. Market segments are identified by crossing the two variables—products (which relate to customer needs) and markets (which relate to customer groups):

Markets (Customer Groups)

		I	II	III
Products	1			
(Customer Needs)	2			
	3			
	4			

The product-market grid implies five different patterns of market coverage that a firm can adopt: (1) single product-market concentration—one product-market combination is targeted (i.e., one cell in the grid); (2) product specialization—one product for all customer groups is produced and marketed (i.e., a row in the grid); (3) market specialization—a range of products are produced and marketed to one customer group (i.e., a column in the grid); (4) selective specialization—a number of product/market combinations are targeted (i.e., two or more cells); (5) full coverage—every product is marketed for every customer group (i.e., all cells). [GSD]

product/market matrix A two-by-two matrix in which the column designations are current products and new products, and the row designations are current markets and new markets. The matrix thus defines four types of new product opportunities ranging from the upper-left quadrant of improved versions of current products to current users to the lower-right quadrant of diversification. (See also **product-market expansion grid.**) [DW]

product-related buying criteria See **buying criteria**

production 1. (economic definition) The addition of utilities to goods or the rendering of services possessing utility. 2. (marketing definition) The creation of form utility, i.e., all activities used to change the appearance or composition of a good or service with the intent of making it more attractive to potential and actual users. [DLS]

production cost The cost of producing a print ad, radio commercial, television commercial, or other advertising materials. [JE]

production era A time period in the United States during which firms emphasized manufacturing or producing products, usually at the expense of marketing strategy. (See also **production orientation.**) [DLS]

production function The technical relationship, given a state of technical knowledge, relating to the amount of output capable of being produced by different sets of specified inputs. [DLS]

production orientation A business philosophy that emphasizes the output of products, usually at the expense of marketing strategy. (See also **production era.**) [DLS]

production scheduling A process that specifies a target output for the production capability of the firm. It is an important operational tool in planning the short-term resource and location focus in a manufacturing environment. [DJB/BJL]

production structure See **PIMS Program**

production unit accounting (PUA) A specific philosophy of making use of expense figures beyond their accumulation into expense centers. It involves utilizing the expense data through units of measure to determine productivity for the purpose of controlling expense. It is common in department store expense management. [WRD]

productivity 1. (economic definition) A measure of the economic output per unit of input of some resource, e.g., the economic output per hour of human labor. [DLS] 2. (environments definition) A ratio of output per unit of input employed. It is measured by the U.S. Bureau of Labor Statistics as output per hour and output per combined unit of labor and capital per hour (multifactor productivity) for the business sector as a whole and for its major subsectors. [WL/MBC]

productivity sales goal An objective for a salesperson based on the salesperson's efficiency assessed by dividing outputs by inputs such as sales per call. [BAW]

professional advertising See **business-to-business advertising**

professional discount A discount granted to people in a specified professional field, especially those who are users of products in that field. For example, this includes discounts given to physicians by drugstores, especially to those who favor the store with prescription references. [WRD]

professional services marketing The marketing of advisory services offered by licensed or accredited individuals or organizations. [ARA]

profit See **net operating income**

profit analysis See **LITMUS**

Profit Impact on Market Strategies See **PIMS Program**

profit maximization objective A firm sets as its major objective the maximization of long-run profits. If not stated, this is often the assumed objective of a firm. There are, however, many other variables that may provide the basis of objectives for a firm. Other objectives relate to such variables as sales growth, market share, risk diversification, innovation, etc. (See also **objective.**) [GSD]

profit-volume ratio The dollar contribution per unit divided by the unit price. The profit-volume ratio indicates the rate at which fixed costs are recovered and, after the break-even point has been reached, the rate at which profits are earned as sales volume increases. [KM]

profiteering The taking advantage of a situation such as famine or natural disaster to charge exorbitant prices and realize excessive profits. [WL/MBC]

profits The excess of total revenues over total costs in a given time period. [KM]

program See **project**

program delivery See **rating**

programmed merchandise agreement A joint venture in which a specific retailer and supplier develop a comprehensive merchandising plan to market the supplier's product lines. [WRD]

programmed merchandising The careful planning and concentration of purchases with a limited number of preferred, or key, vendors. It is usually for an entire line of merchandise and for extended periods of time, such as a year. [WRD]

project A unit of activity in the product development process that usually deals with creating and marketing one new product. A project involves a multidisciplinary group of people, tightly or loosely organized, dedicated to the new product assignment that created the project. A project is often part of a larger unit of work, a program, which delivers a stream of new products, one from each project. [DW]

projection The ego defense of projecting onto others the needs, hostilities, and anxieties that are subconscious to the individual. It is a mode of coping with these perceived undesirable feelings. [HHK/MCC]

projective technique 1. (consumer behavior definition) A psychological method of uncovering subconscious material within subjects. Ambiguous stimuli such as the Thematic Apperception Test, sentence completion test, word association tests, or Rorschach ink blots are presented to subjects who are asked to verbalize their perceptions and reactions. The assumption is that if psychological needs, values, and anxieties affect perception of reality, those can be uncovered by analysis of responses to vague stimuli. (See also **laddering.**) [HHK/MCC] 2. (marketing research definition) A method of questioning respondents using a vague stimulus that respondents are asked to describe, expand on, or build a structure around; the basic assumption is that an individual's organization of the relatively unstructured stimulus is indicative of the person's basic perceptions of the phenomenon and reactions to it. (See also **sentence completion, story telling,** and **word association.**) [GAC]

promise of performance See **warranty**

promotion See **channel flows**

promotion mix The various communication techniques such as advertising, personal selling, sales promotion, and public relations/product publicity available to a marketer that are combined to achieve specific goals. [DES/BEB]

promotion models Models to estimate the effect of a promotion (e.g. temporary price change, etc.) include models based on market response functions, or a combination of empirical data with management subjective judgment as in BRANDAID. Promotion models often are stochastic and based on behavioral assumptions regarding retailers and consumers. Many of these models decompose the value of the promotion into components such as increased loyalty among current customers, attraction of deal prone switchers, etc. Inventory control-based promotion models have also been proposed, incorporating the inventory carrying costs of consumers and retailers. The increased availability and popularity of scanner data have focused attention on promotion models. (See also **LITMUS, NEWPROD,** and **NEWS.**) [DCS/YJW]

promotion, word-of-mouth The product/service information, experience, and opinions discussed by consumers in social contexts. [DES/BEB]

promotional advertising Advertising intended to inform prospective customers of special sales. It announces the arrival of new and seasonal goods, and it features, creates, and promotes a market for the merchandise items in regular stock. [WRD]

promotional allowance 1. (retailing definition) An allowance given by vendors to retailers to compensate the latter for money spent in advertising a particular item in local media, or for preferred window and interior display space used for the vendor's product. [WRD] 2. (sales promotion definition) The payments, price reductions, or other inducements used to reward channel members for participation in advertising and/or sales promotion programs. (See also **trade sales promotion.**) [DES/BEB]

promotional campaign The combination of various advertising, public relations, sales promotion, and personal selling activities used by the marketer over a period of time to achieve predetermined goals. [DES/BEB]

promotional department store A departmentalized store concentrating on apparel that sells a substantial portion of its merchandise in response to frequent promotions. [WRD]

promotional discount See **promotional allowance**

promotional elasticity of demand A measure of the change in quantity demanded relative to the change in promotional activity. [DLS]

promotional package The collection of sales promotion materials and offers developed by the seller to influence retailers, wholesalers, or salespeople to support a particular promotional theme. (See also **trade sales promotion.**) [DES/BEB]

promotional stock A retailer's stock of goods offered at an unusually attractive price in order to obtain volume trade. It generally represents special purchases from vendors. [WRD]

proof-of-purchase Some element of the product or package used as evidence that the consumer has purchased the product. Common proofs-of-purchase are labels, boxtops, ingredient listings, etc. [DES/BEB]

propaganda The ideas, information, or other material commonly disseminated through the media in an effort to win people over to a given doctrine or point of view. [DES/BEB]

propensity to consume The relationship between consumption and saving at all levels of income. (See also **consumption function** and **marginal propensity to consume.**) [DLS]

proposal evaluation and selection See **buygrid framework**

proposal solicitation See **buygrid framework**

proprietary The private or exclusive ownership of such things as a process, design, or patent that competitors cannot duplicate. In the pharmaceutical industry, proprietary products are those over-the-counter products that are differentiated from prescription products. [WL/MBC]

proprietary drugs Drug products not requiring a physician's prescription, patent medicines, or over-the-counter remedies. [WRD]

proprietary store An establishment selling the same merchandise as a drug store, except that prescriptions are not filled and sold. [WRD]

prospect A potential qualified customer who has the willingness, financial capacity, authority, and eligibility to buy the salesperson's offering. (See also **center of influence method, cold-canvassing, curiosity approach, endless chain method, introduction approach, product approach,** and **referral approach.**) [BAW]

prospecting The process of identifying and qualifying potential customers. [BAW]

prosperity A phase of the business cycle characterized by high-level production, increased demand for capital goods, and a tendency toward full employment. (See also **depression, recession,** and **recovery.**) [DLS]

protection department The operating unit of a retail store that is responsible for protecting the merchandise or other assets from pilferage (internal or external). Those working in the department may be store employees or outside people. It is sometimes referred to as a loss prevention department or function. (See also **security.**) [WRD]

protectionism The use of legal controls to protect domestic businesses and industries from foreign competition. [WJK]

protective tariff An import duty or tax applied to goods imported from abroad with an intention to exclude these products or greatly reduce imports of them. [DLS]

prototype The first physical form or service description of a new product, still in rough or tentative mode. Occasionally a prototype may precede research and development if making it is easy (e.g., cake mixes). With complex products, there may be component prototypes as well as one finished prototype. On services, the prototype is simply the first full description of how the service will work, and comes from the systems design or development function. [DW]

proximo dating This specifies the date in the following month on which payment must be made in order to take the cash discount—e.g., terms of "2%, 10th proximo, net 60 days," meaning that the bill must be paid prior to the tenth day of the month following purchase in order to take the discount, but that a credit period of 60 days from the first of the month is allowed. (See also **advance dating, dating, end of month dating, extra dating, future dating, memorandum purchase and dating, ordinary dating, receipt-of-goods dating,** and **season dating.**) [WRD]

pruning decision The act of deciding which products to delete from the line. (See also **abandonment.**) [DW]

PSA See **public service announcement**

psychic income The intangible gratification or value that is derived from products, services, or activities, such as the improvement in a consumer's self image as a result of purchasing certain highly desirable products. [WL/MBC]

psychoanalytic theory A psychological theory developed by Sigmund Freud that emphasizes unconscious motivation. [JPP/JCO]

psychogenic drives See **psychological drives**

psychographic analysis 1. (consumer behavior definition) A technique that investigates how people live, what interests them, and what they like; it is also called life style analysis or AIO because it relies on a number of statements about a person's activities, interests, and opinions. (See also **psychographic segmentation.**) [JPP/JCO] 2. (marketing research definition) A technique that investigates how people live and what interests them. [GAC]

psychographic segmentation The process of dividing markets into segments on the basis of consumer life styles. (See also **AIO, psychographic analysis,** and **VALS.**) [JPP/JCO]

psychographics See **database**

psychological drives Those drives that are not based on the basic biological needs of the individual but rather are social in origin. The need for self-actualization, status, and belongingness are examples. (See also **consumer motivation.**) [HHK/MCC]

psychological perceived risk See **perceived risk**

psychological pricing A method of setting prices intended to have special appeal to consumers. (See also **odd-even pricing.**) [DLS]

psychological stress See **ego defenses**

PUA See **production unit accounting**

public affairs A management function concerned with the relationship between the organization and its external environment, and involving the key tasks of intelligence gathering and analysis, internal communication, and external action programs directed at government, communities, and the general public. [DES/BEB]

public convenience and necessity A phrase used in the regulated transportation environment that describes the certificate required to qualify as a common carrier. A carrier desiring to enter into business in the pre-1980 regulated transportation environment was required to prove public convenience and necessity. [DJB/BJL]

public domain The status of works on which copyrights have expired or do not exist, or which do not have copyright protection. It is also land owned by the government. [DC]

public market A wholesale or retail market primarily for foodstuffs, supervised or administered by a municipality that rents space or stalls to dealers. It is also called a municipal market or a community market. [WRD]

public nonprofit marketer A nonprofit marketer that is a unit of a national, state, or local government. [ARA]

public opinion The consensus view of a population on a topic. [DES/BEB]

public policy A course of action pursued by the government pertaining to people as a whole on which laws rest. [DC]

public relations That form of communication management that seeks to make use of publicity and other nonpaid forms of promotion and information to influence the feelings, opinions, or beliefs about the company, its products or services, or about the value of the product or service or the activities of the organization to buyers, prospects, or other stakeholders. (See also **content analysis, corporate relations, marketing public relations, pass strategy, promotion mix,** and **promotional campaign**.) [DES/BEB]

public relations manager This manager oversees plans and programs designed to promote a favorable image for a company or institution among its various publics such as customers, dealers, investors, government, employees, and the general public. The marketing aspects of the public relations job are concerned with obtaining publicity for marketing programs (such as for a new product launch). The responsibility for product publicity may reside with the public relations manager or with the product publicity manager. The public relations manager would normally report to corporate management whereas the product publicity manager would normally report to the marketing manager. [VPB]

public sector Those marketing activities that are carried out by government agencies for public service rather than for profit. (See also **private sector.**) [WL/MBC]

public service announcement (PSA) 1. (advertising definition) An advertisement or commercial that is carried by an advertising vehicle at no cost as a public service to its readers, viewers, or listeners. (See also **Advertising Council.**) [JE] 2. (sales promotion definition) An announcement aired free of charge that promotes either government programs, nonprofit organizations, or community service activities. [DES/BEB] 3. (social marketing definition) A promotional message for a nonprofit organization or for a social cause printed or broadcast at no charge by the media. [ARA]

publicist The person responsible for managing the publicity program for a product, service, or organization. [DES/BEB]

publicity The non-paid-for communication of information about the company or product, generally in some media form. (See **content analysis, feature story, junket, letters to the editor, marketing public relations, media relations, NEXIS, promotion mix, public relations, publicist,** and **satellite media tour.**) [DES/BEB]

publicity functional expense See **functional expense classification**

publics 1. (legislation definition) Groups of people with common interest in a specific area, domain, topic or organization. [DC] 2. (sales promotion definition) Those groups that have an actual or possible interest in or impact on the company's efforts to achieve its goals. (See also **corporate relations** and **stakeholder.**) [DES/BEB]

puffery 1. (advertising definition) An exaggerated advertising claim that would be generally recognized as such by potential customers. [JE] 2. (consumer behavior definition) An advertising term implying gross exaggeration but usually not considered deception because it is assumed not to be believable. Examples are the mile-high ice cream cone or the world's softest mattress. [HHK/MCC] 3. (sales definition) The exaggerated statements made by a salesperson about the performance of a product or service. [BAW]

pull strategy 1. (physical distribution definition) A manufacturing strategy aimed at the end consumer of a product. The product is pulled through the channel by consumer demand initiated by promotional efforts, inventory stocking procedures, etc. [DJB/BJL] 2. (sales promotion definition) The communications and promotional activities by the marketer to persuade consumers to request specific products or brands from retail channel members. (See also **push strategy.**) [DES/BEB]

pulsing An advertising timing or continuity pattern in which there is noted variation of media spending in the media schedule. There is some spending during all periods of the schedule, but there are periods in which the spending is notably heavier than others. This approach stands in contrast to a continuous media pattern in which equal amounts of spending are allocated to all time periods of the schedule. (See also **continuity, continuous media pattern,** and **flighting.**) [JE]

punch card See **trade card**

punishment See **law of effect**

purchase See **AIDA** and **hierarchy of effects model**

purchase analysis See **value analysis**

purchase contract A written agreement between the buying and supplying organizations that specifies the terms of the transaction: product specifications, price, payment schedule, delivery terms, penalties and the like. It differs from the purchase order in that it is generally written by and signed by both parties. [GLL/DTW]

purchase decision, in organizational buying That phase of the organization's buying process in which alternative offers of suppliers are evaluated and a selection of one (or more) supplier is made. [GLL/DTW]

purchase history See **database**

purchase incidence decision See **nested logit model**

purchase intention A decision plan to buy a particular product or brand created through a choice/decision process (See also **behavioral intention**). [JPP/JCO]

purchase order A (generally standard) document that is issued by a purchasing organization to a supplier requesting items in the quantities, prices, time, and other terms agreed upon. (See also **purchase contract.**) [GLL/DTW]

purchase requisition An internal document issued by the user (or requiring) department to the purchasing department, specifying goods or services required. It authorizes the expenditure, and often includes suggested suppliers and prices. [GLL/DTW]

purchase returns and allowances See **returns and allowances from suppliers**

purchase stage, in organizational buying See **buygrid framework**

purchasing A generic term used to describe a title, a function, or a process by which a firm acquires the factors necessary to produce and distribute goods and services. (See also **procurement.**) [DJB/BJL]

purchasing agent 1. (industrial definition) A member of the purchasing department responsible for one or more categories of products purchased. [GLL/DTW] 2. (retailing definition) An independent middleman, buying broker for a principal or principals (usually wholesalers), paid a commission or fee for services. (See also **gatekeeper.**) [WRD]

purchasing department The organizational unit responsible for learning the needs of operating units, locating and selecting supplier(s), negotiating price and other pertinent terms, and following up to ensure delivery. (See also **procurement.**) [GLL/DTW]

purchasing manual An internal document specifying rules for the relationships between the purchasing department, using departments, and suppliers. It details the principles and approved procedures associated with procurement. [GLL/DTW]

purchasing power A consumer's ability to buy goods and services as distinguished from the amount of money a consumer has. (See also **buying power.**) [WL/MBC]

purchasing power parity An economic principle stating that a change in the relationship between price levels in two countries will require an adjustment in the currency exchange rate to offset the price level differences. [WJK]

pure competition A market model in which (1) a lower price is the only element that leads buyers to prefer one seller to another, and (2) the amount that each individual seller can offer constitutes such a small proportion that acting alone it is powerless to affect the price. (See also **duopoly, imperfect competition, monopolistic competition, monopoly, monopsony, oligopolistic competition, oligopolistic environment, oligopoly, oligopsony, perfect competition,** and **workable competition.**) [DLS]

Pure Food and Drug Act (1906) This act banned adulteration and misbranding of foods and drugs sold in interstate commerce. (See also **consumer protection legislation** and **Food and Drug Administration.**) [DC]

purposive sample See **judgment sample**

push money Cash or other incentives paid directly to retail salespeople by the manufacturer to encourage sales of the manufacturer's brand over competitive brands. It also is used to influence the retail sale of specific products in a line. (See also **spiff.**) [DES/BEB]

push strategy 1. (physical distribution definition) A manufacturing strategy aimed at other channel members rather than the end consumer. The manufacturer attempts to entice other channel members to carry its product through trade allowances, inventory stocking procedures, pricing policies, etc. [DJB/BJL] 2. (sales promotion definition) The communications and promotional activities by the marketer to persuade wholesale and retail channel members to stock and promote specific products. (See also **pull strategy.**) [DES/BEB]

PX See **post exchange**

Q-sort technique A general methodology for gathering data and processing the collected information; the subjects are assigned the task of sorting a number of statements by placing a specific number of statements in each sorting category; the emphases are on determining the relative ranking of stimuli by individuals and in deriving clusters of individuals who display similar preference orderings of stimuli. [GAC]

QR See **quick response** and **quick-response delivery system**

quadratic programming See **mathematical programming**

qualified market See **served market**

qualifying The process of determining whether a suspect has the characteristics that enables the suspect to be classified as a prospect. [BAW]

qualitative data See **focus group**

quality See **product quality**

quality control A function located somewhere in or close to the operations unit. Its primary purpose is to verify that the goods or services produced meet the specifications established for them. For goods, the process involves statistical sampling and measurement of parts of the output from manufacturing. For services, quality control involves actual field sampling of ongoing operations. A secondary purpose of quality control is to analyze the operations function, seek causes for product deficiencies, answer customer complaints, etc. [DW]

quality of life A sense of well being about a person's or society's way of life and life style, often estimated by social indicators. The governing factors include income, wealth, safety, recreation facilities, education, health, aesthetics, leisure time, and the like. [WL/MBC]

quantitative models See **decision calculus models**

quantity discount A reduction in price for volume purchases. (See also **cumulative quantity discount** and **noncumulative quantity discount.**) [KM]

question mark See **growth-share matrix**

questionnaire A document that is used to guide what questions are to be asked respondents and in what order, and sometimes lists the alternative responses that are acceptable. (See also **communication.**) [GAC]

quick response (QR) A finished product inventory management system that times replenishment to actual daily sales. Under this system, the retailer maintains lean inventories through frequent store deliveries of small lots. Point-of-sale information is exchanged daily between the retail outlet and distributors or manufacturers in order to time product delivery closer to actual demand. [DJB/BJL]

quick-response delivery system (QR) A system designed to reduce the leadtime for receiving merchandise, thereby lowering inventory investment, improving customer service levels, and reducing distribution expenses. It is also known as just-in-time inventory management system. [WRD]

quota 1. (global marketing definition) A trade term that denotes a specific numerical or value limit applied to a particular type of good either in the case of exports or imports of goods. [WJK] 2. (sales definition) A target level of performance and/or activity that the salesperson is expected to achieve. Comment: A quota can be established for various performance measures such as sales, gross margin, and new accounts. The quota can be used in a variety of sales management functions including forecasting sales, motivating salespeople, and evaluating their performance. [BAW]

quota sample A nonprobability sample chosen in such a way that the proportion of sample elements possessing a certain characteristic is approximately the same as the proportion of the elements with the characteristic in the population; each field worker is assigned a quota that specifies the characteristics of the people he or she is to contact. (See also **convenience sample, judgment sample, sequential sample,** and **snowball sample.**) [GAC]

quota-bonus compensation A plan that involves a basic salary and commissions paid on sales in excess of a predetermined quota. [WRD]

quotation A promise from a potential supplier stating the supplier's willingness to supply and deliver the item(s) required (by a potential buyer) within a certain period of time at a certain price. It is a response to a buyer's request for quotation. [GLL/DTW]

racetrack layout See **loop layout**

rack jobber A wholesale middleman operating principally in the food trade, supplying certain classes of merchandise that do not fit into the regular routine of food store merchandise resource contacts. The rack jobber commonly places display racks in retail stores providing an opening inventory on a consignment or on a guaranteed-sale basis, periodically checks the stock, and replenishes inventories. The term is somewhat archaic with trade acceptance of the term service merchandiser. (See also **wagon distributor**.) [WRD]

radio wrap-around The radio equivalent of a video news release, a radio story lasting 90 seconds or less and including an announcer who introduces sound bits from one or more news sources. [DES/BEB]

radio-frequency technology (RF) A specific information technology application that allows the positive identification of merchandise both while in-transit and during the materials handling process. [DJB/BJL]

raincheck A promise given to customers when merchandise is out of stock to sell them merchandise at the sale price when the merchandise arrives. [WRD]

random digit dialing A technique used in studies employing telephone interviews in which the numbers to be called are randomly generated. (See also **plus-one dialing**.) [GAC]

random model See **stochastic model**

random utility model See **nested logit model**

randomized response model An interviewing technique in which potentially embarrassing and relatively innocuous questions are paired, and the question the respondent answers is randomly determined. [GAC]

range The maximum distance a consumer is ordinarily willing to travel for a good or service; as such it determines the outer limit of a store's trade area or market area. [WRD]

rapport A close, harmonious relationship between a salesperson and customer. [BAW]

rate 1. (advertising definition) The cost of a unit of space or time in an advertising media vehicle. [JE] 2. (physical distribution definition) A charge usually expressed in dollar terms for the performance of some transportation or distribution service. [DJB/BJL]

rate card A printed listing of the charges associated with different amounts of time or space, different placements in the vehicle, and other conditions of sales. Often rate cards serve as the starting point for negotiation in the fashion of the sticker on the window of a new car. [JE]

rate differential The difference between the local advertising and national advertising rates charged by a local advertising vehicle. [JE]

rate of return pricing A method of determining prices by adding a markup that will produce a predetermined return on investment. [WRD]

rate regulation The process by which rates are administered. In a highly regulated economy, this could include extensive rules and policies on pricing and related services. Regulation occurs at the federal, state, and local levels. [DJB/BJL]

rating The percentage of the total potential audience who are exposed to a particular media vehicle. In television, a rating is the number of households with their television sets tuned to a particular program for a specified length of time divided by the total number of households that have television. In print media, ratings are computed using survey data about actual readership rather than information about circulation. [JE]

ratio of output and/or input measures An objective measure of sales force performance that incorporates common ratios used to evaluate salespeople. These ratios include expense ratios, account development and servicing ratios, and call activity and/or productivity. (See also **input evaluation measure, output evaluation measure,** and **sales force evaluation**.) [AJD]

ratio scale A measurement in which the numbers assigned to the attributes of the objects have a natural or absolute zero and that therefore allow the comparison of absolute magnitudes of the objects. (See also **comparative rating scale, constant sum method, graphic-rating scale, Guttman scale, interval scale, itemized rating scale, nominal scale, ordinal scale, Stapel scale,** and **summated rating**.) [GAC]

rational appeals 1. (consumer behavior definition) The concept of rational or irrational appeals does not exist in modern consumer behavior thinking but rather this is a term carried over from economics. From the point of view of the consumer, all behavior is rational although it may not appear so to the observer. [HHK/MCC] 2. (industrial definition) Claims that attempt to show that a specific product will yield certain functional benefits. Rational appeals form the core of most organizational sales messages while more emotional appeals, addressing self-image, life style and the like, are more often used to position products in the consumer marketplace. (See also **buying motives**.) [GLL/DTW]

rational motivations See **buying motives**

rationalization An ego defense in which unattainable goals are perceived to be undesirable (sour grapes) and those that are attainable are perceived to be remarkably adequate (sweet lemons). [HHK/MCC]

rationing A system of allocating goods and services that are in short supply, other than by price, to prevent prices from rising to unreasonable levels and prevent inequitable distribution. It is often used in periods of emergency. [WL/MBC]

raw materials 1. (industrial definition) The natural products (coal, iron, crude oil, fish) and farm products (wheat, cotton, fruits) that are sold in their natural state. They are processed only to the level required for economical handling and transport. (See also **industrial products**.) [GLL/DTW] 2. (product development definition) The products such as lumber and minerals that are bought for use in the production of other products, either as part of the finished item or in the industrial process. [DW]

R&D See **research and development**

repurchase rate The volume of purchase and the amount of time that typically occur between consumer or retailer purchasing occasions for a specific product. [DES/BEB]

reach The number of different persons or households exposed to a particular advertising media vehicle or a media schedule during a specified period of time. It is also called cumulative audience, cumulative reach, net audience, net reach, net unduplicated audience, or unduplicated audience. Reach is often presented as a percentage of the total number of persons in a specified audience or target market. [JE]

reaction formation See **ego defenses**

reactive moves See **market penetration**

readership test A test of advertising effectiveness of print media in which a sample of readers of a particular issue of a publication are asked whether they noticed and/or read particular ads. It is also called a recognition test. [JE]

readiness-to-buy stage See **buyer readiness stage**

real cost The cost of a product or service adjusted for changes in purchasing power and taking into consideration alternative uses of funds. [WL/MBC]

real dollars See **constant dollar value**

real income The power of one's income to command other goods in the market. (See also **discretionary buying power, disposable personal income, money income, national income, personal disposable income,** and **personal income**.) [DLS]

real self concept The knowledge, attitudes, and perceptions people have about themselves as they actually are. (See also **ideal self concept** and **self concept**.) [JPP/JCO]

rebate A return of a portion of the purchase price in the form of cash by the seller to the buyer. (See also **consumer sales promotion, demand creation, fulfillment,** and **refund**.) [KM]

rebuy purchase See **buyclasses** and **buygrid framework**

recall loss A type of error caused by a respondent forgetting that an event happened. (See also **telephone error**.) [GAC]

recall test A test of advertising effectiveness in which a sample of members of the audience are contacted at a specific time after exposure to a media vehicle and asked to recall advertising messages they remember seeing and/or hearing in the media vehicle. It is called **unaided recall** if there is no prompting with elements of the ads or commercials being examined. With prompting, the results are called **aided recall**. [JE]

receipt See **cash flow**

receipt-of-goods dating (ROG) This denotes that the discount period does not begin until the day the customer receives the shipment. (See also **advance dating, dating, end of month dating, extra dating, future dating, memorandum purchase and dating, ordinary dating, proximo dating,** and **season dating**.) [WRD]

recession A turning point in a business cycle characterized by dropping production and increasing unemployment. (See also **depression, prosperity,** and **recovery**.) [DLS]

reciprocity 1. (industrial definition) A buying arrangement in which two organizations agree to purchase one another's products. [GLL/DTW] 2. (sales definition) A special relationship between two companies that agree to purchase products from each other. [BAW]

recognition test See **readership test**

recovery A phase of the business cycle characterized by increasing gross national product, lessening unemployment, and a leveling out of previously falling prices. It is popularly called an upturn or revival. (See also **depression, prosperity,** and **recession**.) [DLS]

red tape See **bureaucratic organization**

redemption See **coupon redemption**

redemption rate The number or percentage of sales promotion offers that are acted on by consumers or retailers out of the total number possible. (See also **coupon redemption**.) [DES/BEB]

redemption store An establishment operated by a trading stamp company redeeming stamps for merchandise. [WRD]

redlining The arbitrary exclusion of certain classes of customers, often those from poor neighborhoods, from such economic activities as borrowing money or getting real estate mortgages. [WL/MBC]

reducing market attractiveness See **market defense**

reference group 1. (consumer behavior definition) A reference group is one that the individual tends to use as the anchor point for evaluating his/her own beliefs and attitudes. One may or may not be a member and may or may not aspire to membership in a reference group; nevertheless, it can have great influence on one's values, opinions, attitudes, and behavior patterns. A reference group may be positive; that is, the individual patterns his or her own beliefs and behavior to be congruent with those of the group. Or, it may be negative. A negative reference group is just as influential. The church, labor union, political party, or sorority are examples of both positive and negative reference groups for specific individuals. It also is a term coined by Herbert Hyman to designate a group that an individual uses as a "point of reference" in determining his or her own judgments, preferences, beliefs, and behavior. The size of a reference group can be a single individual (although perhaps in this case the term *group* should not be used) to a very large aggregate of persons such as a political party or religious institution. [HHK/MCC] 2. (consumer behavior definition) The people who serve as a point of reference and who influence an individual's affective responses, cognitions, and behavior. (See also **aspirational group** and **dissociative group**.) [JPP/JCO]

reference price The price that buyers use to compare the offered price of a product or service. The reference price may be a price in a buyer's memory, or it may be the price of an alternative product. (See also **anchor, anchoring effect,** and **transaction value**.) [KM]

reference product See **anchor** and **anchoring effect**

referral A lead for a prospect given to the salesperson by an existing customer [BAW]

referral approach A method used by salespeople to approach prospects in which the salesperson uses the name of a satisfied customer or friend of the prospect to begin the sales presentation. (See also **center of influence method, cold-canvassing, curiosity approach, endless chain method, introduction approach,** and **product approach**.) [BAW]

refund 1. (pricing definition) A return of the amount paid for an item. [KM] 2. (sales promotion definition)

An offer made by the seller to return a certain amount of money to the purchaser when the product is purchased alone or in combination with some other product. (See also **bounce back offer, consumer sales promotion, fulfillment, rebate,** and **take one pad**.) [DES/BEB]

refusals A nonsampling error that arises because some designated respondents refuse to participate in the study. (See also **item nonresponse, noncoverage error, nonobservation error, nonresponse error, not-at-home, observation error, office error,** and **overcoverage error**.) [GAC]

regiocentrism orientation An attitude or orientation toward internationalization with the focus on regional orientation. (See also **ethnocentric orientation, geocentric orientation,** and **polycentric orientation**.) [WJK]

regional brand See **local brand, national brand,** and **private brand**

regional edition The subdivision of a national magazine's circulation into geographic regions, so that advertisers can purchase only the portion of the publication's circulation that applies to their immediate needs. A region can be a group of neighboring states, a single state, or in some instances, regions within specific states. A demographic edition operates on the same principle, except that the subdivisions are based on various demographic characteristics of the publication's circulation. [JE]

regional sales manager See **field sales manager**

regional shopping center 1. (geography definition) This type of shopping center ranges from 300,000 to more than 1,000,000 square feet. It provides shopping goods, general merchandise, apparel, furniture, and home furnishings in full depth and variety. It is built around at least one full-line department store with a minimum of 100,000 square feet. [DLH] 2. (retailing definition) One of several standard classes of shopping centers recognized by The Urban Land Institute. It provides for general merchandise, apparel, furniture, and home furnishings in depth. Typically, it has one or two full-line department stores larger than 100,000 square feet and total center store area ranging from 300,000 square feet to 850,000 square feet. It is a class of planned shopping centers, usually with major department store units and with usually 50 to 100 stores, serving a very large trading area. It is larger than a community shopping center. (See also **arcade shopping center, factory outlet center, mall-type shopping center, neighborhood shopping center, off-price shopping center, strip-type shopping center,** and **super regional shopping center**.) [WRD]

regression analysis A statistical technique used to derive an equation that relates a single, continuous criterion variable to one or more continuous predictor variables. (See also **cluster analysis, conjoint analysis, correlation analysis, discriminant analysis, factor analysis, logit model,** and **statistical demand analysis**.) [GAC]

regression models See **forecasting models** and **PAR ROI**

regulation The efforts by governmental units to create and enforce conditions that specify acceptable business practice. [WL/MBC]

rehearsing desired behavior See **behavioral self-management**

Reilly's law A model used in trade area analysis to define the relative ability of two cities to attract customers from the area between them. [WRD]

reinforcement 1. (consumer behavior definition) A consequence that occurs after a behavior that increases the probability of future behavior of the same type. [JPP/JCO] 2. (consumer behavior definition) A term from learning theory denoting the reward available to an organism for the response that the experimenter was trying to create or encourage. (See also **law of effect**.) [HHK/MCC]

rejection operator See **linear learning model**

relationship marketing Marketing with the conscious aim to develop and manage long-term and/or trusting relationships with customers, distributors, suppliers, or other parties in the marketing environment. [GLL/DTW]

relationship value The bonds, both actual and perceptual, that are created between the customer, the marketer, and the brand by a specific sales promotion event. [DES/BEB]

relationship-oriented behavior See **consideration**

relative precision A degree of precision desired in an estimate of a parameter is expressed relative to the level of the estimate of the parameter. [GAC]

reliability The similarity of results provided by independent but comparable measures of the same object, trait, or construct. (See also **equivalence** and **stability**.) [GAC]

religious organization See **hierarchical organization**

remarking The practice of remarking merchandise due to price changes, lost or mutilated tickets, or customer returns. [WRD]

reorder point calculations See **automatic reordering system**

reorder unit The unit in which an item is reordered, the exact amount depending on trade practices—e.g., dozen, gross, nearest hundredweight, or foot. [WRD]

rep See **media representative**

repair items See **maintenance, repair, and operating items and supplies**

repeat See **awareness-trial-repeat**

repeat sale The subsequent sale of a product after the initial purchase. The level of repeat sales for a product is often used as a measure of customer satisfaction—the higher the level of repeat sales, the more satisfied customers are. [GLL/DTW]

repeat usage of product See **consumer sales promotion**

repetition See **habit formation, sleeper effect,** and **trial**

replacement level fertility A total fertility rate of 2,120 or 2.12 births per 1,000 women. It is the rate at which a population reaches zero population growth. (See also **completed fertility, crude birth rate,** and **fertility rate**.) [WL/MBC]

replacement sale A sale that takes place when a product becomes physically or economically obsolete. The timing of replacement is influenced by a customer's business prospects, its cash flow, product alternatives in the market, as well as the seller's financing terms and sales efforts. [GLL/DTW]

replenishment cycle A term used in inventory management that describes the process by which stocks are resupplied from some central location. This process often involves the development of quantitatively based inventory models designed to optimize this resupply process. [DJB/BJL]

replenishment time See **leadtime**

reply card An addressed card inserted between pages of a magazine or newspaper. (See also **preprint advertising**.) [JE]

reply envelope An addressed envelope inserted between pages of a magazine or newspaper. (See also **preprint advertising**.) [JE]

repossession The recovery of merchandise by the store after delivery, owing to a customer's failure to complete payment. [WRD]

repression See **ego defenses**

request for proposal (RFP) A request issued by a potential buyer desiring bids from several potential vendors for a product or service satisfying specifications describing the buyer's needs. [BAW]

request for quotation (RFQ) A document transmitted to a potential supplier requesting price and delivery terms on a specific item or set of items. A supplier responds to an RFQ with a quotation. [GLL/DTW]

requisition See **purchase requisition**

resale price maintenance The determination or suggestion by the manufacturer of the price at which an item will be resold by wholesalers and/or retailers. [WRD]

resale price maintenance laws Federal and state statutes permitting agreements between a supplier and a retailer that state that the latter should not resell commodities below a specified minimum price. (See also **fair trade laws, McGuire-Keogh Fair Trade Enabling Act,** and **Miller-Tydings Resale Price Maintenance Act**.) [DC]

research and development (R&D) The function of working through various sciences and technologies to design new products. This usually involves some basic research for creating new technologies, and some applied research for converting those basic discoveries (and others) into specific new products. The applied (or developmental) phase begins after new product concepts have been screened and desirable attributes set up for them. It ends when scientific personnel deliver to manufacturing the necessary process specifications and finished product specifications. R&D departments also have many other duties not so directly related to new products. [DW]

research design A framework or plan for a study that guides the collection and analysis of the data. (See also **causal research, descriptive research,** and **exploratory research**.) [GAC]

research process A sequence of steps in the design and implementation of a research study, including problem formulation, determination of sources of information and research design, determination of data collection method and design of data collection forms, design of the sample and collection of the data, analysis and interpretation of the data, and the research report. [GAC]

reseller market A market composed of the individuals and organizations that acquire goods for the purpose of reselling or renting them to others at a profit. (See also **organizational market**.) [GLL/DTW]

reservation price The highest price a buyer is willing to pay for a product or service. (See also **price thresholds** and **maximum acceptable price**.) [KM]

reserve system of stock control A method of controlling the amount of stock in the reserve stockroom by keeping records of all goods sent to the selling floor and all goods received from vendors. Stock in reserve is determined without counting the goods, but by adding the number of pieces received to the past physical inventory and subtracting the number sent to the selling floor. [WRD]

resident buying office An office that represents many retailers in the same line of business in the central wholesale market providing information about market developments and guidance in purchasing and actual placing of some orders for their clients. (See also **associated buying office** and **buying committee**.) [WRD]

residual market value The image-enhancing communication about the product or service that remains with the consumer after the sales promotion event is over. [DES/BEB]

resource allocation and budgeting See **implementation**

resource allocation models Models for guiding the allocation of marketing resources. Mathematical programming, decision calculus models, and the analytic hierarchy process are often used. (See also **marketing mix models, product and business portfolio models, sales force models,** and **STRATPORT**.) [DCS/YJW]

resource rating The evaluation of resources through the statistical measurement and rating of vendors according to their respective contributions to store volume and profits and quality or dependability of service. [WRD]

respect needs See **hierarchy of needs**

respondent A person in a survey who is asked for information using either written or verbal questioning, typically employing a questionnaire to guide the questioning. (See also **subject**.) [GAC]

respondent conditioning See **classical conditioning**

response latency An amount of time a respondent deliberates before answering a question. [GAC]

responsiveness See **social styles matrix**

restraint of trade A concept with origin in common law and that embraces acts, contracts, conspiracies, combinations, or practices that operate to prejudice the public interest by unduly restricting competition or unduly obstructing the due course of trade. [DC]

retail accordion theory A theory of retail institutional change that suggests that retail institutions go from outlets with wide assortments to specialized narrow line store merchants and then back again to the more general wide assortment institution. It is also referred to as the general-specific-general theory. (See also **central place theory, concentric zone theory, dialectic process, gravity model, natural selection theory, retail life cycle,** and **wheel of retailing theory**.) [WRD]

retail advertising See **local advertising**

retail establishment A single or separate place of business principally engaged in the performance of marketing functions, where in or out sales are made primarily to ultimate consumers. [WRD]

retail inventory method of accounting A type of accounting system whereby the closing inventory at cost is determined by the average relationship between cost and retail value of all goods available for sale during the period. (See also **additional markup, gross additional markup, gross cost of merchandise handled, gross cost of merchandise sold, initial markup, maintained markup, markup, retailing the invoice, and total cost of goods sold.**) [WRD]

retail life cycle A theory of retail competition that states that retailing institutions, like the products they distribute, pass through an identifiable cycle. This cycle can be partitioned into four distinct stages: (1) innovation, (2) accelerated development, (3) maturity, and (4) decline. (See also **central place theory, concentric zone theory, dialectic process, gravity model, natural selection theory, retail accordion theory,** and **wheel of retailing theory**.) [WRD]

retail reductions The total of markdowns, discounts to employees and other classes of customers, and stock shortages. [WRD]

retail salesperson A salesperson employed by a retailer who is involved in selling goods and services to the ultimate consumer in retail stores. [BAW]

retail store A place of business (establishment) open to and frequented by the general public, and in which sales are made primarily to ultimate consumers, usually in small quantities, from merchandise inventories stored and displayed on the premises. (See also **retail structure** and **unplanned center**.) [WRD]

retail structure The spatial distribution of retail stores and store types, including the composition of groupings of stores, spacing, and relationship to market. [DLH]

retailer A merchant middleman who is engaged primarily in selling to ultimate consumers. One retailer may operate a number of establishments. [WRD]

retailer sales promotion See **demonstrations, as retailer sales promotion**

retailer sponsored cooperative A form of contractual vertical marketing system that is an example of backward integration. Independent retailers organize contractually to form a cooperative that gives them greater market power in dealing with suppliers. [WRD]

retailer's handling charge A sum of money above the face value of a coupon paid by the manufacturer to the retailer as a fee for accepting and initially processing manufacturer-originated coupons. (See also **coupon redemption**.) [DES/BEB]

retailing A set of business activities carried on to accomplishing the exchange of goods and services for purposes of personal, family, or household use, whether performed in a store or by some form of nonstore selling. [WRD]

retailing mix Those variables that a retailer can combine in alternative ways to arrive at a strategy for attracting its consumers. The variables usually include merchandise and services offered, pricing, advertising and promotion, store design, location, and visual merchandising. [WRD]

retailing the invoice 1. The practice of writing the unit selling prices on vendors' invoices that serves as the buyer's authorization. 2. It also refers to extensions of price-quality relationships to ascertain total retail value for purposes of the retail inventory method of accounting. [WRD]

return to stock When a customer returns merchandise to the store for an exchange, credit, or money-back, this process of placing the merchandise into stock again is accompanied by a transaction to return to stock so that the item and the dollar amount are added back to inventory levels. [WRD]

returns and allowances from suppliers The sum of purchased goods returned to the supplier and unplanned reductions in purchase price. This represents a reduction in the cost of purchased items or total purchases. It is also referred to as purchase returns and allowances. [WRD]

returns and allowances to customers The dollar sum of goods returned to the store and of reductions in price allowed customers by the store. It is deducted from gross sales to get net sales. It is also referred to as sales returns and allowances. [WRD]

reusable containers A form of premium in which the product is packed in a container that has additional uses or value after the product has been consumed. (See also **package**.) [DES/BEB]

reverse logistics The process of returning products in a physical channel. In many logistics systems, there are two-way flows of product and service. In some systems, products must be returned to a central location for repair and refurbishing. In other systems, products may be recalled and returned to a central processing area. [DJB/BJL]

reverse marketing A proactive, market-oriented approach to procurement. [GLL/DTW]

reverse reciprocity A selling arrangement in which two organizations agree to sell their scarce products to one another. [GLL/DTW]

revival See **recovery**

revolving credit A consumer credit plan that combines the convenience of a continuous charge account and the privileges of installment payment. It is commonly used for purchase of merchandise on a nonsecured basis. (See also **installment account**.) [WRD]

reward See **dealer loader, frequent shopper program, game, incentive plan,** and **self-liquidator.**

RF See **radio-frequency technology**

RFP See **request for proposal**

RFQ See **request for quotation**

rider See **apron**

risk analysis As a stage in the preparation of a strategic plan, internal vulnerabilities of the business and external threats need to be identified. The risks with the highest probability of occurring and/or those that would cause the most damage need to be identified in order that appropriate action may be taken. The importance of any specific risk factor is equal to the negative (or positive) consequences of the factor multiplied by the likelihood of its occurrence. [GSD]

risk reduction See **perceived risk**

risk surrogate See **beta coefficient**

risking See **channel flows**

rituals Actions or behaviors performed by consumers to create or affirm desired symbolic cultural meanings. (See also **culture**.) [JPP/JCO]

roadrailer A transportation innovation that allows a truck chassis to be outfitted with a set of rail trucks (wheels) that allows the truck to be used directly on the rails. This provides significant intermodal flexibility and service improvement. [DJB/BJL]

Robinson-Patman Act (1936) This is an amendment to the Clayton Act that prohibits price discrimination when the effect "may be substantially to lessen competition or create a monopoly"; prohibits payments of broker's commission when an independent broker is not employed; forbids sellers to provide allowances or services to buyers unless these are available to all buyers on "equally proportional terms"; and prohibits a buyer from inducing or receiving a prohibited discrimination in price.

(See also **antitrust laws** and **Clayton Act**.) [DC]

robotics The use of sophisticated custom-designed machines to do specific tasks in the production, materials handling, and distribution areas of a business. [DJB/BJL]

ROG dating See **receipt-of-goods dating**

role set The set of people who have a vested interest in how the salesperson performs the job. These people include the individual's immediate superior, other executives in the firm, purchasing agents and other members of customers' organizations, and the salesperson's family. They all try to influence the salesperson's behavior, either formally through organizational policies, operating procedures, training programs, and the like, or informally through social pressures, rewards, and sanctions. [AJD]

roles The behavior that is expected of people in standard situations. Roles are the patterns of needs, goals, beliefs, attitudes, values, and behavior that are expected of an individual occupying a particular position in society. [HHK/MCC]

ROP See **run of press coupon** and **run-of-press**

ROP color See **run-of-press color**

Rorschach ink blot See **projective technique**

rough A dummy of a print advertising layout or an early version of a television storyboard prepared by art directors and copywriters to help them realize the advertising idea and discuss it with others in the advertising agency and sometimes with clients. (See also **comprehensive layout, mechanical,** and **thumbnail**.) [JE]

routine call pattern A method used by salespeople to schedule sales calls regularly on customers. (See also **call frequency, circular routing, leapfrog routing, routing,** and **zoning**.) [BAW]

routing 1. (physical distribution definition) A process of directing either an employee or a vehicle along some predesignated path. The path is usually designed to minimize cost or effort given some overall objective of the system. [DJB/BJL] 2. (sales definition) A plan describing how a salesperson will travel through the salesperson's sales territory. (See also **call frequency, circular routing, leapfrog routing, routine call pattern,** and **zoning**.) [BAW]

routinized choice behavior A choice involving little cognitive and behavioral effort. (See also **extensive problem solving** and **limited problem solving**.) [JPP/JCO]

routinized response behavior After a sufficient number of trials or purchases of a particular brand, the decision process requires very little cognitive effort and little or no decision making is involved. The behavior becomes habitual or routine. (See also **extensive problem solving** and **habit**.) [HHK/MCC]

rule of reason 1. (economic definition) A principle for determining the legality of business practices. Illegality is determined by evidence concerning the country, competitors, and consumers. (See also ***per se*** **rules**.) [DLS] 2. (legislation definition) A standard applied to the Sherman Antitrust Act that interprets it to prohibit only "unreasonable restraints of trade" rather than every restraint of trade. The courts have not consistently defined the term "unreasonable." [DC]

rule of thumb See **heuristic**

run of press coupon (ROP) A couponed advertisement placed in a publication in which the location is at the discretion of the publisher. [DES/BEB]

run-of-press (ROP) The positioning of ads anywhere within the pages of a newspaper or magazine as the staff of the publication prepares the various pages for printing. This contrasts with advertisers paying premium prices for ads that are to be placed in specific locations in a magazine or newspaper. (See also **preprint advertising** and **run-of-press color**.) [JE]

run-of-press color The use of color ink for ads printed during the regular printing process for a publication. This contrasts with color preprint advertising in which color ads are printed separately and inserted between the pages of a publication during the regular printing process. (See also **run-of-press**.) [JE]

runners The styles, especially in fashion apparel, for which there are many repeat wholesale purchases of the same item. [WRD]

rural population That part of the total population not classified as urban. (See also **urban population**.) [WL/MBC]

safety needs See **hierarchy of needs** and **Maslow's need hierarchy**

safety stock A measurement used in inventory management. It is the average amount of inventory on hand when a new shipment arrives. Higher levels of safety stock to protect against out of stock condition require additional dollar investment in inventory. [DJB/BJL]

safety stock merchandise Inventory used as a safety cushion for cycle stock so the retailer won't run out of stock if demand exceeds the sales forecast. [WRD]

salary Compensation paid periodically to a salesperson, independent of performance. (See also **bonus, combination compensation plan, commission,** and **incentive compensation.**) [BAW]

salary plus commission See **combination compensation plan**

sale-leaseback The practice of retailers building new stores and selling them to real estate investors who then lease the buildings back to the retailers on a long-term basis. (See also **sell-and-lease agreement.**) [WRD]

saleable sample A regular or specially sized quantity of the product offered at a low price to induce trial. (See also **sample.**) [DES/BEB]

sales See **product performance tracking**

sales activity goal See **activity goal, sales**

sales agent See **manufacturers' agent**

sales analysis A procedure involving the gathering, classifying, comparing, and studying of company sales data. It may simply involve the comparison of total company sales in two different time periods. Or it may entail subjecting thousands of component sales (or sales-related) figures to a variety of comparisons among themselves, with external data, and with like figures for earlier periods of time. (See also **cost analysis, sales force evaluation,** and **sales management.**) [AJD]

sales approach See **approach, sales**

sales aptitude The overall limit of an individual's ability to perform a given sales job. Sales aptitude is a function of such enduring personal and psychological characteristics as physical factors, mental abilities, and personality characteristics. [AJD]

sales budget The portion of a firm's total marketing budget allocated for sales force training, compensation, travel, entertainment expenses, and the costs of sales force administration. [AJD]

sales call A meeting between a customer and a salesperson who engages in selling. [BAW]

sales call allocation grid A method used to classify customers and determine the sales effort to direct toward them. The dimensions are the strength of the firm's position with the customer and the customer's sales potential. [BAW]

sales contest 1. (sales definition) A

short-term incentive program designed to motivate sales personnel to accomplish specific sales objectives. Comment: In general, a sales contest is used by firms to stimulate extra effort for obtaining new customers, promoting the sales of specific items, generating larger orders per sales call, etc. [BAW] 2. (sales definition) A short-term incentive program designed to motivate salespeople to accomplish very specific sales objectives. Although a contest should not be considered part of the firm's ongoing compensation plan, it does offer salespeople the opportunity to gain financial as well as nonfinancial rewards. Contest winners often receive prizes in cash or merchandise or travel that have monetary value. Winners also receive nonfinancial rewards in the form of recognition and a sense of accomplishment. [See also **incentive** and **incentive plan.**) [AJD]

sales demonstration An aspect of the sales presentation that provides a sensory appeal to show how the product works and what benefits it offers to the customer. [BAW]

sales dual career path See **dual career path, sales**

sales engineer A salesperson who has extensive product knowledge and uses this knowledge as a focal aspect of the sales presentation. [BAW]

sales force administration See **sales management**

sales force compensation A financial reward or inventive program based on salesperson performance and tenure. A major purpose of any sales force compensation program is to motivate or influence the sales force to do what management wants, in the way they want it done, and within the desired time. The three major methods of compensating salespeople are (1) straight salary plan, (2) straight commission plan, and (3) combination compensation plan consisting of a combination of salary and incentive pay in the form of commissions, bonuses, or both. [AJD]

sales force composite A method of developing a sales forecast that uses the opinions of each member of the field sales staff regarding how much the individual expects to sell in the period as input. [GAC]

sales force efficiency See **cost analysis** and **sales analysis**

sales force evaluation An assessment of the overall personal selling effort. The evaluation process helps to measure whether the selling effort is on target with respect to the goals established and also provides strong clues of where and how the selling effort can be improved. Sales analysis and cost analysis are major techniques sales managers use to evaluate sales force efforts. To supplement these analyses, objective measures such as output evaluation measures, input evaluation measures, and ratio of output and/or input measures can be employed. (See also **sales report.**) [AJD]

sales force management See **sales management**

sales force management audit A periodic and in-depth review of the adequacy of a firm's sales management process. It is conducted to identify current and potential strengths, weaknesses, and problems at all levels of the sales organization. [AJD]

sales force models The models for allocation of sales efforts include 1) models such as CALLPLAN for allocation of time among various customer and prospect segments; 2) models such as DETAILER, or those more geared for resource allocation such as the analytic hierarchy process, for allocation of sales efforts across products; and 3) models for design of and allocation of resources among sales territories. These models include various applications of linear programming and integer programming as well as specialized models such as GEOLINE. In addition to these types of models, a number of compensation/incentive models have been prepared typically as an optimization model. (See also **BRANDAID, mathematical programming,** and **resource allocation models.**) [DCS/YJW]

sales force organization An arrangement of activities and job positions involving the sales force. The starting point in organizing a sales force is determining the goals or objectives to be accomplished; these are specified in the firm's overall marketing plan. The selling activities necessary to accomplish the firm's marketing objectives can then be divided in such a way that the objectives can be achieved with as little duplication of effort as possible. The organizational structure provides for specialization of labor, stability, and continuity in selling efforts and coordination of the various activities assigned to different salespeople and departments within the firm. (See also **horizontal structure of the sales organization** and **vertical structure of the sales organization.**) [AJD]

sales force recruitment and selection The activities necessary to attract and hire potential members of the sales force. The starting point in the recruitment process is a thorough analysis of the job to be filled and a description of the qualifications that a new hiree should have. The next step is to find and attract a pool of qualified job applicants. The final stage in the hiring process is to evaluate each applicant through personal history information, interviews, reference checks, and/or formal tests and then based upon this evaluation, select the appropriate applicant to fill the position. [AJD]

sales force selection See **sales force recruitment and selection**

sales force size See **equalized workload method** and **incremental productivity method**

sales force supervision See **sales management**

sales forecast An estimate of the dollar or unit sales for a specified future period under a proposed marketing plan or program. (See also **Box-Jenkins method, jury of executive opinion, sales force composite, statistical demand analysis, time series analysis,** and **users' expectations method.**) [GAC]

sales interaction See **sales call**

sales interview See **sales call**

sales job satisfaction A feeling (positive or negative) that a salesperson has about his or her work situation. This includes all of the characteristics of the job itself that salespeople find rewarding, fulfilling, satisfying, or frustrating and unsatisfying. [AJD]

sales lead See **lead, sales**

sales management The planning, direction, and control of the personal selling activities of a business unit, including recruiting, selecting, training, equipping, assigning, routing, supervising, paying, and motivating as these tasks apply to the sales force. Sales management involves three interrelated processes: (1) formulation of a strategic sales program; (2) implementation of the sales program; and (3) evaluation and control of sales force performance. In formulating the strategic sales program, sales management involves a number of activities including development of account management policies, demand forecasts, and quotas and budgets; sales organization; sales planning; territory design; deployment; and routing. In implementing the sales program, sales management activities include supervising, selecting, recruiting, training, and motivating the sales force. In addition, implementation requires the development of compensation systems and sales force incentive programs. The evaluation and control of sales force performance involves the development and enforcement of methods for monitoring and evaluating sales force performance. Sales management activities typically required for evaluation and control include behavioral analysis, cost analysis, and sales analysis. [AJD]

Sales Management Survey of Buying Power A survey published annually by *Sales and Marketing Management* that contains market data for states, a number of counties, cities, and standard metropolitan statistical areas. Included are statistics on population, retail sales, and household income, and a combined index of buying power for each reported geographic area. The index of buying power is a weighted index calculated with the formula: 5 (percentage of disposable personal income in an area) + 2 (percentage of U.S. population) + 3 (percentage of total retail sales)/10. [AJD]

sales manager The sales manager is responsible for planning, organizing, directing, and controlling the personal selling function. There are usually several levels of sales management ranging from the general sales manager to the first line field supervisor of salespeople. (See also **field sales manager.**) [VPB]

sales models See **decision calculus models, LITMUS, MEDIAC, STEAM, Tracker,** and **Vidale-Wolfe model**

sales organization, forms of Sales forces may be centralized at the corporate level or decentralized at the division level. In either case they may be organized to sell the full product line through one salesperson in each territory, or they may be organized to specialize by product, market, or type of account. (See also **centralized sales organization, decentralized sales organization, full-line sales organization, partially integrated division, sales organization specialized by account, sales organization specialized by market,** and **sales organization specialized by product.**) [VPB]

sales organization specialized by account Each salesperson is assigned to one or more accounts of the same type, often without regard to geographic location. An account specialist, for example, may call only on chain store headquarters, or only on automobile company headquarters. This may be an appropriate strategy when the account potential is large and when experienced salespeople are needed to deal with high level customer executives. Although this is the highest cost sales organization strategy, it is usually justified by the large sales potential of the accounts assigned in this manner. (See also **centralized sales organization; decentralized sales organization; full-line sales organization; partially integrated division; sales organization, sales organization specialized by market;** and **sales organization specialized by product.**) [VPB]

sales organization specialized by market In this organization, different salespeople specialize in the sale of the product line to different markets, such as consumer, institutional, and industrial markets. They may report to the same supervisor or there may be separate sales organizations for each market. Specialization may be an appropriate strategy when market knowledge is more important than product knowledge. Sales costs are higher than for a full-line strategy because two or more salespeople travel over the same geographic area, and more supervisors are needed if there is more than one sales force. (See also **centralized sales organization; decentralized sales organization; full-line sales organization; partially integrated division; sales organization, forms of; sales organization specialized by account;** and **sales organization specialized by product.**) [VPB]

sales organization specialized by product In this organization, different salespeople specialize in the sales of different products. They may report to the same supervisor or there may be a separate sales organization for each product line. This may be an appropriate strategy when technical expertise is required for each line, or when there are too many products for one person to sell effectively. Sales costs are higher, however, than they are for a full-line strategy because two or more salespeople travel over the same geographic area; also more supervisors are needed if there is more than one sales force. (See also **centralized sales organization; decentralized sales organization; full-line sales organization; partially integrated division; sales organization, forms of; sales organization specialized by account;** and **sales organization specialized by market.**) [VPB]

sales per call See **productivity sales goal**

sales planning See **sales forecast, sales potential, sales quota,** and **strategic sales program**

sales potential The portion of the market potential that a particular firm can reasonably expect to achieve. [GAC]

sales presentation See **presentation, sales**

sales program See **sales management**

sales promotion The media and nonmedia marketing pressure applied for a predetermined, limited period of time at the level of consumer, retailer, or wholesaler in order to stimulate trial, increase consumer demand, or improve product availability. (See also **accelerated purchase, buy one-get one free, consumer sales promotion, co-op mailing, cross ruff, demand creation, everyday low pricing, free goods, fulfillment, incentive, incremental sales, misredemption, promotion mix, promotional campaign, relationship value, residual market value, special event, sweepstakes,** and **trade sales promotion.**) [DES/BEB]

sales promotion, in organizational buying Those activities other than advertising and personal selling aimed at stimulating product sales. Some of the components of sales promotion are trade shows, premiums, incentives, give-aways, and specialty advertising (in which a firm's name may be printed on a calendar, for example). [GLL/DTW]

sales promotion manager A staff specialist responsible for providing market communication ideas, programs, and materials not otherwise defined as personal selling, advertising, or publicity. The sales promotion manager may report to the marketing manager, advertising manager, or there may be an advertising and sales promotion manager reporting to the marketing manager. [VPB]

sales promotion payment See **clearinghouse**

sales quota A sales goal or objective that is assigned to a marketing unit. The marketing unit in question might be an individual salesperson, a sales territory, a branch office, a region, a dealer or distributor, or a district. Sales quotas apply to specific periods and may be expressed in dollars or physical units. Thus, management can specify quarterly, annual, and longer term quotas for each of the company's field representatives in both dollars and physical units. It might even specify these goals for individual products and customers. (See also **activity quota, financial quota,** and **sales volume quota.**) [AJD]

sales report A report submitted by salespeople that tells management what is happening in the field. Most managers expect salespeople to report competitive activities, reactions of customers to company policies and products, as well as any other information management should know. In addition, sales reports can provide records for evaluating sales force performance. Sales reports often include such information as the number of calls made, orders taken, miles traveled, days worked, new prospects called on, and new accounts sold. (See also **sales force evaluation.**) [AJD]

sales representative The term sales representatives is a generic term that includes both direct salesperson and sales agent. [BAW]

sales response function The relationship between the sales volume of a business and the determinants of the sales volume of that business. The determinants of most interest to a business are those over which they have some control, i.e., the decision variables that comprise the marketing mix. [GSD]

sales returns and allowances See **returns and allowances to customers**

sales skill level An individual's level of sales-related knowledge or proficiency at carrying out the specific tasks necessary to perform a sales job. Sales skills are proficiency levels that can change rapidly with learning and experience. [AJD]

sales taxes See **compensatory import charges**

sales territory 1. (sales definition) A segment of the firm's market assigned to a salesperson or a group of salespeople. Comment: While a sales territory is typically defined by customers within a geographic boundary, it can be defined by customer types. [BAW] 2. (sales definition) A group of present and potential customers that is assigned to a salesperson, branch, dealer, or distributor for a given period of time. The key word in this definition is customers. Good sales territories are made up of customers who have money to spend and the willingness to spend it. Although the key to sales territory design is customers, the notion of a territory is typically operationalized using geographical boundaries. In cases in which products are highly technical and sophisticated, product specialists rather than geographic boundaries define sales territories. [AJD]

sales training A formal or informal program designed to educate the sales force and convey management expectations of job responsibilities. Sales training provides managers with the opportunity to communicate high performance expectations through training and to equip the sales force with the skills needed to reach high performance levels. A well-designed training program moves beyond passive learning techniques and shows the sales force how to sell. Behavior modeling is one successful approach to sales training. Some common objectives of sales training are to impart product knowledge, teach selling skills, increase productivity, improve morale, lower turnover, improve customer relations, and improve time and territory management. [AJD]

sales volume quota A quota that emphasizes sales or some aspect of sales volume. Sales volume quotas can be expressed in dollars, physical units, or points (a certain number of points is given for each dollar or unit sales of particular products.) The point system is typically used when a firm wants to give selective emphasis to certain products in the line. (See also **activity quota, financial quota,** and **sales quota.**) [AJD]

salesperson A person who is primarily involved in the personal process of assisting and/or persuading a potential customer to buy a product or service to the mutual benefit of both buyer and seller. (See also **sales representative.**) [BAW]

salesperson career cycle The sequence of stages that a salesperson passes through during his or her sales career. The salesperson has unique tasks, challenges, and concerns in each stage. The career cycle is characterized by four stages. In the exploration stage, individuals are concerned about finding a career in which they can succeed. In the establishment stage, sales personnel seek to attain stabilization within their occupation and desire professional success (e.g., a promotion). The maintenance stage is typified by salespeople's interest in maintaining their present position, status, and performance level. In the disengagement stage, salespeople are likely to psychologically and/or physically withdraw from their jobs. [AJD]

salesperson motivation The amount of effort the salesperson desires to expend on each activity or task associated with the job. Job tasks include calling on potential new accounts, developing sales presentations, filling out reports, etc. (See also **expectancy, instrumentality,** and **valence.**) [AJD]

salesperson role The set of activities or behaviors that are to be performed by any person occupying the position of salesperson in a firm. [AJD]

salesperson-related buying criteria See **buying criteria**

salient beliefs Those beliefs that are activated from memory in a situation to influence comprehension or decision making. [JPP/JCO]

sample 1. (marketing research definition) The selection of a subset of elements from a larger group of objects. [GAC] 2. (sales promotion definition) A small portion of a product that is made available to prospective purchasers to demonstrate the product's value or use and to encourage future purchase. (See also **consumer sales promotion, cross ruff, free sample, saleable sample,** and **trial.**) [DES/BEB]

sample survey A cross-sectional study in which the sample is selected to be representative of the target population and in which the emphasis is on the generation of summary statistics such as averages and percentages. [GAC]

sampling control A term applied to studies relying on questionnaires that concerns the researcher's dual abilities to direct the inquiry to a designated respondent and to secure the desired cooperation from the respondent. [GAC]

sampling distribution The distribution of values of some statistic calculated for each possible distinguishable sample that could be drawn from a parent population under a specific sampling plan. [GAC]

sampling error The difference between the observed values of a variable and the long-run average of the observed values in repetitions of the measurement. (See also **nonsampling error.**) [GAC]

sampling form A list of sampling units from which a sample will be drawn; the list could consist of geographic areas, institutions, individuals, or other units. (See also **sampling frame.**) [GAC]

sampling frame The list of sampling units from which a sample will be drawn; the list could consist of geographic areas, institutions, individuals, or other units. (See also **sampling form.**) [GAC]

sampling plan The procedure that will be used to select a sample. [GAC]

sampling units The nonoverlapping collections of elements from the population. (See also **sampling forms** and **sampling frame.**) [GAC]

satellite media tour A publicity method that allows a celebrity or company spokesperson to participate in up to 25 interviews per day with representatives of the media. The person being interviewed sits in a television studio and is connected to remote locations via satellite hook-up, increasing the reach of the publicity program at a relatively low cost. [DES/BEB]

satellite tracking A specific information technology application that allows two-way communication between channel members for the purpose of tracking merchandise throughout the delivery process. [DJB/BJL]

satisfaction See **expectation-disconfirmation model** and **law of effect**

satisfaction/dissatisfaction A positive or negative reaction to a purchase decision or product after purchase. (See also **consumer satisfaction, expectation-disconfirmation model,** and **postpurchase evaluation.**) [HHK/MCC]

satisficing An action whose goal is to do something less than optimal, i.e., an action that is satisfactory and will "get me by." [DLS]

SAU See **standard advertising unit**

savings An amount, if any, left after a government, a firm, or a household has accounted for all expenditures. (See also **personal savings.**) [DLS]

SBU See **strategic business unit**

scanner 1. (marketing research definition) An electronic device that automatically reads imprinted Universal Product Codes as the product is pulled across the scanner, looks up the price in an attached computer, and instantly prints the price of the item on the cash register tape. [GAC] 2. (sales promotion definition) An electronic device that records retail purchase data (prices, brands, product sizes, etc.) at the point of sale by means of reading the universal product code. [DES/BEB]

scanner market testing See **test marketing**

scanning The process in point-of-sale systems (point-of-sale service) wherein the input into the terminal is accomplished by passing a coded ticket over a reader or having a hand-held wand pass over the ticket. [WRD]

scenario A narrative sketch, description of possible developments or outline of a conceivable state of affairs at some future period. It is designed to focus attention on future causal processes and decision points. [WL/MBC]

schema A network of associated meanings that represents a person's general knowledge about some concept. [JPP/JCO]

scope of planning activities See **planning**

scoring models See **screening of ideas**

scrambled merchandising A deviation from traditional merchandising that involves the sale of items not usually associated with a retail establishment's primary lines—e.g., supermarkets handling nonfood items, drug stores selling variety goods and sometimes, hardware. It is also called scrambled retailing. [WRD]

scrambled retailing See **scrambled merchandising**

screening of ideas The step just prior to research and development and systems design in the product development process. It involves use of scoring models, checklists, or personal judgments and is based on information from experience and various market research studies (including concept testing). Screening calls for judgments that predict the organization's ability to make the item and its ability to market the item successfully. It culminates in directions to guide technical personnel in their developmental efforts. (See also **research and development.**) [DW]

script A mental directory of appropriate actions in particular situations. [JPP/JCO]

SD-BL See **sight draft-bill of lading**

SDR See **special drawing rights**

sealed-bid pricing A mechanism for awarding a sale or contract. Confidential bids are due at a certain time and the award is normally made to the lowest bidder if that bidder's specifications conform to the request for quotation. (See also **bidding.**) [GLL/DTW]

search heuristics See **product line optimization**

season dating A form of advance dating allowed on merchandise of a seasonal nature, granted by a manufacturer to induce early buying of seasonal goods so as to keep the plant occupied in slack seasons. (See also **dating, end of month dating, extra dating, future dating, memorandum purchase and dating, ordinary dating, proximo dating,** and **receipt-of-goods dating.**) [WRD]

seasonal demand A product demand that fluctuates and peaks at regular points in time. [DLS]

seasonal discount A special discount to all retailers who place orders for seasonal merchandise well in advance of the normal buying period. [WRD]

seasonal variations The regular changes occurring in the production or sales of products due to such factors as climate, vacations, holidays, and customs. [WL/MBC]

secondary data The statistics not gathered for the immediate study at hand but for some other purpose. (See also **primary data.**) [GAC]

secondary package See **multiple packaging** and **package**

secondary readers See **pass-along readers**

secondary shopping district A cluster of stores outside the central business district that serves a large population within a section or part of a large city. It is similar in character to the main shopping district of a smaller city. [WRD]

secondary trade zone The geographic area of secondary importance in terms of customer sales, typically generating about 20 percent or so of a store's sales.

(See also **analog approach** and **tertiary trade zone.**) [WRD]

Securities and Exchange Commission The federal agency that administers the Securities Act of 1933 and the Securities Exchange Act of 1934, and other acts relating to holding companies and investments. (See also **advertising, regulation of.**) [DC]

security An operating unit that is responsible for protecting merchandise and other assets from pilferage (internal or external). Those working in security may be employees or outside agency people. (See also **protection department.**) [WRD]

security needs See **hierarchy of needs**

segment descriptors See **market segmentation**

segmentation See **market segmentation**

segmentation basis See **market segmentation**

selective advertising An approach to developing advertising messages that seeks to present the unique or differentiating characteristics of a particular brand of product or service. [JE]

selective attention See **selective perception**

selective demand The demand for a specific brand marketed by a firm. (See also **primary demand.**) [DLS]

selective distribution A form of market coverage in which a product is distributed through a limited number of wholesalers or retailers in a given market area. (See also **exclusive distribution** and **intensive distribution.**) [GLF]

selective exposure 1. (consumer behavior definition) A process by which people avoid stimuli in their environments, such as leaving the room while commercials are on TV. (See also **selective perception.**) [JPP/JCO] 2. (consumer behavior definition) The conscious or unconscious exposure to a limited set of information, messages, or media. [HHK/MCC]

selective perception 1. The conscious or unconscious increase in attention for stimuli and information consistent with a person's attitudes or interests, or conscious or unconscious discounting of inconsistent stimuli. 2. The ability of the individual to protect himself or herself from the chaos and confusion of excessive and conflicting incoming stimuli. By selectively perceiving and organizing these stimuli, order is created. The needs, values, beliefs, opinions, personality, and other psychological and physical factors are brought into play leading to selective attention, selective exposure, and selective retention, along with the ability to distort and add information to meet the needs of the perceiver to cognitively reorganize reality. [HHK/MCC]

selective retention See **selective perception**

selective specialization See **market coverage strategies**

selective specialization coverage See **product-market grid**

self concept 1. (consumer behavior definition) The ideas, attitudes, and perceptions people have about themselves. [JPP/JCO] 2. (consumer behavior definition) The image one has of oneself. Research indicates that the self concept is a relatively important variable in how a person judges and evaluates other persons or products. For example, the person with a self concept of "upwardly mobile urban professional" may well prefer and purchase a different model or brand of automobile than the individual with a self concept of a middle-aged dowager. (See also **ideal self concept** and **real self concept.**) [HHK/MCC]

Self reference criterion (SRC) The unconscious reference to one's own cultural values or one's home country frame of reference. [WJK]

self regulation Control of itself by a business organization or association independent of government supervision, laws, or the like. [DC]

self selection The method used in retailing by which the customer may choose the desired merchandise without direct assistance of store personnel. (See also **self service.**) [WRD]

self service 1. A type of operation in which the customer is exposed to merchandise that may be examined without sales assistance, unless the customer seeks such assistance. It is usually accompanied by central or area checkouts or transaction stations. This is typical of supermarkets and discount stores. 2. retailers offering minimal customer service. (See also **self selection.**) [WRD]

self sufficiency See **inner-directedness**

self-actualization See **hierarchy of needs** and **psychological drives**

self-actualization needs See **Maslow's need hierarchy**

self-fulfilling forecast A forecast that motivates behavior causing the forecast itself to be realized. [WL/MBC]

self-fulfillment See **hierarchy of needs**

self-image See **value-expressive function of attitudes**

self-liquidator A gift, premium, or other reward offered to consumers by the seller at the seller's net cost, generally including postage, handling, and taxes. [DES/BEB]

self-price elasticity See **elasticon**

self-rating scales See **behavioral analysis**

self-regulation An industry or profession's internal efforts to establish standards of quality, truthfulness, and propriety for its promotional efforts. [DES/BEB]

sell-and-lease agreement A term applied to an arrangement whereby a business enterprise owning and occupying real estate sells it to an investor, such as an insurance company, and makes a long-term lease on the property and often, in addition, an option or agreement to buy, effective at the termination of the lease. (See also **sale-leaseback.**) [WRD]

sell-through analysis A comparison between actual and planned sales to determine whether early markdowns are required or whether more merchandise is needed to satisfy demand. [WRD]

seller identification See **buygrid framework**

seller's welfare models See **product line optimization**

sellers market A combination of economic conditions that favor sellers in negotiated transactions, usually because of high levels of demand, scarcity of supply, etc. It is the opposite of buyers market. [WRD]

selling The personal or impersonal process whereby the salesperson ascertains, activates, and satisfies the needs of the buyer to the mutual, continuous benefit of both buyer and seller. [BAW]

selling agent An agent who operates on an extended contractual basis. The agent sells all of a specified line of merchandise or the entire output of the principal, and usually has full authority with regard to prices, terms, and other conditions of sales. The agent occasionally renders financial aid to the principal. [WRD]

selling functional expense See **functional expense classification**

selling space An area set aside for displays of merchandise, interactions between sales personnel and customers, demonstration, and so on. [WRD]

semantic differential A self-report technique for attitude measurement in which subjects are asked to check which cell between a set of bipolar adjectives or phrases best describes their feelings toward the object. (See also **snake diagram, Stapel scale,** and **summated rating.**) [GAC]

semantic differential scale A scale anchored by two words that emphasize different meanings; the word anchors are opposites of one another. For example, it is a measurement scale anchored by "good" and "bad" or "happy" and "sad." [HHK/MCC]

semantic knowledge The general meanings people have acquired about their world. (See also **episodic knowledge.**) [JPP/JCO]

semimanufactured goods The industrial products that are at least one stage past being raw materials and are sold for use as components of other products. They comprise parts and processed materials. [DW]

sensitivity analysis See **LITMUS**

sensitivity coefficient The average percentage change in consumption corresponding to a 1 percent change in disposable personal income. [WL/MBC]

sensory pleasures See **hedonistic consumption**

sentence completion A questionnaire containing a number of sentences that respondents are directed to complete with the first words that come to mind. (See also **projective technique, storytelling,** and **word association.**) [GAC]

sentence completion test See **projective technique**

sep See **color separation**

sequence bias The distortion in the answers to some questions on a questionnaire because the replies are not independently arrived at but are conditioned by responses to other questions; the problem is particularly acute in mail questionnaires because the respondent can see the whole questionnaire. [GAC]

sequential choice models See **Elimination-By-Aspects model**

sequential sample A nonprobability sample formed on the basis of a series of successive decisions. If the evidence is not conclusive after a small sample is taken, more observations are taken; if still inconclusive after these additional observations, still more observations are taken. At each stage, then, a decision is made as to whether more information should be collected or whether the evidence is sufficient to draw a conclusion. (See also **convenience sample, judgment sample, quota sample,** and **snowball sample.**) [GAC]

served market The business develops, manufactures, and markets products appropriate to a selected segment of the market. It should be noted that the market for which the product is developed (called the qualified market) and the market that is targeted in marketing efforts will often not overlap precisely. The overlap between the qualified market and the target market represents the served market. (See also **PIMS Program** and **product-market definition.**) [GSD]

service desk A station within a store where customers take merchandise for exchange or credit and receive information or other services, depending upon company policy. [WRD]

service mark A trademark for a service. [DW]

service merchandiser See **rack jobber**

service quality An area of study that has developed to define and describe how services can be delivered in such a manner as to satisfy the recipient. High quality service is defined as delivery of service that meets or exceeds customers' expectations. [WRD]

service shopping See **comparison shopping**

service(s) 1. Products, such as a bank loan or home security, that are intangible or at least substantially so. If totally intangible, they are exchanged directly from producer to user, cannot be transported or stored, and are almost instantly perishable. Service products are often difficult to identify, because they come into existence at the same time they are bought and consumed. They comprise intangible elements that are inseparable; they usually involve customer participation in some important way; they cannot be sold in the sense of ownership transfer; and they have no title. Today, however, most products are partly tangible and partly intangible, and the dominant form is used to classify them as either goods or services (all are products). These common, hybrid forms, whatever they are called, may or may not have the attributes just given for totally intangible services. 2. Services, as a term, is also used to describe activities performed by sellers and others that accompany the sale of a product and aid in its exchange or its utilization (e.g., shoe fitting, financing, an 800 number). Such services are either presale or post-sale and supplement the product, not comprise it. If performed during sale, they are considered to be intangible parts of the product. (See also **customer service** and **product hierarchy.**) [DW]

sets in use The percentage of television or radio households in which the sets are actually being used (turned on) during a given time period. In television, this concept is sometimes called HUTs, which stands for households using television. [JE]

SGU See **GEOLINE**

shaping A process of reinforcing successive approximations of a desired behavior, or of other required behaviors, in order to increase the probability of the desired response. [JPP/JCO]

share See **share of audience**

share of audience The proportion of sets in use that are tuned to a particular radio station, television station, or cable television channel during a given time period. It is computed by dividing the rating by the sets in use. [JE]

share of market See **product performance tracking**

shareholder wealth maximization (SWM) The goal of the firm in financial economics. Comment: SWM is an assumption derived from certain axioms about individual behavior due to Von Neumann and Morgenstern. From these axioms it can be deduced that individuals will behave as if they were attempting to maximize an expected utility function. The empirical accuracy and ethical adequacy of SWM is an issue of some controversy. [PFA]

shelf life The length of time a product

can safely remain in storage between production and consumption. After this period, deterioration makes the product unfit for sale and/or consumption. Virtually every good has a shelf life, but services (if totally intangible) do not. Shelf life is not related to product obsolescence. [DW]

shelf stock In a complex distribution system, inventory occurs at the plant and at field locations. Shelf stock refers to inventory that has been accumulated for display at the point of final sale. [DJB/BJL]

shelf talker A printed card or other sign used in retail stores to call attention to a shelved product. It commonly is attached to the shelves or railings of display cases. [DES/BEB]

Shell International Directional Policy Matrix See **product and business portfolio models**

Sherman Antitrust Act (1890) This act prohibits contracts, combinations, and conspiracies that restrain interstate or foreign trade, and prohibits monopolization, attempts to monopolize, and conspiracies to monopolize. (See also **antitrust laws; contract, tying; Hart-Scott-Rodino Antitrust Improvements Act; Miller-Tydings Resale Maintenance Act;** and **rule of reason.**) [DC]

shippers' cooperative A nonprofit organization that pools members' shipments so that they can be moved at low carload or truckload rates instead of the more expensive LCL or LTL rates. [WRD]

Shipping Act (1984) This act permits ocean common carriers to file agreements with the Federal Maritime Commission that fix or regulate transportation rates, pool traffic revenues, allot ports, and restrict the number of ships between ports. [DC]

shipping costs See **buyers' costs**

shop-worn goods See **as is** and **clearance sale**

shoplifting The stealing of a store's merchandise by customers. (See also **pilferage.**) [WRD]

shopping center A group of architecturally unified commercial establishments built on a site that is planned, developed, owned, and managed as an operating unit related in its location, size, and type of shops to the trade area it serves. [DLH]

shopping product A product such as a better dress or hair treatment for which the consumer is willing to spend considerable time and effort in gathering information on price, quality, and other attributes. Several retail outlets are customarily visited. Comparison of product attributes and complex decision processes are common. (See also **consumer product, convenience product, emergency product, fashion product, impulse product, specialty product,** and **staple good.**) [DW]

shopping radius See **trading area**

short delivery A discrepancy in the amount of goods delivered, the number being less than shown on the purchase order or invoice. [WRD]

short-line distributor See **specialty wholesaler**

short-range plans See **tactics**

short-run See **planning**

shortage See **inventory stock shortage**

shotgun approach See **majority fallacy**

shrink-wrap A packaging process that allows the shipper to extend a clear plastic covering over a package or set of packages. The clear plastic is then circulated through a heat tunnel where the film shrinks to adhere closely to the package or collection of packages. [DJB/BJL]

shrinkage 1. (physical distribution definition) The absence of book inventory. The presence of shrinkage suggests that there is less inventory than expected at some specific location in the channel. [DJB/BJL] 2. (retailing definition) The difference between the recorded value of inventory (at retail) based on merchandise bought and the actual retail value of actual inventory in stores and distribution centers divided by retail sales during a time period. Shrinkage is caused by theft by employees and/or customers, merchandise being misplaced or damaged, and clerical errors. [WRD]

SIC See **Standard Industrial Classification**

sight draft-bill of lading (SD-BL) A sight draft is an instrument attached to the bill of lading and must be honored before the buyer can take possession of the shipment. It resembles C.O.D. terms and may be said to constitute one way of forcing them. [WRD]

signaling intentions to defend See **market defense**

similar store approach See **analog approach**

simple random sample A probability sample in which each population element has a known and equal chance of being included in the sample and in which every combination of n population elements is a sample possibility and is just as likely to occur as any other combination of n units. (See also **cluster sample, stratified sample,** and **systematic sample.**) [GAC]

simple tabulation A count of the number of cases that fall into each category when the categories are based on one variable. (See also **tabulation.**) [GAC]

simulated test market A form of market testing in which consumers are exposed to new products and to their claims in a staged advertising and purchase situation. Output of the test is an early forecast of sales and/or market share, based on mathematical forecasting models, management assumptions, and input of specific measurements from the simulation. [DW]

simulated test market models See **new product forecasting models**

simulated test marketing Test marketing done by firms in shopping malls or consumers' homes as a prelude to a full-scale marketing test for the product. (See also **controlled test market** and **standard test market.**) [GAC]

simulation models See **distribution models** and **SPRINTER Mod III**

single column tariff The simplest type of tariff that consists of a schedule of duties in which the tariff rate applies to imports from all countries on the same basis. (See also **tariff system** and **two column tariff.**) [WFK]

single market concentration See **market coverage strategies**

single price policy/store The offering of all goods at a single price—e.g., everything for $5, or $10, etc. It is not to be confused with one price policy. [WRD]

single product-market concentration coverage See **product-market grid**

single sourcing See **sourcing**

single-zone pricing The practice of setting one price for all buyers regardless of their distance from the seller. (See also **multiple-zone pricing system.**) [KM]

site selection model See **distribution models**

situation A particular occasion; the stream of interactions between a consumers' affect and cognitions and goal-directed behaviors in an environment. [JPP/JCO]

situation analysis The systematic collection and study of past and present data to identify trends, forces, and conditions with the potential to influence the performance of the business and the choice of appropriate strategies. The situation analysis is the foundation of the strategic planning process. The situation analysis includes an examination of both the internal factors (to identify strengths and weaknesses) and external factors (to identify opportunities and threats). It is often referred to by the acronym SWOT. [GSD]

situation assessment See **adaptive planning** and **planning**

situational involvement The interest or concern with a product brought about by the situation or context. For example, consumers may become situationally involved with buying a hot water heater if their old one breaks. (See also **enduring involvement.**) [JPP/JCO]

situations See **SPIN**

size lining This is related to the concept of price lining. It is the selection of predetermined size points at which merchandise will be offered. For assistance to customer selection, sizes should be according to customer behavior—e.g., junior sizes together. [WRD]

size scale A chart of the proper quantity of an item to order in each size. [WRD]

skimming See **penetration pricing**

skimming price policy A method of pricing that attempts to first reach those willing to buy at a high price before marketing to more price-sensitive customers. (See also **penetration price policy.**) [DLS]

SKU See **stockkeeping unit**

sleeper effect A controversial finding in the communications literature that asserts that the influence of advertising or other communications material can increase once the message is no longer broadcast or presented to the respondent. The research findings are divided on its existence with sufficient evidence to prove and to disprove the existence of the phenomenon depending on who is interpreting the findings. The belief is that the influence of advertising or other communications increases with number of repetitions. However, as repetitions increase, so does noxiousness, lessening the effectiveness of the persuasion. Once the communication ceases to exist, its noxious character no longer exists and the prior repetitions influence an increase in effectiveness. [HHK/MCC]

slipsheet A materials handling device usually composed of a flat piece of cardboard or board on which product is stacked. The multiple units of product are moved as a unit load in the transportation and distribution system. [DJB/BJL]

slogan The verbal or written portion of an advertising message that summarizes the main idea in a few memorable words. It is sometimes called a tag line. [JE]

slotting allowance 1. (retailing definition) A fee paid by a vendor for space in a retail store. [WRD] 2. (sales promotion definition) The fee a manufacturer pays to a retailer in order to get distribution for a new product. It covers the costs of making room for the product in the warehouse and on the store shelf, reprogramming the computer system to recognize the product's UPC code, and including the product in the retailer's inventory system. [DES/BEB]

slow-moving goods See **clearance sale** and **close-out**

small group theory A set of conceptualizations and hypotheses relating to the behavior of individuals within a small group of psychologically interrelated individuals. It is the study of the influence of others in a small group of interdependent individuals on the beliefs, attitudes, and behavior of the individual. (See also **social factors in consumer behavior.**) [HHK/MCC]

SMSA See **standard metropolitan statistical area**

snake diagram A diagram (so called because of its shape) that connects with straight lines the average responses to a series of semantic differential statements, thereby depicting the profile of the object or objects being evaluated. [GAC]

snowball sample A judgment sample that relies on the researcher's ability to locate an initial set of respondents with the desired characteristics; these individuals are then used as informants to identify still others with the desired characteristics. (See also **convenience sample, nonprobability sample, quota sample,** and **sequential sample.**) [GAC]

social accounting See **social audit**

social advertising The advertising designed to educate or motivate target audiences to undertake socially desirable actions. [ARA]

social audit A systematic assessment and report of some domain of a company's activities that have social impact; thus, it is an assessment of social performance. (See also **social indicator.**) [WL/MBC]

social benefits See **social consciousness**

social character A term coined by David Riesman to describe values and behavioral characteristics of people in various stages of cultural development. (See also **inner-directedness, national character,** and **other-directedness.**) [HHK/MCC]

social class A status hierarchy by which groups and individuals are classified on the basis of esteem and prestige. For example, one classification divides our society into upper-class Americans (14 percent of the population), middle-class (32 percent of the population), working-class (38 percent of the population) and lower-class (16 percent of the population). (See also **social factors in consumer behavior, social mobility,** and **status.**) [JPP/JCO]

social consciousness Marketing managers' concern for meeting social purposes, pursuing social benefits, and adhering to social criteria as compared with achieving the sales, profit, and other wealth-producing goals of capitalism. Social actions are often taken at the expense of immediate profits. [WL/MBC]

social cost The cost to a society as a whole resulting from a firm's decisions and actions, such as the development and launching of a new product that impacts negatively upon the environment. [WL/MBC]

social criteria See **social consciousness**

social drive See **psychological drives**

social engineering The use of knowledge and techniques of social and behavioral sciences to improve the social systems in a community. [WL/MBC]

social factors in consumer behavior The variables other than individual psychological and cognitive factors that have an influence on the behavior of the consumer in the market place. They include the small group, subculture such as ethnic groups, and social class. [HHK/MCC]

social impact See **social audit**

social impact of marketing The external effects of the processes and outcomes of marketing on the well-being of society in general or of specific population segments. Comment: The economics term "externalities" connotes the same effects. The social impacts may be positive or negative. Examples of general impacts would be the effects on public health of the promotion of cigarette smoking. Segment impacts would be advertising portraying the elderly as forgetful, frightened, and physically infirm; or racially discriminatory real estate marketing. These would be negative impacts. An example of a positive impact would be automobile commercials that portray drivers as always wearing seat belts. (See also **social marketing** and **social responsibility of marketing.**) [ARA]

social indicator Information in the form of statistical data and statistical series that can be used for social audit purposes. The data and information that facilitate the evaluation of how well a society or institution is doing in relation to social values and goals. (See also **quality of life.**) [WL/MBC]

social influence See **personal influence** and **social factors in consumer behavior**

social man A person whose buying decisions are highly influenced by sociological factors. (See also **economic man.**) [DLS]

social marketing 1. (environments definition) The branch of marketing that is concerned with the use of marketing knowledge, concepts, and techniques to enhance social ends, as well as the social consequences of marketing strategies, decisions, and actions. [WL/MBC]
2. (social marketing definition) Marketing designed to influence the behavior of a target audience in which the benefits of the behavior are intended by the marketer to accrue primarily to the audience or to the society in general and not to the marketer. Comment: Social marketing is sometimes confused with social impact of marketing. Social marketing can be carried on by for-profit, public, and private nonprofit organizations or by individuals. Examples would be attempts to influence individuals to stop smoking (by the private nonprofit American Cancer Society) or report crimes (by the public U.S. Department of Justice). An attempt of one friend to influence another to go on a diet is also social marketing. [ARA]

social marketing perspective The orientation or perspective that focuses on social purposes and reflects on whether or not a company should market a good or a service as compared to whether or not it can do so economically. [WL/MBC]

social marketing report A report on those marketing activities that have social impact, usually in the form of disclosures to relevant publics, overall rating schemes, or internal performance review. [WL/MBC]

social mobility The ability of the individual to climb above, or slip below, the social class or position in society into which he or she was originally reared. Social mobility can be increased through education, occupation, or fortuitous circumstances. (See also **social class** and **status.**) [HHK/MCC]

social mobilization campaign In social marketing, a campaign directed at the community level designed to stimulate word-of-mouth and social pressures to bring about change in individual behavior. [ARA]

social motives See **psychological drives**

social needs See **psychological drives**

social perceived risk See **perceived risk**

social performance See **social audit**

social purposes See **social consciousness**

social responsibility Concern for the ethical consequences of a person's or institution's acts as they might affect the interests of others. Corporate social responsibility is seriously considering the impact of the company's actions and operating in a way that balances short-term profit needs with society's long-term needs, thus ensuring the company's survival in a healthy environment. [DC]

social responsibility of marketing The obligation of marketing organizations to do no harm to the social environment and, wherever possible, to use their skills and resources to enhance that environment. Comment: Social responsibility of marketing also is called societal marketing. This term is frequently confused with social marketing. [ARA]

social stratification See **social class**

social styles matrix A method of classifying customers based on their preferred communication style. The two dimensions used to classify customers are assertiveness and responsiveness. [BAW]

socialism See **economic organization**

socialization 1. (consumer behavior definition) A process by which an individual learns the values and appropriate behavior patterns of a group, institution, or culture. [JPP/JCO] 2. (consumer behavior definition) The process by which an individual is acculturated into the mores, norms, values, and beliefs of a society or subdivision. It often applies to the learning and conditioning of children. [HHK/MCC]

societal marketing See **social responsibility of marketing**

socioeconomic Both the social and economic characteristics, status, or relationships such as social class, education, profession, as well as income and wealth. [WL/MBC]

Soft Drink Interbrand Competition Act (1980) This act permits the use of exclusive geographic areas by the soft-drink industry for bottling and distribution. [DC]

soft goods These are generally felt to be the clothing portion of nondurable goods. They may also include bolt goods and notions. [DW]

soft sell The opposite of hard sell. (See also **high-pressure selling.**) [BAW]

sogo-sosha Japanese general trading companies. [WJK]

solitary survivor stage See **family life cycle**

solo coupon A certificate for a price reduction or other inducement made for a single product or service. It commonly is distributed separately from other products by media advertising, direct mail, or other method. (See also **coupon, in-store coupon,** and **specialty distributed coupon.**) [DES/BEB]

sortation The general process in materials handling of sorting packages by origin or destination. Sortation is a generic word that describes a process of breaking down shipments into specific destinations, based on customer locations or other destination designators. [DJB/BJL]

sorting A function performed by intermediaries in order to bridge the discrepancy between the assortment of goods and services generated by the producer and the assortment demanded by the consumer. This function includes four distinct processes: accumulation, allocation, assorting, and sorting out. (See also **concentration** and **dispersion.**) [GLF]

sorting out A sorting process that breaks down a heterogeneous supply into separate stocks that are relatively homogeneous. (See also **accumulation, allocation, assorting,** and **dispersion.**) [GLF]

sound bite The basic element of a broadcast news story, consisting of a newsmaker speaking on camera in 10 to 20 second blocks. (See also **radio wrap-around.**) [DES/BEB]

source credibility The believability or veracity of the communication or source of a communication or advertising message. Although it is usually assumed that more credible sources will of necessity be more believable and therefore more influential, research does not unequivocally support the contention. [HHK/MCC]

sourcing 1. (global marketing definition) The what, where, and how of production to supply the customers targeted in the marketing plan. [WJK]
2. (industrial definition) Another term for procurement. Single, dual, and multiple sourcing refer to the number of suppliers from whom one buys a particular product. [GLL/DTW]

span of control The number of people a manager can supervise before managerial effectiveness declines. Comment: The number varies by the complexity of the positions supervised and the degree of decision making authority that is delegated to persons reporting to the manager. There has been a general increase in the space of control as companies have down-sized during the late 1980s and early 1990s. When the span of control is exceeded it usually is necessary to insert another level of supervision. (See also **centralized management, decentralized management,** and **flat organization.**) [VPB]

spatial competition See **institutional boundary**

special drawing rights (SDR) The "paper gold" created by the International Monetary Fund. The SDR is an international reserve asset that is exchanged by member countries of the IMF to offset trade surpluses and deficits. [WJK]

special event A sales promotion program comprising a number of sales promotion techniques built around a seasonal, cultural, sporting, musical event, or other activity. (See also **consumer sales promotion.**) [DES/BEB]

specialty advertising The placement of advertising messages on a wide variety of items of interest to the target market such as calendars, coffee cups, pens, hats, note paper, paper weights, T-shirts, watches, etc. In contrast to premiums, specialty advertising items are usually given to members of the audience. [JE]

specialty department store A large store with a department store format that focuses primarily on apparel and soft home goods. [WRD]

specialty distributed coupon The coupons distributed through nontraditional media, such as the back of cash register tapes, egg cartons, shopping bags, pizza boxes, etc. (See also **in-store coupon** and **solo coupon.**) [DES/BEB]

specialty product A product that has unique attributes or other characteristics that make it singularly important to the buyer. Multiple-store searching, reliance on brand, and absence of extensive product comparisons are the rule. Cigarettes, deodorants, and specialized insurance policies are examples. (See also **consumer product, convenience product, emergency product, impulse product, shopping product,** and **staple good.**) [DW]

specialty store 1. A store that handles a limited variety of goods, as compared to single-line stores. 2. A departmentalized apparel store, as distinct from a department store. 3. Increasingly, a store that caters to narrowly defined core customer target markets. [WRD]

specialty wholesaler A wholesaler who stocks a narrow range of products, not often a great depth of assortment choice. [WRD]

specific duties These duties are expressed as a specific amount of currency per unit of weight, volume, length, or a number of other units of measurement. (See also **ad valorem duty, compound duties, countervailing duties,** and **tariff system.**) [WJK]

specific tasks See **implementation**

speculation This concept holds that changes in the form and movement of goods to forward inventories should be made at the earliest possible time in the marketing process in order to reduce the costs of the marketing system. (See also **postponement.**) [GLF]

SPI See **PIMS Program**

spiff 1. (sales definition) A payment made by a producer's salesperson to a reseller's salesperson to motivate the reseller to sell the producer's products. [BAW] 2. (sales promotion definition) A cash payment made to salespeople at the retail level to influence them to promote and sell the manufacturer's brand or a specific item in the line rather than a competitive item. (See also **push money.**) [DES/BEB]

SPIN A sales technique involving a logical sequence of questions about situations, problems, implications, and need payoff that salespeople use to identify the prospect's needs. [BAW]

split run The placement of two or more different ads for the same advertiser in alternate copies of the same media vehicle in order to compare the effectiveness of the different advertising messages. [JE]

split shipment A vendor ships part of a shipment to a retailer and back orders the remainder because the entire shipment could not be shipped at the same time. [WRD]

sponsor See **advertiser**

spot broadcast The purchasing by a national advertiser of radio and television time on a local or market-by-market basis. This contrasts with the purchase of nationwide exposure by using national television networks or national cable television channels. [JE]

spot check This is used particularly in receiving operations when goods come in for reshipping to branch stores in packing cartons. Certain cartons are opened in the receiving area of the central distribution point and spot checked for quality and quantity. [WRD]

spot market The market for immediate delivery or, in the interbank market, for delivery within two business days of the transaction. [WJK]

spot purchase See **spot sale**

spot sale The sale or purchase of a commodity for immediate delivery, often on a cash basis. [WRD]

spotter See **bird dog**

spreading activation Through this usually unconscious process, interrelated aspects of consumers' knowledge are activated during comprehension and decision making. (See also **activation**). [JPP/JCO]

SPRINTER Mod III A model for analyzing the response to a new product over time using test market data. It simulates product awareness, intention to buy, product search, brand choice, and postpurchase behavior. Besides facilitating a go/no go decision, the model is designed to help improve decisions regarding the level of marketing mix variables (Urban 1970). (See also **ASSESSOR, LITMUS, marketing mix models, new product forecasting models, NEWPROD, NEWS, STEAM,** and **Tracker.**) [DCS/YJW]

spurious correlation A condition that arises when there is no relationship between two variables but the analyst concludes that a relationship exists. (See also **correlation analysis.**) [GAC]

SRC See **self reference criterion**

stability A technique for assessing the reliability of a measure by measuring the same objects or individuals at two different points in time and then correlating the scores; the procedure is known as test-retest reliability assessment. [GAC]

staff authority This includes two types of authority—advisory and functional. Advisory is implied authority based on the staff person's experience or expertise. A staff person with advisory authority cannot order something done but can recommend that it be done in a certain way. Functional authority is the authority held by functional managers (e.g., finance and personnel) to issue orders to people not under their direct (line) supervision; however, this authority encompasses only those functions designated by the chief executive. [VPB]

staged advertising and purchase situation See **simulated test market**

stages in the buying process See **buygrid framework**

stagflation An economic condition characterized by a combination of slow growth (stagnation) and upward-creeping prices (inflation). [DLS]

Staggers Rail Act (1980) This act allows competition and demand to establish rates for rail transportation; it prohibits predatory pricing and undue concentration of market power. [DC]

stakeholder One of a group of publics with which a company must be concerned. Key stakeholders include consumers, employees, stockholders, suppliers, and others who have some relationship with the organization. [DES/BEB]

standard advertising unit (SAU) The system of standard sizes of newspaper space adopted by newspapers in order to introduce a measure of uniformity to the complex process of buying space in a variety of newspapers in an assortment of market areas. [JE]

standard geographic units See **GEOLINE**

Standard Industrial Classification (SIC) A system developed by the U.S. Department of Commerce to assign products and establishments to categories. It divides the U.S. economy into 11 divisions, including one for nonclassifiable establishments. Within each division, major industry groups are classified by two-digit numbers. Within each major two-digit SIC industry group, industry subgroups are defined by a third digit, and detailed industries are defined by a fourth digit. More detailed product categories range up to seven digits, as in the example below. [GLL/DTW]

D	Manufacturing
34	Manufacturers of fabricated metal products
344	Manufacturers of fabricated structural metal products
3441	Manufacturers of fabricated structural steel products
34411	Manufacturers of fabricated structural metal for buildings

Standard International Trade Classifcation A numeric-based commodity code for products moving by air transportation. It was developed by the United Nations and is used by U.S. air carriers. [DJB/BJL]

standard memorized presentation See **canned sales presentation**

standard metropolitan statistical area (SMSA) An integrated economic and social unit having a large population nucleus. This is an old term now replaced by metropolitan statistical area. (See also **consolidated metropolitan statistical area** and **primary metropolitan statistical area**). [DLS]

standard package In some trades, custom or law has stipulated one or several package sizes that the goods are customarily sold in. Bread and sodas are typical, though few product categories today adhere only to the standard sizes. [DW]

standard test market A market in which companies sell their products through normal distribution channels when testing these products or the marketing efforts supporting these products. (See also **controlled test market** and **simulated test marketing.**) [GAC]

standardization See **grade labeling**

standardized portfolio models See **product and business portfolio models**

standards See **non tariff barriers**

standing order An arrangement with a vendor to make shipments periodically in specified quantities in which the vendor may be authorized to ship a certain quantity each month or week for a set period. [WRD]

Stapel scale A self-report technique for attitude measurement in which the respondents are asked to indicate how accurately each of a number of statements describes the object of interest. (See also **comparative rating scale, constant sum method, graphic-rating scale, Guttman scale, interval scale, itemized rating scale, nominal scale, ordinal scale, ratio scale, semantic differential,** and **summated rating.**) **[GAC]**

staple good A convenience product such as sugar or potatoes that is bought often and consumed routinely. Staples often offer little differentiation and are sold importantly on the basis of price. These sometimes are called commodity products, but industrial products can be commodities, too. (See also **consumer product, emergency product, impulse product, shopping product,** and **specialty product.**) [DW]

staple merchandise The merchandise for which a fairly active demand continues over a period of years and which the retailer finds necessary to carry continually in stock. (See also **basic stock list.**) [WRD]

staple stock list The list of items that

are to be carried regularly in stock. [WRD]

star See **growth-share matrix**

stationary first order Markov model See **Markov model**

stationary process See **Bernoulli process**

Statistical Abstract of the United States An annual publication of the U.S. Bureau of the Census, published since 1878 as the standard summary of statistics on the economic, social, and political organization of the U.S. It is both a convenient statistical reference and a guide to other statistical publications. [WL/MBC]

statistical demand analysis A method of developing a sales forecast that attempts to determine the relationship between sales and the important factors affecting sales, typically using regression analysis, and the use of that relationship to forecast sales for the future. [GAC]

statistical efficiency A measure used to compare sampling plans; one sampling plan is said to be superior (more statistically efficient) than another if, for the same size sample, it produces a smaller standard error of estimate. [GAC]

status The positioning of an individual within a group, organization, or society. (See also **psychological drives, social class,** and **social mobility.**) [HHK/MCC]

STEAM A model for predicting the sales over time for a new frequently purchased consumer product based on panel data. The approach explicitly considers heterogeneity across households in their purchase behavior, and models repeat purchase as a function of the household's depth of repeat level (Massy 1969). (See also **ASSESSOR, LITMUS, new product forecasting models, NEWPROD, NEWS, SPRINTER Mod III,** and **Tracker.**) [DCS/YJW]

stereotype A generalized belief about what people or events will be like, what attributes they will possess, how they will behave, etc., based upon group or type membership. For example, a possible stereotype is that older people will be less active than younger people. [HHK/MCC]

stimulus response sales approach A sales presentation method that emphasizes the importance of saying the right things at the right time by means of a well-prepared sales presentation (stimulus) in order to elicit the desired response (sale). (See also **canned sales presentation; customized sales presentation; need satisfaction selling; outlined presentation;** and **presentation, sales.**) [BAW]

stochastic dominance models See **product and business portfolio models**

stochastic model Strictly speaking, this is any model having a stochastic, i.e., probabilistic or random, component. This component can stem from a variety of sources. It arises in models for a single individual making a single decision (e.g., to represent the effect of uncertainty). Randomness also is incorporated in modeling multiple events for a single individual (e.g., to represent the effect on each event of omitted variables—i.e., factors that have an impact but that are not explicitly part of the model). Finally, a probabilistic component can be used in modeling a single event for each of several individuals. Here the randomness represents the (unmeasured) heterogeneity across individuals. In each case the result is a process that, from the standpoint of the observer, appears to have a random component. Often the term stochastic model denotes a more narrow subset of models; namely probability mixture models (Lilien and Kotler 1983; Massy, Montgomery, and Morrison 1970). (See also **brand choice models** and **promotion models.**) [DCS/YJW]

stochastic programming See **mathematical programming**

stock balance This balance is concerned with planning and controlling merchandise investment so that it is balanced with expected sales. The three perspectives from which one can view stock balance are (1) stock width (breadth), (2) stock support (depth), and (3) total dollars invested in stock. [WRD]

stock bin control A system for maintaining assortments of staple merchandise by reordering periodically on a basis of empty spaces or observed low stock conditions in bins or on stock shelves. [WRD]

stock breadth perspective See **stock balance**

stock control This includes all the activities that are carried on to maintain a balance between inventories and sales. [WRD]

stock depth The number of units in individual merchandise items needed to meet sales of each assortment factor. (See also **stock balance,**) [WRD]

stock or inventory control A system or approach to the management of material that is received, stored, and distributed within the firm and between the firm and its vendors or customers. (See also **inventory control.**) [DJB/BJL]

stock rotation A term used in inventory management to describe the process of moving stock to ensure freshness and shelf life of inventory. [DJB/BJL]

stock shortage This includes all unexplained or unrecorded shrinkages in the value of merchandise available for sale. It is the amount by which a physical inventory is short of a book inventory figure. [WRD]

stock support perspective See **stock balance**

stock turnover 1. (physical distribution definition) The number of times average stockkeeping units are sold during a specific time period (usually one year). (See also **inventory turnover**.) [DJB/BJL] 2. (retailing definition) An index of the velocity with which merchandise moves into and out of a store or department. The rate of stock turnover is the number of times during a given period, usually on an annual basis, that the average inventory on hand has been sold and replaced. It is computed by dividing sales by average inventory, with both stated in comparable valuations, either cost or selling price. [WRD]

stock width perspective See **stock balance**

stock-out 1. (physical distribution definition) A stock-out occurs when buyers are unable to fulfill their purchase intentions in a specific buying situation. [DJB/BJL] 2. (retailing definition) A situation in which a retail store does not have enough items of a particular kind in stock to meet customer demand; thus, the product is not available to consumers. [WRD]

stock-sales ratio The ratio between the stock on hand at the beginning or end of a period and the sales for that period. It is determined by dividing stock, preferably at the beginning of the period, usually monthly, by sales. It is distinguished from inventory turnover or stock turnover, which are ratios or averages for a period of time, usually annually. [WRD]

stockholder See **agency theory** and **corporate relations**

stockkeeping unit (SKU) 1. (physical distribution definition) A specific unit of inventory that is carried as a separate identifiable unit. A pint bottle and a quart bottle of the same product would be separate SKUs for inventory purposes. [DJB/BJL] 2. (retailing definition) The lowest level of identification of merchandise. [WRD]

stockpiling The situation in which consumers buy multiple units of products that are on deal and hoard those products for future use. [DES/BEB]

store atmosphere The affective (emotional) and cognitive states consumers experience in a store, but may not be fully conscious of when shopping. [JPP/JCO]

store brand The private brand that is owned by a retailer. [DW]

store image 1. (consumer behavior definition) The total of what consumers think about a particular store. [JPP/JCO] 2. (retailing definition) The way in which a store is defined in a shopper's mind. It is based on the store's physical characteristics, retailing mix, and a set of psychological attributes. [WRD]

store layout The interior retail store arrangement of departments or groupings of merchandise. It should be organized to provide for ease of customer movement through the store and to provide for maximum exposure and attractive display of merchandise. (See also **block plan, boutique store layout, bubble plan, free-flow pattern, free-form, gridiron pattern,** and **loop layout.**) [WRD]

store loyalty 1. (consumer behavior definition) The degree to which a consumer consistently patronizes the same store when shopping for particular types of products. [JPP/JCO] 2. (retailing definition) A condition in which a customer regularly patronizes a specific retailer. [WRD]

store patronage The degree to which a consumer shops at a particular store relative to competitive outlets. [JPP/JCO]

storyboard A sequence of illustrations of the key scenes in a proposed television commercial. They are used by advertising agencies to obtain client advice and approval before continuing to the more advanced, and expensive, stages of television commercial production. (See also **comprehensive layout, dummy, layout, mechanical, rough,** and **thumbnail.**) [JE]

storytelling A questionnaire method of data collection relying on a picture stimulus such as a cartoon, photograph, or drawing, about which the subject is asked to tell a story. (See also **projective technique, sentence completion,** and **word association.**) [GAC]

straight commission plan A sales force compensation plan that uses commissions as the sole basis for pay. A commission is payment for achieving a given level of performance. Salespeople are paid for results. Usually, commission payments are based on the salesperson's dollar or unit sales volume. However, they may be based on the profitability of sales so as to motivate the sales force to expend effort on the most profitable products or customers. (See also **combination compensation plan** and **straight salary plan.**) [AJD]

straight rebuy See **buyclasses** and **buygrid framework**

straight salary plan A sales force compensation plan that relies exclusively on salary as a financial reward for salespeople. A salary is a fixed sum of money paid at regular intervals. The amount paid to the salesperson is a function of the amount of time worked rather than any specific performance. Two sets of conditions favor the use of a straight salary compensation plan. These are (1) when management wishes to motivate people to achieve objectives other than short-run sales volume, and (2) when the individual salesperson's impact on sales volume is difficult to measure in a reasonable time. (See also **combination compensation plan** and **straight commission plan.**) [AJD]

strategic alliances Cooperation strategy between companies to jointly pursue a common goal. They are also referred to as collaborative agreements or global strategic partnerships. [WJK]

strategic business planning See **strategic market planning**

strategic business plans See **strategic market planning**

strategic business unit (SBU) From a strategy formulation point of view, diversified companies are best thought of as being composed of a number of businesses (or SBUs). These organizational entities are large enough and homogeneous enough to exercise control over most strategic factors affecting their performance. They are managed as self-contained planning units for which discrete business strategies can be developed. [GSD]

strategic fit The degree to which the growth strategy that allows the business to achieve its performance objectives can be implemented within the constraints imposed by past strategic commitments, resource availability, and other historical rigidities. Often, tradeoffs and changes are required in the growth strategy prior to implementation. [GSD]

strategic intent An ambitious organizational goal that is not proportional to current resources and capabilities and remains stable over time. To ensure long-term success, management envisions a desired leadership position and then establishes the criterion that the organization will use to chart its progress. The concept encompasses an active management process that includes focusing the organization's attention on the essence of winning; motivating people by communicating the value of the target; leaving room for individual and team contributions; sustaining enthusiasm by providing new operational definitions as circumstances change; and using intent consistently to guide resource allocations. [GSD]

strategic management process An approach to management that incorporates the following elements: (1) focusing planning processes on the search for competitive advantage; (2) the integration of strategic planning with operational and functional levels; (3) orientation toward funding and implementing strategies rather than discrete projects; and (4) greater emphasis and continued focus on strategic issues. [GSD]

strategic market planning The planning process that yields decisions in how a business unit can best compete in the markets it elects to serve. Strategic market decisions are based on assessments of product market and pertain to the basis for advantage in the market. The plan that is the output of the process serves as a blueprint for the development of the skills and resources of a business unit and specifies the results to be expected. In many companies these are called strategic business plans. (See also **strategic planning.**) [GSD]

strategic moves See **market defense**

strategic planning The consideration of current decision alternatives in light of their probable consequences over time. The practice of strategic planning incorporates four distinguishing features: (1) an external orientation; (2) a process for formulating strategies; (3) methods for analysis of strategic situations and alternatives; and (4) a commitment to action. (See also **mission statement, situation analysis,** and **strategic market planning.**) [GSD]

Strategic Planning Institute See **PIMS Program**

strategic sales program A program that organizes and plans the company's overall personal selling efforts and integrates these with the other elements of the firm's marketing strategy. The strategic sales program should take into account the environmental factors faced by the firm. (See also **sales management.**) [AJD]

strategic thinking See **adaptive planning**

strategic thrust A compelling theme that knits together otherwise independent activities and focuses the energies of functional groups on things that matter in the market. The essence of this theme is a shared understanding of why the business is better than the competition and what has to be done to keep it in front. (See also **strategy.**) [GSD]

strategic window The limited time period in which the fit between the factors critical for success in a market and the distinctive competences of a business competing in that market is at an optimum. The implication is that businesses should prepare for and respond appropriately to the "opening" and "closing" of strategic windows. [GSD]

strategy This describes the direction the business will pursue within its chosen environment and guides the allocation of resources and effort. It also provides the logic that integrates the perspectives of functional departments and operating units, and points them all in the same direction. The strategy statement for a strategic business unit is composed of three elements: (1) a business definition that specifies the area in which the business will compete; (2) a strategic thrust that describes whether a competitive advantage is to be gained by focusing the scope or by exploiting an asymmetry in the position of the business; and (3) supporting functional strategies that are activities designed for consistency and comparability with other activities and the strategic thrust. (See also **marketing strategy.**) [GSD]

strategy development See **planning**

stratified sample A probability sample that is distinguished by the two-step procedure in which (1) the parent population is divided into mutually exclusive and exhaustive subsets and (2) a simple random sample of elements is chosen independently from each group or subset. (See also **cluster sample, disproportionate stratified sampling, simple random sample,** and **systematic sample.**) [GAC]

STRATPORT A decision support system for the allocation of a firm's financial resources across its strategic business units (SBUs). The approach models the impact of general marketing expenditures on both market share and on the firm's cost structure. Given a specific portfolio strategy, the system can evaluate the profit and cash flow implications of following that strategy over time. Alternately, the approach can determine the optimal allocation of marketing expenditures across SBUs in order to maximize net present value over a specified time horizon (Larreche and Srinivasan 1981, 1982). (See also **deci-**

sion calculus models and resource allocation models.) [DCS/YJW]

strengths and weaknesses analysis See **situation analysis**

strict liability 1. (legislation definition) A doctrine under which a seller is held liable for injury caused by a defective product even though the seller exercised all possible care in the preparation and sale of the product and the user had not bought the product from or entered into any contractual relation with the seller. [DC] 2. (product development definition) An extreme variant of product liability (in common practice today) in which the producer is held responsible for putting a defective product on the market. Under strict liability, there need be no negligence, sale no longer has to be direct from producer to user (privity of contact), and no disclaimer statement relieves the producer of this responsibility. [DW]

string-street location A location on a major thoroughfare upon which various kinds of stores are strung for a number of consecutive blocks. [WRD]

strip-type shopping center A shopping center in which stores are aligned along a thoroughfare, usually set back some distance from the street to permit front parking. (See also **arcade shopping center, community shopping center, factory outlet center, mall-type shopping center, neighborhood shopping center, off-price shopping center, regional shopping center,** and **super regional shopping center.**) [WRD]

structured questionnaire A degree of standardization imposed on the data collection instrument. A highly structured questionnaire, for example, is one in which the questions to be asked and the responses permitted subjects are completely predetermined, while a highly unstructured questionnaire is one in which the questions to be asked are only loosely predetermined and respondents are free to respond in their own words and in any way they see fit. [GAC]

stub control A perpetual inventory system of unit control in which sales information is obtained from stubs of price tickets rather than from sales checks, scanning of bar codes, or other sources. [WRD]

style A distinctive mode of presentation or performance in any art, product, or activity. Styles may be permanent, but move into and out of fashion. [DW]

style-out A method of pinpointing the determinants of consumer demand for fashion merchandise, whereby buyers and/or merchandise managers physically inspect fast-selling and slow-selling items to determine their customer-attracting features or lack of same. [WRD]

subculture The segments within a culture that share distinguishing meanings, values, and patterns of behavior that differ from those of the overall culture. (See also **acculturation** and **social factors in consumer behavior.**) [JPP/JCO]

subhead A part of the written component of print advertising that is designed to guide the reader's attention to specific details about the advertised item or to help organize issues presented in the body copy. (See also **headline.**) [JE]

subject A person from whom information is secured in a marketing research study, either by questioning or by observing him or her in some way. (See also **respondent**.) [GAC]

sublimation See **ego defenses**

subliminal advertising Advertising messages that are supposedly disguised so that they are not able to be overtly seen and/or heard yet are nevertheless effective in persuading members of the audience. There is no scientific evidence to indicate that this approach is effective communication and, if there were convincing evidence of effectiveness, the approach would likely be prohibited as a deceptive business practice. [JE]

subliminal perception 1. (consumer behavior definition) A psychological view that suggests that attitudes and behaviors can be changed by stimuli that are not consciously perceived. [JPP/JCO] 2. (consumer behavior definition) The perception of or response to a stimulus that the perceiver is unaware of perceiving and can not recognize. The stimulus is below the perceiver's limen, or perceptual threshold. [HHK/MCC]

submissive selling style A selling style often used by excellent socializers who like to spend time talking about nonbusiness activities. These salespeople usually are reluctant to obtain commitments from prospects. [BAW]

subsidiary company See **multibusiness organization**

subsistence economy An economy in which exchange is notable by its absence because goods and services are produced and consumed by the same families. [DLS]

substantiation An FTC requirement that advertisers have a reasonable basis for their advertising claims. [DC]

substitute Substitutes-in-kind are products that look alike and represent the same application of a distinct technology to the provision of a distinct set of customer functions. Substitutes-in-use are products that have shared functionality based on the customer's perceptions of all the ways in which their needs can be satisfied in a given usage or application situation. The attractiveness of a substitute product depends on (1) its initial price, (2) customer switching costs, (3) postpurchase costs of operation, and (4) the additional benefits the customer perceives and values. (See also **cannibalization.**) [GSD]

substitute products The products that are viewed by the user as alternatives for other products. The substitution is rarely perfect, and varies from time to time depending on price, availability, etc. (See also **complementary products** and **product class.**) [DW]

substitutes-in-kind See **substitute**

substitutes-in-use See **substitute**

suggested retail A recommended list price submitted by a manufacturer or other vendor to a retailer. [WRD]

summated rating A self-report technique for attitude measurement in which subjects are asked to indicate their degree of agreement or disagreement with each of a number of statements; a subject's attitude score is the total obtained by summing the scale values assigned to each category checked. (See also **comparative rating scale, constant sum method, graphic-rating scale, Guttman scale, interval scale, itemized rating scale, nominal scale, ordinal scale, ratio scale, semantic differential,** and **Stapel scale.**) [GAC]

summative evaluation See **impact evaluation**

super regional shopping center One of several standard classes of shopping centers recognized by The Urban Land Institute. It provides for extensive variety of general merchandise, apparel, furniture, and home furnishings. Typically, it has three or more full-line department stores of more than 100,000 square feet each, and total store area of center may be about 600,000 square feet to more than 1,500,000 square feet. (See also **arcade shopping center, community shopping center, factory outlet center, mall-type shopping center, neighborhood shopping center, off-price shopping center, regional shopping center,** and **strip-type shopping center.**) [WRD]

superego See **ego, ego defenses,** and **id**

supermarket A large departmentalized retail establishment offering a relatively broad and complete stock of dry groceries, fresh meat, perishable produce, and dairy products, supplemented by a variety of convenience, nonfood merchandise and operated primarily on a self service basis. [WRD]

superstation A television station in a particular city that sends its signal via satellite to subscribing cable television stations anywhere in the world. Television station WGN in Chicago is an example of such a superstation. The cable system disseminates the signal to its subscribers. [JE]

superstore A very large store that is typically of a supermarket character and offers an unusually wide range of the merchandise lines carried, with appeal to the mass market. This term may apply in any line of trade. [WRD]

supervision See **span of control**

supervisor ratings See **behavioral analysis**

supplement A special, preprinted section of a newspaper or magazine that is then inserted during the regular printing process for the publication. Supplements usually contain both editorial matter and ads. Supplements inserted in a variety of newspapers (often appearing on Sundays) are called syndicated supplements. [JE]

supplier decision See **buying decisions**

supplier management The process whereby industrial buyers make suggestions about the suppliers' policies, procedures, and strategies to improve the quality of products and services furnished. [WL/MBC]

supplies The industrial products that are consumed in the process of producing other products. They facilitate the production process and do not go into the product itself. They frequently are referred to as maintenance, repair, and operating items and supplies. [DW]

supply 1. (economic definition) A schedule of the amounts of a good that would be offered for sale at all possible prices at any one instance of time. 2. (business definition) The number of units of a product that will be put on the market over a period of time. [DLS]

supply curve A graph of the quantity of a product expected to be offered to the market by suppliers at various prices, given that other factors are held constant. (See also **demand curve.**) [DLS]

supply house A middleman selling industrial goods to manufacturers or other business or institutional users. Generally, this is a distributor, wholesaler, or jobber. [WRD]

supply-pushed innovation Innovation that is based at least partly on the abilities and outputs of technical engineering and research and development functions. It involves making what the organization is able to make. It is commonly called technology-driven innovation and contrasts with demand-pulled innovation. [DW)

support arguments See **cognitive response**

surcharge An additional charge for performing service that is assessed over and above the base rate. [DJB/BJL]

sustainable competitive advantage A sustainable competitive advantage exists when a firm is implementing a value-creating strategy not simultaneously being implemented by any current or potential competitors *and* when these other competitors are unable to duplicate the benefits of this strategy. The sustainability of a competitive advantage depends upon the possibility of competitive duplication. Invisible assets may allow a firm to sustain a competitive advantage. [GSD]

sustainable growth rate A measure of the capacity of a business to grow within the constraints of its current financial policies. The maximum sustainable growth rate, which reflects the ability of the business to fund new assets needed to support increased sales, is estimated by:

$$SGR = \frac{P(1-d)(1+L)}{t - P(1-d)(1+L)}$$

where:
- P = profit margin after tax
- d = dividend payout ratio (for a business unit this is computed from the corporate overhead charge plus any dividend paid to corporate)
- L = debt to equity ratio
- t = ratio of assets (physical plant and equipment plus working capital) to sales. [GSD]

sweepstakes The offering of prizes to participants, where winners are selected by chance and no consideration is required. (See also **contest** and **game.**) [DES/BEB]

switch trading A mechanism that can be applied to barter or countertrade. A professional switch trader, switch trading house, or bank steps into a simple barter arrangement, clearing arrangement, or countertrade arrangement when one of the parties is not willing to accept all the goods or the clearing credits in a transaction. The switching mechanism provides a secondary market for countertraded or bartered goods and credits. [WJK]

switcher A consumer who alternates purchases in a product category between two or more brands. [DES/BEB]

SWM See **shareholder wealth maximization**

SWOT See **situation analysis**

symbolic interaction A sociological theory that focuses on the formation of self through interactions with other people. The meaning attached to products is a function of the interaction of the self and others to the object. [HHK/MCC]

symbolic meaning The psychological and social meanings products have for consumers that go beyond product attributes. [JPP/JCO]

syncratic decision making A pattern of decision making within a family in which most decisions are made jointly by both spouses. (See also **autonomic decision making.**) [JPP/JCO]

syndicated barter See **barter**

syndicated research The information collected on a regular basis that is then sold to interested clients (for example, Nielsen Television Ratings). [GAC]

syndicated supplement See **supplement**

synectics The joining together of different and seemingly irrelevant elements and people into a problem-stating and problem-solving group. [WL/MBC]

systematic risk See **beta coefficient**

systematic sample A probability sample in which every *k*th element in the population is designated for inclusion in the sample after a random start. (See also **cluster sample, simple random sample,** and **stratified sample.**) [GAC]

systems design See **prototype** and **screening of ideas**

systems selling An approach aimed at providing better service and satisfaction to customers, through the design of well-integrated groups of interlocking products, together with the implementation of a system of production, inventory control, distribution, and other services, to meet major customers' needs for a smooth-running operation. (See also **approach, sales; balance sheet method; benefit approach; compliment approach; consultative selling; customer orientation; formula selling; high-pressure selling; multilevel selling;** and **problem solution approach.**) [BAW]

tabulation A procedure by which the number of cases that fall into each of a number of categories are counted. (See also **simple tabulation.**) [GAC]

tachistoscope A device that provides the researcher timing control over a visual stimulus; in marketing research, the visual stimulus is often a specific advertisement. [GAC]

tactics Short-term actions undertaken to achieve implementation of a broader strategy. [GSD]

tag line See **slogan**

take one pad A packet of coupons, refund blanks, or other promotional offers attached to or placed near the product being promoted. [DES/BEB]

take transaction The sale of goods that are turned over to the customer immediately upon closing the sale rather than delivered. [WRD]

takeover The process by which a firm or group of investors acquires control of a corporation via merger or a tender offer. The empirical evidence suggests that both the shareholders of the acquired firm and the bidding firm or group gain in the transaction on average—although the major portion of the gain goes to the target firm's stockholders. [PFA]

tare The weight of a container deducted from the gross weight of the package to determine net weight and allowance for freight. [WRD]

target market The particular segment of a total population on which the retailer focuses its merchandising expertise to satisfy that submarket in order to accomplish its profit objectives. (See also **advertising strategy.**) [WRD]

target market identification The process of using income, demographic, and life style characteristics of a market and census information for small areas to identify the most favorable locations. [DLH]

target return pricing A method of pricing that attempts to cover all costs and achieve a target return. [DLS]

tariff A published set of rates for transportation and distribution services. [DJB/BJL]

tariff system The system of duties applied to goods and services from foreign countries. It may be a single rate of duty for each item applicable to all countries or groups of countries or two or more rates applicable to different countries or groups of countries. (See also **ad valorem duty, Brussels Nomenclature, compound duties, countervailing duties, preferential tariff, single column tariff, specific duties,** and **two column tariff.**) [WJK]

task force, in new product development This task force (or team) is established for a new product idea to shepherd it through the various development stages until it is abandoned or approved for commercialization. The task force is composed of personnel (on loan, full time or part time) from departments such as marketing, research and development, and finance. Other specialists may join the task force as needed. The task force disbands when the project is abandoned or when commercialization is authorized. Comment: The advantage of the task force is that disagreements among functional specialists are more readily resolved when members must work together to achieve goals. Also, they have direct communications with their own functional departments which have new product assignments. The disadvantage is that there may not be enough competent people to staff the task forces assigned to the many new product projects going on at the same time. (See also **team, as in organization** and **venture team, in new product development.**) [VPB]

task-oriented behavior See **initiating structure**

TC See **total cost**

team, as in organization A team is an organizational device bringing together persons with different skills to work toward a goal as defined by the manager appointing the team. The manager may be a working member of the team or the team may work on its own, selecting its leader from within the team. The manager, in either case, is responsible for monitoring progress of the team as it works to achieve the goal in a specified period of time. Comment: Teams often are used to solve problems requiring skills and experience of members from various parts of the company, and whose knowledge exceeds that of the manager who might otherwise have to make the decision alone. (See also **matrix organization; task force, in new product development;** and **venture team, in new product development.**) [VPB]

team selling The practice of involving a group of people familiar with the viewpoints and concerns of key decision makers of the customer's organization to sell and service a major account. Comment: This is especially prevalent in the sale of complex industrial products, where a particular salesperson cannot be an expert on all aspects of the purchase process. [BAW]

tear sheet An advertisement torn from a newspaper or magazine, sent to an agency or advertiser as evidence of insertion. [WRD]

technical salesperson See **sales engineer**

technological base The technical skills and equipment available to a country for converting its resources to a standard of living. [DLS]

technological change The discovery and application of new products, new and improved machines, tools, equipment, and methods of production. [DLS]

technological forecasting The prediction of innovations and advances in a particular technology. Both exploratory research methods and normative research methods are used, the former to project future developments based on the past, and the latter to focus more on planning and planned technological innovation. [WL/MBC]

technological improvements See **experience curve effect**

technological mapping The gathering and analysis of information about the direction and timing of possible competitive technological developments. [WL/MBC]

technology 1. (economic definition) A nation's accumulated competence to provide goods and services. [DLS]
2. (environments definition) The purposeful application of scientific knowl-

edge; an environmental force that consists of inventions and innovations from applied scientific and engineering research. [WL/MBC] (See also **business definition** and **product-market definition.**)

technology assessment The analysis and evaluation of the potential impact on society of the introduction, modification, or development of a technology, both direct and indirect, intended and unintended. [WL/MBC]

technology planning The development of plans and procedures to implement technology transfer. [WL/MBC]

technology transfer The transfer of a capability to use, modify, or adapt a process, among organizations or countries. [WL/MBC]

technology-driven innovation See **supply-pushed innovation**

Telephone Disclosure and Dispute Resolution Act (1992) An act authorizing the Federal Trade Commission to provide rules to prohibit unfair and deceptive acts and practices in connection with pay-per-call services. (See also **consumer protection legislation.**) [DC]

telephone error A type of error resulting from the fact that most people remember an event as having occurred more recently than in fact is the case. (See also **recall loss.**) [GAC]

telephone interview A telephone conversation between a representative of the research organization, the interviewer, and a respondent or interviewee. (See also **plus-one dialing** and **random digit dialing.**) [GAC]

telephone sales representative See **TSR**

telephone selling Selling that involves interacting with customers using a telephone. (See also **inside salesperson.**) [BAW]

temporary import surcharges Import charges to provide additional protection for local industry and in response to balance of payments deficits. [WJK]

tender offer See **takeover**

terminal values One of two major types of values proposed by Milton Rokeach. Terminal values represent preferred end states of being or global goals that consumers are trying to achieve in their lives. (See also **instrumental values.**) [JPP/JCO]

terms of access All the conditions that apply to the importation of goods manufactured in a foreign country such as import duties, import restrictions or quotas, foreign exchange regulations, and preference arrangements. [WJK]

terms of purchase The conditions in a purchase agreement with a vendor that include the type(s) of discounts available and responsibility for transportation costs. [WRD]

terms of sale The conditions in a sales contract with customers including such issues as charges for alterations, delivery, or gift wrapping, or the store's exchange policies. [WRD]

territorial allocation The rights given to the wholesaler or retailer (by the manufacturer) to sell the manufacturer's product or brand in a defined geographic area that is, at least to some extent, removed, isolated, or protected from other wholesalers and retailers also selling the manufacturer's items. [GLF]

territorial rights See **territorial allocation**

territory management The development and implementation of a strategy for directing selling activities toward customers in a sales territory aimed at maintaining the lines of communications, improving sales coverage, and minimizing wasted time. Territory management includes the allocation of sales calls to customers and the planning, routing, and scheduling of the calls. (See also **call frequency, circular routing, leapfrog routing, routine call pattern,** and **zoning.**) [BAW]

territory potential An estimate of the maximum possible sales opportunities that could be realized in a sales territory. [BAW]

territory, sales See **sales territory**

tertiary package See **multiple packaging** and **package**

tertiary trade zone The outermost ring of a trade area. It includes customers who only occasionally shop at a store or shopping center. It is also known as fringe trade area. (See also **analog approach** and **secondary trade zone.**) [WRD]

test market The trading area selected to test a company's new or modified product, service, or promotion. (See also **market testing.**) [WRD]

test market-based forecasting models See **new product forecasting models**

test marketing One form of market testing. It usually involves actually marketing a new product in one or several cities. The effort is totally representative of what the firm intends to do later upon national marketing (or regional market rollout). Various aspects of the marketing plan may be tested (e.g., advertising expenditure levels or, less often, product form variants), by using several pairs of cities. Output is a mix of learning, especially a sales and profit forecast. In some areas, test marketing is currently being stretched to include scanner market testing, in which the marketing activity is less than total, but the term is best confined to the full-scale activity. [DW]

test-pretest reliability assessment See **stability**

Textile Fiber Products Identification Act (1958) An act that applies to yarns, fabrics, and household articles made from fiber other than wool, and requires that such products bear labels revealing the amount of each fiber they contain and forbids misbranding of such products. [DC]

Thematic Apperception Test See **projective technique**

Theory of Reasoned Action 1. (consumer behavior definition) A theory developed by Martin Fishbein that assumes consumers consciously consider the consequences of alternative behaviors and choose the one that leads to the most desirable consequences. The theory states that behavior is closely related to behavorial intentions which are in turn the result of attitudes toward performing the behavior and social normative beliefs. [JPP/JCO] 2. (consumer behavior definition) An extension of learning theory proposing that prediction of a person's likelihood to perform an action must be based upon measurement of the person's attitude toward performing the behavior, rather than measurement of the person's attitude toward the behavioral object in general. For example, a person could have a positive attitude toward Nike athletic shoes, but may not purchase them because they are priced too high. The theory of reasoned action claims that measurement of the person's attitude toward purchasing Nike shoes would allow greater predictability than measuring the person's attitude toward Nike shoes in general. [HHK/MCC]

third party provider A for-hire firm

that performs logistics service functions such as warehousing and transportation. The majority of these firms customize their offerings to meet individual customer needs. (See also **integrated service provider** and **physical distribution agency.**) [DJB/BJL]

third sector Collectively, all private nonprofit marketers. (See also **independent sector, nongovernmental organization,** and **private nonprofit marketer.** [ARA]

thumbnail A rough sketch of the layout for a piece of print advertising. (See also **comprehensive layout, dummy, mechanical, rough,** and **storyboard.**) [JE]

time horizon See **implementation**

time rate of demand The quantity of product that the market will absorb at a particular price per period of time. [DLS]

time series The historical records of the fluctuations of economic variables. [DLS]

time series analysis An approach to developing a sales forecast that relies on the analysis of historical data to develop a prediction for the future. [GAC]

time series models See **forecasting models**

time utility The increased satisfaction created by marketing through making products available at the time consumers want them. (See also **place utility** and **possession utility.**) [DLS]

tip sheet A summary of material to be covered in a publicity interview or photo shoot. [DES/BEB]

title The legal evidence of ownership or right of possession. (See also **price structure.**) [WRD]

TOFC See **trailer-on-flatcar**

token order The placing of a small order with the possibility of a larger one in the future. [WRD]

ton-mile A transportation term denoting the movement of one ton, i.e., 2,000 pounds, one mile. [DLS]

total cost (TC) 1. (economic definition) The sum of total fixed cost and total variable cost for a given level of output. (See also **fixed cost, total; profits;** and **variable cost, total.**) [DLS] 2. (physical distribution definition) In a physical distribution system, total cost includes all the costs of transportation, warehousing, order processing, packaging, etc. [DJB/BJL]

total cost of goods sold The gross cost of goods sold plus alteration room and workroom net cost, if any, less each discount earned on purchases. (See also **gross margin of profit** and **retail inventory method of accounting.**) [WRD]

total disposable personal income See **disposable personal income**

total dollars invested in stock perspective See **stock balance**

total fertility rate The number of births that 1,000 women would have in their lifetimes if at each year of age, they experienced birthrates occurring in the specified year. (See also **completed fertility, crude birth rate, fertility rate,** and **replacement level fertility.**) [WL/MBC]

total fixed cost See **fixed cost, total**

total personal income See **personal income**

total revenue The price per unit multiplied by sales volume and summed over all products and services. (See also **profits.**) [KM]

total variable cost See **variable cost, total**

traceable costs See **direct costs**

Tracker A model using three waves of survey data to predict 12-month test market sales for a new consumer nondurable product. The approach views potential customers as proceeding sequentially through stages of awareness, initial product trial, and repeat purchase. The overall prediction of sales over time is constructed by predicting the time trend of these three quantities (awareness-trial-repeat) using the survey data (Blattberg and Golanty 1978). The effectiveness of the model's product awareness predictions has been investigated by Mahajan, Muller, and Sharma (1984). (See also **ASSESSOR, LITMUS, new product forecasting model, NEWPROD, NEWS, SPRINTER Mod III,** and **STEAM.**) [DCS/YJW]

tractor-trailer The power unit and the van of a motor truck. This term usually refers to the two units that are commonly used for over-the-road surface transportation. [DJB/BJL]

trade acceptance A noninterest-bearing bill of exchange or draft covering the sale of goods, drawn by the seller on, and accepted by, the buyer. [WRD]

trade advertising See **business-to-business advertising**

trade allowance A short-term special offer, made by marketers to channel members as an incentive to stock, feature, or in some way participate in the cooperative promotion of a product. (See also **trade sales promotion.**) [DES/BEB]

trade area 1. (geography definition) A geographical area containing the customers of a particular firm or group of firms for specific goods or services. [DLH] 2. (retailing definition) A geographic sector containing potential customers for a particular retailer or shopping center. (See also **trading area.**) [WRD]

trade balance A sub-balance of a country's balance of payments showing the relationship between total exports and total imports for a given period of time. (See also **trade deficit.**) [DLS]

trade card A special card issued to the customer as successive purchases are made. It entitles the holder to a prize or purchase credit when a certain total is reached. It is also called a punch card. [WRD]

trade channel See **channel of distribution**

trade coupon A coupon that may only be redeemed at a particular store or group of stores. [DES/BEB]

trade credit The supplying of goods (by wholesalers and manufacturers) on terms that are intended to permit sale by the retailer before payment is due. [WRD]

trade deficit The difference between the value of products exported to a country and the products imported from that country over a given period of time. (See also **trade balance.**) **[DLS]**

trade discount The discount allowed to a class of customers (manufacturers, wholesalers, retailers) on a list price before consideration of credit terms. It applies to any allowance granted without reference to the date of payment. (See also **functional discount.**) [WRD]

trade dress The total appearance and image of a product including size, texture, shape, and color combination. Duplication of trade dress of another good is actionable under common law and the Lanham Trademark Act. [DC]

trade name A trademark that is used to

identify an organization rather than a product or product line. (See also **logo**.) [DW]

trade premium A prize, usually merchandise, given by jobbers' retailers for their cooperation in achieving sales. [WRD]

trade regulation rule A rule issued by the Federal Trade Commission that states that particular practices are unfair or deceptive acts within the meaning of Section 5 of the FTC Act. The Magnuson-Moss Warranty–Federal Trade Commission Improvement Act gave the FTC the power to promulgate substantive trade regulation rules, that is, rules having the force of law as opposed to interpretive rules merely stating the FTC's interpretation of its statutory mandate. [DC]

trade sales promotion Marketers' activities directed to channel members to encourage them to provide special support or activities for the product or service. (See also **accelerated purchase, advertising/display allowance, buy-back allowance, buy one-get one free, buying allowance, count and recount promotion, dating, deal, deal merchandise, dealer loader, dealer tie-in, display, end-aisle display, free merchandise, incentive plan, off-invoice allowance, pass-along deal, pass-through rate, price off, promotional allowance, promotional package, sales promotion, trade allowance,** and **trade show.**) [DES/BEB]

trade salesperson A salesperson employed by the manufacturing firm whose primary responsibility is to sell to channel members. [BAW]

trade secret According to the 1939 Restatement of Torts, a trade secret may consist of any formula, pattern, device, or compilation of information that is used in one's business and that gives the person an opportunity to obtain an advantage over competitors who do not know or use it. A trade secret may be any commercially valuable information, whether in the form of an invention, an industrial or commercial idea, or a compilation of data. Trade secret law is a common law doctrine and varies somewhat from state to state. [DC]

trade show 1. (sales definition) An exhibition in which a number of manufacturers display their products. [BAW] 2. (sales promotion definition) A periodic gathering at which manufacturers, suppliers, and distributors in a particular industry, or related industries, display their products and provide information for potential buyers (retail, wholesale, or industrial). (See also **trade sales promotion.**) [DES/BEB]

trade up See **consumer sales promotion**

trademark A legal term meaning the same as brand. A trademark identifies one seller's product and thus differentiates it from products of other sellers. A trademark also aids in promotion and helps protect the seller from imitations. A trademark may be eligible for registration, as it is in the United States through the Patent and Trademark Office of the Department of Commerce. If registered, the trademark obtains additional protection, mainly exclusive use, but special efforts are necessary to keep the registration and the exclusive use. (See also **brand name, copyright, individual brand, service mark,** and **trade name.**) [DW]

Trademark Law Revision Act (1988) This act revises the Lanham Trademark Act. It is designed to increase the value of the federal registration system for U.S. companies, to remove the current preference for foreign companies applying to register trademarks in the United States, and to improve the law's protection of the public from counterfeiting, confusion, and deception. [DC]

trading area A district the size of which is usually determined by the boundaries within which it is economical in terms of volume and cost for a marketing unit or group to sell and/or deliver products. It is also referred to as shopping radius. (See also **trade area.**) [WRD]

trading stamps A type of continuity plan in which a consumer collects stamps or certificates issued with each purchase at participating retail stores. Stamps are generally redeemed for prizes from a catalog. [DES/BEB]

trading-up 1. A seller's practice of handling and promoting more expensive or higher-grade merchandise in order to elevate the prestige of the firm. 2. A salesperson's effort to interest a customer in better-grade and more expensive goods than the customer expects to buy. [WRD]

Traffic Audit Bureau An organization that audits freight bills tendered to the buyer of the transportation service for accuracy. If inaccurate, a claim is filed by the payer of the transportation service to recover cost of overcharges. [DJB/BJL]

traffic (customer) When applied to retailing, this refers to those people who frequent the store (or the shopping area) within a particular period of time. Traffic may be heavy, light, or medium. [WRD]

traffic item A consumer product in demand and with high replacement frequency that regularly brings traffic to a store or department. [WRD]

traffic management A corporate function that is responsible for determining the mode of transportation and utilization of transportation equipment as well as general administration of the movement of goods by the firm. A traffic manager usually heads the traffic management function. [DJB/BJL]

traffic manager See **traffic management**

trailer-on-flatcar (TOFC) A shipment of goods in a truck trailer on a rail flatcar. Shipments moving as TOFC receive special rates. (See also **container-on-flatcar, intermodal transportation,** and **piggyback.**) [DJB/BJL]

transaction code The unique identifying number that defines the specific data being transmitted via an electronic data interchange transaction. Numbers are assigned to various types of document transactions such as purchase orders, warehouse shipping orders, and motor carrier shipment information. [DJB/BJL]

transaction set The electronic equivalent of common paper forms such as purchase orders, invoices, and receipts. [DJB/BJL]

transaction value The subjectively weighted difference between the buyer's reference price and the actual price to be paid. [KM]

transactions cost analysis An approach to analyzing the economics of vertical relationships. The basic premise is that firms will internalize those activities they are able to perform at lower cost, and will rely on the market for those activities for which other providers have an advantage. The costs of transactions are determined by the frequency with which they recur, the environmental uncertainty surrounding them, and the specificity of the assets they require. [GSD]

transfer (interdepartmental merchandise) An intrafirm transaction accounting for the movement of merchandise from one selling department or location to another, which is a transfer-in for the department or other selling unit receiving the goods and a transfer-out for the department or location sending the goods. [WRD]

transfer pricing The pricing of goods and services that are sold to controlled entities of the same organization, e.g., movements of goods and services within a multinational or global corporation. [WJK]

transformational advertising The advertising that associates product usage with certain feelings, images, or meanings that then transform the experience of using the product. For example, a transformational ad could make the experience of using a product warmer or more exciting. (See also **informational advertising.**) [HHK/MCC]

transformational leadership A leadership style wherein sales managers use inspiration and charisma, seek to intellectually stimulate the salespeople, and treat each salesperson as an individual. The goal of transformational leadership is to move the salespeople beyond their own self interests toward those of the organization. The inspiring and charismatic sales manager can create feelings of extraordinary esteem, affection, admiration, respect, and trust within sales personnel. Intellectually stimulating salespeople entails creating a readiness for changes in salespeople's thinking and encouraging the sales personnel to think of new ways to solve old problems. Treating salespeople as individuals involves establishing and exhibiting genuine concern for each salesperson. (See also **consideration, contingent reward leadership, initiating structure, laissez faire leadership,** and **management-by-exception leadership.**) [AJD]

transit rate A rate that allows the through shipment of goods to be interrupted for intermediate processing. Even though the goods are stopped enroute to the ultimate destination, a through rate is charged similar to a rate that would be charged if the goods had not stopped enroute to their ultimate destination. [DJB/BJL]

transition probability matrix See **Markov model**

transnational corporation A stage of development of the global/transnational corporation. (See also **international corporation** and **multinational corporation.**) [WJK]

transportation A marketing function that adds time and place utility to the product by moving it from where it is made to where it is purchased and used. It includes all intermediate steps in the process. [DJB/BJL]

transportation costs See **buyers' costs**

transportation mode A specific class of related carriers such as truck, rail, air, or water. It is a generic class of transportation carrier. [DJB/BJL]

trend analysis The use of analytical techniques, such as time series analysis, to discern trends. [WL/MBC]

trend extrapolation The projection of patterns identified in data about the past into the future. [WL/MBC]

trial A psychological term denoting the number of a practice run, such as a 5-trial learning experience, or a series of repetitions of a learning experience. It also is used to imply a sampling of a product before repurchase. (See also **adoption process, awareness-trial-repeat, habit formation,** and **sales promotion.**) [HHK/MCC]

trial close An attempt made by the salesperson to close the sale. [BAW]

trickle down theory The belief that clothing fashions trickle down from the higher socioeconomic classes to the lower classes as consumers attempt to emulate individuals with greater social status. Research evidence generally does not support a trickle down theory. The diffusion of fashion appears to trickle across social classes rather than trickle down or up. [HHK/MCC]

truckload The shipment by truck of a full load. A truckload usually qualifies for lower freight rate than smaller shipments. [DJB/BJL]

true panel See **panel (true)**

Truth-in-Lending Act (1968) This act requires full disclosure of terms and conditions of finance charges. (See also **Consumer Credit Protection Act.**) [DC]

TSR An abbreviation that is used for a telephone sales representative. [BAW]

turnkey operation Also called system selling, this is a complete system solution, in which the seller provides the buyer with a complete working operation, including all equipment, assembly, operating expenses, personnel training, and the like. It is common in foreign licensing in which a firm provides experts to set up a foreign company, ultimately turning the operation over to the host entirely. [GLL/DTW]

turnover table See **brand-switching matrix**

twig A store (smaller than a branch) that specializes in a particular category or few categories of merchandise when the firm does not believe a wider offering in that market is reasonable—e.g., a home furnishings twig. [WRD]

two column tariff A system of tariffs in which the initial single column of duties is supplemented by a second column of duties that shows reduced rates agreed through tariff negotiations with other countries. (See also **single column tariff** and **tariff system.**) [WJK]

two step flow of communication The belief that the process of influence of communications material is not directly from the communicator to the audience or interpreters, but rather influence is a two step process from the mass communications, such as advertising, to the opinion leader in the group and from the opinion leader to the other individuals. (See also **personal influence.**) [HHK/MCC]

two-stage area sampling See **area sampling**

two-stage cluster sampling See **cluster sample**

tying clause A limitation in a contract requiring price maintenance or exclusive purchase of certain products from one party by the other. [WRD]

type face Any one of a wide variety of systematically designed styles or patterns used to present letters of the alphabet, numbers, and punctuation marks. A font is a particular point size and style variation (such as italic) with a given type face. (See also **typesetting.**) [JE]

Type I error The rejection of a null hypothesis when it is true; it is also known as alpha error. [GAC]

type I Fisher-Tippett extreme value distribution See logit model

Type II error The failure to reject a null hypothesis when it is false; it is also known as beta error. [GAC]

type membership See **stereotype**

typesetting The process of choosing appropriate type faces (or fonts), reproducing the headlines and other text in an appropriate size (or point size), and placing the type in the proper place on the page. [JE]

UCS See **uniform communications system**

ultimate consumer A consumer who buys goods for personal or family use or for household consumption. [WRD}

ultimate user See **consumer**

UN See **United Nations**

unadvertised brand A brand that is not advertised. Frequently unadvertised brands are the private brands of retail food chains. [DW]

unaided recall See **recall test**

unaware stage See **buyer readiness stage**

unconditioned stimulus See **classical conditioning**

UNCTAD See **United Nations Conference on Trade and Development**

underdeveloped country A country where 1987 GNP per capita ranged from $500 to $1000. This country exhibits the symptoms of the first stages of industrialization, which are (1) small factories are erected to supply the domestic market with such items as batteries, tires, footwear, clothing, building materials, and packaged foods; (2) the proportion of the population engaged in agricultural activities declines and the degree of urbanization increases; and (3) the available educational effort expands and literacy rises. (See also **developing country, industrialized country, postindustrialized country,** and **preindustrialized country.**) [WJK]

underprivileged family A family in a social class that does not have enough money to purchase the necessities, i.e., shelter, clothing, and transportation, appropriate for its class status. An underprivileged family is not able to acquire what is expected for its class status and usually is defined as having at least 15 percent lower income than the median for the social class. (See also **overprivileged family.**) [HHK/MCC]

understored A market condition that exists when a market has too few stores to provide satisfactorily for the needs of the consumer. (See also **overstored.**) [WRD]

undifferentiated marketing See **market segmentation strategies**

undifferentiated oligopoly An oligopoly that produces and markets standardized products—e.g., cement or paperboard boxes. (See also **differentiated oligopoly.**) [DLS]

unduplicated audience See **reach**

uneven exchange An exchange of goods made by a customer when the value of the new goods received is different from that of the goods returned. [WRD]

unfair competition 1. (environments definition) The rivalry among sellers through the use of practices deemed to be unfair by judicial, legal, or administrative agencies such as selling products below cost to drive a competitor out of business, or dumping goods in foreign markets. It is defined in antitrust laws as acts to mislead and confuse consumers, such as the deceptive substitution of one product for another in order to gain unfair advantage over competitors. [WL/MBC] 2. (retailing definition) A business practice that is not considered ethical in a trade or industry. According to federal and other laws, it is a certain situation and/or practice that unduly injures competitors and works contrary to the public interest as interpreted in the business community and the nation's laws. [WRD]

unfair trade practices acts Sales-below-cost statutes that vary widely from state to state and most frequently prohibit the sale of branded and unbranded goods below cost when the intent is to destroy competition or to injure a competitor. [DC]

unfashionable merchandise See **distress merchandise**

Uniform Commercial Code A code adopted by most states that provides consistency in commercial law and deals with all the aspects of a commercial transaction as well as other commercial matters such as bulk sales, investment securities, and the bank collection process. [DC]

uniform communications system (UCS) A communications standard adopted by the food industry for electronic transmission of information between buyer and seller. [DJB/BJL]

uniform freight classification A system that allows the grouping of related products into specific rate categories. These ratings are based on handling characteristics, bulk, value, and perishability of the product. These ratings are used as the basis for standardized rates for classes of products. [DJB/BJL]

unique selling proposition (USP) An approach to developing the advertising message that concentrates on the uniquely differentiating characteristics of the product or service to be sold. The key idea is to concentrate on a characteristic of the product that is both important to the customer and a unique strength of the advertised product when compared to competing products. [JE]

unit business manager See **category manager**

unit control The control of stock in terms of merchandise units rather than in terms of dollar value. [WRD]

unit load A shipment that contains multiple units but moves as a single entity. For example, shipments that are palletized or slipsheeted or containerized are unit load shipments. [DJB/BJL]

unit packing Packing merchandise in selling units (by the manufacturer) so it can be sold from sample and delivered to the customer without repacking at the store. [WRD]

unit pricing Under unit pricing, products offered for sale include the price per unit such as per ounce, pound, or quart, in addition to the price of the product as packaged. [WRD]

unit sales manager See **field sales manager**

unit train An entire train comprising a single product, typically a bulk commodity such as coal or grain. These trains are faster and less expensive to operate than traditional trains because they bypass railyards. [DJB/BJL]

unitary price elasticity A special situation in which a cut in price increases quantity just enough that total revenue remains unchanged. (See also **elasticity coefficient.**) [DLS]

United Nations (UN) An international organization founded in 1945 of countries whose mission is to promote the cause of peace, prosperity, and human rights for all people. (See also **International Court of Justice.**) [WJK]

United Nations Conference on Trade and Development (UNCTAD) An organization set up by the United Nations to assist the less developed nations. It seeks to accelerate the growth rate of the less developed countries (LDCs) to not less than 5 percent per annum. [WJK]

universal product code (UPC) 1. (retailing definition) A national coordinated system of product identification by which a ten-digit number is assigned to products. The UPC is designed so that at the checkout counter an electronic scanner will read the symbol on the product and automatically transmit the information to a computer that controls the sales register. The code is called OCR-A. [WRD] 2. (environments definition) A set of bars or lines, printed on most items sold in supermarkets and other mass retailing outlets, that permits computers at checkout counters to retrieve the price of the item from its memory or data base. The data generated can be used for a wide variety of marketing decisions such as inventory control, allocation of shelf space, advertising, pricing, and so on. (See also **bar code** and **scanner.**) [WL/MBC]

University of Michigan Survey Research Center See **Consumer Sentiment Index**

unlearning See **extinction**

unplanned buying See **planned buying vs. unplanned buying**

unplanned center A cluster of retail stores within the city in which there is a structured internal pattern of locations, achieved by the independent decisions of stores operating within the land market. [DLH]

unseasonable merchandise See **distress merchandise**

unsought good A product which the consumer does not seek, either from lack of awareness or lack of interest in the particular attributes it has. Because most products are both sought and unsought by different persons this category is not part of the basic classification of goods. [DW]

unwholesome demand The desire for goods, services, and activities that are deemed to reduce individual and social welfare. Comment: Examples include the desire for illegal drugs, excessive amounts of alcoholic beverages, and driving at excessive speeds. [ARA]

UPC See **universal product code**

UPC bar codes See **universal product code**

upper-class See **social class**

upturn See **recovery**

urban population Persons living in places of 2,500 or more inhabitants incorporated as cities, villages, boroughs, or areas designated as such by the Census, with some exceptions. (See also **rural population.**) [WL/MBC]

urbanized area An area consisting of a central city or core together with contiguous, closely settled territories that have a combined total population of at least 50,000. (See also **metropolitan statistical area.**) [WL/MBC]

urbanized core See **census metropolitan area**

Uruguay Round The multilateral negotiations between the member countries of GATT that were held in Uruguay from the mid-1980s to 1993. [WJK]

use date See **open-code dating**

use up rate The volume or length of time required by a consumer to move from one purchase occasion to another. [DES/BEB]

user See **buying roles**

users' expectations method A method of forecasting sales that relies on answers from customers regarding their expected consumption or purchases of the product. It is also known as buyers' intentions method. [GAC]

USP See **unique selling proposition**

utilitarian function of attitudes See **instrumental function of attitudes**

utilitarian reference group influence The compliance of an individual with perceived expectations of others in order to achieve rewards or avoid punishments. (See also **value expressive reference group influence.**) [JPP/JCO]

utility 1. (general definition) The state or quality of being useful. 2. (economic definition) The usefulness received by consumers from buying, owning, or consuming a product. (See also **place utility, possession utility,** and **time utility.**) [DLS]

valence A salesperson's desire to receive additional amounts of a given reward (e.g., a pay increase). Valences can influence salespeople's level of motivation. (See also **expectancy, instrumentality,** and **salesperson motivation.**) [AJD]

validity A term applied to measuring instruments reflecting the extent to which differences in scores on the measurement reflect true differences among individuals, groups, or situations in the characteristic it seeks to measure, or true differences in the same individual, group, or situation from one occasion to another rather than constant or random errors. (See also **construct validation, content validity, convergent validity, discriminant validity, external validity, internal validity,** and **pragmatic validity.**) [GAC]

VALS An acronym standing for values and life styles. VALS is a psychographic segmentation approach developed at Stanford Research Institute International. (See also **inter-directedness** and **other-directedness.**) [JPP/JCO]

value The power of any good to command other goods in peaceful and voluntary exchange. [DLS]

value added 1. (environments definition) An economic concept referring to the value that a firm adds to the cost of its inputs as a result of its activities, thereby arriving at the price of its outputs. [WL/MBC] 2. (product development definition) A measure of the contribution to a product's worth by any organization that handles it on its way to the ultimate user. Value added is measured by subtracting the cost of a product (or the cost of ingredients from which it was made) from the price that the organization got for it. For resellers, this means the firm's gross margin; for manufacturing firms, it means the contribution over cost of ingredients. Presumably whatever work that firm did is reflected in the higher price someone is willing to pay for the product, hence that firm's value added. [DW]

value added by marketing The increase in value due to performance of marketing activities by a firm. Value added by marketing is computed by subtracting the market value of purchased goods from the market value of goods sold. [DLS]

value adding resellers (VARs) Retail intermediaries who modify equipment, integrate several components into a system solution, or provide additional services to offer customized solutions to the customer. VARs are found especially in markets for computer equipment and other forms of information technology. [GLL/DTW]

value analysis 1. (industrial definition) An analytical procedure to study the costs versus the benefits of a currently purchased material, component, or design in order to reduce the cost/benefit ratio as much as possible. It is also called value engineering. When performed by a seller, it is often referred to as value-in-use analysis. [GLL/DTW] 2. (product development definition) A systematic study of a product wherein the analyst keeps asking, "Can the cost of this part, this subassembly, or this step be reduced in any way, or even eliminated?" Value analysis is usually performed by engineers who are seeking new, less expensive ways to design or create the product being studied. It may be performed on the products the firm produces, or on products that it purchases from its suppliers. [DW]

value based pricing A price setting process based on the value the product provides to the customer. [GLL/DTW]

value chain analysis An approach to assessing the positions of competitive advantage. A value chain first classifies the activities of a business into the discrete steps performed to design, produce, market, deliver, and service a product. Supporting these specific value-creation activities are firm-wide activities such as procurement, human resource management, technology, and the infrastructure of systems and management that ties the value chain together. To gain advantage a business must either perform enough of these activities at a lower cost to gain an overall cost edge while offering a parity product, or perform them in a way that leads to differentiation and a premium price. [GSD]

value engineering See **value analysis**

value expressive reference group influence An individual's use of groups to enhance or support his or her self concept. (See also **utilitarian reference group influence.**) [JPP/JCO]

value pricing A method of setting prices based upon the perceived value the product gives a specific consumer or group of consumers. (See also **value-in-use pricing.**) [DLS]

value-added system See **business definition** and **product-market definition**

value-added taxes See **compensatory import charges**

value-expressive function of attitudes A function of attitudes that allows the individual to express his or her self concept. The value-expressive function is served by attitudes that demonstrate one's self image to others. It is one of the functions of attitudes proposed by the functional theory of attitudes. (See also **ego-defensive function of attitudes, instrumental function of attitudes,** and **knowledge function of attitudes.**) [HHK/MCC]

value-in-exchange The amount of money or goods actually paid for a product or service. (See also **value-in-use.**) [KM]

value-in-use The amount of money or goods that buyers would be willing to pay for a product or service. Value-in-use is always greater than value-in-exchange. (See also **consumers' surplus.**) [KM]

value-in-use-analysis See **value analysis**

value-in-use pricing A method of setting prices in which an attempt is made to capture a portion of what a customer would save by buying a firm's product. (See also **demand-oriented pricing, perceived-value pricing,** and **value pricing.**) [DLS]

value-oriented pricing See **demand-oriented pricing** and **perceived-value pricing**

values 1. (consumer behavior definition) The beliefs about the important life goals that consumers are trying to achieve (See also **terminal values** and **instrumental values.**) [JPP/JCO]
2. (consumer behavior definition) Beliefs widely shared by members of a cul-

ture about what is desirable or good (nutritious food, French wines, free speech, or honesty) and what is undesirable or bad (arson, bigotry, escargot, spinach, or deceit). If a value is accepted by the individual, it can become a major influence on his or her behavior. 3. The important, enduring ideals or beliefs that guide behavior within a culture or for a specific person. For example, health and fitness have recently become important values for Americans. (See also **consistency theory.**) [HHK/MCC]

variable cost, average The sum of all variable costs, i.e., those costs that vary directly with the number of units produced and marketed, divided by the number of units currently produced. (See also **variable cost, total.**) [DLS]

variable cost, total The sum of all costs directly incurred by production and marketing of a given number of units. (See also **total cost** and **variable cost, average.**) [DLS]

variable import levies The import charges levied when the prices of imported products would undercut those of domestic products. The effect of these levies would be to raise the price of imported products to the domestic level. [WJK]

variable price policy A policy of adjusting prices to different customers, depending on their relative purchasing power or bargaining ability. (See also **one price policy.**) [WRD]

variety The number of different classifications of goods carried in a particular merchandising unit. It implies generically different kinds of goods. (See also **assortment.**) [WRD]

variety seeking The choice of an alternative in order to experience diversity or variety in consumption over time. For example, someone may eat a Butterfinger candy bar for a snack one day, but choose a Baby Ruth candy bar the next day specifically to get something different. [HHK/MCC]

variety store An establishment primarily selling a wide variety of merchandise in the low and popular price range usually in limited assortments, such as stationery, gift items, women's accessories, toilet articles, light hardware, toys, housewares, and confectionary. Variety stores were formerly known as limited price variety stores because merchandise was usually not sold outside some specified price ranges. [WRD]

VARs See **value adding resellers**

vehicle See **media vehicle**

vending machine The retail sale of goods or services through coin- or currency-operated machines activated by the ultimate consumer-buyer. (See also **automatic merchandising machine operator, automatic selling,** and **nonstore retailing.**) [WRD]

vendor 1. (industrial definition) An organization that supplies specific goods or services to the business markets and/or organizational markets. [GLL/DTW] 2. (retailing definition) Any firm from which a retailer obtains merchandise. [WRD]

vendor analysis 1. (industrial definition) An organized effort to assess strengths and weaknesses of current or new suppliers to assure supplier quality. It is usually undertaken by the purchasing department. [GLL/DTW] 2. (retailing definition) An analysis of sales, stocks, markups, markdowns, and gross margin by vendors. [WRD]

venture A risky new product project or business start-up. Ventures are often staffed by managers who are pulled out of their regular functional jobs and assigned to the project. The venture may be totally in-house (located on the customary premises, close to the regular operation) or it may be spun out (relocated at some point well apart from the ongoing operation). If carried out in cooperation with another firm, it is a joint venture. [DW]

venture team, in new product development This is similar to a new product task force, but with an important difference: the team is independent of any functional department. Members stay with the project until it is abandoned or commercialized. In the latter case they may become the management team responsible for running the new product as a separate business. The venture team is authorized to obtain assistance as needed from functional departments or to purchase external assistance. A venture team usually reports to a top corporate officer. Comment: A venture team is appropriate for developing new products that are outside of the company's existing businesses. A venture team is also appropriate for totally new products that usually require more time, expense, and risk than managers of currently operating businesses are willing to support. A venture team is more likely to be used for high technology industrial products than, for example, consumer packaged goods. A venture team requires long-term commitment and support from corporate management. (See also **new product organization, forms of** and **task force, in new product development.**) [VPB]

vertical business system See **business definition** and **value chain analysis**

vertical cooperative advertising Advertising in which the retailer and other previous marketing channel members (e.g., manufacturers or wholesalers) share the cost. (See also **horizontal cooperative advertising.**) [WRD]

vertical integration 1. (channels of distribution definition) The combination of two or more separate stages in the channel through ownership, including mergers or acquisitions. [GLF] 2. (environments definition) The expansion of a business by acquiring or developing businesses engaged in earlier or later stages of marketing a product. In forward vertical integration, manufacturers might acquire or develop wholesaling and retailing activities. In backward vertical integration, retailers might develop their own wholesaling or manufacturing capabilities. [WL/MBC]

vertical market A situation in which an industrial product is used by only one or a very few industry or trade groups. The market is narrow but deep in the sense that most prospective customers in the industry may need the article. [WRD]

vertical marketing system 1. (channels of distribution definition) The channel systems consisting of horizontally coordinated and vertically aligned establishments that are professionally managed and centrally coordinated to achieve optimum operating economies and maximum market impact. The three types of vertical marketing systems are administered vertical marketing system, contractual vertical marketing system, and corporate vertical marketing system. (See also **vertical marketing system competition.**) [GLF] 2. (physical distribution definition) A long-term channel relationship in which two or more firms acknowledge and desire interdependence. [DJB/BJL]

vertical marketing system competition The competition between rival vertical marketing systems. For example, the total vertical marketing system of General Motors competing with that of Ford Motor Company. [WRD]

vertical merger The joining or combination of two or more companies at different stages in the production or marketing process, such as the combination of IBM, a manufacturer of computers, with Intel, a manufacturer of microprocessors. (See also **merger.**) [WL/MBC]

vertical price-fixing A conspiracy among marketers at different levels of the channel to set prices for a product. (See also **horizontal price-fixing.**) [DLS]

vertical restraint The arrangement between firms operating at different levels of the manufacturing or distribution chain that restrict the conditions under which firms may purchase, sell, or resell. [GLF]

vertical restriction See **vertical restraint**

vertical structure of the sales organization An enumeration of which managerial positions have the authority for carrying out specific sales management activities. It also provides for effective integration and coordination of selling efforts throughout the firm. (See also **horizontal structure of the sales organization** and **sales force organization.**) [AJD]

vicarious learning The changes in an individual's behavior brought about by observing the actions of others and the consequences of those actions. [JPP/JCO]

VICS See **voluntary inter-industry communications standard**

Vidale-Wolfe model An econometric model that represents the rate of change of sales as a function of the rate of advertising spending. The lagged effect of advertising is incorporated using a sales-decay term (Vidale and Wolfe 1957). The model allows the effect of advertising to have different rise versus decay rates. (See also **advertising models.**) [DCS/YJW]

video news release (VNR) A publicity device designed to look and sound like a television news story. The publicist prepares a 60- to 90-second news release on videotape, which can then be used by television stations as is or after further editing. It is more sophisticated than a news clip. (See also **B-roll** and **radio wrap-around.**) [DES/BEB]

videotex retailing An interactive electronic system in which a retailer transmits data and graphics over cable or telephone lines to a consumer's TV or terminal. [WRD]

vision A guiding theme that articulates the nature of the business and its intentions for the future. These intentions are based on how management believes the environment will unfold and what the business can and should be in the future. A vision has the following characteristics: (1) informed—grounded in a solid understanding of the business and the forces shaping the future, (2) shared—created through collaboration, (3) competitive—creates an obsession with winning throughout the organization, and (4) enabling—empowers individuals to make meaningful decisions about strategies and tactics. [GSD]

visual front An open storefront design that has no vision barrier between the interior and exterior. [WRD]

visual merchandising A situation in which reliance is upon the use of informative labels, descriptive signs, or a self service type of display, as opposed to dependence upon a salesperson for information. [WRD]

visual system of stock control A method of controlling the amount of stock on hand by systematic observation rather than by records. [WRD]

VNR See **video news release**

voice pitch analysis A type of analysis that examines changes in the relative frequency of the human voice that accompany emotional arousal. [GAC]

voluntary chain See **voluntary group**

voluntary group A contractual vertical marketing system in which a wholesaler bands together its independent retail customers into a voluntary group. A complete range of services is offered to retail members including centralized advertising and promotion, store location and store layout, training, financing, and accounting. [GLF]

voluntary inter-industry communications standard (VICS) A communications standard adopted by the mass merchandising industry for electronic transmission of information between buyer and seller. [DJB/BJL]

wagon distributor A wholesaler whose inventory of merchandise is carried on trucks that are operated by driver-salespeople. The retailer's requirements for merchandise are determined at the time of the sales call and orders are filled immediately from the stock carried on the truck. It is a somewhat archaic team. (See also **rack jobber.**) [WRD]

want book 1. The information collected by retail salespeople to record out-of-stock or requested merchandise. 2. A notebook in which store employees record the names of items called for by customers but are not in stock. (See also **want slip.**) [WRD]

want slip A slip on which the salesperson records customer requests for items that cannot be supplied from stock. (See also **want book.**) [WRD]

wants The wishes, needs, cravings, demands, or desires of human beings. [DLS]

warehouse A physical facility used primarily for the storage of goods held in anticipation of sale or transfer within the marketing channel. [DJB/BJL]

warehouse, automated A facility where machine power such as conveyors, automatic sortation, ASAR, and other materials handling applications have been implemented to speed the receiving, handling, picking, and shipping of product within the facility. [DNB/BJL]

warehouse, bonded A warehouse that is bonded to insure the owners of the stored goods against loss. [WRD]

warehouse, chain store An establishment that is operated by a retail multiunit organization primarily for the purpose of assembling and distributing goods and performing other wholesale functions for the stores of such an organization. [WRD]

warehouse club See **wholesale club**

warehouse, contract A facility where the user of the warehouse contracts with a third party for some mix of labor, management, and materials handling capability over a specified contract period. The contract period usually exceeds one year. [DJB/BJL]

warehouse, field A warehouse facility used to store and transfer merchandise enroute from manufacturing location to other channel members. [DJB/BJL]

warehouse, private A private, or corporate, warehouse is a facility that is operated by the buyer or the seller of the product. It may be used to store raw materials in anticipation of production, work in process, or finished goods awaiting shipment to the buyer. [DJB/BJL]

warehouse, public 1. (physical distribution definition) A for-hire facility that is available to any business requiring storage or handling of goods. The public warehouse usually operates on a monthly contract and charges for storage plus a handling fee for receiving goods and moving goods out of storage. [DJB/BJL] 2. (retailing definition) A storage facility generally privately owned that does not take title to the goods it handles. It may issue receipts that can be used as security for loans. (See also **warehouse receipts.**) [WRD]

warehouse receipts The receipts that every public warehouse issues to depositors for goods placed in storage. [WRD]

warehouse retailing The retailing of certain types of merchandise, particularly groceries, drugs, hardware, home improvement, and home furnishings, in a superstore type of warehouse atmosphere. The facilities are typically in low-rent, isolated buildings with a minimum of services offered, and the consumer performs the bulk of the functions in a self service mode. [WRD]

warehouse store A large discount retailer that offers merchandise in a no-frills or warehouse type of environment. [WRD]

warranty A statement or promise made to the customer that a product being offered for sale is fit for the purpose being claimed. The promise concerns primarily what the seller will do if the product performs below expectations or turns out to be defective in some way. The promise (warranty) may be full (complete protection) or limited (some corrective steps), under terms of the Magnuson-Moss Warranty-Federal Trade Commission Improvement Act (1975). It may also be expressed (orally or in writing) or only implied, and it may have time restrictions. (See also **product liability.**) [DW]

waybill An official shipping document that identifies shipper and consignee, routing, description of goods, cost of shipment, and weight of shipment. [DJB/BJL]

weak product A term used (rarely) in reference to a product in the decline stage of the product life cycle or otherwise so short of market value that it is destined for early abandonment. [DW]

wealth 1. All material objects that have an economic value possessed by a nation. 2. The aggregate of all possessions of economic goods owned by a person. [DLS]

wearout A condition of inattention and possible irritation that occurs after an audience or target market has encountered a specific advertisement too many times. [JE]

Webb-Pomerene Association Organizations jointly owned, maintained, or supported by competing U.S. manufacturers especially and exclusively for export trade. Special legislation gives them qualified exemption from antitrust laws. [WJK]

Weber's law This states that product purchasers and users are more interested in the relative differences between products than in the absolute characteristics of products standing alone. [DW]

weeks' supply method of stock planning A method of stock planning whereby one plans for a certain number of weeks' supply. In utilizing this method, it is assumed that the same stock turnover can be maintained throughout the selling season; thus, inventory carried is in direct proportion to expected sales. [WRD]

what-if analysis See **decision support system**

Wheel of Consumer Analysis A simple model of the key factors in understanding consumer behavior and guiding marketing strategy. It consists of three parts: affect and cognition, behavior, and the environment. [JPP/JCO]

wheel of retailing theory A theory of retail institutional change that explains retail evolution with an institutional life cycle concept. (See also **central place theory, concentric zone theory, dialectic process, gravity model, natural selection theory, retail accordian theory,** and **retail life cycle.**) [WRD]

Wheeler Lea Act (1938) This act was an amendment to the Federal Trade Commission Act that added the phrase "unfair or deceptive acts or practices in commerce are hereby declared unlawful" to the Section 5 prohibition of unfair methods of competition, in order to provide protection for consumers as well as competition. [DC]

white goods 1. Large kitchen appliances. 2. Sheets and other bedding items. [DW]

wholesale club A general merchandise wholesaler and/or retailer that offers a limited merchandise assortment with little service at low prices and sells only to club member ultimate consumers and member trade people. It is sometimes called a warehouse club. (See also **closed-door discount house.**) [WRD]

wholesale distributor See **wholesale merchant**

wholesale establishment A recognizable place of business that is primarily engaged in performing marketing functions, including the functions of exchange on the wholesale level of distribution. [WRD]

wholesale market center A concentration of vendors' sales offices or display rooms in one place, usually a city or an area within a city. Sometimes it is identified by a concentration of production facilities, as well as sales offices. [WRD]

wholesale merchant An establishment primarily engaged in buying and selling merchandise in the domestic market and performing the principal wholesale functions. (See also **distributor.**) [WRD]

wholesale price index (WPI) A relative measure maintained by the U.S. government of average price changes in commodities sold in wholesale markets in the United States. (See also **producer price index.**) [DLS]

wholesaler A merchant establishment operated by a concern that is primarily engaged in buying, taking title to, usually storing and physically handling goods in large quantities, and reselling the goods (usually in smaller quantities) to retailers or to industrial or business users. (See also **distributor, jobber, middleman,** and **supply house.**) [WRD]

wholesaler sponsored cooperative A form of contractual vertical marketing system that is an example of forward integration. Retailers achieve vertical system advantages by affiliating with a sponsoring wholesaler. [WRD]

wholesaling 1. All transactions in which the purchaser is actuated by a profit or business motive in making the purchase, except for transactions that involve a small quantity of goods purchased from a retail establishment for business use, which is considered a retail purchase. 2. For U.S. Census of Business purposes, include the foregoing as based on the institutional structure of business establishments primarily engaged in wholesale trade. [WRD]

will-call The products ordered by customers in advance of the time delivery is desired. [WRD]

win-win negotiation A negotiating philosophy in which the negotiators attempt to uncover bases of agreement that benefit both parties. (See also **good guy-bad guy routine** and **low-balling.**) [BAW]

WOM See **word-of-mouth communication**

Wool Products Labeling Act (1939) An act administered by the FTC that requires labels be affixed to products containing wool showing the percentages of new wool, reused or reprocessed wool, and other fibers or fillers that are used. [DC]

word association A questionnaire containing a list of words to which respondents are instructed to reply with the first word that comes to mind. (See also **projective technique, sentence completion,** and **storytelling.**) [GAC]

word association test See **projective technique**

word-of-mouth communication (WOM) 1. (consumer behavior definition) This occurs when people share information about products or promotions with friends. [JPP/JCO] 2. (consumer behavior definition) The information imparted by a consumer or individual other than the sponsor. It is sharing information about a product, promotion, etc., between a consumer and a friend, colleague, or other acquaintance. For example, a consumer may tell a friend about a particularly good price he or she received on a product. Research has found that word-of-mouth communication about products is more likely to be negative than positive. [HHK/MCC]

word-of-mouth promotion See **promotion, word-of-mouth**

workable competition An economic model of a market in which competition is less than perfect, but adequate enough to give buyers genuine alternatives. (See also **duopoly, imperfect competition, monopolistic competition, monopoly, monopsony, oligopolistic competition, oligopolistic environment, oligopoly, oligopsony, perfect competition,** and **pure competition.**) [DLS]

working-class See **social class**

workload analysis A procedure for determining the total amount of sales effort required to cover each sales territory, after considering the sales potential and the number of accounts to be served. Comment: The number of sales calls to be made on each, the duration of each sales call, and the estimated amount of nonselling and travel time are explicitly considered. [BAW]

workroom A service department such as apparel alterations, drapery manufacture, furniture polishing and repair, or carpet workroom. [WRD]

World Bank See **International Bank for Reconstruction Development**

world organization See **geocentric orientation**

WPI See **wholesale price index**

yield management The practice of pricing to maximize the amount of revenue received per unit sold. It is commonly associated with the pricing practices of airlines, hotels, and other sellers of "perishable" products. [KM]

young single stage See **family life cycle**

zapping The act of using a remote control to change television channels when an advertisement begins. Advertisers are concerned that this will be harmful, but it is still unclear what effect zapping will have on advertising effectiveness. (See also **zipping.**) [HHK/MCC]

zero defects A condition in which a production unit makes every product without defect. It is usually only a theory or a reference point, but it is actually sought in such categories as aerospace, serums, U.S. mint, and others. [DW]

zero order model A probabilistic model in which the probability of occurrence of any given outcome at a particular point in time does not depend on any previous outcomes of the process. Models of this kind are often used to represent brand choice behavior or media exposure patterns (Lilien and Kotler 1983). Evidence that this simple zero order assumption for brand choice behavior cannot be rejected, given empirical choice patterns, has been provided by Bass, Givon, Kalwani, Reibstein, and Wright (1984). (See also **Bernoulli process** and **brand choice models.**) [DCS/YJW]

zero population growth See **replacement level fertility**

ZIP code A geographical classification system developed by the U.S. government for mail distribution. A nested, numeric code with a range of five to nine digits. [DJB/BJL]

zipping The act of fast forwarding through commercials while watching a previously taped show on a VCR. Advertisers are concerned about the effect of zipping on advertising effectiveness, but any effect is not yet known. In fact, viewers may pay more attention to advertising while zipping to be able to stop fast forwarding in time when the show resumes. (See also **zapping.**) [HHK/MCC]

zone in transition See **concentric zone theory**

zone of better residences See **concentric zone theory**

zone of rate freedom (ZORF) A zone within which a carrier can raise or lower rates without regulatory or other administrative action. [DJB/BJL]

zone of working persons' homes See **concentric zone theory**

zone pricing The delivered cost based on factory price plus averaged freight rate for the section or territory to which goods are shipped (same delivered cost to all in the zone). [WRD]

zoning 1. (retailing definition) The regulation of the construction and use of buildings in certain areas of a municipality. [WRD] 2. (sales definition) A method for scheduling sales calls that divides a territory into areas or zones. The salesperson then makes calls in each zone for a prespecified length of time. (See also **call frequency, circular routing, leapfrog routing, routine call pattern,** and **routing.**) [BAW]

ZORF See **zone of rate freedom**

ZPG See **replacement level fertility**

References

Aaker, D. A. (1975), "ADMOD: An Advertising Decision Model," *Journal of Marketing,* 12 (February), 37–45.

Adams, J. S. (1963), "Toward an Understanding of Inequity," *Journal of Abnormal and Social Psychology,* 67 (July), 422–436.

Assmus, G. (1975), "Newprod: The Design and Implementation of a New Product Model," *Journal of Marketing,* 39 (January), 16–23.

Barney, J. (1991). "Firm Resources and Sustained Competitive Advantage," *Journal of Management,* 17 (1), 99–120.

Bass, F. M. (1969), "A New Product Growth Model for Consumer Durables," *Management Science,* 15, 215–227.

Bass, F. M. (1985), *Leadership and Performance Beyond Expectations,* New York: The Free Press.

Bass, F. M., M. M. Givon, M. U. Kalwani, D. J. Reibstein, and G. P. Wright (1984), "An Investigation into the Order of the Brand Choice Process," *Marketing Science,* 3, 267–287.

Bell, D. E., R. L. Keeney, and J. D. C. Little (1975), "A Market Share Theorem," *Journal of Marketing Research,* 12, 136–141.

Bettman, J. R. (1979), *An Information Processing Theory of Consumer Choice,* Reading, MA: Addison-Wesley.

Blackburn, J. D., and K. J. Clancy (1982), "LITMUS: A New Product Planning Model," in A. A. Zoltners (ed.) *Marketing Planning Models,* TIMS Studies in the Management Sciences, Vol. 18, New York: North-Holland, pp. 43–61.

Black's Law Dictionary with Pronunciations, 6th ed. (1990), St. Paul, MN: West Publishing Co.

Blattberg, R. C., and J. Golanty (1978), "Tracker: An Early Test Market Forecasting and Diagnostic Model for New Product Planning," *Journal of Marketing Research,* 15, 192–202.

Bowersox, D. J., and M. B. Cooper (1992), *Strategic Marketing Channel Management,* New York: McGraw-Hill, Inc.

Boyd, Jr., H., and O. Walker, Jr. (1990) *Marketing Management,* Homewood, IL: Richard D. Irwin.

Burke, R. R., A. Rangaswamy, J. Wind, and J. Eliashberg (1990), "A Knowledge-Based System for Advertising Design," *Marketing Science,* 9, 212–229.

Castleberry, S. B., and J. F. Tanner (1986), "The Manager-Salesperson Relationship: An Exploratory Examination of the Vertical-Dyad Linkage

Model,'' *Journal of Personal Selling and Sales Management,* 6 (November), 29–37.

Chakravarthi, D., A. A. Mitchell, and R. Staelin (1981), ''Judgement Based Marketing Decision Models: Problems and Possible Solutions,'' *Journal of Marketing,* 45, No. 4, 13–23.

Clark, K., and T. Fujimoto (1991), *Product Development Performance,* Boston: Harvard Business School Press.

Cooper, R., and E. Kleinschmidt (1991), ''New Product Processes at Leading Industrial Firms,'' *Industrial Marketing Management,* 20, 137–148.,

Corstjens, M. L., and D. A. Gautschi (1983), ''Formal Choice Models in Marketing,'' *Marketing Science,* 2, 19–56.

Crawford, M. (1994), *New Products Management,* Burr Ridge, IL: Richard D. Irwin.

Cron, W. L. (1984), ''Industrial Salesperson Development: A Career Stages Perspective,'' *Journal of Marketing,* 48 (Fall), 41–52.

Currim, I. S. (1982), ''Predictive Testing of Consumer Choice Models Not Subject to Independence of Irrelevant Alternatives,'' *Journal of Marketing Research,* 19, 208–222.

Daganzo, C. (1979), *Multinomial Probit: The Theory and Its Application to Demand Forecasting,* New York: Academic Press.

Day, G. S. (1986), *Analysis for Strategic Market Decisions,* New York: West Publishing Co.

Dubin, J. A. (1986), ''A Nested Logit Model of Space and Water Heat System Choice,'' *Marketing Science,* 5, 112–124.

Ehrenberg, A. S. C. (1972). *Repeat-Buying: Theory and Applications,* Amsterdam: North-Holland.

Feldman, D. C., and B. A. Weitz (1988), ''Career Plateaus in the Salesforce: Understanding and Removing Blockages to Employee Growth,'' *Journal of Personal Selling and Sales Management,* 8 (November), 23–32.

Fudge, W. K., and L. M. Lodish (1977), ''Evaluation of the Effectiveness of a Model Based Salesman's Planning System by Field Experimentation,'' *Interfaces,* 8, No. 1, Part 2, 97–106.

Gilman, J. (1992), *Inventivity: The Art and Science of Research Management,* New York: Van Nostrand Reinhold.

Goodhardt, G. J., A. S. C. Ehrenberg, and C. Chatfield (1984), ''The Dirichlet: A Comprehensive Model of Buying Behavior,'' *The Journal of the Royal Statistical Society: Series A,* 147, 621–655.

Green, P. E., J. D. Carroll, and S. M. Goldberg (1981), "A General Approach to Product Design Optimization via Conjoint Analysis," *Journal of Marketing,* 45 (Summer) 17-37.

Green, P. E., and A. M. Krieger (1985), "Models and Heuristics for Product Line Selection," *Marketing Science,* 4, 1-19.

Green, P. E., and A. M. Krieger, and C. M. Schaffer (1985), "Quick and Simple Benefit Segmentation," *Journal of Advertising Research,* 25 (June/July), 9-17.

Greene, J. D. (1982), *Consumer Behavior Models for Non-Statisticians,* New York: Praeger Publishers.

Griffin, A., and J. Hauser (1993), "The Voice of the Customer," *Management Science,* 36(7), 867-83.

Guadagni, P. M. (1983), "A Nested Logit Model of Product Choice and Purchase Incidence," in F. S. Zufryden (ed.) *Advances and Practices of Marketing Science,* Providence, RI: The Institute of Management Sciences, pp. 90-100.

Hamel, G. K., and C. K. Prahalad (1989), "Strategic Intent," *Harvard Business Review,* May-June, 63-76.

Hauser, J. R. (1986), "Agendas and Consumer Choice," *Journal of Marketing Research,* 23, 199-212.

Hauser, J. R., and S. P. Gaskin (1984), "Application of the 'Defender' Consumer Model," *Marketing Science,* 3, 327-351.

Hauser, J. R., and S. M. Shugan (1983), "Defensive Marketing Strategies," *Marketing Science,* 2, 319-360.

Hess, S. W., and S. A. Samuels (1971), "Experiences with a Sales Districting Model: Criteria and Implementation," *Management Science,* 18, No. 4, Part II, 41-54.

Huff, D. L. (1962), "A Note on the Limitation of Intraurban Gravity Models," *Land Economics,* 38, No. 1.

Huff, D. L. (1963), "A Probabilistic Analysis of Shopping Center Trade Areas," *Land Economics,* 39, No. 1.

Huff, D. L. (1964), "Defining and Estimating a Trading Area," *Journal of Marketing,* 28 (July), 34-38.

Huff, D. L. (1966), "A Programmed Solution for Approximating an Optimum Retail Location," *Land Economics,* 42, No. 3.

Huff, D. L., and R. Battsell (1977), "Delimiting the Areal Extent of a Market Area," *Journal of Marketing Research,* Vol. 14.

Huff, D. L. (1981), "Retail Location Theory," Elizabeth Hirshman and Ronald

Stampfl (eds.), *Theory in Retailing: Traditional and Nontraditional Sources,* Proceedings, American Marketing Association.

Jain, S. (1993), *Marketing Planning and Strategy,* Cincinnati: South-Western Publishing Co.

Jeuland, A. P., F. M. Bass, and G. P. Wright (1980), "A Multibrand Stochastic Model Compounding Heterogeneous Erlang Timing and Multinomial Choice Processes," *Operations Research,* 28, 255–277.

Kahn, B. K., M. U. Kalwani, and D. G. Morrison (1986), "Measuring Variety Seeking and Reinforcement Behavior Using Panel Data," *Journal of Marketing Research,* 23, 89–100.

Kalwani, M. U., and D. G. Morrison (1977), "A Parsimonious Description of the Hendry System," *Management Science,* 23, 467–477.

Katzenbach, J. R., and D. K. Smith (1992), "Why Teams Matter," *The McKinsey Quarterly,* 3.

Kerr S., and J. M. Jermier (1978), "Substitutes for Leadership: Their Meaning and Measurement," *Organizational Behavior and Human Performance,* 22 (December), 375–403.

Krench, D., and R. S. Crutchfield (1948), "Theory and Problems," *Social Psychology,* New York: McGraw-Hill, Inc.

Krench, D., R. S. Crutchfield, and E. Ballachoy (1962), *Individual in Society,* New York: McGraw-Hill, Inc.

Kuehn, A. A. (1962), "Consumer Brand Choice—A Learning Process," *Journal of Advertising Research,* 2 (December), 10–17.

Larreche, J. C., and V. Srinivasan (1981), "STRATPORT: A Decision Support System for Strategic Planning," *Journal of Marketing,* 45, No. 4, 39–52.

Larreche, J. C., and V. Srinivasan (1982), "STRATPORT: A Model for the Evaluation and Formulation of Business Portfolio Strategies," *Management Science,* 28, 979–1001.

Leiberman, M. B., and D. B. Montgomery (1988), "First-Mover Advantages," *Strategic Management Journal,* 9, 41–58.

Lattin, J. M., and L. McAlister (1985), "Using a Variety-Seeking Model to Identify Substitute and Complementary Relationships Among Competing Products," *Journal of Marketing Research,* 22, 330–339.

Lilien, G. L. (1979), "Advisor 2: Modeling the Marketing Mix for Industrial Products," *Management Science,* 25, No. 2, 191–204.

Lilien, G. L., and P. Kotler (1983), *Marketing Decision Making: A Model-Building Approach,* New York: Harper and Row.

Little, J. D. C. (1970), "Models and Managers: The Concept of a Decision Calculus," *Management Science,* 16, B466–B485.

Little, J. D. C. (1975), "BRANDAID: A Marketing Mix Model, Part I: Structure; Part II: Implementation," *Operations Research,* 23, 628–673.

Little, J. D. C., and L. M. Lodish (1966), "A Media Selection Model and Its Optimization by Dynamic Programming," *Industrial Management Review,* 8 (Fall), 15–23.

Little, J. D. C., and L. M. Lodish (1969), "A Media Planning Calculus," *Operations Research,* 17, 1–34.

Little, J. D. C., and L. M. Lodish (1981), "Commentary on 'Judgement Based Marketing Decision Models'," *Journal of Marketing,* 45, No. 4, 24–29.

Lodish, L. M. (1971), "CALLPLAN: An Interactive Salesman's Call Planning System," *Management Science,* 18, No. 4, Part II, 25–40.

Luce, R. D. (1977), "The Choice Axiom after Twenty Years," *Journal of Mathematical Psychology,* 15, 215–233.

Mahajan, V., P. E. Green, and S. M. Goldberg (1982), "A Conjoint Model for Measuring Self and Cross-Price/Demand Relationships," *Journal of Marketing Research,* 19, 334–342.

Mahajan, V., E. Muller, and S. Sharma (1984), "An Empirical Comparison of Awareness Forecasting Models of New Product Introduction," *Marketing Science,* 3, 179–197.

Mahajan, V., and Y. Wind (1986), *Innovation Diffusion Models of New Product Acceptance,* Cambridge, MA: Ballinger Publishing Co.

Massy, W. F. (1969), "Forecasting Demand for New Convenience Products," *Journal of Marketing,* 6, 405–412.

Massy, W. F., D. B. Montgomery, and D. G. Morrison (1970), *Stochastic Models of Buying Behavior,* Cambridge, MA: MIT Press.

McFadden, D. (1986), "The Choice Theory Approach to Market Research," *Marketing Science,* 5, 275–297.

Montgomery, D. B., A. J. Silk, and C. E. Zaragoza (1971), "A Multiple-Product Sales Force Allocation Model," *Management Science,* 18, No. 4, Part II, 3–24.

Moorthy, K. S. (1985), "Using Game Theory to Model Competition," *Journal of Marketing Research,* 22, 262–282.

Morrison, D. G., and D. C. Schmittlein (1981), "Predicting Future Random Events Based on Past Performance," *Management Science,* 27, 1006–1023.

Nakanishi, M., and L. G. Cooper (1974), "Parameter Estimation for a Multiplicative Competitive Interaction Model-Least Squares Approach,'' *Journal of Marketing Research,* 11, 303–311.

Parfitt, J. H., and B. J. K. Collins (1968), ''Use of Consumer Panels for Brand Share Prediction,'' *Journal of Marketing Research,* 5, 131–146.

Parry, M., and M. Song (1993), ''Determinants of R&D-Marketing Integration in High-Tech Japanese Firms,'' *Journal of Product Innovation Management,* 10, 4–23.

Parsons, L. J., and R. L. Schultz (1976), *Marketing Models and Econometric Research,* Amsterdam: Elsevier Scientific Publishing.

Pringle, L. G., R. D. Wilson, and E. I. Brody (1982), ''NEWS: A Decision Oriented Model for New Product Analysis and Forecasting,'' *Marketing Science,* 1, 1–30.

Robertson, T. S., and H. H. Kassarjian (eds.) (1991), *Handbook of Consumer Behavior,* Englewood Cliffs, NJ: Prentice Hall.

Rubinson, J. R., W. R. Vanhonacker, and F. M. Bass (1980), ''On 'A Parsimonious Description of the Hendry System','' *Management Science,* 26, 215–226.

Sauers, D. A., J. B. Hunt, and K. Bass (1990), ''Behavioral Self-Management as a Supplement to External Sales Force Controls,'' *Journal of Personal Selling and Sales Management,* 10 (Summer), 17–28.

Saxe, R., and B. A. Weitz, ''The Customer Orientation of Sales People: Measurement and Relationship to Performance,'' *Journal of Marketing Research,* 19, (August 1982), 343–351.

Silk, A. J., and G. L. Urban (1978), ''Pre-Test Market Evaluation of New Packaged Goods: A Model and Measurement Methodology,'' *Journal of Marketing Research,* 15, 171–191.

Smith, P., and D. Reinertsen (1991), *Developing Products in Half the Time,* New York: Van Nostrand Reinhold.

Spiro, R. L., and B. A. Weitz, ''Adaptive Selling: Conceptualization, Measurement, and Validity,'' *Journal of Marketing Research,* 27 (February 1990), 61–69.

Stalk, G., and T. Hout (1990), *Competing Against Time,* New York: The Free Press.

Sujan, H., B. A. Weitz, and M. Sujan, ''Knowledge, Motivation, and Adaptive Behavior: A Framework for Improving Selling Effectiveness,'' *Journal of Marketing,* 50 (October 1986), 174–191.

The Hendry Corporation (1970), *Hendrodynamics: Fundamental Laws of Consumer Dynamics,* Chapter I, Hendry Corporation.

The Hendry Corporation (1971), *Hendrodynamics: Fundamental Laws of Consumer Dynamics,* Chapter 2, Hendry Corporation.

Thurstone, L. L. (1927), "A Law of Comparative Judgment," *Psychological Review,* 34, 273–286.

Tull, D. S., B. E. Cooley, M. R. Phillips, Jr., and H. S. Watkins (1991), *The Organization of Marketing Activities of American Manufacturers,* Report No. 91-126. Cambridge, MA: Marketing Science Institute.

Tversky, A. (1972), "Elimination By Aspects: A Theory of Choice," *Psychological Review,* 79, 281–219.

Tversky, A., and S. Sattath (1979), "Preference Trees," *Psychological Review,* 86, 542–573.

Urban, G. L. (1970), "SPRINTER Mod III: A Model for the Analysis of New Frequently Purchased Consumer Products," *Operations Research,* 18, 805-853.

Urban, G., and J. Hauser (1993), *Design and Marketing of New Products,* Englewood Cliffs, NJ: Prentice Hall.

Urban, G. L., and G. M. Katz (1983), "Pre-Test-Market Models: Validation and Managerial Implications," *Journal of Marketing Research,* 20, 221–234.

Urban, G., and E. von Hippel (1988), "Lead User Analyses for the Development of New Industrial Products," *Management Science,* 34 (May), 569–582.

Vidale, H. L., and H. B. Wolfe (1957), "An Operations Research Study of Sales Response to Advertising," *Operational Research Quarterly,* 5, 370–381.

von Hippel, Eric (1988), *The Sources of Innovation,* New York: Oxford University Press.

Wheelwright, S., and K. Clark (1992), *Revolutionizing Product Development,* New York: The Free Press.

Walker, O. C., G. A. Churchill, and N. M. Ford (1977), "Motivation and Performance in Industrial Selling: Present Knowledge and Needed Research," *Journal of Marketing Research,* 14 (May), 156–168.

Wind, Y., V. Mahajan, and R. Cardozo (1981), *New Product Forecasting Models,* Lexington, MA: Lexington Books.

Wind, Y., and T. L. Saaty (1980), "Marketing Applications of the Analytic Hierarchy Process," *Management Science,* 26, 641–658.

Wood, D. F., and J. C. Johnson (1983), *Contemporary Transportation,* 2nd. edition, Tulsa, OK: PennWell Publishing Company.

Yellott, J. I., Jr. (1977), "The Relationship between Luce's Choice Axiom,

Thurstone's Theory of Comparative Judgement, and the Double Exponential Distribution,'' *Journal of Mathematical Psychology,* 15, 109–144.

Yukl, G. A. (1981), *Leadership in Organizations,* Englewood Cliffs, NJ: Prentice Hall.

Zirger, B., and M. Maidique (1990), ''Model of New Product Development: Empirical Test,'' *Management Science,* 36 (July), 867–83.

TITLES OF INTEREST IN MARKETING, DIRECT MARKETING, AND SALES PROMOTION

Successful Direct Marketing Methods, by Bob Stone
Profitable Direct Marketing, by Jim Kobs
Integrated Direct Marketing, by Ernan Roman
Beyond 2000: The Future of Direct Marketing, by Jerry I. Reitman
Power Direct Marketing, by "Rocket" Ray Jutkins
Creative Strategy in Direct Marketing, by Susan K. Jones
Secrets of Successful Direct Mail, by Richard V. Benson
Strategic Database Marketing, by Rob Jackson and Paul Wang
Successful Telemarketing, by Bob Stone and John Wyman
Business to Business Direct Marketing, by Robert Bly
Commonsense Direct Marketing, by Drayton Bird
Direct Marketing Checklists, by John Stockwell and Henry Shaw
Integrated Marketing Communications, by Don E. Schultz, Stanley I. Tannenbaum, and Robert F. Lauterborn
New Directions in Marketing, by Aubrey Wilson
Green Marketing, by Jacquelyn Ottman
Marketing Corporate Image: The Company as Your Number One Product, by James R. Gregory with Jack G. Wiechmann
How to Create Successful Catalogs, by Maxwell Sroge
101 Tips for More Profitable Catalogs, by Maxwell Sroge
Sales Promotion Essentials, by Don E. Schultz, William A. Robinson and Lisa A. Petrison
Promotional Marketing, by William A. Robinson and Christine Hauri
Best Sales Promotions, by William A. Robinson
Inside the Leading Mail Order Houses, by Maxwell Sroge
New Product Development, by George Gruenwald
New Product Development Checklists, by George Gruenwald
Classic Failures in Product Marketing, by Donald W. Hendon
How to Turn Customer Service into Customer Sales, by Bernard Katz
Advertising & Marketing Checklists, by Ron Kaatz
Brand Marketing, by William M. Weilbacher
Marketing Without Money, by Nicholas E. Bade
The 1-Day Marketing Plan, by Roman A. Hiebing, Jr. and Scott W. Cooper
How to Write a Successful Marketing Plan, by Roman G. Hiebing, Jr. and Scott W. Cooper
Developing, Implementing, and Managing Effective Marketing Plans, by Hal Goetsch
How to Evaluate and Improve Your Marketing Department, by Keith Sparling and Gerard Earls
Selling to a Segmented Market, by Chester A. Swenson
Market-Oriented Pricing, by Michael Morris and Gene Morris
State-of-the-Art Marketing Research, by A.B. Blankenship and George E. Breen
AMA Handbook for Customer Satisfaction, by Alan Dutka
Was There a Pepsi Generation Before Pepsi Discovered It?, by Stanley C. Hollander and Richard Germain
Business to Business Communications Handbook, by Fred Messner
Managing Sales Leads: How to Turn Every Prospect Into a Customer, by Robert Donath, Richard Crocker, Carol Dixon and James Obermeyer
AMA Marketing Toolbox (series), by David Parmerlee
AMA Complete Guide to Small Business Marketing, by Kenneth J. Cook
AMA Complete Guide to Strategic Planning for Small Business, by Kenneth J. Cook
AMA Complete Guide to Small Business Advertising, by Joe Vitale
How to Get the Most Out of Trade Shows, by Steve Miller
How to Get the Most Out of Sales Meetings, by James Dance
Strategic Market Planning, by Robert J. Hamper and L. Sue Baugh

For further information or a current catalog, write:
NTC Business Books
a division of *NTC Publishing Group*
4255 West Touhy Avenue
Lincolnwood, Illinois 60646-1975 U.S.A.